grzimek's
Student Animal Life Resource

• • • •

grzimek's
Student Animal Life Resource

• • • •

Birds
volume 4

Broadbills to Fantails

THOMSON

GALE

Detroit • New York • San Francisco • San Diego • New Haven, Conn. • Waterville, Maine • London • Munich

Grzimek's Student Animal Life Resource
Birds

Project Editor
Melissa C. McDade

Editorial
Julie L. Carnagie, Madeline Harris, Heather Price

Indexing Services
Synapse, the Knowledge Link Corporation

Rights and Acquisitions
Sheila Spencer, Mari Masalin-Cooper

Imaging and Multimedia
Randy Bassett, Michael Logusz, Dan Newell, Chris O'Bryan, Robyn Young

Product Design
Tracey Rowens, Jennifer Wahi

Composition
Evi Seoud, Mary Beth Trimper

Manufacturing
Wendy Blurton, Dorothy Maki

LIBRARY OF CONGRESS CATALOGING-IN-PUBLICATION DATA

Grzimek's student animal life resource. Birds / Melissa C. McDade, project editor.
    p. cm.
  Includes bibliographical references and index.
  ISBN 0-7876-9235-2 (set hardcover : alk. paper) — ISBN 0-7876-9236-0 (volume 1) — ISBN 0-7876-9237-9 (volume 2) — ISBN 0-7876-9238-7 (volume 3) — ISBN 0-7876-9239-5 (volume 4) — ISBN 0-7876-9240-9 (volume 5)
  1. Birds—Juvenile literature. I. Grzimek, Bernhard. II. McDade, Melissa C.
  QL673.G79 2005
  598—dc22
                                        2004015729

ISBN 0-7876-9402-9 (21-vol set), ISBN 0-7876-9235-2 (Birds set),
ISBN 0-7876-9236-0 (v.1), ISBN 0-7876-9237-9 (v.2), ISBN 0-7876-9238-7 (v.3),
ISBN 0-7876-9239-5 (v.4), ISBN 0-7876-9240-9 (v.5)

This title is also available as an e-book
Contact your Thomson Gale sales representative for ordering information.

Printed in Canada
10 9 8 7 6 5 4 3 2 1

Contents

BIRDS: VOLUME 3

BIRDS: VOLUME 4

BIRDS: VOLUME 5

Reader's Guide

Grzimek's Student Animal Life Resource: Birds offers readers comprehensive and easy-to-use information on Earth's birds. Entries are arranged by taxonomy, the science through which living things are classified into related groups. Order entries provide an overview of a group of families, and family entries provide an overview of a particular family. Each entry includes sections on physical characteristics; geographic range; habitat; diet; behavior and reproduction; animals and people; and conservation status. Family entries are followed by one or more species accounts with the same information as well as a range map and photo or illustration for each species. Entries conclude with a list of books, periodicals, and Web sites that may be used for further research.

ADDITIONAL FEATURES

Each volume of *Grzimek's Student Animal Life Resource: Birds* includes a pronunciation guide for scientific names, a glossary, an overview of birds, a list of species in the set by biome, a list of species by geographic location, and an index. The set has 640 full-color maps, photos, and illustrations to enliven the text, and sidebars provide additional facts and related information.

NOTES

The classification of animals into orders, families, and even species is not a completed exercise. As researchers learn more about animals and their relationships, classifications may change. In some cases, researchers do not agree on how or whether to make a change. For this reason, the heading "Number of species" in the introduction of an entry may read "About 36 species" or "34 to 37 species." It is not a question of whether some animals exist or not, but a question of how they are classified. Some researchers are more likely to "lump" animals into the same species classification, while others may "split" animals into separate species.

Grzimek's Student Animal Life Resource: Birds has standardized information in the Conservation Status section. The IUCN Red List provides the world's most comprehensive inventory of the global conservation status of plants and animals. Using a set of criteria to evaluate extinction risk, the IUCN recognizes the following categories: Extinct, Extinct in the Wild, Critically Endangered, Endangered, Vulnerable, Conservation Dependent, Near Threatened, Least Concern, and Data Deficient. These terms are defined where they are used in the text, but for a complete explanation of each category, visit the IUCN web page at http://www.iucn.org/themes/ssc/redlists/RLcats2001booklet.html.

ACKNOWLEDGEMENTS

Special thanks are due for the invaluable comments and suggestions provided by the *Grzimek's Student Animal Life Resource: Birds* advisors:

- Mary Alice Anderson, Media Specialist, Winona Middle School, Winona, Minnesota
- Thane Johnson, Librarian, Oklahoma City Zoo, Oklahoma City, Oklahoma
- Debra Kachel, Media Specialist, Ephrata Senior High School, Ephrata, Pennsylvania
- Nina Levine, Media Specialist, Blue Mountain Middle School, Courtlandt Manor, New York
- Ruth Mormon, Media Specialist, The Meadows School, Las Vegas, Nevada

COMMENTS AND SUGGESTIONS

We welcome your comments on *Grzimek's Student Animal Life Resource: Birds* and suggestions for future editions of this work. Please write: Editors, *Grzimek's Student Animal Life Resource: Birds*, U•X•L, 27500 Drake Rd., Farmington Hills, Michigan 48331-3535; call toll free: 1-800-877-4253; fax: 248-699-8097; or send e-mail via www.gale.com.

Pronunciation Guide for Scientific Names

Acanthisitta chloris uh-kan-thuh-SIT-tuh KLOR-is

Acanthisittidae uh-kan-thuh-SIT-tuh-dee

Acanthiza chrysorrhoa uh-KAN-thih-zuh KRIH-soh-ROH-uh

Acanthizidae uh-kan-THIZ-uh-dee

Accipitridae ak-sip-IT-ruh-dee

Aceros cassidix AH-ser-uhs KAS-sid-iks

Acridotheres tristis AK-rid-uh-THER-eez TRIS-tis

Actenoides concretus ak-TEN-oi-deez con-CREE-tuhs

Actinodura sodangorum AK-tin-uh-DYOOR-uh soh-dan-GOH-rum

Actophilornis africanus ak-tuh-FIL-or-nis AF-rih-kan-uhs

Aechmophorus occidentalis ek-MOH-for-uhs OK-sih-DEN-tal-is

Aegithalidae ee-jih-THAL-uh-dee

Aegithina tiphia ee-JIH-thin-uh TIF-ee-uh

Aegotheles insignis ee-GO-thel-eez IN-sig-nis

Aegothelidae ee-go-THEL-uh-dee

Agelaioides badius ah-jeh-LAY-oid-eez BAD-ee-uhs

Agelaius phoeniceus ah-jeh-LAY-ee-uhs fee-nih-SEE-uhs

Aix sponsa AKS SPON-suh

Ajaia ajaja ah-JAH-ee-uh AH-jah-juh

Alaemon alaudipes al-EE-mon ah-LAUD-ih-peez

Alaudidae ah-LAUD-uh-dee

Alcedinidae al-sed-IN-uh-dee

Alcidae AL-suh-dee

Amytornis striatus am-IT-or-nis stry-AH-tuhs

Anas platyrhynchos AH-nuhs PLA-tee-RIN-koz

Anatidae ah-NA-tuh-dee

Andigena hypoglauca an-DIH-jin-uh HI-poh-GLO-kuh

Anhima cornuta AN-him-uh KOR-nyoo-tuh

Anhimidae an-HIM-uh-dee

Anhinga anhinga AN-hin-guh AN-hin-guh

Anseriformes an-ser-uh-FORM-eez

Anthus spragueii AN-thuhs SPRAG-ee-eye

Aphelocoma californica uh-fel-uh-KOH-muh kal-uh-FORN-
ik-uh

Apodidae a-POD-uh-dee

Apodiformes a-pod-uh-FORM-eez

Aptenodytes forsteri ap-ten-uh-DIE-teez FOS-ter-eye

Apterygidae ap-ter-IJ-uh-dee

Apteryx australis AP-ter-iks au-STRA-lis

Ara macao AR-uh MUH-kow

Aramidae ar-UH-muh-dee

Aramus guarauna AR-uh-muhs GWAR-aw-nuh

Ardea herodias AR-dee-uh hir-OH-dee-uhs

Ardeidae ar-DEE-uh-dee

Arenaria interpres ar-en-AIR-ee-uh IN-ter-preez

Artamidae ar-TAM-uh-dee

Artamus cyanopterus AR-tam-uhs SIGH-an-OP-ter-uhs

Astrapia mayeri as-truh-PEE-uh MAY-er-eye

Atrichornis rufescens a-TRIK-or-nis ROO-fehs-sens

Atrichornithidae a-trik-or-NITH-uh-dee

Attagis gayi AT-uh-jis GAY-eye

Auriparus flaviceps aw-RIP-ar-uhs FLAV-uh-seps

Balaeniceps rex bal-EEN-uh-seps REX

Balaenicipitidae BAL-een-uh-sip-IH-tuh-dee

Balearica regulorum BAL-ih-AR-ik-uh reg-YOO-lor-um

Batis capensis BAT-is KAP-en-sis

Bombycilla cedrorum bom-bih-SILL-uh SEED-roh-rum

Bombycillidae bom-bih-SILL-uh-dee

Botaurus stellaris BOH-tor-uhs STEL-lar-is

Branta canadensis BRAN-tuh kan-uh-DEN-sis

Bubo sumatranus BYOO-boh SOO-mah-TRAN-uhs

Bucconidae buck-ON-uh-dee

Bucerotidae byoo-ser-UH-tuh-dee

Bucorvus leadbeateri BYOO-kor-vuhs LED-bet-er-eye

Buphagus erythrorhynchus BYOO-fag-uhs eh-RITH-roh-RIN-kuhs

Burhinidae bur-HIN-uh-dee

Callaeas cinerea cal-LEE-uhs sin-EAR-ee-uh

Callaeidae cal-LEE-uh-dee

Calypte anna kuh-LIP-tee AN-nuh

Campephagidae kam-pee-FAJ-uh-dee

Campephilus principalis KAM-pee-FIL-uhs PRIN-sih-PAL-is

Campylorhamphus trochilirostris KAM-pie-luh-RAM-fuhs TRO-kil-ih-ROS-tris

Campylorhynchus brunneicapillus KAM-pie-luh-RIN-kuhs BROO-nee-kap-ILL-uhs

Capitonidae kap-ih-TON-uh-dee

Caprimulgidae kap-rih-MUL-juh-dee

Caprimulgiformes kal-rih-mul-juh-FORM-eez

Caprimulgus indicus KAP-rih-MUL-juhs IN-dih-kuhs

Caprimulgus vociferus KAP-rih-MUL-juhs voh-SIF-er-uhs

Carduelis tristis KAR-doo-lis TRIS-tis

Cariama cristata KAR-ee-ah-muh KRIS-tah-tuh

Cariamidae kar-ee-AH-muh-dee

Casuariidae kas-oo-ar-EYE-uh-dee

Casuarius casuarius kas-oo-AR-ee-uhs kas-oo-AR-ee-uhs

Cathartidae kath-ART-uh-dee

Cephalopterus ornatus SEFF-uhl-OP-ter-uhs AWR-nah-tuhs

Cercomacra cinerascens SIR-koh-MAK-ruh si-NEAR-ass-enz

Certhia americana SIR-thee-uh uh-mer-uh-kAN-uh

Certhiidae sirth-EYE-uh-dee

Chaetura pelagica KEE-tur-uh peh-LAJ-ik-uh

Chalcoparia singalensis kal-kuh-PAIR-ee-uh sin-GAHL-en-sis

Chamaea fasciata kam-EE-uh fah-she-AH-tuh

Chamaepetes unicolor kam-ee-PEET-eez YOO-nih-KUH-luhr

Charadriidae kar-ad-RYE-uh-dee

Charadriiformes kar-ad-rye-uh-FORM-eez

Charadrius vociferus kar-ad-REE-uhs voh-SIF-er-uhs

Chionidae ky-ON-uh-dee

Chionis minor KY-on-is MY-ner

Chiroxiphia linearis ky-roh-ZIF-ee-uh lin-EE-air-is

Chlamydera maculata klam-EE-der-uh mak-yoo-LAH-tuh

Chlidonias niger klih-DON-ee-uhs NY-jer

Cicinnurus regius sih-SIN-yoor-uhs RAY-jee-uhs

Ciconia ciconia SIK-uh-nee-uh SIK-uh-nee-uh
Ciconiidae sik-uh-NYE-uh-dee
Ciconiiformes sik-uh-nee-uh-FORM-eez
Cinclidae SIN-kluh-dee
Cinclosoma punctatum sin-cluh-SOH-muh PUNK-tah-tum
Cinclus cinclus SIN-kluhs SIN-kluhs
Cinclus mexicanus SIN-kluhs MEK-sih-KAN-uhs
Cinnyris asiaticus SIN-ny-ris AY-zhi-AT-ik-uhs
Cissa chinensis SIS-suh CHIN-en-sis
Cisticola juncidis sis-tuh-KOH-luh JUNK-id-is
Climacteridae kly-mak-TER-uh-dee
Climacteris rufa kly-MAK-ter-is ROO-fuh
Colibri coruscans KOH-lee-bree KOR-us-kans
Coliidae kol-EYE-uh-dee
Coliiformes kol-eye-uh-FORM-eez
Colinus virginianus KOL-eye-nuhs ver-JIN-ee-an-nuhs
Colius striatus KOL-ee-uhs stry-AH-tuhs
Columba livia KUH-lum-buh LIV-ee-uh
Columbidae kuh-LUM-buh-dee
Columbiformes kuh-lum-buh-FORM-eez
Coracias garrulus kor-UH-see-uhs GAR-oo-luhs
Coraciidae kor-uh-SIGH-uh-dee
Coraciiformes kor-uh-sigh-uh-FORM-eez
Coracina typica kor-uh-SEE-nuh TIP-ik-uh
Corvidae KOR-vuh-dee
Corvus corax KOR-vuhs KOR-aks
Corythaeola cristata kor-ih-thee-OH-luh KRIS-tah-tuh
Corythaixoides concolor kor-ih-THAKS-oi-deez CON-kuh-luhr
Cotinga cayana KOH-ting-guh KAY-ah-nuh
Cotingidae koh-TING-guh-dee
Cracidae KRA-suh-dee
Cracticidae krak-TIK-uh-dee
Cracticus torquatus KRAK-tik-uhs TOR-kwah-tuhs
Crax globulosa KRAKS glob-yoo-LOH-suh
Crex crex CREKS CREKS
Cuculidae kyoo-KYOO-luh-dee
Cuculiformes kyoo-kyoo-luh-FORM-eez
Cuculus canorus KYOO-kyoo-luhs KAN-or-uhs
Cyanocitta cristata SIGH-an-uh-SIT-tuh KRIS-tah-tuh
Cyclarhis gujanensis SIGH-klar-is GOO-jan-en-sis

Cygnus olor   SIG-nuhs OH-lor

Cymbirhynchus macrorhynchos   SIM-bih-RIN-kuhs ma-crow-RIN-kuhs

Cypsiurus parvus   sip-SIH-yoor-uhs PAR-vuhs

Dacelo novaeguineae   DAY-sel-oh NOH-vee-GIN-ee-ee

Dendrocolaptidae   den-droh-koh-LAP-tuh-dee

Dendroica kirtlandii   DEN-droy-kuh KIRT-land-ee-eye

Dendropicos goertae   den-droh-PEE-kuhs GER-tee

Dicaeidae   die-SEE-uh-dee

Dicaeum ignipectus   DIE-see-um IG-nih-PEK-tuhs

Dicruridae   die-KRU-ruh-dee

Dicrurus ludwigii   DIE-kru-ruhs LOOT-vig-ee-eye

Dicrurus paradiseus   DIE-kru-ruhs par-uh-DIE-see-uhs

Diomedea cauta eremite   DIE-uh-MED-ee-uh CAW-tuh ER-ih-mite

Diomedea immutabilis   DIE-uh-MED-ee-uh im-myoo-TUH-bil-is

Diomedeidae   die-uh-med-EYE-dee

Donacobius atricapillus   don-uh-KOH-bee-uhs ay-trih-kap-ILL-uhs

Drepanididae   dre-pan-ID-uh-dee

Drepanorhynchus reichenowi   DRE-pan-uh-RIN-kuhs RYE-keh-now-eye

Dromadidae   droh-MAD-uh-dee

Dromaiidae   droh-MAY-uh-dee

Dromaius novaehollandiae   DROH-may-uhs NO-vee-hol-LAND-ee-ee

Dromas ardeola   DROH-muhs ar-dee-OH-luh

Drymodes brunneopygia   dry-MOH-deez BROO-nee-oh-PIJ-ee-uh

Dulidae   DYOO-luh-dee

Dulus dominicus   DYOO-luhs duh-MIN-ih-kuhs

Dumetella carolinensis   dum-uh-TELL-uh kar-uh-LINE-en-sis

Eclectus roratus   EK-lek-tuhs ROH-rat-uhs

Egretta ibis   EE-gret-uh EYE-bis

Emberizidae   em-ber-IZ-uh-dee

Epthianuridae   ep-thy-an-YOOR-uh-dee

Epthianura tricolor   ep-thy-an-YOOR-uh TRY-kuh-luhr

Eremophila alpestris   ER-em-uh-FIL-uh al-PES-tris

Esacus magnirostris   EH-sak-uhs MAG-nuh-ROS-tris

Estrilda astrild ES-tril-duh AS-trild

Estrildidae es-TRIL-duh-dee

Eudyptes chrysolophus YOO-dip-teez krih-soh-LOH-fuhs

Eupetidae yoo-PET-uh-dee

Euplectes orix YOO-plek-teez OR-iks

Eupodotis caerulescens yoo-pod-OH-tis see-ROO-less-sens

Eurylaimidae yoo-rih-lay-IM-uh-dee

Eurypyga helias yoo-RIH-pij-uh HEE-lee-uhs

Eurypygidae yoo-rih-PIJ-uh-dee

Eurystomus orientalis yoo-rih-STOH-muhs or-ih-EN-tal-is

Falco peregrinus FAL-koh PEHR-eh-GRIN-uhs

Falco rusticolis FAL-koh rus-TIH-kol-is

Falconidae fal-KON-uh-dee

Falconiformes fal-kon-uh-FORM-eez

Ficedula basilanica fih-SEH-duh-luh bas-ill-AN-ik-uh

Formicariidae for-mih-kar-EYE-uh-dee

Fratercula arctica frah-TER-kuh-luh ARK-tik-uh

Fregata magnificens FREH-gah-tuh mag-NIH-fih-sens

Fregatidae freh-GAH-tuh-dee

Fringilla coelebs frin-JILL-uh SEE-lebz

Fringillidae frin-JILL-uh-dee

Fulmarus glacialis FULL-mar-uhs glay-SHE-al-is

Furnariidae fur-nar-EYE-uh-dee

Furnarius rufus fur-NAR-ee-uhs ROO-fuhs

Galbula pastazae GAL-bull-uh PAS-tah-zee

Galbula ruficauda GAL-bull-uh roo-fee-KAW-duh

Galbulidae gal-BULL-uh-dee

Gallicolumba luzonica gal-ih-KUH-lum-buh loo-ZON-ik-uh

Galliformes gal-uh-FORM-eez

Gallinago nigripennis gal-uh-NAY-go NY-gruh-PEN-is

Gavia immer GAV-ee-uh IM-mer

Gavia stellata GAV-ee-uh STEL-lah-tuh

Gaviidae gav-EYE-uh-dee

Gaviiformes gav-eye-uh-FORM-eez

Geococcyx californiana GEE-oh-COCK-siks kal-uh-FORN-uh-kuh

Glareola pratincola glar-ee-OH-luh prat-in-KOH-luh

Glareolidae glar-ee-OH-luh-dee

Glaucis hirsuta GLO-kis her-SOO-tuh

Grallina cyanoleuca GRAL-line-uh SIGH-an-uh-LYOO-kuh

Grallinidae gral-LINE-uh-dee

Gruidae GROO-uh-dee

Gruiformes groo-uh-FORM-eez

Grus canadensis GROOS kan-uh-DEN-sis

Grus japonensis GROOS jap-ON-en-sis

Gymnogyps californianus JIM-nuh-jips kal-uh-FORN-uh-kuhs

Haematopodidae hee-muh-toh-POD-uh-dee

Haematopus unicolor hee-muh-TOH-puhs YOO-nih-KUH-luhr

Harpactes oreskios hahr-PAK-teez or-es-KEE-uhs

Heliornis fulica hee-LEE-or-nis FUL-ik-uh

Heliornithidae hee-lee-or-NITH-uh-dee

Hemiprocne coronata HEMI-prok-nee koh-roh-NAH-tuh

Hemiprocnidae hemi-PROK-nuh-dee

Himantopus himantopus hih-MAN-tuh-puhs hih-MAN-tuh-puhs

Himatione sanguinea hih-MAY-shun-ee san-GWIN-ee-uh

Hirundinidae hir-un-DIN-uh-dee

Hirundo pyrrhonota HIR-un-doh pir-uh-NOH-tuh

Hirundo rustica HIR-un-doh RUS-tik-uh

Hydrobatidae hi-droh-BAT-uh-dee

Hydrophasianus chirurgus hi-droh-fay-SEE-an-uhs KY-ruhr-guhs

Hypocolius ampelinus hi-poh-KOL-ee-uhs am-peh-LINE-uhs

Hypothymis azurea hi-poh-THY-mis az-YOOR-ee-uh

Hypsipetes madagascariensis hip-sih-PEET-eez mad-uh-GAS-kar-EE-en-sis

Icteria virens ik-TER-ee-uh VY-renz

Icteridae ik-TER-uh-dee

Icterus galbula IK-ter-uhs GAL-bull-uh

Indicator archipelagicus in-dih-KAY-ter AR-kih-peh-LAJ-ik-uhs

Indicatoridae in-dih-kay-TER-uh-dee

Irena puella eye-REEN-uh poo-ELL-uh

Irenidae eye-REEN-uh-dee

Jacanidae juh-KAN-uh-dee

Jynx torquilla JINKS tor-KWILL-uh

Lagopus lagopus LAG-uh-puhs LAG-uh-puhs

Laniidae lan-EYE-uh-dee

Lanius ludovicianus lan-ee-uhs LOO-doh-vih-SHE-an-uhs

Laridae LAR-uh-dee

Larus saundersi LAR-uhs SON-ders-eye

Laterallus jamaicensis lat-er-ALL-uhs ja-MAY-sen-sis

Leipoa ocellata LYE-poh-uh os-ELL-ah-tuh

Liosceles thoracicus lye-OS-sel-eez tho-RAS-ik-uhs

Lonchura punctulata LON-chur-uh punk-TOO-lah-tuh

Loxia curvirostra LOK-see-uh KUR-vih-ROS-truh

Macrocephalon maleo ma-crow-SEFF-uh-lon MAL-ee-oh

Macronyx ameliae MA-cron-iks am-EEL-ee-ee

Maluridae mal-YOOR-uh-dee

Malurus splendens MAL-yoor-uhs SPLEN-denz

Megaceryle alcyon MEG-uh-ser-EYE-lee al-SIGH-on

Megapodiidae meg-uh-pod-EYE-uh-dee

Megalaima haemacephala meg-uh-LAY-muh hee-muh-SEFF-ah-luh

Melanocharis versteri mel-uh-NOH-kar-is VER-ster-eye

Meleagris gallopavo mel-ee-AY-gris gal-uh-PAY-voh

Melichneutes robustus mel-ik-NOO-teez ro-BUHS-tuhs

Meliphagidae mel-ih-FAJ-uh-dee

Melospiza melodia mel-uh-SPY-zuh meh-LOH-dee-uh

Menura alberti MEN-yoor-uh AL-bert-eye

Menuridae men-YOOR-uh-dee

Meropidae mer-OP-uh-dee

Meropogon forsteni mer-uh-POH-gon FOR-sten-eye

Merops apiaster MER-ops ay-PEE-as-ter

Mesitornis variegata meh-SIT-or-nis VAIR-ree-uh-GAH-tuh

Mesitornithidae meh-sit-or-NITH-uh-dee

Microeca fascinans my-CROW-ek-uh FAS-sin-ans

Mimidae MIH-muh-dee

Mirafra javanica MIR-af-ruh jah-VAH-nik-uh

Mniotilta varia ny-OH-til-tuh VAIR-ee-uh

Moho bishopi MOH-hoh BISH-up-eye

Mohua ochrocephala MOH-hyoo-uh OH-kruh-SEFF-ah-luh

Momotidae moh-MOH-tuh-dee

Momotus momota MOH-moh-tuhs MOH-moh-tuh

Monarchidae mon-ARK-uh-dee

Montifringilla nivalis mon-tih-frin-JILL-uh NYE-val-is

Morus bassanus MOR-uhs BASS-an-uhs

Motacilla cinerea moh-tuh-SILL-uh sin-EAR-ee-uh

Motacillidae moh-tuh-SILL-uh-dee

Muscicapidae mus-kih-KAP-uh-dee

Muscicaps striata   MUS-kih-kaps stry-AH-tuh
Musophagidae   mus-oh-FAJ-uh-dee
Musophagiformes   mus-oh-faj-uh-FORM-eez
Mycteria americana   mik-TER-ee-uh uh-mer-uh-KAN-uh
Nectariniidae   nek-tar-in-EYE-uh-dee
Neodrepanis coruscans   nee-oh-DREH-pan-is KOR-us-kans
Neophron percnopterus   NEE-oh-fron perk-NOP-ter-uhs
Nesomimus macdonaldi   NEZ-oh-MIH-muhs mak-DON-uld-eye
Nonnula ruficapilla   NON-nuh-luh roo-fih-kap-ILL-uh
Notharchus macrorhynchos   NOTH-ark-uhs ma-crow-RIN-kuhs
Nothocercus bonapartei   NOTH-uh-SER-kuhs BOH-nuh-PART-eye
Nucifraga caryocatactes   NYOO-sih-FRAG-uh KAR-ee-oh-KAT-ak-teez
Numenius americanus   nyoo-MEN-ee-uhs uh-mer-uh-KAN-uhs
Numida meleagris   NYOO-mid-uh mel-ee-AY-gris
Numididae   nyoo-MID-uh-dee
Nyctea scandiaca   NIK-tee-uh skan-DEE-uh-kuh
Nyctibiidae   nik-tih-BYE-uh-dee
Nyctibius griseus   nik-TIB-ee-uhs GRIS-ee-uhs
Oceanites oceanicus   OH-shih-NYE-teez OH-shih-AN-uh-kuhs
Odontophoridae   OH-don-tuh-FOR-uh-dee
Opisthocomidae   op-is-thuh-KOM-eh-dee
Opisthocomiformes   op-is-thuh-kom-eh-FORM-eez
Opisthocomus hoazin   op-is-thuh-KOM-uhs HOH-ah-sin
Oriolidae   or-ih-OH-lu-dee
Oriolus oriolus   or-ih-OH-luhs or-ih-OH-luhs
Ortalis vetula   OR-tal-is VET-uh-luh
Orthonychidae   or-thuh-NIK-uh-dee
Orthonyx temminckii   OR-thon-iks TEM-ink-ee-eye
Otididae   oh-TID-uh-dee
Otis tarda   OH-tis TAR-duh
Otus asio   OH-tuhs AS-ee-oh
Oxyruncidae   ok-sih-RUN-kuh-dee
Oxyruncus cristatus   OK-sih-RUN-kuhs KRIS-tah-tuhs
Pachycephala pectoralis   pak-ih-SEFF-ah-luh pek-TOR-al-is
Pachycephalidae   pak-ih-seff-AL-uh-dee

Pachyramphus aglaiae   PAK-ih-RAM-fuhs ag-LAY-ee-ee

Pandion haliaetus   PAN-die-on HAL-ee-ee-tuhs

Parabuteo unicinctus   par-uh-BYOO-tee-oh YOO-nih-SINK-tuhs

Paradisaeidae   par-uh-die-SEE-uh-dee

Pardalotidae   par-duh-LOT-uh-dee

Pardalotus striatus   par-duh-LOT-uhs stry-AH-tuhs

Paridae   PAR-uh-dee

Parulidae   par-YOOL-uh-dee

Parus major   PAR-uhs MAY-jur

Passer domesticus   PASS-er doh-MES-tuh-kuhs

Passerculus sandwichensis   pass-ER-kyoo-luhs SAND-wich-en-sis

Passeridae   pass-ER-uh-dee

Passeriformes   pass-er-uh-FORM-eez

Pelecanidae   pel-uh-KAN-uh-dee

Pelecaniformes   pel-uh-kan-uh-FORM-eez

Pelecanoides urinatrix   pel-uh-KAN-oi-deez yoor-in-AY-triks

Pelecanoididae   pel-uh-kan-OI-duh-dee

Pelecanus erythrorhynchos   pel-uh-KAN-uhs eh-RITH-roh-RIN-kuhs

Pelecanus occidentalis   pel-uh-KAN-uhs ok-sih-DEN-tal-is

Pericrocotus igneus   per-ih-CROW-kot-uhs IG-nee-uhs

Petroicidae   pet-ROY-kuh-dee

Phacellodomus ruber   fay-sell-uh-DOH-muhs ROO-ber

Phaethon lepturus   FEE-thon LEPT-yoor-uhs

Phaethontidae   fee-THON-tuh-dee

Phalacrocoracidae   fal-uh-crow-kor-AY-suh-dee

Phalacrocorax carbo   fal-uh-crow-cor-aks KAR-boh

Pharomachrus mocinno   far-uh-MAK-ruhs MOH-sin-noh

Phasianidae   fay-see-AN-uh-dee

Philepittidae   fil-uh-PIT-tuh-dee

Phoenicopteridae   FEE-nih-kop-TER-uh-dee

Phoenicopteriformes   FEE-nih-KOP-ter-uh-FORM-eez

Phoenicopterus ruber   FEE-nih-KOP-ter-uhs ROO-ber

Phoeniculidae   FEE-nih-KYOO-luh-dee

Phoeniculus purpureus   fee-NIH-kyoo-luhs purh-PURH-ee-uhs

Phyllastrephus scandens   FIL-uh-STRE-fuhs SKAN-denz

Phylloscopus borealis   FIL-uh-SKOH-puhs BOHR-ee-al-is

Phytotoma raimondii   fye-toh-TOH-muh RAY-mund-ee-eye

Phytotomidae fye-toh-TOH-muh-dee

Picathartes oreas PIK-uh-THAR-teez OR-ee-uhs

Picoides borealis PIK-oy-deez BOHR-ee-al-is

Picidae PIS-uh-dee

Piciformes pis-uh-FORM-eez

Pinguinus impennis PIN-gwin-uhs IM-pen-is

Pipra filicauda PIP-ruh fil-eh-KAW-duh

Pipridae PIP-ruh-dee

Pitangus sulphuratus PIT-an-guhs sul-FUR-ah-tuhs

Pitohui kirhocephalus PIT-oo-eey kir-uh-SEFF-ah-luhs

Pitta angolensis PIT-tuh an-GOH-len-sis

Pitta sordida PIT-tuh SOR-dih-duh

Pittidae PIT-tuh-dee

Pityriasis gymnocephala pit-ih-RYE-uh-sis jim-nuh-SEFF-ah-luh

Plectoryncha lanceolata PLEK-tuh-RIN-kuh LAN-see-oh-LAH-tuh

Plectrophenax nivalis PLEK-troh-FEN-aks NYE-val-is

Ploceidae ploh-SEE-uh-dee

Ploceus cucullatus PLOH-see-uhs kyoo-KYOO-lah-tuhs

Ploceus philippinus PLOH-see-uhs fil-ih-PINE-uhs

Podargidae pod-AR-juh-dee

Podargus strigoides POD-ar-guhs STRI-goy-deez

Podiceps cristatus POD-ih-seps KRIS-tah-tuhs

Podicipedidae pod-ih-sih-PED-uh-dee

Podicipediformes pod-ih-sih-ped-uh-FORM-eez

Poecile atricapilla PEE-suh-lee ay-trih-kap-ILL-uh

Pogoniulus chrysoconus po-go-NYE-uh-luhs KRIS-oh-KON-uhs

Polioptila caerulea poh-lih-OP-til-uh see-ROO-lee-uh

Polyborus plancus pol-ih-BOHR-uhs PLAN-kuhs

Pomatostomidae poh-may-tuh-STOH-muh-dee

Pomatostomus temporalis poh-may-tuh-STOH-muhs tem-PER-al-is

Prionops plumatus PRY-on-ops PLOO-mah-tuhs

Procellariidae pro-sell-ar-EYE-uh-dee

Procellariiformes pro-sell-ar-eye-uh-FORM-eez

Promerops cafer PRO-mer-ops KAF-er

Prunella modularis proo-NELL-uh mod-YOO-lar-is

Prunellidae proo-NELL-uh-dee

Psaltriparus minimus sol-TRI-par-uhs MIN-ih-muhs

Psittacidae sit-UH-suh-dee

Psittaciformes sit-uh-suh-FORM-eez

Psittacula krameri sit-UH-kuh-luh KRAY-mer-eye

Psittacus erithacus SIT-uh-kuhs eh-RITH-uh-kuhs

Psittirostra cantans SIT-uh-ROS-truh KAN-tanz

Psophia crepitans SOH-fee-uh KREP-ih-tanz

Psophiidae soh-FYE-uh-dee

Pterocles namaqua TER-oh-kleez nah-MAH-kwuh

Pteroclididae ter-oh-KLID-uh-dee

Pterocliformes ter-oh-cluh-FORM-eez

Pterocnemia pennata ter-ok-NEE-mee-uh PEN-ah-tuh

Ptilonorhynchidae TIL-on-oh-RIN-kuh-dee

Ptilonorhynchus violaceus TIL-on-oh-RIN-kuhs vee-o-LAY-see-uhs

Ptiloris victoriae TIL-or-is vik-TOR-ee-ee

Ptyonoprogne rupestris TY-on-oh-PROG-nee ROO-pes-tris

Puffinus puffinus PUFF-in-uhs PUFF-in-uhs

Pycnonotidae pik-noh-NOH-tuh-dee

Pycnonotus barbatus pik-noh-NOH-tuhs BAR-bat-uhs

Rallidae RALL-uh-dee

Ramphastidae ram-FAS-tuh-dee

Ramphastos toco RAM-fas-tuhs TOH-coh

Raphidae RAF-uh-dee

Raphus cucullatus RAF-uhs kyoo-KYOO-lah-tuhs

Recurvirostra americana re-CURV-ih-ROS-truh uh-mer-uh-KAN-uh

Recurvirostridae re-CURV-ih-ROS-truh-dee

Remizidae rem-IZ-uh-dee

Rhabdornis mysticalis RAB-dor-nis mis-TIH-kal-is

Rhabdornithidae rab-dor-NITH-uh-dee

Rheidae REE-uh-dee

Rhinocryptidae RYE-noh-KRIP-tuh-dee

Rhinoplax vigil RYE-noh-plaks VIH-jil

Rhipidura albicollis rip-ih-DYOOR-uh ahl-bih-KOLL-is

Rhipidura leucophrys rip-ih-DYOOR-uh LYOO-kuh-frees

Rhipiduridae rip-ih-DYOOR-uh-dee

Rhynochetidae rye-noh-KEE-tuh-dee

Rhynochetos jubatus rye-noh-KEE-tuhs JOO-bat-uhs

Rostratula benghalensis ros-TRAT-uh-luh ben-GOL-en-sis

Rostratulidae ros-trat-UH-luh-dee

Rupicola rupicola roo-pih-KOH-luh roo-pih-KOH-luh

Sagittariidae saj-ih-tar-EYE-uh-dee

Sagittarius serpentarius saj-ih-TAR-ee-uhs ser-pen-TAR-ee-uhs

Sarcoramphus papa sar-KOH-ram-fuhs PAH-pah

Sarothrura elegans sar-oh-THROO-ruh EL-eh-ganz

Saxicola torquata sax-ih-KOH-luh TOR-kwah-tuh

Sayornis phoebe SAY-ro-nis FEE-bee

Schetba rufa SKET-buh ROO-fuh

Scolopacidae skoh-loh-PAY-suh-dee

Scopidae SKOH-puh-dee

Scopus umbretta SKOH-puhs UM-bret-tuh

Semnornis ramphastinus SEM-nor-nis ram-FAS-tin-uhs

Sialia sialis sigh-AL-ee-uh SIGH-al-is

Sitta canadensis SIT-tuh kan-uh-DEN-sis

Sitta europaea SIT-tuh yoor-uh-PEE-uh

Sittidae SIT-tuh-dee

Smithornis capensis SMITH-or-nis KAP-en-sis

Somateria spectabilis soh-muh-TER-ee-uh spek-TAB-ih-lis

Sphecotheres vieilloti sfek-UH-ther-eez VYE-ill-oh-eye

Spheniscidae sfen-IS-kuh-dee

Sphenisciformes sfen-is-kuh-FORM-eez

Spheniscus magellanicus SFEN-is-kuhs maj-eh-LAN-ik-uhs

Sphyrapicus varius sfir-AP-ik-uhs VAIR-ee-uhs

Steatornis caripensis stee-AT-or-nis kar-IH-pen-sis

Steatornithidae stee-at-or-NITH-uh-dee

Stercorarius parasiticus ster-koh-RARE-ee-uhs par-uh-SIT-ik-uhs

Stiltia isabella STILT-ee-uh IZ-uh-BELL-uh

Strigidae STRIJ-uh-dee

Strigiformes strij-uh-FORM-eez

Struthio camelus STROO-thee-oh KAM-el-uhs

Struthionidae stroo-thee-ON-uh-dee

Struthioniformes stroo-thee-on-uh-FORM-eez

Sturnidae STURN-uh-dee

Sturnus vulgaris STURN-uhs VUL-gar-is

Sula nebouxii SUL-uh NEB-oo-ee-eye

Sulidae SUL-uh-dee

Sylviidae sil-VYE-uh-dee

Syrrhaptes paradoxus SIR-rap-teez PAR-uh-DOKS-uhs

Taeniopygia guttata tee-nee-uh-PIJ-ee-uh GUT-tah-tuh

Terpsiphone viridis terp-SIF-oh-nee VIR-id-is

Thamnophilus doliatus THAM-nuh-FIL-uhs dol-EE-ah-tuhs

Thinocoridae thin-uh-KOR-uh-dee

Threskiornis aethiopicus THRES-kih-OR-nis EE-thi-OH-pi-kuhs

Threskiornithidae thres-kih-or-NITH-uh-dee

Timaliidae tim-al-EYE-uh-dee

Tinamidae tin-AM-uh-dee

Todidae TOH-duh-dee

Todus multicolor TOH-duhs MULL-tee-KUH-luhr

Tragopan satyra TRAG-uh-pan SAT-eye-ruh

Trichoglossus haematodus TRIK-uh-GLOS-uhs HEE-muh-TOH-duhs

Trochilidae trok-ILL-uh-dee

Troglodytes aedon trog-luh-DIE-teez EE-don

Troglodytes troglodytes trog-luh-DIE-teez trog-luh-DIE-teez

Troglodytidae trog-luh-DIE-tuh-dee

Trogonidae troh-GON-uh-dee

Trogoniformes troh-gon-uh-FORM-eez

Turdidae TUR-duh-dee

Turdus migratorius TUR-duhs my-gruh-TOR-ee-uhs

Turnicidae tur-NIS-uh-dee

Turnix sylvatica TUR-niks sil-VAT-ik-uh

Turnix varia TUR-niks VAIR-ee-uh

Tyrannidae tie-RAN-uh-dee

Tyto alba TIE-toh AHL-buh

Tytonidae tie-TON-uh-dee

Upupa epops UP-up-uh EE-pops

Upupidae up-UP-uh-dee

Uria aalge YOOR-ee-uh AHL-jee

Vanellus vanellus vah-NELL-uhs vah-NELL-uhs

Vangidae VAN-juh-dee

Vireo atricapillus VIR-e-oh ay-trih-kap-ILL-uhs

Vireonidae vir-e-ON-uh-dee

Volatinia jacarina vol-uh-TIN-ee-uh jak-uh-REE-nuh

Zenaida macroura ZEN-ay-duh ma-crow-YOOR-uh

Zosteropidae zos-ter-OP-uh-dee

Zosterops japonicus ZOS-ter-ops jap-ON-ik-uhs

Words to Know

A

Acacia: A thorny tree, or any of several trees, shrubs, or other plants of the legume family that tend to be ornamental.

Adaptation: Any structural, physiological, or behavioral trait that aids an organism's survival and ability to reproduce in its existing environment.

Adaptive evolution: Changes in organisms over time that allow them to cope more efficiently with their biomes.

Adaptive shift: An evolutionary process by which the descendants of an organism adapt, over time, to ecological niches, or natural lifestyles, that are new to that organism and usually filled in other places by much different organisms.

Aftershaft: The secondary feather that branches from the base of the main feather.

Algae: Tiny plants or plantlike organisms that grow in water and in damp places.

Alpine: Used to refer to the mountainous region of the Alps, or to describe other areas related to mountains.

Altitude: The height of something in relation to the earth's surface or sea level.

Altricial: Chicks that hatch at an early developmental stage, often blind and without feathers.

Anisodactyl: Toe arrangement with three toes pointing forward and one toe facing backward.

Anting: A behavior birds use to interact with ants, either by rolling in an ant hill or placing ants into their feathers.

Aphrodisiac: Anything that intensifies or arouses sexual desires.

Aquatic: Related to water.

Arachnid: Eight-legged animals, including spiders, scorpions, and mites.

Arboreal: Living primarily or entirely in trees and bushes.

Arthropod: A member of the largest single animal phylum, consisting of organisms with segmented bodies, jointed legs or wings, and exoskeletons.

Asynchronous hatching: A situation in which the eggs in a nest hatch at different times, so that some chicks (the older ones) are larger and stronger than others.

Australasia: Region consisting of Australia, New Zealand, New Guinea, and the neighboring islands of the South Pacific.

Avian: Relating to birds.

Aviary: Large enclosure or cage for birds.

B

Barb: Stiff filament that forms the framework of a feather.

Bib: Area under the bill of a bird, just above the breast.

Biodiversity: Abundance of species in a particular biome or geographical area.

Biparental: Both male and female of the species incubate, feed, and fledge their young.

Bower: Shady, leafy shelter or recess.

Brackish: Water that is a mix of freshwater and saltwater.

Bromeliads: A family of tropical plants. Many bromeliads grow high on the branches and trunks of trees rather than in the soil.

Brood: Young birds that are born and raised together.

Brood parasite: An animal species, most often a bird, in which the female lays its own eggs in the nests of other bird species. The host mother raises the chick as if it were her own. This behavior has also been observed in fish.

Brushland: Habitat characterized by a cover of bushes or shrubs.

Burrow: Tunnel or hole that an animal digs in the ground to use as a home.

C

Cache: A hidden supply area.

Camouflage: Device used by an animal, such as coloration, allowing it to blend in with the surroundings to avoid being seen by prey and predators.

Canopy: The uppermost layer of a forest formed naturally by the leaves and branches of trees and plants.

Cap: Patch on top of bird's head.

Carcass: The dead body of an animal. Vultures gather around a carcass to eat it.

Carnivore: Meat-eating organism.

Carrion: Dead and decaying animal flesh.

Caruncle: A genetically controlled outgrowth of skin on an animal, usually for dominance or mating displays.

Casque: A horny growth on the head of a bird resembling a helmet.

Cavity: Hollow area within a body.

Churring: Referring to a low, trilled, or whirring sound that some birds make.

Circumpolar: Able to live at the North and South Pole.

Clutch: Group of eggs hatched together.

Collagen: A type of protein formed within an animal body that is assembled into various structures, most notably tendons.

Colony: A group of animals of the same type living together.

Comb: Fleshy red crest on top of the head.

Coniferous: Refers to evergreen trees, such as pines and firs, that bear cones and have needle-like leaves that are not shed all at once.

Coniferous forest: An evergreen forest where plants stay green all year.

Continental margin: A gently sloping ledge of a continent that is submerged in the ocean.

Convergence: In adaptive evolution, a process by which unrelated or only distantly related living things come to resemble one another in adapting to similar environments.

Cooperative breeding: A social organization of breeding where several birds (not just the parents) feed a group of hatchlings.

Courtship: Behaviors related to attracting a mate and preparing to breed.

Courtship display: Actions of a male and female animal that demonstrate their interest in becoming or remaining a pair for breeding.

Covert: Term derived from the word for something that is concealed, and used to describe the small feathers that cover the bases of the larger feathers on a bird's wing and tail.

Crèche: A group of young of the same species, which gather together in order to better avoid predators.

Crepuscular: Most active at dawn and dusk.

Crest: A group of feathers on the top or back of a bird's head.

Critically Endangered: A term used by the IUCN in reference to a species that is at an extremely high risk of extinction in the wild.

Crop: A pouch-like organ in the throat where crop milk is produced.

Crop milk: A cheesy, nutritious substance produced by adult pigeons and doves and fed to chicks.

Crown: Top of a bird's head.

Cryptic: To be colored so as to blend into the environment.

D

Deciduous: Shedding leaves at the end of the growing season.

Deciduous forest: A forest with four seasons in which trees drop their leaves in the fall.

Decurved: Down-curved; slightly bent.

Defensive posture: A position adopted to frighten away potential predators.

Deforestation: Those practices or processes that result in the change of forested lands to non-forest uses, such as human settlement or farming. This is often cited as one of the major causes of the enhanced greenhouse effect.

Distal: Away from the point of attachment.

Distraction display: Behaviors intended to distract potential predators from the nest site.

Diurnal: Refers to animals that are active during the day.

Domesticated: Tamed.

Dominant: The top male or female of a social group, sometimes called the alpha male or alpha female.

Dormant: Not active.

Dorsal: Located in the back.

Dung: Feces, or solid waste from an animal.

E

Ecological niche: The role a living creature, plant or animal, plays in its community.

Ecotourist: A person who visits a place in order to observe the plants and animals in the area while making minimal human impact on the natural environment.

Elevation: The height of land when measured from sea level.

Endangered: A term used by the U.S. Endangered Species Act of 1973 and by the IUCN in reference to a species that is facing a very high risk of extinction from all or a significant portion of its natural home.

Endemic: Native to or occuring only in a particular place.

Epiphyte: Plant such as mosses that grows on another plant but does not depend on that host plant for nutrition.

Estuary: Lower end of a river where ocean tides meet the river's current.

Eucalyptus: Tall, aromatic trees.

Evolve: To change slowly over time.

Extinct: A species without living members.

Extinction: The total disappearance of a species or the disappearance of a species from a given area.

Eyespot: Colored feathers on the body that resemble the eyes of a large animal, which function in helping to frighten away potential predators.

F

Family: A grouping of genera that share certain characteristics and appear to have evolved from the same ancestors.

Feather tract: Spacing of feathers in a pattern.

Feces: Solid body waste.

Fermentation: Chemical reaction in which enzymes break down complex organic compounds into simpler ones. This can make digestion easier.

Fledgling: Bird that has recently grown the feathers necessary to fly.

Flightless: Species that have lost the ability to fly.

Flock: A large group of birds of the same species.

Forage: To search for food.

Frugivore: Animal that primarily eats fruit. Many bats and birds are frugivores.

G

Gape: The width of the open mouth.

Genera: Plural of genus.

Generalist feeder: A species that eats a wide variety of foods.

Genus (pl. genera): A category of classification made up of species sharing similar characteristics.

Granivore: Animal that primarily eats seeds and grains.

Grassland: Region in which the climate is dry for long periods of the summer, and freezes in the winter. Grasslands are characterized by grasses and other erect herbs, usually without trees or shrubs, and occur in the dry temperate interiors of continents.

Gregarious: Used to describe birds that tend to live in flocks, and are very sociable with other birds. The word has come to be used to describe people who are very outgoing and sociable, as well.

H

Habitat: The area or region where a particular type of plant or animal lives and grows.

Hallux: The big toe, or first digit, on the part of the foot facing inwards.

Hatchling: Birds that have just hatched, or broken out of the egg.

Hawking: Hunting for food by sitting on a perch, flying out and capturing the food, and returning to the perch to eat.

Heath: Grassy and shrubby uncultivated land.

Herbivore: Plant eating organism.

Heterodactyl: With toes pointed in opposite directions; usually with first and second inner front toes turned backward and the third and fourth toes turned forward.

Homeotherm: Organism with stable independent body temperature.

Host: A living plant or animal from which a parasite takes nutrition

I

Igapó: Black waters of the Amazon river area.

Incubation: Process of sitting on and warming eggs in order for them to hatch.

Indicator species: A bird or animal whose presence reveals a specific environmental characteristic

Indigenous: Originating in a region or country.

Insectivore: An animal that eats primarily insects.

Introduced: Not native to the area; brought in by humans.

Invertebrate: Animal lacking a spinal column (backbone).

Iridescent: Having a lustrous or brilliant appearance or quality.

IUCN: Abbreviation for the International Union for Conservation of Nature and Natural Resources, now the World Conservation Union. A conservation organization of government agencies and nongovernmental organizations best known for its Red Lists of threatened an

K

Keel: A projection from a bone.

Keratin: Protein found in hair, nails, and skin.

Kleptoparasite: An individual that steals food or other resources from another individual.

L

Lamellae: Plural of lamella; comb-like bristles inside a flamingos bill.

Larva (pl. larvae): Immature form (wormlike in insects; fish-like in amphibians) of an organism capable of surviving on its own. A larva does not resemble the parent and must go through metamorphosis, or change, to reach its adult stage.

Lek: An area where birds come to display courtship behaviors to attract a mate (noun); to sing, flutter, hop and perform other courtship behaviors at a lek (verb).

Lerp: Sugary lumps of secretions of psillid insects, small plant-sucking insects living on Eucalyptus trees.

Lichen: A complex of algae and fungi found growing on trees, rocks, or other solid surfaces.

Litter: A layer of dead vegetation and other material covering the ground.

M

Mandible: Upper or lower part of a bird's bill; jaw.

Mangrove: Tropical coastal trees or shrubs that produce many supporting roots and that provide dense vegetation.

Mantle: Back, inner-wing, and shoulder area.

Mesic: Referring to any area that is known to be wet or moist.

Midstory: The level of tropical forests between ground level (understory) and treetops (overstory).

Migrate: To move from one area or climate to another as the seasons change, usually to find food or to mate..

Mixed-species flock: A flock of birds that includes multiple species.

Mobbing: A group of birds gathering together to defend themselves from another large bird by calling loudly and flying at the intruder.

Molt: The process by which an organism sheds its outermost layer of feathers, fur, skin, or exoskeleton.

Monogamous: Refers to a breeding system in which a male and a female mate only with each other during a breeding season or lifetime.

Montane forest: Forest found in mountainous areas.

Mutualism: A relationship between two species where both gain something and neither is harmed.

N

Nape: Back part of the neck.

Near Threatened: A category defined by the IUCN suggesting that a species could become threatened with extinction in the future.

Nectar: Sweet liquid secreted by the flowers of various plants to attract pollinators (animals that pollinate, or fertilize, the flowers).

Neotropical: Relating to a geographic area of plant and animal life east, south, and west of Mexico's central plateau that includes Central and South America and the West Indies.

Nest box: A small, human-made shelter intended as a nest site for birds. Usually a rectangular wooden box with a round entrance hole.

Nestling: Young bird unable to leave the nest.

New World: Made up of North America, Central America, and South America; the western half of the world.

Niche: A habitat with everything an animal needs.

Nictating membranes: Clear coverings under the eyelids that can be moved over the eye.

Nocturnal: Occuring or active at night.

O

Omnivore: A plant- and meat- eating animal.

Opportunistic feeder: One that is able to take advantage of whatever food resources become available.

Overstory: The level of tropical forests nearest treetops.

P

Palearctic: The area or subregion of Europe, Africa, and the Middle East, that is north of the Tropic of Cancer, and the area north of the Himalayas mountain range.

Pampas: Open grasslands of South America.

Parasite: An organism that lives in or on a host organism and that gets its nourishment from that host.

Pelagic: To live on the open ocean.

Permafrost: Permanently frozen lands.

Plain: Large expanse of land that is fairly dry and with few trees.

Plumage: Feathers of a bird.

Pneumatic: Air-filled cavities in the bones of birds.

Poisonous: Containing or producing toxic materials.

Pollen: Dust-like grains or particles produced by a plant that contain male sex cells.

Pollinate: To transfer pollen from the male organ to the female organ of a flower.

Polyandry: A mating system in which a single female mates with multiple males.

Polygamy: A mating system in which males and females mate with multiple partners.

Polygynous lek: A mating system in which several males display together for the attention of females. A female, after watching the displaying males, may mate with one or more males in the lek.

Polygyny: A mating system in which a single male mates with multiple females.

Precocial: Young that hatch at an advanced stage of development, with feathers and able to move.

Predator: An animal that eats other animals.

Preen: To clean and smooth feathers using the bill.

Preen gland: A gland on the rear of most birds which secretes an oil the birds use in grooming.

Prey: Organism hunted and eaten by a predator.

Primary forest: A forest characterized by a full-ceiling canopy formed by the branches of tall trees and several layers of smaller trees. This type of forest lacks ground vegetation because sunlight cannot penetrate through the canopy.

Promiscuity: Mating in which individuals mate with as many other individuals as they can or want to.

Pupae: Plural of pupa; developing insects inside cocoon.

Q

Quill: Hollow feather shaft.

R

Rainforest: An evergreen woodland of the tropics distinguished by a continuous leaf canopy and an average rainfall of about 100 inches (250 centimeters) per year.

Raptor: A bird of prey.

Regurgitate: Eject the contents of the stomach through the mouth; to vomit.

Resident: Bird species that do not migrate.

Retrices: Plural of retrix; paired flight feathers of the tail, which extend from the margins of a bird's tail.

Rictal bristles: Modified feathers composed mainly of the vertical shaft.

Riparian: Having to do with the edges of streams or rivers.

Riverine: Located near a river.

Roe: Fish eggs.

Roost: A place where animals, such as bats, sit or rest on a perch, branch, etc.

S

Savanna: A biome characterized by an extensive cover of grasses with scattered trees, usually transitioning between areas dominated by forests and those dominated by grasses and having alternating seasonal climates of precipitation and drought.

Scavenger: An animal that eats carrion.

Scrub forest: A forest with short trees and shrubs.

Secondary forest: A forest characterized by a less-developed canopy, smaller trees, and a dense ground vegetation found on the edges of fores

Sedentary: Living in a fixed location, as with most plants, tunicates, sponges, etc. Contrast with motile.

Semi-precocial: To be born in a state between altricial and precocial. Semi-precocial chicks can usually leave the nest after a few days.

Sequential polyandry: A mating system in which a female mates with one male, leaves him a clutch of eggs to tend, and then mates with another male, repeating the process throughout the breeding season.

Serial monogamy: Mating for a single nesting then finding another mate or mates for other nestings.

Serrated: Having notches like a saw blade.

Sexual dichromatism: Difference in coloration between the sexes of a species.

Sexual dimorphism: Differences in size and in shapes of body or body parts between sexes of a species.

Sexually mature: Capable of reproducing.

Sheath: Tubular-shaped covering used to protect a body part.

Snag: A dead tree, still standing, with the top broken off.

Social: Species in which individuals are found with other individuals of the same species.

Solitary: Living alone or avoiding the company of others.

Specialist feeder: A species that eats only one or a few food items.

Species: A group of living things that share certain distinctive characteristics and can breed together in the wild.

Squab: Young pigeons and doves.

Steppe: Wide expanse of semiarid relatively level plains, found in cool climates and characterized by shrubs, grasses, and few trees.

Sternum: The breastbone.

Subalpine forest: Forest found at elevations between 9,190 and 10,500 feet (2,800 and 3,200 meters).

Sub-canopy: Below the treetops.

Subordinate: An individual that has lower rank than other, dominant, members of the group.

Subspecies: Divisions within a species based on significant differences and on genetics. Subspecies within a species look different from one another but are still genetically close to be considered separate species. In most cases, subspecies can interbreed and produc

Subtropical: Referring to large areas near the tropics that are not quite as warm as tropical areas.

Syndactyly: A condition in which two bones (or digits) fuse together to become a single bone.

Syrinx (pl. syringes): Vocal organ of birds.

T

Taiga: Subarctic wet evergreen forests.

Tail coverts: The short feathers bordering the quills of the long tail feathers of a bird. They may be over-tail or under-tail (i.e., top or bottom).

Tail streamer: A central part of a bird's tail that is longer than other parts.

Talon: A sharp hooked claw.

Taxonomy: The science dealing with the identification, naming, and classification of plants and animals.

Temperate: Areas with moderate temperatures in which the climate undergoes seasonal change in temperature and moisture. Temperate regions of the earth lie primarily between 30 and 60° latitude in both hemispheres.

Terrestrial: Relating to the land or living primarily on land.

Territorial: A pattern of behavior that causes an animal to stay in a limited area and/or to keep certain other animals of the same species (other than its mate, herd, or family group) out of the

Tetrapod: Any vertebrate having four legs or limbs, including mammals, birds, reptiles, and others.

Thermal: Rising bubble of warm air.

Thicket: An area represented by a thick, or dense, growth of shrubs, underbrush, or small trees.

Threat display: A set of characteristic motions used to communicate aggression and warning to other individuals of the same species.

Threatened: Describes a species that is threatened with extinction.

Torpor: A short period of inactivity characterized by an energy-saving, deep sleep-like state in which heart rate, respiratory rate and body temperature drop.

Tropical: The area between 23.5° north and south of the equator. This region has small daily and seasonal changes in temperature, but great seasonal changes in precipitation. Generally, a hot and humid climate that is completely or almost free of frost.

Tundra: A type of ecosystem dominated by lichens, mosses, grasses, and woody plants. It is found at high latitudes (arctic tundra) and high altitudes (alpine tundra). Arctic tundra is underlain by permafrost and usually very wet.

U

Understory: The trees and shrubs between the forest canopy and the ground cover.

V

Vertebra (pl. vertebrae): A component of the vertebral column, or backbone, found in vertebrates.

Vertebrate: An animal having a spinal column (backbone).

Vocalization: Sound made by vibration of the vocal tract.

Vulnerable: An IUCN category referring to a species that faces a high risk of extinction.

W

Wattle: A fold of skin, often brightly colored, that hangs from the throat area.

Wetlands: Areas that are wet or covered with water for at least part of the year and support aquatic plants, such as marshes, swamps, and bogs.

Wingbars: Stripes of coloration on the wing.

Wingspan: The distance from wingtip to wingtip when the wings are extended in flight.

X

Xeric forest: Forest adapted to very dry conditions.

Z

Zygodactyl: Two pairs of toes, with two toes pointing forward and two toes facing backward.

Getting to Know Birds

FEATHERS

It is easy to tell that an animal is a bird. If it has feathers, it is one of the more than 8,600 kinds of birds in the world. Birds can also be recognized by their bills, wings, and two legs, but feathers are what make them different from every other animal.

First feathers

Scientists are not sure when feathers first appeared on animals. They might have begun as feather-like scales on some of the dinosaurs. In 1861, fossils of a feathered animal, *Archaeopteryx* (ar-key-OP-tuh-rix), were found in Germany. These are the first animals known to scientists that were covered with feathers. These crow-sized animals with heads like lizards lived on the Earth about 150 million years ago.

How birds use different types of feathers

Feathers in most birds' wings and tail help them fly. Each of these flight feathers has a stiff shaft that goes from one end to the other. Flight feathers are light, but they are surprisingly strong. Birds that can fly can escape enemies and get to food sources and nesting places they wouldn't be able to walk to.

Feathers have many other uses in addition to flight. The outer feathers on a bird's body give it color and shape and help to waterproof the bird. Outer feathers with patterns are useful for camouflaging some birds, and colorful feathers send messages. For example, male birds show off their bright feathers to impress females or wave them as warnings to others. Downy inner feathers trap air to keep the bird warm.

Archaeopteryx is the first animal known to be covered with feathers. (© François Gohier/Photo Researchers, Inc. Reproduced by permission.)

Scientists have names for different types of feathers and also for groups of feathers according to where they grow on a bird's body.

Flight

Most birds' bodies are built for flight. Air sacs in their chests and hollow bones keep them light. They have powerful chest muscles that move their wings. The wing and tail feathers are tough, and birds can turn some of them for steering. A bird usually shuts its wing feathers to trap the air as its wings go down. This lifts the bird into the air and pushes it forward. Then, as it raises the wings, it fans the feathers open to let the air through.

How birds fly depends somewhat on the shape of their wings. Vultures and seabirds have long, narrow wings that are great for soaring high on air currents or gliding over the ocean. Songbirds have short, broad wings that are made for flapping as the birds fly among trees. Falcons have narrow, pointed wings that curve backward. These wings help them fly fast and steer well. But all birds flap their wings at times and glide at other times, depending on what they are doing and how the wind is blowing.

Some birds use their wings in unusual ways. Hummingbirds can flap their wings about fifty times every second. This allows them to hover at one spot as they lap nectar from flowers. Flipper-like wings help penguins to "fly" through the water, and even ostriches use their wings to keep their balance as they run.

The wing of a bird is rounded on top and flat on the bottom, similar to the wing of an airplane. This shape is what gives the bird the lift it needs to stay up in the air.

Birds take off and land facing the wind. Small birds (up to the size of pigeons) can jump up from the ground and fly right off into the air. Larger birds have to jump off something high or run along the ground or the water to get going.

BIRDS' BODIES

Different, but the same

A 400-pound (181-kilogram) ostrich may seem very different from a tiny bee hummingbird that weighs less than an ounce (about 2 grams). But all birds have many things in common besides having feathers. They have bills, two legs, a backbone, they are warm-blooded (keep an even body temperature), and they lay hard-shelled eggs.

Body shapes

Birds have many different shapes. Wading birds such as flamingos have long necks and long legs. Eagles have short necks and legs. But both kinds of birds are able to find their food in the water. Falcons and penguins have sleek, torpedo-shaped bodies that are perfect for catching speedy prey. Turkeys' heavier bodies are just right for their quiet lives in the forest searching for acorns and insects.

Bill shapes

Bird bills come in a wide variety of shapes. They use their bills to gather food, build nests, fix their feathers, feed their young, attract mates, and attack their enemies. The type of food a bird eats depends on its bills' shape. For example, the sturdy bills of sparrows are good for cracking seeds, and hawks' hooked beaks are perfect for tearing up prey.

Legs and feet

Bird legs and feet fit their many different lifestyles. For example, hawks have sharp talons for hunting and ducks have webbed feet to help them swim. Some of the birds that spend most of their lives in the air or on the water are not good at walking. Most birds have four toes, but some have three, and ostriches have only two.

BIRDS' SENSES

Sight

For most birds, sight is their best sense. They can see much better than humans, and they can see in color, unlike many mammals.

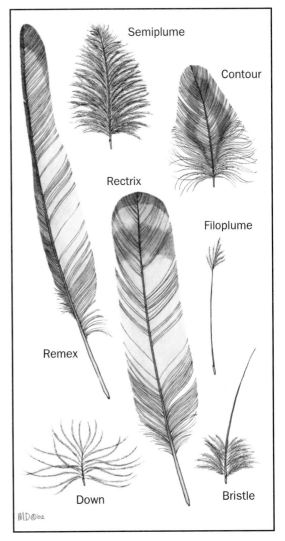

A bird's stiffest feathers are the remex feathers of the wing and the retrix feathers of the tail. The outside of a bird's body is covered with contour feathers that give the body shape and waterproof the bird. Underneath the contour feathers are the semiplume and down feathers that help keep the bird warm. Filoplumes lie alongside the contour feathers and help the bird tell if its feathers are in place. Some birds have bristles around their beaks that allow them to feel insects in the air. (Illustration by Marguette Dongvillo. Reproduced by permission.)

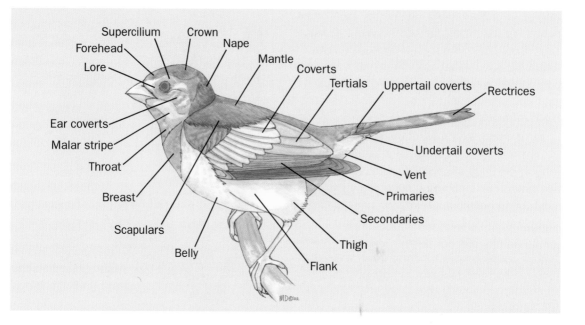

Scientists have names for groups of feathers according to where they grow on a bird's body. (Illustration by Marguette Dongvillo. Reproduced by permission.)

A bird's eyes are big and are usually set on the sides of its head. The eyes focus independently, so that the bird sees two different things at the same time. This gives the bird a very wide view and helps it to watch for predators in most directions. Most birds cannot roll their eyes, but they can turn their heads farther around than mammals can. Owls and other birds of prey have forward-facing eyes that usually work together. This helps them judge distance as they swoop down on prey.

Hearing

Birds have a good sense of hearing—they can hear about as well as mammals. The sound goes in through a little opening near each eye. The holes are usually covered with feathers. They lead to the bird's middle and inner ear, which are very sensitive to sounds. Because owls hunt at night, hearing is especially important to them. Some owls have a disc of stiff feathers on the face. The disc catches sounds, such as the squeaks of a mouse, and leads them to the ears.

Touch

Birds have many nerve endings, which shows that they have a good sense of touch. They can also feel pain, hot, and cold.

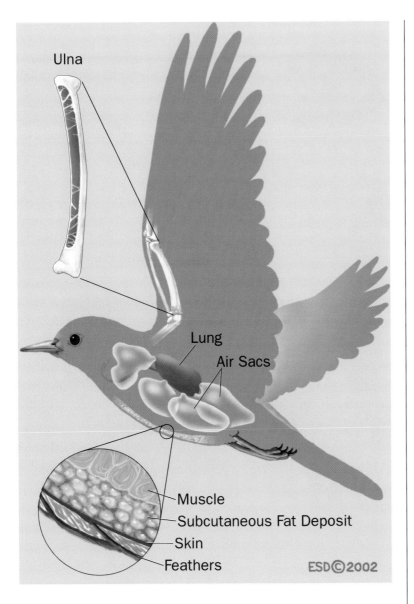

Ulna

Lung

Air Sacs

Muscle

Subcutaneous Fat Deposit

Skin

Feathers

ESD©2002

Birds' bodies have adaptations for flight, including air sacs in the chest and hollow bones to keep them light, and strong chest muscles. (Illustration by Emily Damstra. Reproduced by permission.)

Some long-billed birds have very sensitive bills and can feel their prey in muddy water.

Smell and taste

Most birds' sense of smell seems to be poorly developed. But kiwis, turkey vultures, and several other birds are able to find food by sniffing it. Although birds do not have many taste buds on their tongues, they can often taste well enough to avoid eating harmful foods.

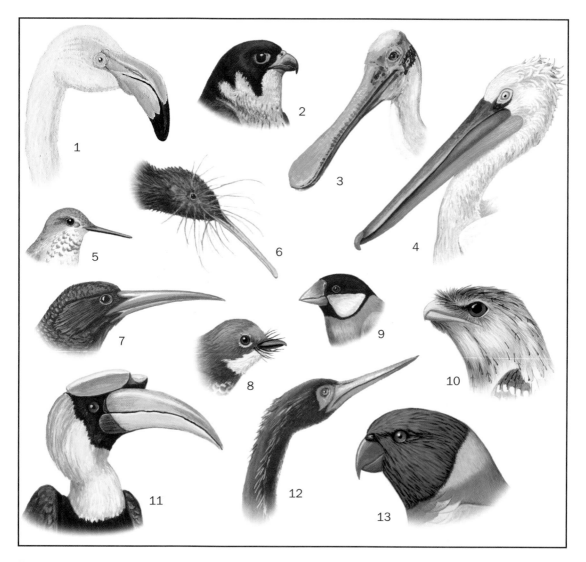

Bills are different shapes and sizes for different eating methods: 1. The greater flamingo filters microorganisms from water; 2. A peregrine falcon tears its prey; 3. Roseate spoonbills sift water for fish; 4. The Dalmation pelican scoops fish in its pouch; 5. Anna's hummingbird sips nectar; 6. The brown kiwi probes the soil for invertebrates; 7. The green woodhoopoe probes bark for insects; 8. Rufous flycatchers catch insects; 9. Java sparrows eat seeds; 10. Papuan frogmouths catch insects; 11. The bicornis hornbill eats fruit; 12. American anhingas spear fish; 13. Rainbow lorikeets crack nuts. (Illustration by Jacqueline Mahannah. Reproduced by permission.)

WHAT'S INSIDE?

Organs and muscles

Birds have many of the same organs that humans have, but they have special features that help with flight and keep them light. Their biggest, strongest muscles control their wings. Birds

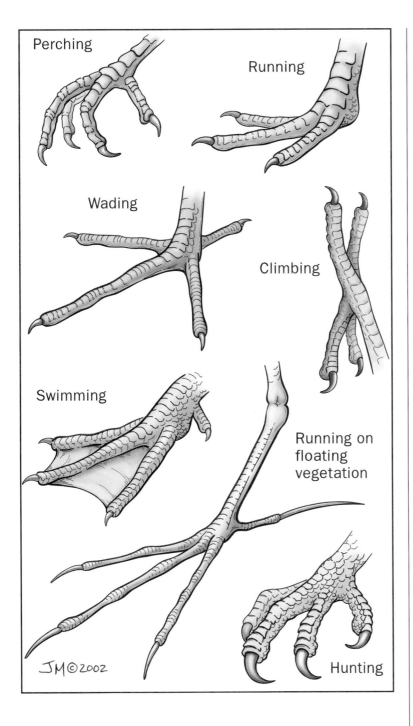

Perching

Running

Wading

Climbing

Swimming

Running on floating vegetation

Hunting

JM©2002

The number of toes, and the arrangement of their toes and feet fit birds' different lifestyles. (Illustration by Jacqueline Mahannah. Reproduced by permission.)

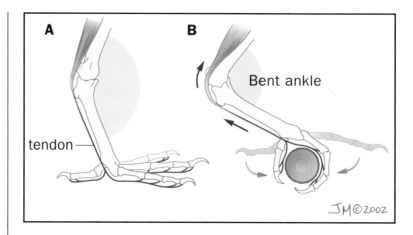

do not have a heavy jaw with teeth to grind their food. Instead, it is ground up in a muscular stomach called a gizzard, and they swallow gravel to help with the grinding. To get the energy they need for flight, birds digest their food quickly. Their fast digestion also keeps them from being weighed down for long by the food they have eaten.

Skeleton

A birds' skeleton is strong, even though it light. Many of the bones are hollow, and some of them are joined together to give the skeleton extra strength. (Loons and other diving birds have some solid bones to help the birds sink in the water.) The breastbone, or sternum, of a flying bird has a part called the keel. The bird's big flight muscles are attached to the keel. What looks like a backward-bending knee on a bird is really its ankle. The bird's knee is hidden high up inside its body feathers.

Body temperature

Birds are warm-blooded, which means their bodies stay at an even temperature no matter how warm or cold it is outside. They make their own heat from the food that they eat. Some birds cope with cold weather by growing extra feathers or a layer of fat, fluffing their feathers to trap more air, and huddling together with other birds. When birds can't find enough food to keep warm, they fly to warmer places. In hot weather, they cool down by panting, swimming in cool water, sitting in the shade, and raising their wings to catch a breeze.

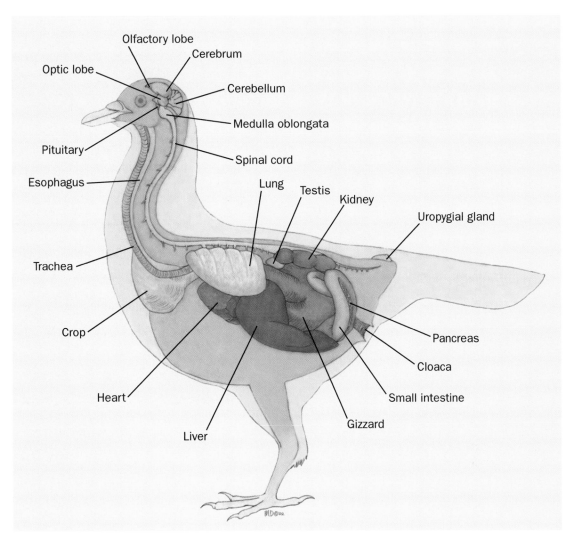

Figure labels: Olfactory lobe, Cerebrum, Optic lobe, Cerebellum, Medulla oblongata, Pituitary, Spinal cord, Esophagus, Lung, Testis, Kidney, Uropygial gland, Trachea, Crop, Heart, Liver, Gizzard, Small intestine, Cloaca, Pancreas

FAMILY LIFE

Singing

Singing is one of the most important ways that songbirds communicate. Birds do not sing just because they are happy. Instead, a male songbird sings to say that he "owns" a certain territory, and he warns birds of the same species to stay away. Songbirds do not have to see each other to know who is nearby. Birds can recognize the songs of their neighbors, because each bird of the same species sounds a little different. Male birds show off to females by singing the most complicated songs they can. Often the best singers are the strongest, healthiest males.

Though birds may look different on the outside, they have the same organs on the inside. (Illustration by Marguette Dongvillo. Reproduced by permission.)

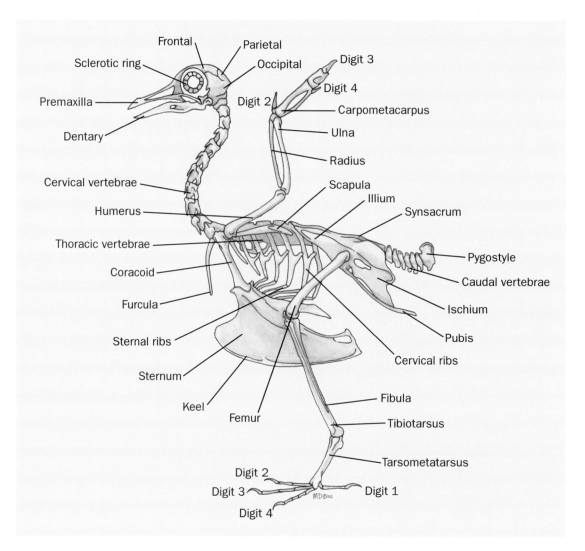

Frontal
Parietal
Occipital
Digit 3
Sclerotic ring
Premaxilla
Digit 2
Digit 4
Carpometacarpus
Ulna
Dentary
Radius
Cervical vertebrae
Scapula
Illium
Humerus
Synsacrum
Thoracic vertebrae
Coracoid
Pygostyle
Caudal vertebrae
Furcula
Ischium
Sternal ribs
Pubis
Sternum
Cervical ribs
Keel
Fibula
Femur
Tibiotarsus
Tarsometatarsus
Digit 2
Digit 3
Digit 1
Digit 4

MD©02

Birds have a strong, light skeleton. (Illustration by Marguette Dongvillo. Reproduced by permission.)

When a female songbird hears her mate singing, her brain tells her body to make hormones (special chemicals). These hormones make eggs start to grow inside her body.

Other ways birds communicate

Singing is just one of the many ways that birds communicate with each other. They have warning calls that tell other birds that a predator is nearby. They chirp to say, "I am here, where are you?" And young birds sometimes beg noisily to be fed. At breeding time, birds have a variety of courtships displays that ask, "Will you be mine?" and state, "We belong together." These include bowing, flight displays, and calling together. Male birds

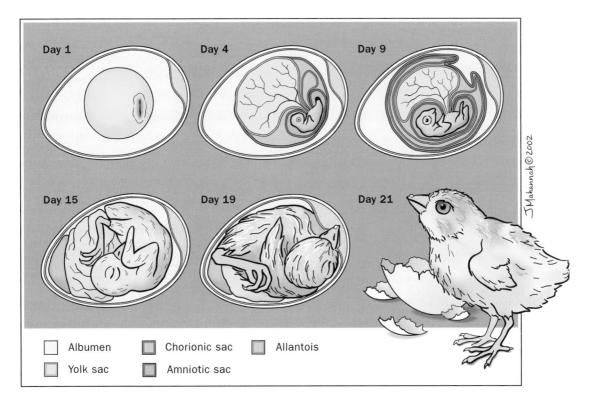

Day 1 | Day 4 | Day 9

Day 15 | Day 19 | Day 21

Albumen Chorionic sac Allantois

Yolk sac Amniotic sac

parade and show off bright feathers or blow up colorful throat sacs to impress females.

Nests

When a bird has found a mate, it is nest-building time. Birds lay their hard-shelled eggs where they can be protected from predators and rain. There are many different kinds of nests. Some birds lay their eggs right on the ground or on the sides of cliffs, some use tree holes or burrows, and some weave complicated stick nests. A few kinds of birds even bury their eggs in mounds of soil and leaves.

Eggs and hatching

Eggs come in many different sizes and colors. Those laid on the ground usually have camouflage colors, and eggs laid in hidden places are often white. The female bird usually incubates the eggs (keeps them warm), especially if she has duller, harder-to-see feathers than the male. Sometimes males and females take turns, and occasionally the males incubate by themselves. Some birds, such as cowbirds, lay their eggs in the nests of other bird species and let the other birds incubate them.

An egg is a perfect package for the chick developing inside it. The albumen (egg white) and yolk provide all the food and water it needs, and are used up as the bird develops. Air moves in and out through hundreds of tiny holes in the shell. Waste from the developing chick is stored in a sac called the allantois (uh-LAN-tuh-wus). The chorionic (kor-ee-AHN-ik) sac lines the inside of the shell, and the amniotic sac surrounds the chick. Time spent in the egg is different for each species, but for this chick, feathers have started to grow by Day 15, and the chick begins making noises by Day 19. There is a little egg tooth on the tip of the chick's bill that it uses to break out of the shell on Day 21. (Illustration by Jacqueline Mahannah. Reproduced by permission.)

Growth of young birds

There are two main types of newly hatched birds. Young chickens, ducks, geese, turkeys, and ostriches are precocial (pre-KOH-shul). Precocial chicks are covered with down feathers and can run or swim after their parents soon after hatching. Before long, they learn to find their own food, but the parents usually protect them for a while longer. Altricial (al-TRISH-ul) birds are helpless when they hatch. Songbirds, seabirds, owls, parrots, and woodpeckers are some of the altricial birds. They are naked, blind, and weak, and they need to be fed by adults at least until they leave the nest.

HABITATS, HABITS, AND PEOPLE

Surviving in a habitat

In order to live in a habitat, birds need food, water, and shelter (such as a hedge to hide in). At breeding time, they also need a place to raise their young. Many different kinds of birds can live in the same habitat because they eat different foods and nest in different places. Some birds, such as crows, can often adapt to changes in their habitat, but other birds are very particular and have to leave if something changes.

Staying alive and keeping fit

Birds have to have their feathers in flying shape at all times so that they can escape predators. Well-cared-for feathers are also necessary for keeping the birds warm and waterproof. Birds often have to stop what they are doing and take time out to fix their messed-up feathers. Sometimes they start with a bath. But they always finish by preening. To preen, the birds nibble along each feather to remove dirt and tiny pests. Most birds also get oil on their beaks from a gland near their tails. They spread the oil on each feather and straighten it by zipping it through their beaks. The oil keeps the feathers from drying out and waterproofs them. When a feather gets too worn, it either falls out or gets pushed out by a new feather growing in its place.

Migration

Migration is one way birds cope with natural changes in their habitats. When the weather gets cold and insects get scarce in fall, for example, insect-eating birds fly to warmer places where

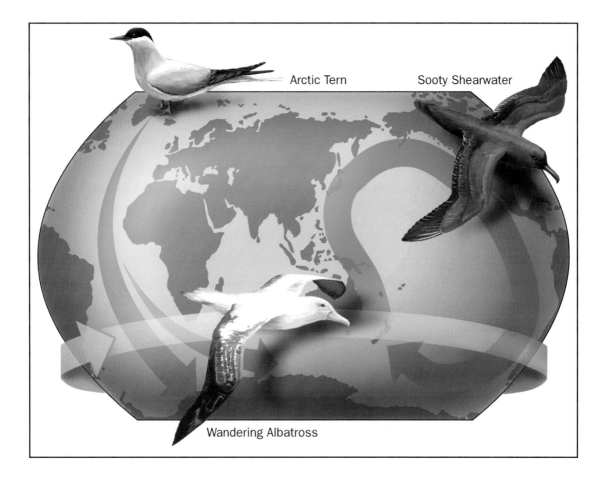

Arctic Tern   Sooty Shearwater

Wandering Albatross

they will be able to find the food they need. Their bodies are programmed to tell them that when the days start getting shorter, they have to eat more so they will have enough fuel for the journey. They follow the same migration routes year after year, and they know the general direction they should go and where to stop. The migrating birds are guided by the stars and by the direction the sun moves across the sky. Birds have a built-in compass and are able to follow magnetic fields in the earth. Some birds also rely on landmarks such as rivers and mountains to follow, and some may use sounds and smells to help them find their way.

Birds and people

Birds are some of the most visible wild animals on Earth, and they play an important part in people's lives. Humans

Seabirds have some of the longest migrations. The arctic tern migrates about 25,000 miles (40,000 kilometers) round-trip each year. The sooty shearwater breeds around New Zealand and the southern tip of South America and migrates in the spring to the northern Pacific and Atlantic Oceans. The wandering albatross moves around the Earth from west to east over the oceans south of the tips of the southern continents. (Illustration by Emily Damstra. Reproduced by permission.)

learned about flight from birds, they eat birds and their eggs, and they keep birds as pets. They appreciate the way birds eat insect pests and weed seeds, and they enjoy watching and listening to birds. Sometimes people kill the birds that eat fish or destroy their crops. People have also harmed birds unintentionally by polluting their habitats or turning them into farms and cities.

Humans now take the disappearance of birds from an area as a warning—there may be harmful poisons in the air or water. Many people are working hard to preserve natural places for birds and all wild animals. They are also having some success with fixing habitats that have been destroyed, but fixing them is much harder than preserving them in the first place.

FOR MORE INFORMATION

Books

Johnson, Jinny. *Children's Guide to Birds*. New York: Simon & Schuster, 1996.

MacKay, Barry Kent. *Bird Sounds*. Mechanicsburg, PA: Stackpole Books, 2001.

Markle, Sandra. *Outside and Inside Birds*. New York: Bradbury Press, 1994.

Perrins, Christopher M. *The Illustrated Encyclopedia of Birds*. New York: Prentice Hall Press, 1990.

Proctor, Noble S., and Patrick J. Lynch. *Manual of Ornithology, Avian Structure and Function*. New Haven, CT: Yale University Press, 1993.

Reid, Struan. *Bird World*. Brookfield, CT: The Millbrook Press, 1991.

Rupp, Rebecca. *Everything You Never Learned About Birds*. Pownal, VT: Storey Communications, Inc., 1995.

Sibley, David Allen, Chris Elphick, and John B. Dunning, Jr., eds. *National Audubon Society: The Sibley Guide to Bird Life & Behavior*. New York: Alfred A. Knopf, 2001.

Taylor, Kim. *Flight*. New York: John Wiley & sons, Inc., 1992.

Periodicals

Able, Kenneth P. "The Concepts and Terminology of Bird Navigation." *Journal of Aviation Biology* 32 (2000): 174–182.

Berger, Cynthia. "Fluffy, Fancy, Fantastic Feathers." *Ranger Rick* (January 2001): 2–10.

Greij, Eldon. "Happy Returns: Landing Safely Is Every Bit as Tricky as Flying." *Birders World* (February 2003): 58–60.

Kerlinger, Paul. "How High? How High a Bird Flies Depends on the Weather, the Time of Day, Whether Land or Water Lies Below—and the Bird." *Birder's World* (February 2003): 62–65.

Miller, Claire. "Guess Where They Nest." *Ranger Rick* (March 1996): 19–27.

Pennisi, Elizabeth. "Colorful Males Flaunt Their Health." *Science* (April 4, 2003): 29–30.

Web sites

"Act for the Environment." National Wildlife Federation. http://www.nwf.org/action/ (accessed on May 3, 2004).

"All About Birds." Cornell Lab of Ornithology. http://www.birds.cornell.edu/programs/AllAboutBirds/ (accessed on May 3, 2004).

American Bird Conservancy. http://www.abcbirds.org (accessed on May 3, 2004).

American Ornithologists' Union. http://www.aou.org (accessed on May 3, 2004).

"Bird and Wildlife Information Center." National Audubon Society. http://www.audubon.org/educate/expert/index.html (accessed on May 3, 2004).

BirdLife International. http://www.birdlife.net (accessed on May 3, 2004).

"Birdlife Worldwide." Birdlife International. http://www.birdlife.net/worldwide/index.html (accessed on May 3, 2004).

National Audubon Society. http://www.Audubon.org (accessed on May 3, 2004).

National Wildlife Federation. http://www.nwf.org (accessed on May 3, 2004).

The Nature Conservancy. http://nature.org (accessed on May 3, 2004).

order
CHAPTER

PHYSICAL CHARACTERISTICS

The order of Passeriformes, commonly called passerines (PASS-ur-eenz), are the largest and most unique family of birds. A few of the many birds in the passerine order are crows, finches, flycatchers, nightingales, swallows, tanagers, vireos, shrikes, wrens, and warblers. They are sometimes called "perching birds" and (less accurately) "song birds." These perching birds include some of the most colorful and mysterious of all birds in the world, such as birds of paradise from New Guinea and the bright orange cock-of-the-rock from tropical South America. They are generally small to medium in size (except for the crows, jays, and lyrebirds) with large wings relative to their body size. Two interesting physical features of the passerines are their distinctive syrinx (SIHR-ingks; or vocal organ) that allows them through complicated muscles to have a wide range of songs and calls, and their very specialized feet and legs that allow them to grip and move in very unique ways.

Passerines have three toes that point forward and one toe that points backward. The first toe, called the hallux (HAL-lux), is often called the hind toe because it always points backward and is never reversible. This arrangement allows them to perch on many different slender structures such as tree branches, grasses, telephone and fence wires, feeders, or anything that has some type of narrow place to perch. Their vocal organ allows the birds to produce a large range of vocalizations (although some species can only grunt and hiss while others produce very complex and melodic sounds that are called songs).

Bills on passerines vary greatly in size and shape due to the type of diet of each species. The types of bills range from tiny, needle-like bills of insect-easting warblers and vireos, to the generally huge, vise-like bills of finches, designed to crack the hard shells of seeds.

Passerines weigh between about 0.18 ounces (5 grams) in kinglets (also very small in weight are the bushtits and pygmy tits) to about 3.1 pounds (1.4 kilograms) in ravens and about 3.7 pounds (1.7 kilograms) in Australian lyrebirds and ravens.

GEOGRAPHIC RANGE

Passerines are very widespread on all continents except Antarctica, but have the greatest numbers in the tropical areas of the world. They are considered the most widely distributed of all birds, living on nearly every oceanic island that can support a bird. Passerines include over half in total numbers of the known birds in the world.

HABITAT

Passerines are found in grasslands, woodlands, scrublands, forests, deserts, mountains, and urban environments. They are widely scattered throughout arid (dry) to wet, and temperate (mild) to tropical climates, especially liking areas filled with trees because most of the birds are arboreal; that is, they live primarily in trees. Although passerines are found in most areas of the world, they avoid areas with permanently frozen land, or permafrost, that are always covered with snow and ice.

DIET

Passerines eat mostly seeds, fruits, nectar, insects, small birds, small lizards, and marine invertebrates (animals without a backbone). They have been known to also eat carrion (decaying animals), and even potato chips and other foods left out by humans. They eat often throughout the day and need a high-energy diet in order to supply their active lifestyle. Crossbills, diggers, and swallows have shapes for their bill, wing, and legs that are especially adapted for foraging. They forage (search for food) by many different methods including taking insects from the bark of trees, catching insects as they fly through the air, and very specialized methods for eating seeds. Most of the birds eat food as they find it, but some do store their food to eat later. Shrikes (sometimes called "butcherbirds") use an unusual way to store foods they catch. They spear insects, small birds, and lizards on thorns or barbed wire, so they can come back later to feed.

BEHAVIOR AND REPRODUCTION

Because of their leg, foot, and toe arrangement, passerines are able to sleep while perched when special features in the foot automatically grip a perch. Being songbirds, passerines are very vocal birds with highly developed vocal chords. In fact, the birds are some of the most complex and rich singers in the bird world. They sometimes copy the songs and calls of other birds, especially the songs of competing males within their own species. Some species even copy the sounds of insects, frogs, and (even) mechanical sounds heard in their environment. Many passerines migrate from their nesting grounds to warmer regions, or from southern temperate regions north to the tropics.

PASSERINES VERSUS NON-PASSERINES

About 60 percent of all bird species are passerines, and the families within this order have a larger than average number of species. These two facts portray the degree of success with which passerine birds evolved and grew in numbers over the many, many years of their existence. Because there are so many passerines, the class Aves (birds) is often informally divided into passerines and non-passerines.

Predators (animals that hunt other animals for food) of passerines include raccoons, feral (wild) cats, and snakes.

There are many different ways that passerines build nests and many different materials that are used to construct nests. Generally, nests are made out of sticks or grass on the ground, in trees, and even sometimes in the banks of fast-flowing rivers. Nests are often camouflaged (KAM-uh-flajd; designed to hide by matching the colors and textures of the surrounding environment) in order to conceal them from predators. Although nests range from being built very simply to very elaborately, they can be classified as being constructed in three different ways: built out of a hole, built so the opening is from above, and built with a dome or roof.

Parental care by both sexes is common in passerines, although females sometimes are left with all of the duties. Cooperative breeding, in which young birds delay breeding and assist other individuals (often their parents) in raising young and defending the territory, is common in several passerine groups. Female passerines lay small eggs that are usually colored or marked in some manner. Clutch size (group of eggs hatched together) varies greatly from one to sixteen eggs. Passerines are born blind, naked, and completely helpless. The incubation period (the time that it takes to sit on eggs before they hatch) is around fourteen days but can last up to twenty-eight days in large species and fifty days in lyrebirds. Some females are able to replace eggs that have been lost or destroyed. The fledgling period (the time necessary for young birds to grow feathers necessary to fly) is eight to forty-five days.

PASSERINES AND PEOPLE

Passerines help to control insects that destroy trees. In fact, the American redstart feeds on regal moths and the red-eyed vireo eats gypsy moths, both of which are very harmful to oak trees, a common tree found in urban areas.

CONSERVATION STATUS

Passerines are by far the most successful group of birds on Earth with respect to numbers and distribution around the world. More than five hundred passerine species, out of 5,100 to 6,000 species worldwide, are considered threatened with extinction, mostly due to habitat loss. (The exact number of passerine species is unknown due to disagreements among bird experts about whether some birds are species or not. About 8,600 total bird species are believed to exist throughout the world.) Bird experts, or ornithologists (people who scientifically study birds), believe that some of the species of passerines will become extinct in the future unless corrective measures are taken to preserve their habitat and reverse other negative conditions brought about mostly by human activities.

FOR MORE INFORMATION

Books:

del Hoyo, Josep, Andrew Elliott, Jordi Sargatal, Jose Cabot, et al., eds. *Handbook of the Birds of the World.* Barcelona: Lynx Edicions, 1992.

Dickinson, Edward C., ed. *The Howard and Moore Complete Checklist of the Birds of the World,* 3rd ed. Princeton, NJ and Oxford, U.K.: Princeton University Press, 2003.

Forshaw, Joseph, ed. *Encyclopedia of Birds,* 2nd ed. San Diego, CA: Academic Press, 1998.

Harrison, Colin James Oliver. *Birds of the World.* London and New York: Dorling Kindersley, 1993.

Perrins, Christopher M., and Alex L. A. Middleton, eds. *The Encyclopedia of Birds.* New York: Facts on File, 1985.

Class: Aves

Order: Passeriformes

Family: Eurylaimidae

Number of species: 15 species

family

CHAPTER

PHYSICAL CHARACTERISTICS

Broadbills are small- to medium-sized, stockily built birds with large eyes; a broad bill (from which they get the name) that is rounded along its sides, flattened from front to back, hooked at the end, and with a wide gap; rounded wings; a rather short, square tail (except for one species with a fine-pointed tail); short legs; strong, syndactylous (sin-DACK-tuh-lus; with fused digits) feet; and long, hooked claws. There is much difference among the species in the color of their plumage (feathers). Most birds are very colorful although some are rather dull looking, with colors ranging from browns with gray or black (in most African species) to green, red, blue, black, or silvery gray with many areas of bright colors (in most Asian species). Some species have an area of bare skin around the eyes that is sometimes pink or blue. Males and females look alike in some species but look different in others. Adults are 4.5 to 10.8 inches (11.5 to 27.5 centimeters) long and weigh between 0.4 and 6 ounces (10 and 171 grams).

GEOGRAPHIC RANGE

Broadbills are found in sub-Saharan Africa, Himalayan portions of India, Thailand, Cambodia, Vietnam, far southern China (also Hainan Island), Borneo, Sumatra, Java, peninsular Malaysia, and the Philippines.

HABITAT

Broadbills inhabit mostly humid tropical and subtropical lowlands (including evergreen or mostly evergreen broad-leaved

phylum

class

subclass

order

monotypic order

suborder

▲ **family**

lowland forests), while a few species are located in montane (mountain) forests and one species is found in dry climates. They move with the change of seasons to mountain areas when food becomes scarce.

DIET

Most broadbills eat insects, but some of the larger species also eat small vertebrates (animals with a backbone) such as lizards, frogs, small crabs, and small fish, and fruits such as figs. Foods are foraged from leaves or branches, caught while in flight, or captured on the ground.

BEHAVIOR AND REPRODUCTION

The behavior and reproduction habits of broadbills are not known very well. The birds are generally arboreal (live in trees) and are believed to be mostly monogamous (muh-NAH-guh-mus; having one mate), but some species may be polygamous (puh-LIH-guh-mus; having more than one mate). Broadbills join single or mixed species flocks, but avian experts do not know whether the birds remain in one territory, range over several territories, or return to a territory after leaving. When defending a territory or during courtship, broadbills perform various displays of songs and flights. Simple songs usually consist of dove-like cooing, croaks, trills, whistles, and a series of bubbly to screaming notes.

Broadbills have a mating and reproduction period that is tied to rainfall amounts. Some species reproduce during the dry season, while others mate during the rainy season. All of the birds make large domed nests in the shape of a pear that is suspended from the tips of branches. In almost all species, both males and females build nests. Such nests are made from twigs, rootlets, and leaf strips from plants such as grasses, bamboo, and palms. Oftentimes, spider webs, moss, cocoons, and other materials hide the nests. At other times, nests are hung above water to make it difficult for predators, animals that hunt them for food, to enter. Females lay two to six white to pinkish eggs that are sometimes unmarked or speckled reddish or purple. Males help females with the care of the young, and some species also use helpers, related, nonbreeding birds that help care for the young.

BROADBILLS AND PEOPLE

People hunt broadbills for their colorful plumage in order to sell them within the pet industry.

CONSERVATION STATUS

Three broadbill species are listed on the IUCN Red List as Vulnerable, facing a high risk of extinction, due to deforestation, mining, and human warfare in their very small ranges. Three other species are listed as Near Threatened, in danger of becoming threatened with extinction.

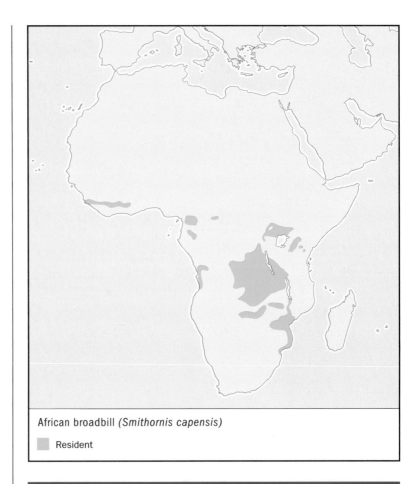

African broadbill (*Smithornis capensis*)

▩ Resident

AFRICAN BROADBILL
Smithornis capensis

Physical characteristics: African broadbills are stocky, short-tailed birds with a distinctive broad, flat bill. They have a brownish head and upperparts, and buffy underparts that are streaked with blackish colors. Males have a black crown (top of head), gray lower nape (back of neck), black upper mandible (top part of the bill) and whitish lower mandible (bottom part), and reddish brown upperparts and tail. The mantle (back, inner-wing, and shoulder area) has broad black streaks. White underparts are deeply streaked with black except on the central belly and rump, and the legs are olive to yellowish green. Females look like males but are duller overall, with a gray crown that has black streaks. Juveniles look like females but with less buff on forehead and a brown crown with faint streaks. Adults are 4.7 to 5.5 inches (12 to 14 centimeters) long and weigh between 0.7 and 1.1 ounces (20 and 31 grams).

Geographic range: African broadbills are found in various scattered spots in central and southern Africa including Cameroon, Gabon, Central Africa Republic, Sierra Leone, Liberia, Ivory Coast, Ghana, Malawi, Democratic Republic of the Congo, Tanzania, Kenya, Zambia, Mozambique, Rwanda, Uganda, Angola, Namibia, and South Africa.

Habitat: African broadbills inhabit the understory (lower vegetation of a forest) of primary and secondary forests, dense deciduous thickets, montane forests, riparian forests (along or near banks of rivers), a variety of woodlands and savannas (flat grasslands), and open agricultural lands. They are usually found at elevations below 2,300 feet (700 meters), but can be found as high as 8,000 (2,440 meters).

During courtship, male and female African broadbills face each other on a horizontal branch and flick their wings, changing between perching and hanging positions. They also use a whistled "huiii" and a mewing-like call during courtship. (Illustration by Bruce Worden. Reproduced by permission.)

Diet: Their diet consists of insects such as caterpillars, butterfly eggs, and ants. They often rush forward to snag prey, sometimes even falling to the ground in order to capture food.

Behavior and reproduction: African broadbills are territorial birds. Both males and females perform elliptical display flights. During courtship, both birds face each other on a horizontal branch and flick their wings, changing between perching and hanging positions. Their call is a "twee-uu," probably to keep in contact with other birds and to show alarm or distress. A whistled "huiii" and a mewing-like call are used during courtship. They build a bag-like nest of plant fibers, dead leaves, moss, and twigs with a rough-looking hanging tail. An entrance is made high on the side. The inside of the nest is lined with soft bark, dry stems, leaves, and grasses, and kept together with spider silk. Their breeding season varies depending on where they are located. Females lay one to three eggs.

African broadbills and people: There is no known significance to humans.

Conservation status: African broadbills are not threatened. They are common in many areas, but scarce in others, mostly due to habitat destruction. ■

Black-and-red broadbill *(Cymbirhynchus macrorhynchos)*

Resident

BLACK-AND-RED BROADBILL
Cymbirhynchus macrorhynchos

Physical characteristics: Black-and-red broadbills are beautiful crimson and black birds. They have a black head, back, and tail feathers; crimson red underparts, rump, and throat; black wings with a white narrow stripe; and a bill that is pale blue on top and yellow below. Adults are 8.3 to 9.4 inches (21 to 24 centimeters) long and weigh between 1.8 and 2.7 ounces (50.0 and 76.5 grams).

Geographic range: They are found in Borneo, Myanmar, southern Thailand, southern Laos, south Vietnam, peninsular Malaysia, and Sumatra.

Habitat: Black-and-red broadbills occupy areas with water within evergreen forests.

Black-and-red broadbills eat mostly insects, but also mollusks, crabs, and small fish. (© Doug Wechsler/VIREO. Reproduced by permission.)

Diet: Their food consists of mostly insects, but also mollusks, crabs, and small fish.

Behavior and reproduction: The behavior and reproduction habits of black-and-red broadbills are not well known. They are usually found in pairs or small groups. Nests are often built in dead stumps or along bends in streams. The breeding season usually occurs in the dry season. Females lay two to three eggs. Males may help females incubate (sit on) the eggs.

Black-and-red broadbills and people: There is no known significance between people and black-and-red broadbills.

Conservation status: Black-and-red broadbills are not threatened. They are fairly common throughout their range, but their habitat is being reduced, mostly due to human activities. ■

FOR MORE INFORMATION

Books:

del Hoyo, Josep, Andrew Elliott, Jordi Sargatal, Jose Cabot, et al., eds. *Handbook of the Birds of the World.* Barcelona: Lynx Edicions, 1992.

Dickinson, Edward C., ed. *The Howard and Moore Complete Checklist of the Birds of the World,* 3rd ed. Princeton, NJ and Oxford, U.K.: Princeton University Press, 2003.

Forshaw, Joseph, ed. *Encyclopedia of Birds,* 2nd ed. San Diego, CA: Academic Press, 1998.

Harrison, Colin James Oliver. *Birds of the World.* London and New York: Dorling Kindersley, 1993.

Perrins, Christopher M., and Alex L. A. Middleton, eds. *The Encyclopedia of Birds.* New York: Facts on File, 1985.

Class: Aves

Order: Passeriformes

Family: Philepittidae

Number of species: 4 species

family
CHAPTER

phylum

class

subclass

order

monotypic order

suborder

▲ **family**

PHYSICAL CHARACTERISTICS

Asities are very small, compact birds with tails so short that individuals look almost spherical, ball-shaped. The velvet and Schlegel's asities grow up to 6 inches (15 centimeters) long and weigh up to 1.5 ounces (40 grams). The common and yellow-bellied sunbird-asities (also called false sunbirds) are smaller, up to 4 inches (10 centimeters) long and up to 0.88 ounces (25 grams) in weight. Both of these species have long, thin, down-curved beaks, like those of nectar-feeding birds. The two asity species have more modest, short, slightly downcurved beaks.

Males sprout brilliant, colorful plumage (feathers) and caruncles (KAR-un-kulz; wart-like skin bumps) at the beginning of the mating season (October through February). After the breeding season, the males revert to duller coloration. Females do not change colors and their colorations are more drab, being various mixtures and patterns of olives, grays, dull greens and dull yellows. The coloration of males outside the breeding season resembles that of the females of the same species, and the caruncles fade and disappear.

GEOGRAPHIC RANGE

These species live in Madagascar, along the east coast and in the sambirano region, another rainforested area in the northwest.

HABITAT

Asities inhabit lowland (sea level), mid-altitude and high altitude tropical primary (original) and secondary (regrown) rainforest, and higher altitude scrub forest (forest with low trees and shrubs). All four species are common and in some areas, plentiful, but since they spend much time in the upper reaches of forests, and because of their small size, asities are difficult to spot and observe.

The velvet asity inhabits most of the east coast of Madagascar, in tropical primary and secondary rain forest from sea level to 5,700 feet (1,900 meters) above sea level. Schlegel's asity lives in tropical deciduous forest in northwestern and western Madagascar. The common sunbird asity lives in the mountainous tropical rainforest belt along most of the east coast, between 1,200 and 4,350 feet (400 to 1,450 meters) above sea level. The yellow-bellied sunbird asity lives in mossy mountain scrub forest that fringes the east coast forest belt between 3,630 and 5,970 feet (1,210 and 1,990 meters) of altitude.

DIET

Asities eat nectar, fruits, insects, spiders, and other small creatures.

BEHAVIOR AND REPRODUCTION

Asities are energetic, lively birds that seem to have little fear of anything around them, including humankind. Some will approach within a few feet of a human being, show a few quick threat displays, then fly off.

Philepittidae singing is simple and not especially loud. Male birds, in flight, can also make fairly loud whirring sounds with their wings. The tenth primary feather of each wing is pointed, and the extended shape creates the sound during flight. A male asity, by adjusting the position of the tenth primary feather, can turn the whirring sound on and off as he wants to. Males use the noise in courtship and defense displays.

Mating behavior in asities is centered on a social behavior system called a polygynous (puh-LIH-juh-nus) lek. One to five males display on vertical branches in an open area twenty to thirty meters across. The males go through several ritualistic displays, competing with others in the lek for the attention and approval of the females. In the most distinctive display, a male will bob up and down on its legs, feet still gripping the branch, while quickly opening and closing the wings. Females gather to watch the displays, each female choosing a male mating partner based on how attracted she is by his courting displays.

In the velvet asity, only females build nests and breeding partners do not form pair-bonds. The other species do establish pair-bonds, and males and females share nest building. A female or breeding pair builds a distinctive, spindle-shaped nest, made from moss, spider webs and plant fibers, suspended from a lower tree branch. The nest, which takes ten or more days to build, is about 10 inches (25 centimeters) in height and 5 inches (12 centimeters) wide. The female lays up to three eggs.

FALSE SUNBIRDS, ASITIES, AND PEOPLE

Asities are not considered pests in any way, since they stay in rainforest and have no interest in human cultivated crops. The tiny, brilliant birds have become a ecotourist draw, especially for dedicated birdwatchers eager to check out Madagascar's unique avian species.

CONSERVATION STATUS

The World Conservation Union (IUCN) lists the yellow-bellied sunbird-asity as Endangered, facing a very high risk of extinction, and Schlegel's asity as Near Threatened, in danger of becoming threatened with extinction. The Endangered designation for the yellow-bellied sunbird-asity may be based on old data in which the species was believed to inhabit only a few mountain forest areas. According to a recent article by Prum and Razafindratsita, more recent surveys have found the yellow-bellied sunbird-asity to be widely distributed and plentiful throughout mountain forests along most of the east coast of Madagascar, and all four species of asity to be plentiful in their ranges and in no danger of extinction. The common sunbird-asity has been found in densities of a thousand individuals per 0.4 square miles (1 square kilometer). Yellow-bellied asities have been recorded in densities of over 2,600 individuals per 0.4 square miles (1 square kilometer).

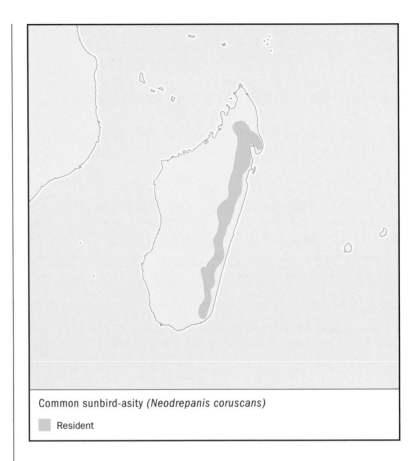

Common sunbird-asity (*Neodrepanis coruscans*)

■ Resident

COMMON SUNBIRD-ASITY
Neodrepanis coruscans

Physical characteristics: Adult body length is about 4 inches (10 centimeters) and adult weight is 0.88 ounces (25 grams). The breeding-season male's coloration is black fringed with royal blue on the crown, nape and shoulders, with yellow fringing of some of the wing feathers, deep yellow on the ventral surface (undersides) with olive-brown streaks on the breast. The caruncles are squarish and turquoise blue except for green closest to the eye. Females have dull yellowish underparts, yellow on the sides and on the underside of the tail, dull blue-green brown upper bodies and heads.

Geographic range: They are found along the east coast of Madagascar.

The male common sunbird-asity's breeding colors are black, blue, and yellow. During the nonbreeding season, his colors are duller blue-green, brown, and dull yellow. (Illustration by Dan Erickson. Reproduced by permission.)

Habitat: Sunbird-asities live in the east coast mid-altitude mountain rainforest from 1,200 to 4,350 feet (400 to 1,450 meters) above sea level.

Diet: Common sunbird-asities eat nectar from many plant sources; and insects and related creatures. Common sunbird asities glean (pluck off) insect prey from flowers, leaves, and bark.

Behavior and reproduction: The typical call of the common sunbird-asity is a high-pitched string of notes that sounds like "see-see-see-see-see-see." The call can be heard from 150 to 300 feet (50 to 100 meters) away. Male common sunbird-asities, curiosity-driven, will often approach to within a few feet of a human being.

Common sunbird asities and people: There is little if any direct interaction between common sunbird asities and humanity, except for mostly foreign bird watchers, who benefit ecotourism in Madagascar and contribute to the local and national economies.

Conservation status: These birds are plentiful and widespread along Madagascar's east coast, with densities of a thousand individuals per 0.4 square miles (1 square kilometer) reported. They are not considered endangered or threatened. ∎

FOR MORE INFORMATION

Books:

Goodman, Steven M., and Jonathan P. Benstead, eds. *The Natural History of Madagascar.* Chicago: University of Chicago Press, 2003.

Lambert, Frank, and Martin Woodcock. *Pittas, Broadbills, and Asities.* Sussex, U.K.: Pica Press, 1996.

Morris, P., and F. Hawkins. *Birds of Madagascar: A Photographic Guide.* New Haven, CT: Yale University Press, 1998.

Safford, R. J. and J. W. Duckworth, eds. *A Wildlife Survey of Marojejy Reserve, Madagascar.* Study Report No. 40. Cambridge, U.K.: International Council for Bird Preservation, 1990.

Periodicals:

Andrianarimisa, A. "A Record of the Sunbird Asity *Neodrepanis coruscans* in the Rèserve Spèciale d'Ambohitantely." *Newsletter of the Working Group on Birds in the Madagascar Region* 5, no. 2 (1995): 8–9.

Goodman, S. M., and M. S. Putnam. "The Birds of the Eastern Slope of the Reserve Naturalle Intégrale d'Andringitra." *Fieldiana: Zoology, new series* no. 85 (1996).

Hawkins, F., R. Safford, W. Duckworth, and M. Evans. "Field Identification and Status of the Sunbird Asities *Neodrepanis* of Madagascar." *Bulletin of the African Bird Club* 4 (1997): 36–41.

Prum, R. O. "Phylogeny, Biogeography, and Evolution of the Broadbills (Eurylaimidae) and Asities (Philepittidae) Based on Morphology." *Auk* 110 (1993): 304–324.

Prum, R. O., and V. R. Razafindratsita. "Lek Behavior and Natural History of the Velvet Asity *Philepitta castenea.*" *Wilson Bulletin* 109, no. 3 (1997): 371–392.

Class: Aves

Order: Passeriformes

Family: Pittidae

Number of species: 30 species

family

CHAPTER

PHYSICAL CHARACTERISTICS

Pittas are medium-sized birds with a large head, short neck, strong bill often hooked at the tip, round body, short rounded wings, short tail, longish legs, and strong, large feet. They are some of the world's most brightly colored birds and are sometimes called the "jewels of the forest" and "jewel thrushes" (because of similarity to thrushes). Many species contain patches of white, chestnut, turquoise, green, red, purple, and black, which are found on the chin, breast, or body areas that are hidden by dull-colored wing feathers. Both sexes contain these same colors, however females are generally duller. Adults are 5.9 to 11 inches (15 to 28 centimeters) long and weigh between 1.6 and 7.1 ounces (45 and 202 grams).

GEOGRAPHIC RANGE

Pittas are found from Africa to the Solomon Islands and from Japan through Southeast Asia to New Guinea and Australia. They are mostly found in peninsular Malaysia, Borneo, Sumatra, and Java. One species is found in India, two species are found from west-central to east-central Africa, and two species live along the northern and eastern coasts of Australia.

HABITAT

Most pittas inhabit the understory (level of tropical forests nearest ground level) of lowland tropical and subtropical forests. They prefer areas that are moist, such as those near rivers and streams or in shaded ravines. Some pittas inhabit moist, montane (mountain) forests from sea level to elevations of 8,200 feet (2,500 meters).

DIET

Food consists of insects, small frogs, snails, snakes, mice, earthworms, and other small vertebrates (animals with a backbone) and invertebrates (animals without a backbone).

BEHAVIOR AND REPRODUCTION

Pittas are terrestrial birds, staying generally on or near the ground. They prefer to walk or run, rather than fly, when alarmed or disturbed, and tend to be shy, usually found alone or in pairs. They do not generally migrate, move seasonally, but some species migrate at night over land and water. The birds defend a territory that varies depending on the species from 0.8 to 2.5 acres (0.3 to 1.0 hectares), but can be as large as 50 acres (20 hectares). Their defense calls are one, two, or sometimes three syllables that sound like a whistle or buzz. A loud pleasant double whistle is heard in the early morning or evening. When unwanted visitors enter their territory, pittas flash a white wing patch, spread the tail, or fan out the bright breast feathers. At other times, pittas stay hidden by lowering their bright breasts and remaining still.

Most pittas are monogamous (muh-NAH-guh-mus; have one mate). They begin to breed at the start of the wet season, except for one species that breeds year-round. Both sexes build a large, bulky, domed nest that is loosely constructed with leaves and twigs that are placed on a platform made of larger sticks. A side entrance is often made in front of a path or clearing that the female faces as she sits on her eggs. The interior is lined with fibers or finer leaves. The nest may be located on the ground or 3 to 50 feet (1 to 15 meters) above the ground, usually in low vegetation. Females lay two to seven eggs, although most species lay three to four eggs. The incubation period (time to sit on eggs before hatching) is fourteen to sixteen days, with both sexes sharing incubating duties. Young are born naked, blind, and unable to move far. Both males and females share the brooding and feeding of young. The fledgling period (time for a young bird to grow feathers necessary to fly) is eleven to seventeen days. Although able to fly, they are still fed by the adults for seven to ten days, and up to thirty days.

PITTAS AND PEOPLE

People make pets out of pittas, hunt them for food, and enjoy watching them because of their colorful feathers.

CONSERVATION STATUS

One species of pitta is listed as Critically Endangered, facing an extremely high risk of extinction; eight species are listed as Vulnerable, facing a high risk of extinction; and four species are listed as Near Threatened, in danger of becoming threatened with extinction.

Hooded pitta (*Pitta sordida*)

■ Resident   ■ Breeding   ■ Nonbreeding

HOODED PITTA
Pitta sordida

Physical characteristics: Hooded pittas have a black head, thin throat, and bill; dark greenish upperparts and wings; light wing bands; dark green underparts; black flight feathers; a black tail with blue-green tips and red underneath; black belly patch and lower belly; and pale brown to pinkish feet. Females are slightly duller than males. Adults are 6.3 to 7.5 inches (16 to 19 centimeters) long and weigh between 1.6 and 2.5 ounces (42 and 70 grams).

Geographic range: Hooded pittas are found throughout Southeast Asia, from the foothills of the Himalayas to Indonesia, the Philippines, and New Guinea.

Habitat: Hooded pittas inhabit forested and wooded areas including primary rainforests, secondary forests, bamboo forests, scrublands, overgrown plantations, and cultivated areas. They are found from sea level to 4,900 feet (1,500 meters).

Diet: Their diet consists mostly of insects, beetles, ants, termites, cockroaches, bugs, various larvae (LAR-vee), earthworms, snails, and berries. They hop quickly along the ground among dead leaves in search of food, and often feed in pairs about 16 to 64 feet (5 to 30 meters) apart.

Behavior and reproduction: Hooded pittas are strong fliers that are found alone or in pairs. When alarmed, or in order to distract other birds, they display such features as bowing, head-bobbing, wing flicking, and wing/tail fanning. They breed from February to August. Their call varies depending on region, but generally is a double-noted fluty whistle like "whew-whew." The dome-shaped nests are usually on the ground, made of roots, leaves (often bamboo), rootlets, moss, and twigs. The inside is lined with finer material. A short path, made of twigs, usually leads up to the entrance. Females usually lay three or four eggs that are white with gray, brown, or dark purple spots. Both sexes share nest construction, incubation, and care of the young. The incubation period is fifteen to sixteen days. The fledgling period is about sixteen days.

Hooded pittas and people: There is no known significance to humans.

Conservation status: Hooded pittas are not threatened. They are common throughout most of their range. ■

Hooded pittas live in forested and wooded areas, where they eat a variety of insects and larvae, as well as earthworms, snails, and berries. (Illustration by Michelle Meneghini. Reproduced by permission.)

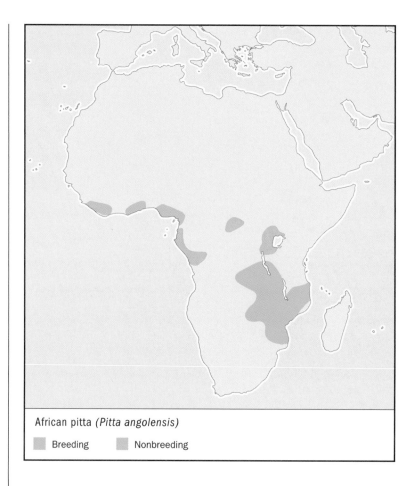

African pitta (Pitta angolensis)

■ Breeding ■ Nonbreeding

AFRICAN PITTA
Pitta angolensis

Physical characteristics: African pittas have a black head with a yellow side stripe; white throat with pink wash; blackish brown bill with a reddish base; deep buff breast and flanks (sides); whitish color under the bill and throat that turns yellow at breast; bright olive green upperparts with blue and black banding on wings; dark azure-blue rump; blackish flight feathers with paler tips; black tail with red underside and blue upperside; and pinkish to grayish white feet. Males and females look alike. Juveniles look similar to adults except they have duller colors. They are 6.7 to 8.7 inches (17 to 22 centimeters) long and weigh between 1.6 and 3.5 ounces (45 and 98 grams).

Geographic range: African pittas are found scattered near the west-central coast of Africa including Sierra Leone, Ghana, Liberia, Nigeria, and Ivory Coast, and in central and southeastern parts of Africa including Tanzania, Malawi, Democratic Republic of the Congo, Cameron, Zambia, Zimbabwe, Rwanda, Burundi, Central African Republic, Uganda, and Kenya.

Habitat: African pittas inhabit areas of dense undergrowth including evergreen bush country; thickets along waterways, swampy areas, and secondary forests; and tall semi-deciduous and evergreen rainforests. They are found from sea level to 4,100 feet (1,250 meters).

Diet: Their food includes insects, insect larvae, ants, termites, beetles, slugs, grubs, snails, millipedes, caterpillars, and earthworms. The birds sit quietly and watch for prey. If none is found, they go to another perch or fly down to the ground to forage among the leaf-litter of the forest floor.

African pittas are mostly terrestrial, hopping quickly on the ground while foraging, and flying short distances when alarmed. (Illustration by Michelle Meneghini. Reproduced by permission.)

Behavior and reproduction: African pittas are mostly terrestrial, often defending the territory by singing from the ground or a perch. They are found alone or in pairs during the breeding season. The birds hop quickly on the ground while foraging, and fly short distances when alarmed. Their main call is a "prrrrt" followed by a short, sharp "ouit" or "wheet." It is believed that they breed during the wet season. Their nest is a loosely made dome that is placed 7 to 26 feet (2 to 8 meters) off the ground usually in thorny vegetation. Nests are made of roots, sticks, twigs, dried leaves, rootlets, and fine fibers, with a side entrance and (sometimes) a platform made of dead leaves and twigs. Females lay one to four eggs, but usually three, which are dull creamy-white, sometimes greenish or pinkish, with reddish brown and purplish spots and lines over gray-lilac markings.

African pittas and people: There are no known significance to humans.

Conservation status: African pittas are not considered to be threatened. They are common in their habitat, however deforestation is hurting much of their environment. ∎

FOR MORE INFORMATION

Books:

del Hoyo, Josep, Andrew Elliott, Jordi Sargatal, Jose Cabot, et al., eds. *Handbook of the Birds of the World.* Barcelona: Lynx Edicions, 1992.

Dickinson, Edward C., ed. *The Howard and Moore Complete Checklist of the Birds of the World,* 3rd ed. Princeton, NJ and Oxford, U.K.: Princeton University Press, 2003.

Forshaw, Joseph, ed. *Encyclopedia of Birds,* 2nd ed. San Diego, CA: Academic Press, 1998.

Harrison, Colin James Oliver. *Birds of the World.* London and New York: Dorling Kindersley, 1993.

Perrins, Christopher M., and Alex L. A. Middleton, eds. *The Encyclopedia of Birds.* New York: Facts on File, 1985.

Class: Aves

Order: Passeriformes

Family: Acanthisittidae

Number of species: 4 species

family
CHAPTER

PHYSICAL CHARACTERISTICS

New Zealand wrens are very small, compact birds. They have straight or slightly upturned, slender, and pointed bills, which are about the same length as the head. Their wings are short and rounded. These birds have large, stout legs with strong, gripping feet and long, slender toes. The third and fourth toes are joined at their base. These birds have almost no tail. Their soft plumage, feathers, consists of greens, browns, and white. Adults are 3 to 4 inches (8 to 10 centimeters) long, with females substantially larger than males, although males are more brightly colored than females.

GEOGRAPHIC RANGE

New Zealand wrens are found on the North and South Islands, and some of the other surrounding islands of New Zealand.

HABITAT

New Zealand wrens are found in forests, beech forests, scrublands, and alpine, high mountain, areas, especially when large amounts of insects are available. They are usually found from sea level to 1,150 feet (350 meters) in elevation.

DIET

The diet of New Zealand wrens consists mostly of insects. They forage, search for food, alone, as a bonded male and female couple, or as a family group. They forage by crawling along the bark of trees and among the leafy parts of trees in

search of insects and small arthropods, invertebrate animals (animals without backbones) with jointed limbs. They sometimes forage on the ground.

BEHAVIOR AND REPRODUCTION

New Zealand wrens are weak fliers, with soft songs and calls. When landing on a perch from a short flight they often bob their body up and down. Their breeding season is from August to March. They are monogamous (muh-NAH-guh-mus), having only one mate, birds that form long-lasting pair bonds. The mating pair builds a complex nest in tree and rock crevices, narrow cracks or openings, in tree hollows or behind loose bark, in holes within tree trunks, earthen banks, walls within human-made structures, and fence posts, and sometimes on the ground in protected places. The nest consists of loosely woven materials such as moss, roots, leaves, ferns, and plant debris. There is a side entrance into the nest, which is often lined with feathers. Females usually lay two to five white eggs. Males feed nesting females and both parents feed their young. After the young leave the nest, they remain with the parents for several weeks.

NEW ZEALAND WRENS AND PEOPLE

With very few predators, animals that hunt them for food, in their customary habitats, most New Zealand wrens are not able to cope with new predators, such as those introduced by humans. It is also difficult for most of them to adapt to modifications within their environments.

CONSERVATION STATUS

Two species of New Zealand wrens are listed as Extinct, no longer existing. The two remaining species are fairly common and protected by laws.

Rifleman (*Acanthisitta chloris*)

Resident

RIFLEMAN
Acanthisitta chloris

Physical characteristics: Riflemen are the smallest living bird species in New Zealand. They have greenish upperparts and whitish undersides with yellow wash on the sides. Females are generally duller than males and are brown striped. Males have a bright yellow-green back while females have a back that is striped with darker and lighter browns and flecked with red-brown spots. Both sexes have a slightly upturned bill, with the female bill being a little more upturned. They have white bellies and white markings above the eyes. Their wings have a yellow bar with a white spot at the end of the bar and yellowish rumps and flanks. Males are generally smaller than females,

with adults about 3 inches (8 centimeters) in length and weighing between 0.2 and 0.3 ounces (6.3 and 9.0 grams).

Geographic range: Riflemen are found on both main islands (North Island and South Island) of New Zealand, except for the northern portion of the North Island. They are also found on Stewart Island, just off the southeastern coast of South Island, and the Great Barrier and Little Barrier Islands.

Habitat: Riflemen are located in various habitats including forests, scrublands, farmlands, and disturbed and regenerating habitats. They adapt easily to new environments composed of plant species not native to their normal habitats.

Diet: Their diet consists of insects, spiders, and other small invertebrates, animals without backbones. Males take prey from tree leaves while females find food within tree bark. The female's slightly more upcurved bill helps the female pry and loosen bark away from trees. They often work their way up and around tree trunks in a spiral route that takes them from the base of a tree up to 20 to 30 feet (6 to 9 meters) off the ground.

Behavior and reproduction: Riflemen are lively, diurnal, active during the day, birds. Their call is a sharp, high-pitched, cricket-like "zipt" or "zsit" that is sounded either singly or in a rapid series of separate notes. Most of their activity consists of foraging in trees, going from one tree to another, usually in an established route. Riflemen are not very strong fliers, so, they limit their flights to short ones from tree to tree, and rarely go out of their small familiar territory. They rarely go to the ground. Sometimes when perching on a branch, riflemen will quickly flick their wings.

Riflemen are monogamous birds, forming long-lasting pair bonds. Their breeding season is from August to January. Males do most of the construction of the nest. The typical nest is a rather complex structure in a tree crevice, sometimes with a dome-like roof and inside lined with spider webs and mosses. Females lay two to four white eggs. About ten days before and during the egg laying process, males will bring food to females up to nine times an hour. Both parents usually raise two broods, young birds that are born and raised together, each year. The incubation period, time that it takes to sit on eggs before they hatch, is nineteen to twenty-one days. The nestling period, time necessary to take care of young birds unable to leave nest, is twenty-three to twenty-five days, but can last up to sixty days. Eggs weigh about 20 percent of the female's weight, and are laid every other day. Males incubate during the day and females incubate at night. Hatchlings are born in an undeveloped condition, so they take longer than most birds to develop into a stage where they can fly away.

Parents often use one to three adult or juvenile helpers to help feed nestlings and fledged offspring, those able to fly. For a first clutch, group of eggs hatched together, helpers are not usually related to the parents. They help to feed and defend the chicks, and to clean the nest. Some helpers only help with one nest, but others divide their time between several nests. With helpers, parents often have less work to do. Fledged young birds from the first brood often help to feed the chicks of the second brood. The nest for the second brood is often started before the first brood has left the first nest. This nest is smaller, loosely built, and unlined. Males do not bring food to females before and during the second egg-laying period. The second clutch of eggs is usually one egg less than the first clutch.

Riflemen and people: There is no known significance between riflemen and people.

Conservation status: Riflemen are fairly common and protected by New Zealand laws and a strong conservation program. They are the most successful species of the New Zealand wrens.   ■

FOR MORE INFORMATION

Books:

del Hoyo, Josep, Andrew Elliott, Jordi Sargatal, Jose Cabot, et al., eds. *Handbook of the Birds of the World.* Barcelona: Lynx Edicions, 1992.

Dickinson, Edward C., ed. *The Howard and Moore Complete Checklist of the Birds of the World,* 3rd ed. Princeton, NJ and Oxford, U.K.: Princeton University Press, 2003.

Forshaw, Joseph, ed. *Encyclopedia of Birds,* 2nd ed. San Diego, CA: Academic Press, 1998.

Harrison, Colin James Oliver. *Birds of the World.* London and New York: Dorling Kindersley, 1993.

Perrins, Christopher M., and Alex L. A. Middleton, eds. *The Encyclopedia of Birds.* New York: Facts on File, 1985.

OVENBIRDS
Furnariidae

Class: Aves
Order: Passeriformes
Family: Furnariidae
Number of species: 218 species

family
CHAPTER

PHYSICAL CHARACTERISTICS

Ovenbirds, also called horneros (or-NEYR-ohz), are small-to medium-sized, rust-to-brown colored birds. They have slender, pointed bills that range in length from short to long. Their wings are relatively short and are rounded or pointed at the tips. Ovenbirds have medium length legs and feet with front toes that are joined at the base. These birds have rufous, reddish, heads and white throats in many species. There is a light stripe over the eyes. They have brownish backs, light brown-and-white speckled or streaked bellies, rufous wings with brownish red or white bands, and rufous tails. Males and females are similarly colored. Adults are 5 to 11 inches (13 to 28 centimeters) long and weigh 0.3 to 1.6 ounces (9 to 46 grams).

GEOGRAPHIC RANGE

Ovenbirds are found from central Mexico to Patagonia in southern South America.

HABITAT

Ovenbirds inhabit forests of various types, brushlands, pampas (grasslands), alpine areas (high mountain regions), and semi-deserts.

DIET

Their diet consists of mostly insects, spiders, other invertebrates, animals without backbones, and sometimes small seeds. They forage, search for food, among litter on the ground, in

phylum
class
subclass
order
monotypic order
suborder
▲ **family**

OVENBIRDS ARE NAMED FOR A NEST

Rufous horneros build rounded nests out of moist clay, like a traditional clay baker's oven. They first build a base, often on a stout tree branch. They bring in small clumps of clay, mud, and some straw and hair to the construction site with their bill. The outer walls are built next, followed by the roof, which is dome-shaped. An entrance hole is left on one of the sides. Inside, a lining is made of fine fibers of soft grass and other plant tissues.

foliage, leaves, and on bark and epiphytes (EPP-uh-fytes), plants such as mosses that grow on another plant but do not depend on that host plant for nutrition, of shrubs and trees.

BEHAVIOR AND REPRODUCTION

Ovenbirds do not migrate, and are found usually alone or as a breeding pair, but sometimes in small groups. Some species are found primarily on the ground and others remain mostly in trees. When foraging on the ground they tend to walk and hop. While foraging in trees, some species are very quick as they search through foliage and finer branches, while other species are very agile as they forage on tree trunks. Some species are strong flyers, while others are weak and unable to fly long distances. Their calls are harsh and scolding, and their songs consist of a series of whistles and trills.

Ovenbirds build various shapes and types of nests. Many species build loose nests of plant fibers such as twigs and moss inside a cavity in a tree, among rocks, or in dense foliage. Other species make nests of lumps of moist clay, each about 0.1 ounces (3 grams) in weight, which is carried inside the bill. When completed, the nest looks like an oven, often weighing about 10 pounds (4 kilograms). One mated pair of ovenbirds may work on several nests at the same time. Other species dig tunnels from 3 to 10 feet (1 to 3 meters) long into an earthen bank or cliff. Still other species build small, spherical, hanging nests in trees, which are entered from a hole underneath. The last species group builds the largest of ovenbird nests, up to 3 feet (1 meter) in height, with several chambers enclosed inside the nest.

Females lay two to six eggs that are usually white but can be blue or greenish. Both parents share in egg incubation, sitting on the eggs, and in the care of nestlings, young birds unable to leave nest, and fledglings, birds that has recently grown the feathers needed for flight. The incubation period is fifteen to twenty-two days, and the nestling period, time necessary to take care of young birds unable to leave nest, is thirteen to twenty-nine days.

OVENBIRDS AND PEOPLE

The ovenbird species called the rufous hornero is the national bird of Argentina. Birdwatchers like to view these birds. There is little other significance between ovenbirds and people.

CONSERVATION STATUS

Three species of ovenbirds are listed as Critically Endangered, facing an extremely high risk of extinction, no longer existing, in the wild. Nine species are listed as Endangered, facing a very high risk of extinction in the wild in the near future, and fifteen species are Vulnerable, facing a high risk of extinction in the wild. There are eighteen species considered Near Threatened, in danger of becoming threatened with extinction.

Rufous hornero (*Furnarius rufus*)

■ Resident

RUFOUS HORNERO
Furnarius rufus

Physical characteristics: Rufous horneros are large ovenbirds with slightly rounded to nearly square tails. They have short-to-medium, pointed bills that are almost straight. The upper part of the bill is a brownish gray, to grayish or dark brownish while the lower part of the bill is pale horn to pinkish with a dark tip. They have rufous-brown foreheads and dull brown crowns, top of head. This species has

a tan stripe over the eyes. Their throats are whitish with very rufous hindnecks, back of the neck. The back and rump are rufous-brown with some pale edgings and the belly is pale buff or tan. Their flanks, sides, are tawny, copper color. The primary feathers are dull brownish with light rufous wingbands. Their tails are somewhat rufous in color and their lower legs and toes are grayish, brownish, or blackish. Males and females are similar in color. Juveniles are paler on the undersides. Adults are 6.3 to 9.1 inches (16 to 23 centimeters) long and weigh between 1.1 and 2.3 ounces (31 and 65 grams).

Geographic range: They are widely found in Bolivia, much of southern Brazil, Paraguay, Uruguay, and northern and central Argentina.

Habitat: Rufous horneros usually inhabit scrublands, pastures, agricultural lands, urban parks, and gardens. They are often found near streams, rivers, ponds, or lakes; usually in lowlands but they can be found to about 8,200 feet (2,500 meters), and occasionally up to 12,150 feet (3,500 meters).

Diet: Their diet consists of insects, other small invertebrates, and seeds. The bird forages on the bare ground and among leaf litter, often probing into soft dirt with its bill.

Behavior and reproduction: Rufous horneros do not migrate. They are usually found alone or in pairs on the ground where they run and hop, and perch in open spaces within shrubs. Their song is a loud, fast, rhythmic series of notes such as "kweep!" and their calls include a sharp "jeet!," "jeah," or "krip," often sounded as a series of notes. Pairs of birds often sing back and forth with each other.

The breeding season of the monogamous (muh-NAH-guh-mus), having only one mate, birds is in the spring-summer, September to February. Rufous horneros will defend their breeding territory, where they construct a large nest made up of thousands of small clumps of moist mud, clay, some dung, and straw carried to a nest site with their bills. The inside of the nest is lined with bits of grasses and stems. The spherical, oven-shaped structure is usually placed on a tree stump, fencepost, telephone pole, or rooftop; but can also be placed on older nests, bare ground, or rock. The entrance is usually placed on the side of the nest. Two to five eggs are laid from September to December. The incubation period is fourteen to eighteen days. Both males and females incubate eggs and take care of the nestlings. The nestling period is twenty-three to twenty-six days.

Rufous horneros and people: The rufous hornero is the national bird of Argentina. They are often found near human dwellings.

Conservation status: Rufous horneros are not threatened with extinction. They are widespread and abundant throughout their habitat.   ■

Greater thornbird (*Phacellodomus ruber*)

██ Resident

GREATER THORNBIRD
Phacellodomus ruber

Physical characteristics: Greater thornbirds are the reddest in color and among the largest in size of the ovenbirds. This species has a stout, plump, body and a long tail. They have a short, pointed bill that is slightly downcurved. The upper part of the bills is blackish and the lower part of the bill is pale gray to grayish green. They have a rufous-brown to grayish brown face with a light brown stripe over the eyes.

There is a reddish chestnut crown with faint pale shaft streaks; a rufous cap on the head; and a reddish brown to olive-brown hindcrown. Wings are rufous-chestnut. They have brown backs, rufous tails and whitish bellies and throats. Their rumps are brown tinged with red and their toes are gray to olive. Sexes are similar in appearance. Juveniles lack the crown patch and have a mottled, speckled, brownish breast. Adults are 7.5 to 8.3 inches (19 to 21 centimeters) long and weigh between 1.2 to 1.8 ounces (35 and 51 grams).

Geographic range: They are found in Bolivia, central Brazil, Paraguay, northern Argentina, and, possibly, in far northern Uruguay.

Habitat: Greater thornbirds inhabit the undergrowth of humid tropical forests, thickets on the banks of waterways, woodlands and scrublands. They especially like to be near ponds and other surface waters. They are found from sea level to elevations up to 4,600 feet (1,400 meters).

Diet: Their food includes insects, ants, and other small invertebrates. They are usually found foraging on the forest floor, around dense vegetation, and near the edges of water bodies such as marshes.

Behavior and reproduction: Greater thornbirds move about cautiously, not wanting to be seen. They usually move about alone or in pairs. Their song is a long series of loud, abrupt, accelerating notes such as "chip," with a sharp call of "check check" and "chweet." Their breeding season is from October to January. They build large, bulky nests that look similar to a cylinder or cone. The birds use sticks, twigs, and branches, often thorny ones, as materials to build the nest, which often contains several chambers and has a side entrance at the lower end. The interior of the nest is usually lined with fine grasses and feathers. The nest is usually attached to an outer, drooping branch of a tree or other low vegetation. Females lay three to five eggs, but five eggs are rare. Both sexes incubate the eggs and raise the nestlings.

Greater thornbirds and people: There is no known significance between people and greater thornbirds.

Conservation status: Greater thornbirds are not threatened with extinction. They are widespread and locally abundant throughout most of their habitats. They are protected in parts of their range, such as Pantanal National Park in Brazil and Esteros del Iberá and Calilegua National Parks in Argentina. ■

FOR MORE INFORMATION

Books:

del Hoyo, Josep, Andrew Elliott, Jordi Sargatal, Jose Cabot, et al., eds. *Handbook of the Birds of the World.* Barcelona: Lynx Edicions, 1992.

Dickinson, Edward C., ed. *The Howard and Moore Complete Checklist of the Birds of the World,* 3rd ed. Princeton, NJ and Oxford, U.K.: Princeton University Press, 2003.

Forshaw, Joseph, ed. *Encyclopedia of Birds,* 2nd ed. San Diego, CA: Academic Press, 1998.

Harrison, Colin James Oliver. *Birds of the World.* London and New York: Dorling Kindersley, 1993.

Perrins, Christopher M., and Alex L. A. Middleton, eds. *The Encyclopedia of Birds.* New York: Facts on File, 1985.

Class: Aves
Order: Passeriformes
Family: Dendrocolaptidae
Number of species: 52 species

family
CHAPTER

PHYSICAL CHARACTERISTICS

Woodcreepers range in length from 5.5 to 14 inches (14 to 36 centimeters). They have a slender body and long rounded wings. Tails are long with feather shafts that are sharp and stiff. Woodcreepers have short legs and strong claws. Bill shape varies tremendously in the group. Some species have curved sickle-shaped bills while other species have short bills. Woodcreepers are generally brown, brownish olive, brownish red or brownish yellow in color. Many species have stripes, bands, or spots. Males and females are similar in coloration and general appearance.

GEOGRAPHIC RANGE

Woodcreepers are found throughout the Central American and South American tropics. They occur from southern Mexico to northern Argentina. The greatest species diversity of woodcreepers is found in tropical Amazonia, the Amazon River basin area.

HABITAT

Woodcreepers are found in many types of rainforests, montane (mountain) forests, and brush lands.

DIET

The diet of most woodcreepers includes insects, spiders, and other invertebrates, animals without a backbone. Some species may eat larger prey such as small lizards. A few species also eat small fruits. In some species, individuals forage, or look for food, in mixed-species flocks that include other species of birds. Most woodcreepers forage, look for food, in trees, searching for insects and other prey hidden in the bark of the trunk and branches or among the mosses, lichens, and other plants that grow on branches. Woodcreepers walk, or "creep" up the tree trunk looking for food. Once they reach the top of one tree, they fly to the base of another tree and begin to forage upwards again. The woodcreepers' stiff tails help support them as they ascend a tree. Some species are also able to catch insects mid-flight, and others are known for following army ants and catching prey that the ants have flushed out.

BEHAVIOR AND REPRODUCTION

Woodcreepers stay in their breeding area all year long. They do not migrate. Some species of woodcreepers live in male-female pairs all year long, while others are solitary except during the breeding season.

At night, woodcreepers generally roost in natural tree-cavities or old woodpecker holes, with each individual occupying a separate hole.

Woodcreepers sing primarily at dusk, often while they are feeding. Their songs are simple and clear, frequently made up of either soft trills or a series of loud, ringing tones.

Woodcreepers nest in holes in tree-trunks, sometimes those which were once used by woodpeckers. They build nests from small pieces of plant material. The female generally lays two or three white eggs. Eggs hatch in fifteen to twenty-one days. The young fledge, or grow the feathers needed to fly, in nineteen to twenty-three days. Older nestling and fledgling woodcreepers spend the nights in holes separate from the parents. Both parents participate in all phases of reproductive activity, including building the nest, incubating the eggs, and feeding the hatched young.

WOODCREEPERS AND PEOPLE

Woodcreepers, along with other tropical birds, attract tourists and birdwatchers to rainforest habitats. They have no other known impact on or importance to humans.

CAVITY NESTERS

Woodcreepers are one of many groups of birds known as cavity nesters, birds that nest in tree cavities, or holes. Tree cavities occur naturally or are purposely excavated, dug out. Species that excavate their own nest cavities are known as primary cavity nesters, and include groups such as woodpeckers. Woodcreepers, on the other hand, are secondary cavity nesters, species that are unable to excavate their own cavities. Secondary cavity nesters use either naturally occurring cavities or cavities that have been excavated by other species.

CONSERVATION STATUS

The moustached woodcreeper is considered Vulnerable, facing a high risk of extinction in the wild. It occupies areas of eastern Brazil, where populations have declined due primarily to large-scale logging and habitat destruction for farming. Another species, the greater scythebill, is considered Near Threatened, likely to qualify for a threatened category in the near future, because of habitat destruction. In addition, a number of other woodcreeper species have also suffered recent declines in numbers but are not yet considered in danger of extinction.

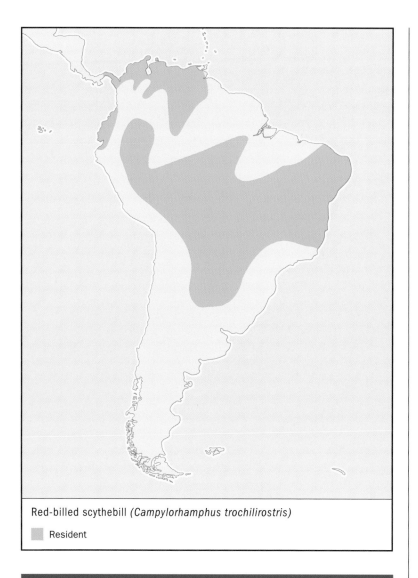

Red-billed scythebill (*Campylorhamphus trochilirostris*)

■ Resident

RED-BILLED SCYTHEBILL
Campylorhamphus trochilirostris

Physical characteristics: The red-billed scythebill is one of the larger woodcreeper species, with a body 9.5 to 11 inches (24 to 28 centimeters) in length. It has a long tail and a long, slender, downwardly-curved bill. Its back and tail are brownish red in color, while the belly is a lighter cinnamon-brown shade. The head and throat are covered with brown and white streaks.

Red-billed scythebills eat insects and other invertebrates by picking them off the trunks and branches of trees. (© Doug Wechsler/VIREO. Reproduced by permission.)

Geographic range: The red-billed scythebill has a wide range, occurring in portions of Panama, Venezuela, Colombia, Ecuador, Peru, Bolivia, Brazil, Paraguay, and northern Argentina.

Habitat: The red-billed scythebill is one of the most widely-distributed woodcreeper species. It inhabits rainforests, forests, and forests in mountainous regions up to a height of 6,600 feet (2,000 meters).

Diet: Red-billed scythebills eat insects and other invertebrates by picking them off the trunks and branches of trees.

Behavior and reproduction: Red-billed scythebills are either solitary or found in pairs. While looking for food, they sometimes join flocks that include other bird species. Two or three eggs are laid in an abandoned woodpecker hole or other tree cavity. Both parents help incubate eggs and feed nestlings.

Red-billed scythebills and people: Red-billed scythebills are not known to have any special significance to humans.

Conservation status: The red-billed scythebill is not considered threatened. ▪

FOR MORE INFORMATION

Books:

Perrins, Christopher, ed. *Firefly Encyclopedia of Birds.* Buffalo, NY: Firefly Books, 2003.

Web sites:

"Dendrocolaptidae (Woodcreepers)." The Internet Bird Collection. http://www.hbw.com/ibc/phtml/familia.phtml?idFamilia=107 (accessed on April 25, 2004).

"Family Dendrocolaptidae (Woodcreepers)." Animal Diversity Web. http://animaldiversity.ummz.umich.edu/site/accounts/classification/Dendrocolaptidae.html#Dendrocolaptidae (accessed on April 25, 2004).

"Woodcreepers." Bird Families of the World, Cornell University. http://www.es.cornell.edu/winkler/botw/dendrocolaptidae.html (accessed on April 25, 2004).

ANT THRUSHES
Formicariidae

Class: Aves
Order: Passeriformes
Family: Formicariidae
Number of species: 244 species

PHYSICAL CHARACTERISTICS

Ant thrushes, also called antbirds, antcatchers, antpittas, antshrikes, or antwrens, are a family of small to medium-sized perching songbirds found in the rainforests of Central and South America. There are two major divisions within the ant thrush family, based on where the birds spend most of their time. About fifty-six species live on or near the forest floor and as a group are called ground antbirds. About 188 species live in the canopy, or forest treetops. These birds are sometimes called typical antbirds.

The bodies of antbirds vary in length from 4 to about 15 inches (10 to 38 centimeters). Some antbirds have short, stiff tails that they hold upright, while others have tails as long as their body that droop. Ground antbirds tend to be larger than canopy-dwelling antbirds and have longer, stronger legs and short toes for running and hopping. Antbirds that live in the canopy have developed special longer toes that allow them to grip thin branches for long periods without using much energy.

Antbirds do not migrate, or move seasonally from one region to another. As a result, they have evolved, changed over time, to have stubby, rounded, relatively weak wings that are best suited for flying only short distances.

Antbirds eat mainly insects. Their bills are specially designed for this task. Antbird bills curve slightly downward and in some of the larger species have a hook at the tip. Larger species of antbirds also have a "tooth," or rough spot, inside the bill that helps them to hold on to or tear up food. Smaller antbirds have a smooth bill and no "tooth."

Antbirds are not the most colorful birds in the rainforest. In fact, they are rather dull. They range in color from black to gray to brown. Male and female ground antbirds usually look quite similar. However, canopy-dwelling males are often black or gray with some white feathers, while females are brown and often marked with a pattern of light and dark spots. Their coloring makes them difficult to see on the forest floor or among the shifting shadows and sunlight of the canopy.

GEOGRAPHIC RANGE

Antbirds are found in tropical and subtropical rainforests from southern Mexico to northern Argentina. However, the greatest number of species is found in the rainforest of the Amazon River basin in Brazil and the Orinoco River basin in Venezuela.

HABITAT

Antbirds live in damp, shrubby, forested regions and woodland areas in the tropics, including areas where the original trees have been cut down and new trees are appearing. Species in this family can be found from sea level to high on forested mountains, up to 10,900 feet (3,300 meters).

DIET

Antbirds are insectivores, or insect eaters. They eat many different insects and insect-like bugs including crickets, beetles, spiders, centipedes, and lice. Larger antbirds also eat snails, frogs, lizards, small snakes, mice, and young birds. They use their strong bill and "tooth" to kill this larger food. Some species eat fruit and seeds in addition to insects.

BEHAVIOR AND REPRODUCTION

Antbirds were given their name because of their special feeding behavior. In the rainforest colonies of ants often move together in huge swarms or columns when they are hunting for food. As the ants move, they stir up insects and small animals, such as mice and lizards. Antbirds have learned to take advantage of the movement of these ants, especially swarms of red army ants and black rain ants. The antbirds follow a column

SOS FOR DANGER

Most species of ant thrushes have white spots on their back that are hidden under their wings when they are resting or calm. When these birds think that they are in danger, they flash these white spots in a quick off-and-on pattern. Scientists believe this is a kind of Morse code that lets other birds in the area know that something threatening is nearby.

In 1980 the Central
American country of Belize
featured the barred ant-
shrike on its 25 cent postage stamp.

of moving ants and pick off insects and small animals that are trying to get away from the hungry ants. In a sense, the ants do the birds' hunting for them.

Ant colonies are so important to antbirds that that older male birds will drive younger, weaker birds out of their territory in order to keep them away from the ant colonies. During nesting season, antbirds usually wait for ant columns to pass their nests, but other times of they year they actively look for and follow moving ant colonies.

Antbirds also perform a grooming or cleaning behavior that involves ants. The birds pick up ants in their bills and rub them into their feathers. This is called "anting." Scientists believe that when the ants are crushed, their bodies release formic acid, which kills parasites, organisms that live on other organisms, living on the birds' feathers. A few antbird species also allow live ants to crawl through their feathers and eat insects that are attached to their skin.

Although much is not known about the reproductive behavior of antbirds, it appears that they mate with a single partner for life. The location and shape of antbird nests varies depending on the species. Ground antbirds often build closed, rounded nests directly on the forest floor. Other species build deep cup-shaped nests on low branches. Some species use holes in trees or rotting logs.

Antbirds usually lay two light-colored eggs that hatch within fourteen to seventeen days. Both parents share the job of incubating, sitting on the nest to provide warmth for chick development, the eggs. Young antbirds are able to leave the nest and hunt for food soon after they are born.

ANT THRUSHES AND PEOPLE

The ant thrush family is of interest mainly to ornithologists, scientists who study birds, and birdwatchers interested in ecotourism, travel for the purpose of studying wildlife and the environment.

CONSERVATION STATUS

In 2003, four species of antbirds were considered Critically Endangered, facing an extremely high risk of extinction, or dying out, in the wild. These were the fringe-backed fire-eye, the Rio de Janeiro antwren, the Alagoas antwren, and the Rondonia bushbird. Sixteen other species were considered

Endangered, facing a very high risk of extinction, and eleven species were classified as Vulnerable, facing a high risk of extinction. The main reason these birds are at risk for extinction is loss of habitat due to human activities such as farming, mining, and development.

Barred antshrike (*Thamnophilus doliatus*)

▢ Resident

BARRED ANTSHRIKE
Thamnophilus doliatus

Physical characteristics: Barred antshrikes, sometimes called Chapman's antshrikes, are small, noisy birds about 6 inches (15 centimeters) long. Males are black with white bars and a black crest of feathers on their head. Females have black stripes, but are cinnamon or reddish brown colored, instead of white, and have a brown crest. Both males and females have yellow eyes, long tails, and strong black bills.

Geographic range: The barred antshrike is one of the most common antbirds. It can be found living year-round from southern Mexico to northern Argentina east of the Andes Mountains. Although it is widespread in Brazil, it is not found in the center of the Amazon rainforest.

Habitat: Barred antshrikes live on the edges of the tropical rainforest, but not deep in the center of the forest. These birds can be found in scrubland, along roads, in open woodland and clearings, and in gardens or abandoned lots. They live in both humid and dry areas at elevations between 330 and 6,600 feet (100 and 2,000 meters).

Barred antshrikes live on the edges of the tropical rainforest and hunt for food with mixed groups of other species of birds. (© J. Dunning/VIREO. Reproduced by permission.)

Diet: Like all antbirds, barred antshrikes eat insects and insect-like bugs. They normally hunt for food with mixed groups of other birds in an area between the lowest bushes and the treetops.

Behavior and reproduction: Barred antshrikes mate for life with a single partner and tend to stay together throughout the year. They usually lay two eggs in a nest made of grasses. Nests are often built in low bushes. Both parents incubate the eggs and care for the young.

Barred antshrikes and people: Barred antshrikes have no special significance and little economic impact on people. They are of interest mainly to birdwatchers and ecotourists.

Conservation status: Barred antshrikes are not threatened. They are common birds found across a wide area of Central and South America. ■

Gray antbird (*Cercomacra cinerascens*)

■ Resident

GRAY ANTBIRD
Cercomacra cinerascens

Physical characteristics: The gray antbird is a small bird of about 6 inches (16 centimeters) with a rather long tail. It is dark gray with a white band at the tip of the tail.

Geographic range: Gray antbirds are found in the rainforests of northern South America, including Guyana, the southern part of

Venezuela, parts of Colombia and Ecuador, eastern Peru and northern Bolivia. They are most abundant in the Amazon River basin of Brazil.

Habitat: Gray antbirds live in the forest canopy in dense rainforests and on heavily forested mountain slopes below an elevation of 2,300 feet (700 meters).

Diet: Gray antbirds eat insects and insect-like bugs.

Behavior and reproduction: Gray antbirds form pairs that stay together, although they sometimes hunt for food in a group with birds of other species. Little is known about their nesting habits.

Gray antbirds and people: Gray antbirds are of interest mainly to birdwatchers and ecotourists.

Conservation status: Gray antbirds are not threatened; they are abundant in many places. They are found across a wide area of northern South America. ∎

FOR MORE INFORMATION

Books:

Hilty, Steven L. *Birds of Venezuela.* Princeton, NJ: Princeton University Press, 2003.

Ridgley, Robert S., and Guy Tudor. *The Birds of South America.* Vol 2, *The Suboscine Passerines.* Austin, TX: University of Texas Press, 1994.

Web sites:

Gleyzer, Artem, Seth Weith-Glushko, and Abhiram Vijay. "Project:Antbird." Academy for the Advancement of Science and Technology and The National Zoo. http://www.bergen.org/Smithsonian/Antbirds/homeantb. htm (accessed on April 24, 2004).

Robertson, Don. "Bird Families of the World." CREARGUS@Monterey Bay. http://www.montereybay.com/creagrus/index.html (accessed on April 27, 2004).

family
CHAPTER

PHYSICAL CHARACTERISTICS

Tapaculos are a diverse family of small perching birds that live in Central and South America. They range in size from about 4 to 9 inches (10 to 23 centimeters) and weigh anywhere from 0.4 to 6.5 ounces (11 to 185 grams). Tapaculos are one of the most primitive families of songbirds.

Tapaculos are also one of the most varied families of birds. The fifty or so species have only a few physical characteristics in common. Tapaculos are very poor flyers. They have short, rounded wings, but unusually strong feet and large claws. Internally the sternum, or breastbone, of these birds is different from the sternum of birds that are better flyers. In most birds, even domestic chickens, the sternum has a projection or bulge called a keel. The keel creates more surface area for the muscles used in flight to attach to the bone. Birds like tapaculos that are nearly flightless do not need this extra area where flight muscles can attach, so their breastbones do not have a keel.

Tapaculos are generally solid color grayish or brown birds, although some have lighter-colored spots or patterns. In most species, the males and females look similar, although the females tend to be slightly smaller. Most tapaculos have short tails. Their feathers fall out easily and it is thought that this is a way of fooling predators, animals that are hunting them.

Different species of tapaculo may be difficult or impossible to tell apart by sight. Some species look alike and can only be identified based on their song, their weight, and the habitat in which they live. Others are so similar that they can only be told

phylum

class

subclass

order

monotypic order

suborder

▲ **family**

WHO IS IN AND WHO IS OUT?

Tapaculos are some of the hardest birds to classify. Scientists are still not sure exactly how many species there are in this family. New species are being discovered, and in 1997 several species were reclassified. In the past, tapaculos were considered separate species if they had different songs or lived in different environments and did not interbreed. Today genetic and biochemical evidence suggests that some of these classifications may be wrong and the number of tapaculo species may change again.

apart by genetic testing. Ornithologists, scientists who study birds, are not in complete agreement about how many species of tapaculos exist and how they should be classified.

GEOGRAPHIC RANGE

Tapaculos are found from Costa Rica in southern Central America to Tierra del Fuego, Argentina, at the southern tip of South America. Many species live in the Andes Mountains in western South America. They are mostly absent from the hot, humid rainforest of the Amazon and Orinoco river basins in Brazil and Venezuela.

HABITAT

Most species of tapaculos prefer high, cool, tropical mountain rainforests. Only one kind of tapaculo lives in the lowland Amazon rainforest. Several members of this family have adapted to life in dry, desert climates or dry grasslands. Some species have extremely limited habitats, which puts them at risk for extinction, or dying out. For example, one type of tapaculo lives only in the tall grass of certain marshes in Brazil. Species tend to separate by elevation, height of land above sea level, so that in the Andes, a single mountain may be home to four or five species of tapaculos all living at different elevations that do not overlap.

DIET

Tapaculos eat mainly insects and spiders. Some species also eat berries. These birds feed by walking or hopping across the forest floor, then scraping their feet against the ground, turning over the moss and leaves with their strong claws to look for bugs. A few species hop through low branches eating the insects they find there.

BEHAVIOR AND REPRODUCTION

Tapaculos have not been well studied, and not much is known about their behavior. They tend to be shy birds that spend much of their time on the forest floor. They are so hard to observe, in fact, that scientists know several species only by their song. It appears that these birds identify each other and choose their mates by sound rather than sight. This may be one reason why their feathers are dull and why some species look the same, but sound different.

In the tapaculos that have been studied, it appears that birds who mate form permanent pairs, but if one member of the pair dies, another mate is chosen almost immediately. The nests of fewer than half the species of all tapaculos have been observed. Of those that are known, most species build their nests in the ground at the end of tunnels. The birds either dig the tunnels themselves or take over empty animal burrows. Some species use hollow logs instead of digging tunnels. A few build cup nests in low branches.

Normally tapaculos lay two or three eggs. In some species both males and females sit on, incubate, the eggs for about two weeks before they hatch. The young birds are naked when they hatch and are cared for by both parents until they are ready to leave the nest several weeks later.

TAPACULOS AND PEOPLE

Because they are such shy birds, tapaculos are often overlooked by people who are not trained birdwatchers. They are mainly studied by ornithologists interested in the evolution of different families of birds.

CONSERVATION STATUS

Two species of tapaculos are Critically Endangered, facing an extremely high risk of extinction in the wild, and may be extinct. Streseman's bristlefront and the Bahai tapaculo both live in eastern Brazil and are in danger of dying out because of loss of habit from deforestation of their naturally small range.

One other tapaculo, the tall-grass wetland tapaculo, that lives in the marshes of southern Brazil, is Endangered, facing a high risk of extinction, due to human development. The population of Tacarcula tapaculos is holding steady, but is considered Vulnerable, facing a high risk of extinction, because of clearing of forests and potential road building in its habitat along on the border of Panama and Colombia. Five other species are considered Near Threatened, in danger of becoming threatened with extinction, and face declining populations.

Rusty-belted tapaculo (*Liosceles thoracicus*)

▨ Resident

RUSTY-BELTED TAPACULO
Liosceles thoracicus

Physical characteristics: The rusty-belted tapaculo is one of the larger tapaculos. They are about 7.5 inches (19 centimeters) long and weigh about 1.5 ounces (42 grams). Rusty-belted tapaculos live on the forest floor. Their dark gray-brown back helps them blend in well with their environment. Their throat and breast are white, with a rusty reddish breast band that gives them their name. They have a black, white, and rusty pattern on their undersides.

Geographic range: Rusty-belted tapaculos live in South America in southeastern Colombia, western Brazil, and neighboring parts of Peru and Ecuador.

Habitat: Unlike many tapaculos that prefer higher, cooler elevations, rusty-belted tapaculos live in humid lowland rainforests on the forest floor.

Diet: Like all tapaculos, these birds eat insects. They feed by walking or hopping slowly along the forest floor looking for prey.

Rusty-belted tapaculos live in humid lowland rainforests on the forest floor. (Illustration by Brian Cressman. Reproduced by permission.)

Behavior and reproduction: Rusty-belted tapaculos build underground nests among the roots of trees. Little is known about their reproductive behavior, because they are shy and difficult to observe.

Rusty-belted tapaculos and people: These birds have little interaction with people and are rarely seen. They are of interest mainly to ornithologists and birdwatchers.

Conservation status: Rusty-belted tapaculos are not threatened or in danger of extinction. ■

FOR MORE INFORMATION

Books:

Ridgley, Robert S., and Guy Tudor. *The Birds of South America.* Vol 2, *The Suboscine Passerines.* Austin, TX: University of Texas Press, 1994.

Web sites:

"Birds, Mammals, and Amphibians of Latin America." NatureServe. http://www.natureserve.org/infonatura (accessed on May 4, 2004).

Robertson, Don. "Bird Families of the World." CREAGRUS@Monterey Bay. http://www.montereybay.com/creagrus/index.html (accessed on May 4, 2004).

TYRANT FLYCATCHERS
Tyrannidae

Class: Aves

Order: Passeriformes

Family: Tyrannidae

Number of species: About 420 species

family

phylum

class

subclass

order

monotypic order

suborder

▲ **family**

PHYSICAL CHARACTERISTICS

There are more species in the family of tyrant flycatchers than in any other family of birds in the Western Hemisphere. Members of this family are found throughout North, Central, and South America. The family includes both migratory species that move from one climate to another as the seasons change and non-migratory species that remain in the same area year round. Only about thirty-seven of the more than four hundred species of tyrant flycatchers live in North America.

Tyrant flycatchers are perching birds with bodies that range in size from 3.5 to 11 inches (9 to 28 centimeters) and weigh from about 0.2 to 2.4 ounces (5.7 to 68 grams). This family includes some species that look very different from each other and other species that look so similar they cannot be told apart just by looking at them. In addition, males and females of many species look alike. Most members of this family are dull with brown, gray, or olive-green backs and ivory or light gray undersides. There are exceptions to this color pattern, including the vermilion flycatcher and the great kiskadee, both of which are brightly colored. Most species have moderate-length tails, although a few, such as the scissor-tailed flycatcher, have pairs of 6 inch long (15 centimeter) tail feathers that stream out behind them, almost doubling the bird's length.

Despite the diversity found in this family, tyrant flycatchers do have certain characteristics in common. All these birds eat insects, and they have developed short, wide bills with a slight hook at the end that help them catch and hold their food. Stiff stripped-down feathers consisting mainly of the feather shaft are found around the bill of most tyrant flycatchers. These are called rictal (RIK-tuhl) bristles. Originally it was thought that rictal bristles helped the birds catch insects while flying, but recent experimental evidence disproved this theory. Ornithologists, scientists who study birds, now think the bristles may help to keep insects out of the birds' eyes as they fly.

Tyrant flycatchers are good flyers. Those species that migrate have longer, more pointed wings designed for more efficient flight than those species that stay in one area year round. In non-migratory species the wings are shorter and rounder, a design that makes lifting off a branch easier. Because flycatchers spend little time on the ground, their feet and legs are weak.

GEOGRAPHIC RANGE

Tyrant flycatchers are found from the southernmost tip of South America to north of the Arctic Circle in North America. Species that summer in the Arctic usually migrate to Central or South America in the winter. The only area in the Western Hemisphere where tyrant flycatchers are not found is in the extreme northern edge of Canada.

HABITAT

Tyrant flycatchers live wherever insects live. They have adapted to tropical rainforests and deserts of the southwestern United States. They can be found in all types of forests, along steams, in grasslands, deserts and around human-made structures. They are most likely to be found in areas where trees, posts, or other spots to perch are combined with open areas.

DIET

Tyrant flycatchers are insectivores, eating mainly insects. However, certain species also eat berries, fruit, caterpillars, and worms. Some of the larger species eat small fish, frogs, lizards, and even mice or small birds, in addition to insects. Flycatchers' bills are adapted to the type of food they eat. The larger the food, the larger and stronger the bill must be. Bigger birds may beat their food against a branch until it is dead, then hold it down with one foot while pulling it apart with their bill.

When hunting for food, most tyrant flycatchers sit on a perch above the ground and remain still until they see an insect. They then fly out and snap the insect out of the air. As their bill closes,

it makes clicking sound loud enough to be heard by human observers. The bird then returns either to the same or a different perch and waits for the next insect. This type of feeding is called hawking. Some tyrant flycatchers such as phoebes (FEE-beez) eat insects, caterpillars, and worms off the ground. These birds sit on a low perch until they see their prey, then fly down to the ground to pick it up, and return to a perch. They do not walk or hop along the ground hunting for food.

BEHAVIOR AND REPRODUCTION

Songs and calls are important in helping tyrant flycatchers recognize their own species, especially when several different members of this family live in the same area and look similar. Most species of tyrant flycatchers form pairs only for a single breeding season, choosing a different mate the next year. The female does most of the nest building, although the male sometimes keeps her company as she gathers material for the nest.

Tyrant flycatchers build many different types of nests in a variety of different locations. Many species build open cup-like nests in trees or shrubs. Some species nest in holes in trees, while others, such as phoebes, build nests of mud and plant material under bridges or under the eaves of empty buildings. Other species build bag-type nests that hang from branches over streams. Generally tyrant flycatchers select nest sites that offer some protection from predators and the weather.

Tyrant flycatchers lay two to eight eggs, and have one or two broods, or groups of young, a year. The female sits on the nest and incubates, sits on and warms, the eggs for about two weeks. The eggs hatch over several days, rather than all at the same time. Newborn tyrant flycatchers are almost naked and take two to three weeks to fledge, or develop feathers. During this time, both parents feed the young birds.

Tyrant flycatchers are territorial while they are breeding. They actively defend the area where they are nesting against other birds of the same or competing species and do their best to drive them away. Some tyrant flycatchers are very aggressive. The family gets the name tyrant from the behavior of kingbirds, which sometimes fearlessly attack larger birds.

Tyrant flycatchers that nest at the extreme edges of their range—either in the Arctic or near at the southern tip of South America—migrate hundreds of miles to warmer climates in order to find food when cold weather sets in. Other species that live in less extreme climates move much shorter distances or not at all. Migrating birds tend to return to the same nesting area each year.

TYRANT FLYCATCHERS AND PEOPLE

Tyrant flycatchers are neither dangerous nor particularly useful to humans, although they do eat large numbers of insects and may help to control the insect population.

CONSERVATION STATUS

Two tyrant flycatchers found in Brazil, the Alagoas tyrannulet and the Minas Gerais tyrannulet are Critically Endangered, facing an extremely high risk of extinction in the wild, because of rapid habitat loss and small populations that are widely separated. Nine other members of the tyrant flycatcher family, eight in South America and one in Cuba, are Endangered, facing a very high risk of extinction, for similar reasons. Fifteen additional species, none of which are in North America, are Vulnerable, facing a high risk of extinction.

Rose-throated becard *(Pachyramphus aglaiae)*

Resident   Breeding

SPECIES ACCOUNTS

ROSE-THROATED BECARD
Pachyramphus aglaiae

Physical characteristics: The rose-throated becard is one of the more colorful members of the tyrant flycatcher family. It is a moderate sized bird about 6.5 to 7.3 inches (16 to 19 centimeters) long with strong black bills. Males and females look different. Males have a dark gray head, gray back, light gray undersides, and a bright rose-colored throat patch. Females are dark brown on top and tan underneath with no rose color on them at all. Young birds have the same color pattern as adult females.

Geographic range: Rose-throated becards live year round from northern Mexico through Panama in southern Central America. During spring and summer breeding season, they can also be found in the United States in southeastern Arizona and the Rio Grande valley of Texas.

Habitat: Rose-throated becards live along the edge of forests, in wooded canyons and mountainous areas. They prefer places with tall trees, such as sycamores (SIK-ah-mohrz), near open areas.

Diet: Rose-throated becards eat insects, insect larvae (LAR-vee), and some berries. They hawk for food, sitting on a perch, then flying out to snap an insect out of the air.

Behavior and reproduction: Rose-throated becards choose a single mate and lay two to six eggs once each year. Female do most of the nest building. The nest is round and hangs from a tree branch. Females incubate the eggs for just over two weeks. Both parents feed the young, which leave the nest around three weeks after birth.

Rose-throated becards and people: Rose-throated becards are attractive to birdwatchers, but have little other known importance to people.

Conservation status: Large populations of rose-throated becards exist. They are not in immediate danger of extinction. ■

Female rose-throated becards do most of the nest building and incubate the eggs, but the males help feed the young. (Illustration by Wendy Baker. Reproduced by permission.)

Great kiskadee (*Pitangus sulphuratus*)

☐ Resident

GREAT KISKADEE
Pitangus sulphuratus

Physical characteristics: Great kiskadees, also called kiskadee fly-catchers, are one of the larger, more colorful tyrant flycatchers. These birds are about 9.8 inches (25 centimeters) long. Males and females look the same. They have a black and white lined head, brown back and wings, white throat patch, and bright yellow undersides.

Geographic range: Great kiskadees are found in the United States in southwest Texas, and from northern Mexico through Central America, and in South America east of the Andes Mountains and as far south as Paraguay.

Habitat: Great kiskadees live in semi-open country with scattered trees. They are often found at the edge of forests and along streams.

Diet: Great kiskadees eat insects, but also will eat small fish, tadpoles, lizards, and mice. They will dive into the water after food, which they bring to their perch and beat against a branch until it is dead before tearing it apart. If they cannot find their preferred food, great kiskadees will eat fruits and berries.

Behavior and reproduction: Great kiskadees are aggressive and will chase larger birds out of their territory. These are large, active, noisy birds with a loud, harsh, call that sounds like their name. They mate with a single partner and build round nests on trees or utility poles. The female lays two to five eggs, two or three times a year. The young hatch in about two weeks and are fed by both parents before they fledge, grow feathers, and leave the nest about three weeks after birth.

Great kiskadees and people: Great kiskadees are often found around houses and gardens. They are common in many areas, but do not have a special significance to people.

Conservation status: Great kiskadees are abundant in much of their range, although their populations are declining in Texas due to development. They are in no danger of becoming extinct. ■

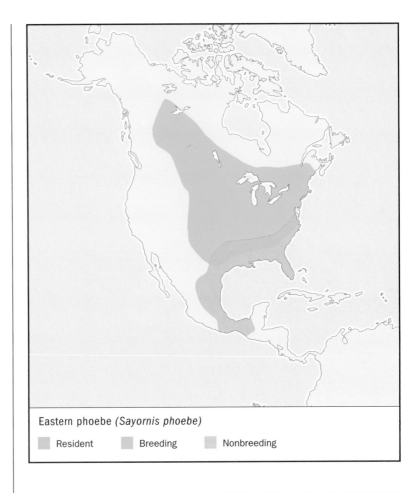

Eastern phoebe *(Sayornis phoebe)*

Resident   Breeding   Nonbreeding

EASTERN PHOEBE
Sayornis phoebe

Physical characteristics: Eastern phoebes are about 7 inches (18 centimeter) long with gray-brown heads and backs, white undersides, and black bills, legs, and feet. Males and females look alike.

Geographic range: Eastern phoebes are found east of the Rocky Mountains in the United States and Canada. They are migratory birds, moving north to nest in the summer and south to winter in coastal South Carolina, Georgia, Florida, and along the Gulf of Mexico as far south as the Yucatán Peninsula in Mexico.

Habitat: Eastern phoebes live in open land along the edge of forests and along rivers and streams. They survive very well close to human-made structures such as bridges, roads, and farms.

Diet: Eastern phoebes hawk for insects. They will also eat small fish and berries.

Behavior and reproduction: Eastern phoebes mate two or three times a year, usually with the same partner. They build a cup-shaped nest out of mud attached to a vertical wall, such as a cliff, pole, or building.

Eastern phoebes and people: Eastern phoebes often live near human structures and take advantage of them as places to build nests. They eat large numbers of insects, but are not especially significant to people.

Conservation status: Eastern phoebes are common in many parts of their range and are in no immediate danger of extinction. ■

Eastern phoebes build their cup-shaped nests out of mud attached to a vertical wall, such as a cliff, pole, or building. (© N. Barnes/VIREO. Reproduced by permission.)

FOR MORE INFORMATION

Books:

Hilty, Steven L. *Birds of Venezuela.* Princeton, NJ: Princeton University Press, 2003.

Ridgley, Robert S., and Guy Tudor. *The Birds of South America.* Vol 2, *The Suboscine Passerines.* Austin, TX: University of Texas Press, 1994.

Sibley, David. *The Sibley Guide to Bird Life and Behavior.* New York: Alfred A. Knopf, 2001.

Web sites:

Deeble, B. "Rose-Throated Becard." The Nature Conservancy. http://www.conserveonline.org/2001/05/m/en/rtbe.doc (accessed on May 4, 2004).

Robertson, Don. "Bird Families of the World." CREAGRUS@Monterey Bay. http://www.montereybay.com/creagrus/index.html (accessed on May 4, 2004).

SHARPBILL

Oxyruncidae

Class: Aves

Order: Passeriformes

Family: Oxyruncidae

One species: Sharpbill (*Oxyruncus cristatus*)

phylum

class

subclass

order

monotypic order

suborder

▲ family

PHYSICAL CHARACTERISTICS

Sharpbills are small, sturdy, quiet birds 6 to 7 inches (15 to 18 centimeters) in length that live in scattered areas of South America. Sharpbills have olive green backs, black wings, and black tails. Their undersides are ivory with distinctive dark tear-shaped spots on the upper part of the breast. In the center of the head is a bright orange or red crest that is normally hidden, but is raised when the bird is excited. Males and females look similar, although the colors of the female may be duller. Some ornithologists, scientists that study birds, separate this species into five different groups based on their geographic location and small differences in color and size. However, these differences are minor.

Sharpbills get their name from the distinctive shape of their gray bill, which is sharply pointed. The bill is surrounded by rictal (RIK-tuhl) bristles, stiff stripped-down feathers consisting mainly of the feather shaft. Originally it was thought that rictal bristles helped the birds catch insects while flying, but experimental evidence disproved this theory. Ornithologists (scientists who study birds) now think the bristles may help to keep insects out of the birds' eyes as they fly.

Ornithologists have not decided exactly where sharpbills belong in the classification of bird families. Sharpbills were first scientifically described in 1820 and were put in their own family, which contains only this species. Since then, they have been reclassified by some ornithologists as contingas or as tyrant flycatchers. Genetic research started in the 1980s seemed to suggest that they could be part of the tyrant flycatcher family, but as recently as 2002, there was no firm conclusion about how they should be classified.

GEOGRAPHIC RANGE

The range of the sharpbill is unusual, because it is discontinuous, or broken. Sharpbills are found in isolated patches throughout Central and South America. They live year round in parts of Costa Rica and Panama, Argentina, Bolivia, Brazil, Ecuador, French Guiana, Guyana, Paraguay, Peru, Suriname, and Venezuela. The broken up nature of their range suggests that at one time they may have been found over a much greater, continuous area.

HABITAT

Sharpbills live and breed in humid mountain rainforests at elevations of 1,300 to 5,900 feet (400 to 1,800 meters) above sea level. They are found in both dense forest and along the forest edges. Although they do not migrate, or move seasonally to find food, in the traditional sense, some scientists have reported that they do move down the mountain toward lowland rainforests when they are not breeding.

DIET

Sharpbills eat mainly fruit, insects, and insect eggs. They get their name from their pointed bill that allows them to hunt for food using what is called "pry and gape" behavior. When a sharpbill is feeding, it often hangs upside down on a branch and uses its pointed bill to pry into fruit, tightly rolled leaves, or moss growing on the tree. It then forces its bill apart (gapes) and collects seeds or insects from inside the fruit, leaves, or moss. This type of feeding behavior is uncommon. It is an example of a physical trait, the bill, and a behavioral trait, the feeding technique, evolving, changing over time, together to give the bird an advantage over competing species.

WHAT IS A TAXONOMIST?

A taxonomist is a scientist who studies the orderly classification of plants and animals. Taxonomists first look to see if two groups of plants or animals can interbreed, produce living offspring. This is the main way to define separate species. Taxonomists also look at the physical and behavioral characteristics a species shares with other species in determining their genus (JEE-nus), the first grouping above individual species, and the family, a grouping of genera (JEN-uh-rah; plural of genus). Today, taxonomists use biochemical and genetic tests to determine the relationship among species, genera, and families. Single species like sharpbills that do not seem to be closely related to any other species provide a challenge for taxonomists. Often they are reclassified several times as more information becomes available.

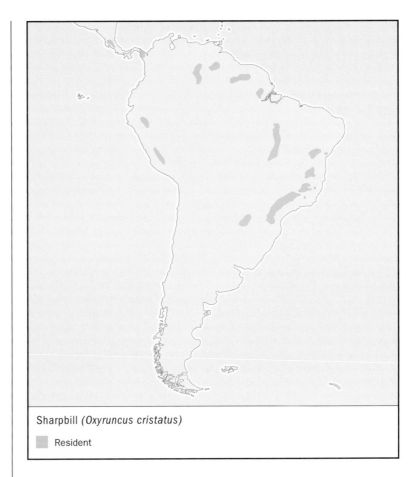

Sharpbill (*Oxyruncus cristatus*)

■ Resident

BEHAVIOR AND REPRODUCTION

Sharpbills are quiet birds that tend to stay still, making only short flights between perches. Their coloring allows them to blend in well with the environment, making them hard to observe. They live alone, rather than in flocks.

Although sharpbills were first described in 1820, the first sharpbill nest was not found until 1980, so not much is known about the mating and nesting behavior of these birds. It is believed that sharpbills mate from late February to May. The nest that was found in 1980 contained two eggs and was a shallow cup located near the top of tree about 100 feet (30 meters) tall, making observations difficult for scientists. Much remains to be learned about the behavior of these birds.

SHARPBILLS AND PEOPLE

Sharpbills are of interest mainly to ornithologists and birdwatchers.

To feed, the sharpbill forces its pointed bill into fruit, tightly rolled leaves, or moss growing on a tree. It then forces its bill apart and collects seeds or insects from inside the fruit, leaves, or moss. (Illustration by Bruce Worden. Reproduced by permission.)

CONSERVATION STATUS

Not enough is known about these birds to determine their conservation status. However, the broken up nature of their range suggests that they once were found in a wider area than they are today.

FOR MORE INFORMATION

Books:

Hilty, Steven L. *Birds of Venezuela.* Princeton, NJ: Princeton University Press, 2003.

Ridgley, Robert S., and Guy Tudor. *The Birds of South America.* Vol. 2, *The Suboscine Passerines.* Austin, TX: University of Texas Press, 1994.

Periodicals:

Brooke, M., D. Scott, and D. Teixeira. "Some Observations Made at the First Recorded Nest of the Sharpbill *Oxyruncus cristatus.*" *Ibis* (1983): 259–261.

Web sites:

"Birds Mammals and Amphibians of Latin America." NatureServe. http://www.natureserve.org/infonatura (accessed on May 4, 2004).

Class: Aves

Order: Passeriformes

Family: Pipridae

Number of species: 54 species

family

CHAPTER

phylum

class

subclass

order

monotypic order

suborder

▲ **family**

PHYSICAL CHARACTERISTICS

Manakins are some of the most brightly colored, energetic, attractive birds of the Western Hemisphere. They are generally small, around the size of hummingbirds. Most are less than 5 inches (13 centimeters) long and weigh only 0.35 to 0.70 ounces (10 to 20 grams). Manakins live up to fifteen years, an unusually long life for birds this small.

Female and young manakins of both sexes tend to be olive-green or black. Males, however, have intense jewel-like colors, with white, red, blue, or yellow areas on the top of the head, neck, and across the back, depending on the particular species. Young males go through several molts, or sets of feathers, before they achieve the full color of adults. In some species the males have long tail feathers that almost double the length of their body. Others have modified wing feathers that can be used by the males to make whirring or snapping sounds as part of their courtship and mating rituals.

GEOGRAPHIC RANGE

Manakins are found continuously from Mexico to Argentina and on the Caribbean islands of Trinidad and Tobago. Manakins live year round in the same location. They do not migrate, or relocate seasonally.

HABITAT

Manakins prefer the understory, which is the part of the forest midway between the forest floor and the tops of the trees.

They live in thick, subtropical woodlands and lowland tropical rainforests.

DIET

Manakins eat fruits and berries. They also eat insects that they snap out of the air during quick, short flights.

BEHAVIOR AND REPRODUCTION

Manakins do not form bonded pairs when they mate, nor do the males stay with the female after mating to help build a nest or raise the young. The dominant, or strongest and most attractive, male mates with many females during the breeding season. Younger, less attractive males may not mate at all.

Manakins are best known for their spectacular courtship rituals. When a male wants to attract a female, he removes the leaves and twigs on the ground in a small area, often about 3 square feet (1 square meter). This area is called the lek or lek court. In some species, males clear areas next to each other, creating very large lek courts.

In most species of manakin, two unrelated males form a lek partnership where they sing and dance in a complex, coordinated pattern unique to their species. This activity is called lekking. Females come to the lek to watch and choose a mate. They may visit many lek courts and watch many displays before mating. Often male lek partnerships last for years. One bird is definitely dominant and gets to mate with the majority of females. The other bird is a sort of apprentice, apparently learning from the dominant male and perfecting his own display.

Lekking can go on for quite a while and requires a lot of energy. Some species of manakin have modified feathers that they use to make snapping or whirring noises while making short flights during lekking. Others do their coordinated song and dance full of hops and flutters along horizontal branches. In the end, the female makes her decision, and flies away to mate with the chosen male.

Females build a nest of grass, usually over water. They lay one or two eggs and incubate (keep warm for hatching) them for seventeen to twenty-one days. The chicks fledge, grow their flying feathers, in thirteen to fifteen days.

MANAKINS AND PEOPLE

Both their beauty and their behavior make manakins attractive to birdwatchers and ecotourists who want to observe the natural world while leaving it as undisturbed as possible. In this way, manakins may have an indirect economic impact on tourism in some countries. In addition, the colorful males are often printed on souvenirs such as T-shirts and are represented on the postage stamps of several countries.

CONSERVATION STATUS

As of 2003, the Araripe manakin of Brazil was considered Critically Endangered, facing a extremely high risk of extinction in the wild. This manakin has been found only in one location, and its small population is under pressure from human development. Wied's tyrant-manakin, also found in Brazil, is Endangered, facing a very high risk of extinction. Two other Brazilian species are considered Vulnerable, facing a high risk of extinction.

Long-tailed manakin (*Chiroxiphia linearis*)

▇ Resident

LONG-TAILED MANAKIN
Chiroxiphia linearis

Physical characteristics: The female and male long-tailed manakin look very different. Females are about 5.5 inches (14 centimeters) in length, while males are 8.5 to 10.5 inches (21 to 27 centimeters) long. The difference in length is due to the male's much longer central tail feathers. Females are olive green with orange legs and feet. Males are black with a blue back and red crest on the head. Young males do not develop full adult coloration until they are four years old.

Geographic range: Long-tailed manakins are found in the western part of southern Mexico, and along the western edge of Guatemala, El Salvador, Honduras, Nicaragua, and Costa Rica.

Habitat: Long-tailed manakins live in thick, dense forests, along forest borders, and along the edge of mangrove swamps.

Two or three male long-tailed manakins often make their displays for females together at a lek. The dominant male mates with the females, and the other males work on perfecting their displays. (Kenneth W. Fink/Bruce Coleman Inc. Reproduced by permission.)

Diet: Like other manakins, these birds eat berries and insects.

Behavior and reproduction: Long-tailed manakins put on one of the more spectacular displays of lekking. A pair, or occasionally three males, do a coordinated dance in which the birds sit on a horizontal branch. One jumps and hovers above the branch. When he lands, the other bird jumps and hovers. This dance is accompanied by a song, with each bird singing a distinct part. One male is dominant, and almost always gets to mate with the female.

Scientists have wondered why the non-dominant male participates in this time and energy consuming courtship ritual when he does not get to mate, despite all the effort he has put out. They have concluded that pairs of male long-tailed manakins stay together in a loose relationship for up to ten years. The non-dominant male practices his singing and dancing and waits for the dominant male to die or leave the lek. He then becomes the dominant male, mating with the females and taking on an apprentice of his own. This pattern is made possible because these birds live for up to fifteen years.

Long-tailed manakins and people: Long-tailed manakins are one of the better-studied species in this family. Scientists have recorded the courtship behavior of this bird in detail. These birds may have an indirect positive impact on the local economy by attracting bird-watchers and ecotourists to the region.

Conservation status: Long-tailed manakins are common in the locations where they live. They are not in danger of extinction. ■

Wire-tailed manakin (*Pipra filicauda*)

■ Resident

WIRE-TAILED MANAKIN
Pipra filicauda

Physical characteristics: Wire-tailed manakins are about 4.5 inches (11 centimeters) long. The females are dull olive-colored birds, but the males are brilliantly colored. Males have red from the top of their head through their upper back, a black back, bright yellow undersides, and long, thin tail feathers.

Geographic range: These birds are found in northeastern Peru, southeastern Colombia, eastern Ecuador, and in the rainforests of Venezuela and Brazil.

The wire-tailed manakin gets its name from its long, thin tail feathers. (© J. Alvarez A./VIREO. Reproduced by permission.)

Habitat: Wire-tailed manakins prefer the edges of humid, tropical forests, forest clearings, and the edges of agricultural land.

Diet: Wire-tailed manakins eat berries and fruit. They hunt for food near the top part of the forest close to the canopy.

Behavior and reproduction: Wire-tailed manakins do not clear a lek space on the ground. Instead, they create perches about 4 to 6 feet (1.2 to 1.8 meters) above the ground in the understory. Each male may have several of these display perches. Although they have a distinctive call, wire-tailed manakins are mostly silent while they are lekking. Their courtship ritual consists of short flights, swoops, and jumps along a branch. They also lift the feathers of their lower back like a fan.

Wire-tailed manakins and people: Wire-tailed manakins are quieter and less noticeable than some of the other members of this family. They are of interest mainly to serious birdwatchers and ecotourists.

Conservation status: Wire-tailed manakins are not threatened. ■

FOR MORE INFORMATION

Books:

Hilty, Steven L. *Birds of Venezuela.* Princeton, NJ: Princeton University Press, 2003.

Kircher, John. *A Neotropical Companion: An Introduction to the Animals, Plants, and Ecosystems of the New World Tropics,* 2nd ed. Princeton, NJ: Princeton University Press, 1999.

Ridgley, Robert S., and Guy Tudor. *The Birds of South America.* Vol 2, *The Suboscine Passerines.* Austin, TX: University of Texas Press, 1994.

Sibley, David. *The Sibley Guide to Bird Life and Behavior.* New York: Alfred A. Knopf, 2001.

Periodicals:

McDonald, David B., and Wayne K. Potts. "Cooperative Display and Relatedness Among Males in a Lek-Mating Bird." *Science* (November 11, 1995): 1030–1033.

"The Buddy System." *Discover* (April 1995): 18–19.

Web sites:

Robertson, Don. "Bird Families of the World." CREAGRUS@Monterey Bay. http://www.montereybay.com/creagrus/index.html (accessed on May 4, 2004).

"Manakins and the Plant Family Melastomataceae." Ecology Online. http://www.ecology.info/manakins-melastomataceae.htm (accessed on May 4, 2004).

family

CHAPTER

phylum

class

subclass

order

monotypic order

suborder

▲ **family**

PHYSICAL CHARACTERISTICS

Cotingas are a family of brightly colored Central and South American birds that are so closely related to tyrant flycatchers that there has been some disagreement about which family some of the species belong to. Cotingas are also related to the manakin family.

Members of the cotinga family vary greatly in size and physical appearance. They range from tiny, 3-inch (8-centimeter) birds to 20-inch (50-centimeter) birds the size of crows. In the smaller species, the females tend to be larger and heavier than the male birds, but in the larger species, the females are smaller than the males. Males and females usually look different. The males are more colorful than the females.

Male cotingas tend to be brightly colored with shiny, jewel-like feathers of red, orange, blue, green, and purple, depending on the species. These birds are some of the most attractive, colorful birds in the world. In addition to their brilliant feathers, many species of cotinga have evolved odd decorative features, probably important in attracting a mate. These include oversized head crests, inflatable throat sacs, and wattles, which are extra flaps of skin and feathers that hang from the neck.

Cotingas are also known for their voices, which can be quite loud. For example, the call of the screaming piha, sometimes called the "voice of the Amazon," sounds like a loud wolf whistle. It can be heard for more than half a mile (1 kilometer). Bellbirds, another group of cotingas, make a distinctive ringing sound as if someone had hit a metal bell. These are some of the loudest of any birdcalls. Although cotingas can be loud, they are often shy and difficult to see. Species that are brightly colored tend to have quieter calls than those that have duller, darker feathers.

GEOGRAPHIC RANGE

Cotingas live in southern Mexico, almost all of Central America, and in South America as far south as Argentina. The greatest number of species live in the Amazon River basin of Brazil and the Orinoco River basin of Venezuela.

HABITAT

Most cotingas prefer lowland tropical rainforests where they live in the middle and upper levels of the forest. Some of the larger species prefer living along rivers and streams. Only a few species live in mountainous areas at higher elevations.

DIET

Cotingas have evolved large mouths that can open wide in order to eat fruit and other berries. Smaller species eat fruits almost exclusively. Larger species also eat insects, especially when fruits are less available. The seeds inside many fruits pass unharmed through the digestive system of the birds. Smaller seeds are eliminated. Larger seeds are regurgitated (re-GER-jih-tate-ud), vomited. The birds help to spread the seeds over a large area, increasing the range and diversity of plants in the areas where they live.

BEHAVIOR AND REPRODUCTION

Some species of cotinga, especially those of medium size, participate in spectacular courtship rituals, behaviors that lead to mating. When a male wants to attract a female, he removes the leaves and twigs on the ground in a small area. This area is called the lek or lek court. Several males will then go to these areas and sing, call, and dance by hopping, making short flights, and fanning or making noise with their feathers. This activity is called lekking. Some species lek on branches above the ground rather then on the forest floor.

Females are attracted to the lek by the calls or wing sounds the males make. They watch the display, and then choose a mate. Once the female makes her choice, she flies away with the chosen male. The male will mate with as many females as possible during the breeding season. He does not stay with the female and rarely helps with building a nest. Females incubate,

sit on and warm, the eggs and raise the young alone. Not every species of cotinga leks. Some use fancy flying maneuvers (mah-NOO-verz) to attract mates, while others display their interest in mating individually rather than in groups.

Cotingas build a variety of different types of nests ranging from heaps of twigs in the fork of a tree to shallow woven cups. Generally birds in this family lay a single egg that hatches after about a month. The chicks are born blind and without feathers. The mother feeds the chicks for about a month until they mature enough to leave the nest.

Cotingas tend to be non-aggressive, passive, with their own and other bird species except when nesting. They do not protect a particular territory, and they often feed in the same tree as other birds.

COTINGAS AND PEOPLE

Because of their bright, beautiful colors, cotingas have been hunted for their feathers, which are used as ornaments by native people. They may also be hunted for food. The feathers of some species are used in making fishing flies, lures for fish. The beauty of these birds draws birdwatchers and ecotourists, travel for the purpose of studying wildlife and the environment, from around the world, and may add indirectly to the local tourist economy.

CONSERVATION STATUS

The kinglet calyptura, also called the kinglet cotinga, is Critically Endangered, facing an extremely high risk of extinction in the wild. It lives in only one place in Brazil and its population is tiny. This bird had not been seen in over one hundred years and was thought to be extinct until it was re-discovered in 1996.

Four other species of Brazilian cotinga, the white-winged cotinga, the yellow-billed cotinga, the banded cotinga, and the buff-throated purpletuft are all Endangered, facing a very high risk of extinction in the wild. Ten other species are considered Vulnerable, facing a high risk of extinction. The population of these birds is declining rapidly because their habitat is being destroyed, and their small populations are being fragmented, separated.

Spangled cotinga (Cotinga cayana)

▢ Resident

SPANGLED COTINGA
Cotinga cayana

Physical characteristics: Spangled contingas are 8.5-inch (22-centimeter) long birds that live in the rainforest. The males are brightly colored. Their backs are brilliant turquoise blue spattered with black. They have black wings, a black tail, and a large purple patch under their throat. The females are dull, with dark brown backs and light brown, spotted breasts.

Geographic range: Spangled cotingas are found in the Amazon River basin of Brazil, the rainforest of Venezuela, French Guiana, Guyuana, eastern Colombia, and northwestern Bolivia.

Spangled cotingas prefer fruit and berries, and often search for food in the same trees as other members of the cotinga family. (Illustration by Emily Damstra. Reproduced by permission.)

Habitat: Spangled cotingas live in the canopy under the treetops of lowland rainforests, rarely above 2,000 feet (600 meters) in elevation.

Diet: Like all cotingas, these birds prefer fruit and berries. They often search for food in the same trees as other members of the cotinga family.

Behavior and reproduction: Not much is known about the mating behavior of spangled cotingas, however, it is believed that they form loose leks during the mating season. During courtship, males often spread themselves flat along a branch, moving their wings and calling to females. Females build loose platform nests of sticks in the tops of trees and care for the young alone.

Spangled cotingas and people: These birds are hunted for their feathers, which are used in making flies for fishing and as decoration by native tribes.

Conservation status: The spangled cotinga is not currently threatened with extinction. ■

Amazonian umbrellabird (*Cephalopterus ornatus*)

■ Resident

AMAZONIAN UMBRELLABIRD
Cephalopterus ornatus

Physical characteristics: Amazonian umbrellabirds are black birds with a whitish eye and strong black claws. They are about the size of a crow, 18 inches (46 centimeters) in length. Their most impressive physical feature is the tall crest of hair-like feathers with white shafts that stands up over its head like an umbrella. In fact, the bird's Latin scientific name roughly means "fancy head." This bird also has a long wattle of feathers that hangs down from its throat to its belly. Amazonian umbrellabirds are known for their loud, carrying voice.

The Amazonian umbrellabird has a tall crest of hair-like feathers with white shafts that stands up over its head like an umbrella. (Illustration by Emily Damstra. Reproduced by permission.)

Geographic range: Amazonian umbrellabirds are found in the Amazon river basin of Brazil and Venezuela, northwest Bolivia, and eastern Colombia.

Habitat: This species prefers to live along rivers. However, near the edge of the Andes mountains, it lives in the forest at elevations up to 4,300 feet (1,300 meters).

Diet: Umbrellabirds primarily eat fruit and berries, but will eat insects, spiders, and insect larvae when fruit is not available.

Behavior and reproduction: Amazonian umbrellabirds are slow-flying birds that spend a lot of time sitting still on branches. During mating season, males form leks spread far apart. The female builds a loose nest of twigs high in a tree and raises a single chick.

Amazonian umbrellabirds and people: These birds are heard more often than they are seen. They are mainly of interest to birdwatchers.

Conservation status: Amazonian umbrellabirds are not threatened or at risk of becoming extinct at any time in the foreseeable future. ■

Guianan cock-of-the-rock (*Rupicola rupicola*)

■ Resident

GUIANAN COCK-OF-THE-ROCK
Rupicola rupicola

Physical characteristics: Male Guianan cocks-of-the-rock are bright orange birds with large orange crests on their heads. They have black and white wing bars and black on their tails. Females are a drab brown color.

Geographic range: Guianan cocks-of-the-rock are found in southern Guyana, Colombia, Venezuela and in northern Brazil.

Habitat: Guiana cocks-of-the-rock live in lowland forests below 4,900 feet (1,500 meters).

Male Guianan cocks-of-the-rock have a large orange crest on their heads. Females are a drab brown color. (Illustration by Emily Damstra. Reproduced by permission.)

Diet: Cocks-of-the-rock prefer fruit and berries, but will eat insects if other food is scarce.

Behavior and reproduction: Male cocks-of-the-rock clear spots on the forest floor to form large leks where they sing loudly and perform mating dances for females. Predators such as hawks, jaguars, ocelots, and boa constrictors are attracted to these leks. Successful males will mate with many females during the breeding season. Females raise their young alone, building cup-shaped nests of clay and plants along rock faces or in holes on cliffs. They lay two eggs that hatch in about a month.

Guianan cocks-of-the-rock and people: In the early twentieth century, hunters captured these birds and sold them as pets. Today they are attractive to birdwatchers and ecotourists who want to observe nature without disturbing it. In this way they may add to the local tourist economy. Native tribes hunt these birds for their feathers and as food. Fly fishermen use their feathers in making fishing flies.

Conservation status: Guianan cocks-of-the-rock are not threatened or at risk of extinction. ■

FOR MORE INFORMATION

Books:

Hilty, Steven L. *Birds of Venezuela.* Princeton, NJ: Princeton University Press, 2003.

Kircher, John. *A Neotropical Companion: An Introduction to the Animals, Plants, and Ecosystems of the New World Tropics,* 2nd ed. Princeton, NJ: Princeton University Press, 1999.

Ridgley, Robert S., and Guy Tudor. *The Birds of South America.* Vol 2, *The Suboscine Passerines.* Austin, TX: University of Texas Press, 1994.

Web sites:

"Cotingas, Bellbirds, Becards, Cock-of-the-rock." Cornell University. http://www.eeb.cornell.edu/winkler/botw/families.htm (accessed on May 4, 2004).

"Ecology of the Cock-of-the-Rock." Ecology Online. http://www.ecology.info/cock-of-the-rock.htm (accessed on May 4, 2004).

family

C H A P T E R

phylum

class

subclass

order

monotypic order

suborder

▲ **family**

PHYSICAL CHARACTERISTICS

Adult plantcutters are generally between 7 and 8 inches (18 and 20 centimeters) long, and have short, thick, cone-shaped bills. Their bodies are stocky, although they weigh only 1.5 ounces (40 grams). The birds' wings and legs tend to be short, although plantcutters have long tails and strong, large feet. In the males and females of the Peruvian and red-breasted species, the head peaks in a short crest. The rufous-tailed plantcutter is similar looking, but lacks a crest and has more red in its tail.

Male plantcutters are more brightly colored than the females, and show off their cinnamon or rusty breasts and bellies and distinctive black eye stripes at mating time. Neither sex is particularly colorful, however, blending into their dry environment with ashy gray (male) and buff-brown (female) backs. Both sexes have white bars on their wings and tail ends and either yellow or crimson irises.

These birds are locally known in South America as *cotarramas*, *cortaplantas*, and *raras* ("rare ones"). Their name derives from the highly unusual rows of sharp, forward-leaning, tooth-like projections on the edges of their bills on both sides. Made of keratin (KARE-ah-tin), like the bill itself, these projections allow the birds to pulverize and eat the leafy foods on which they feed.

GEOGRAPHIC RANGE

The Peruvian plantcutter lives only in the dry forest and scrublands of Peru's northwest coasts. The rufous-tailed and red-breasted plantcutters occupy a larger area, and may be

found in Argentina's southern temperate zone and Chile, and north to subtropical Bolivia and Paraguay.

HABITAT

The Peruvian plantcutter lives exclusively in the dry forests of Peru's northwest coast, whereas the rufous-tailed and red-breasted varieties live mainly in open farmland, grassland, open forest, and scrubland.

DIET

All three species of plantcutter are herbivores (plant eaters), eating leaves of the plants and trees found in their habitats. They also eat fruit on occasion, and since humans have occupied their territories have developed a fondness for grape and cereal-crop leaves.

Unlike other species of herbivorous birds, of which there are only a few, the plantcutter has not evolved a complex digestive system to process its tough, fibrous food. They use the tooth-like ridges on the edges of their beaks to chew their food into a pulp, which allows their digestive tracts to absorb the nutritious interiors of the plants' cells.

The plantcutter species has extremely efficient intestines that can process large amounts of vegetation in a relatively short time. This adaptation lets the birds maintain a high metabolic level, and thus a high energy and activity level.

BEHAVIOR AND REPRODUCTION

Unlike the majority of vegetarian birds, whose biology demands that they conserve energy to compensate for their low-calorie diet, plantcutters are energetic and lively. They patrol their territories throughout the day, looking for new food sources and invaders.

The reproductive life of the plantcutter species remains something of a mystery to ornithologists, although we know that the females lay two to four eggs in a loosely constructed nest.

PLANTCUTTERS AND PEOPLE

South American farmers and vintners (grape growers) often complain about plantcutter raids on their grape and cereal crops. However, tourist revenue from avid birdwatchers hoping for a glimpse of the rare Peruvian plantcutter helps to offset any animosity.

CONSERVATION STATUS

While the red-breasted and rufous-tailed plantcutters vigorously occupy a large area of South America, the Peruvian plantcutter is one of the most Endangered birds in the world, facing a very high risk of extinction, because of the rapid destruction of its small habitat for grazing, mining, and agriculture.

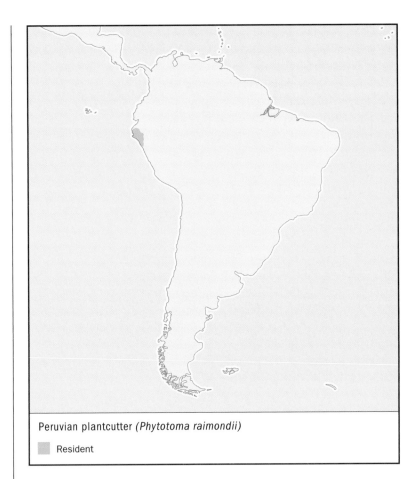

Peruvian plantcutter (*Phytotoma raimondii*)

Resident

PERUVIAN PLANTCUTTER
Phytotoma raimondii

Physical characteristics: Adult Peruvian plantcutters are 7 to 8 inches (18 to 20 centimeters) in length and weigh approximately 1.5 ounces (40 grams). Both males and females have bright yellow eyes and a short crest, but the male is more colorful, with red patches on his lower breast and forehead. The birds' short wings make them agile fliers, and their strong feet allow them to grasp their leafy food tightly as they shred it with their tough, ridged beaks.

Geographic range: The Peruvian plantcutter lives only in coastal northwestern Peru, from the city of Tumbes south to the capital, Lima.

Habitat: Adapted to the dry environment known as the Tumbesian ecosystem, the Peruvian plantcutter prefers desert scrub, low woodlands (both open and dense), and occasionally thickets near or next to rivers. Its habitat is always populated with caper shrubs, acacia (uh-KAY-shah) trees, the *Prosopis* tree, and climbing vines in the cucumber family. The Peruvian plantcutter is notoriously sensitive to any changes in its environment, including noise, light, and contamination.

Diet: Although it eats occasional bits of fruit, the Peruvian plantcutter gets most of its nutrition from the leaves and buds of the *Prosopis* tree and various shrubs. In terms of diet, the bird has adapted to its dry environment by extracting most of its water from the foliage it eats.

The Peruvian plantcutter gets most of its nutrition from the leaves and buds of the Prosopis tree and various shrubs. The bird has adapted to its dry environment by extracting most of its water from the foliage it eats. (Illustration by Michelle Meneghini. Reproduced by permission.)

Behavior and reproduction: The Peruvian species of plantcutter is a high-energy and active bird, patrolling its territory during the day to flush out interlopers and find new sources of food. Its throbbing, sad song has prompted locals to nickname it the "toothache bird."

Scientists know very little about the reproductive habits of the bird. However, field biologists have observed that they build loose nests and that the females lay between two and four eggs. The eggs are a mottled brown color to help camouflage (KAM-uh-flaj; hide) them from predators, animals that hunt them for food. The females incubate the eggs, keep them warm, by sitting on them for an unknown period of time.

Peruvian plantcutters and people: The Peruvian plantcutter has become a rallying symbol for Peru's emerging conservation movement. Champions of the bird have been fighting to save the estimated 500 to 1,000 remaining birds by educating the public and trying to block agricultural interests from developing the plantcutter's last population stronghold near Talara.

Conservation status: There are only four recent records of sightings of this bird, leading to its classification by the World Conservation Union (IUCN) as Endangered. The Peruvian plantcutter is extremely choosy about its habitat. The species has failed to colonize some apparently suitable territory, which has puzzled experts.

A nongovernment conservation group called ProAvesPeru is the leader in the effort to save the Peruvian plantcutter. Sponsored and supported by the Audubon Society of Latin America, ProAvesPeru's main goal is to establish the Talara Reserve. Another ally of the plantcutter is Gunnar Engblom, a Swedish ornithologist who in 1999 conducted the first ecological study of the bird's habitat.

The main threats to Peruvian plantcutters are gold mining, animal grazing, illegal logging for firewood, and the installation of new crops such as sugar cane.

FOR MORE INFORMATION

Books:

Feduccia, Alan. *The Origin and Evolution of Birds.* New Haven, CT: Yale University Press, 1999.

Sibley, C. G., and B. L. Monroe. *Distribution and Taxonomy of Birds of the World.* New Haven, CT: Yale University Press, 1990.

Skutch, Alexander F. *Life Histories of Central American Birds.* Vol. 3. Berkeley, CA: Cooper Ornithological Society, 1969.

Periodicals:

Lopez-Calleja, M. V., and F. Bozinovic. "Energetics and Nutritional Ecology of Small Herbivorous Birds." *Revista Chilena de Historia Natural* 73 (September 2000): 411–420.

Prum, R. O., et al. "A Preliminary Phylogenic Hypothesis for the Cotingas (Cotingidae) Based on Mitochrondrial DNA." *Auk* 117 (2000).

Web sites:

"Birder's Exchange Recipients." American Birding Association. http://www.americanbirding.org/programs/consbexr3.htm (accessed on April 27, 2004).

"Tambogrande Referendum Has Domino Effect in Peru." Americas Program. http://www.americaspolicy.org/citizen-action/focus/0207 tambogrande_body.html (accessed on April 27, 2004).

"Conservation of the Critically Endangered Peruvian Plantcutter in Talara Province, NW Peru." Audubon Latin America. http://www. audubon.org/local/latin/bulletin6/initiatives.html (accessed on April 27, 2004).

"Birdlife Species Factsheet (extended): Peruvian Plantcutter (*Phytotoma raimondii*)." Birdlife International. http://www.birdlife.net (accessed on April 27, 2004).

"Conservation of the Threatened Peruvian Plantcutter." Communications for a Sustainable Future. http://csf.colorado.edu/mail/elan/jan99/ 0053.html (accessed on April 27, 2004).

"Phytotomidae." Cornell University, Department of Ecology and Evolutionary Biology. http://www.eeb.cornell.edu/winkler/botw/phytotomidae.html (accessed on April 27, 2004).

"Phytotomidae: Plantcutters." John Penhallurick's Bird Data Project. http://www.worldbirdinfo.net (accessed on April 27, 2004).

LYREBIRDS
Menuridae

Class: Aves
Order: Passeriformes
Family: Menuridae
Number of species: 2 species

family

CHAPTER

phylum

class

subclass

order

monotypic order

suborder

▲ **family**

PHYSICAL CHARACTERISTICS

The male superb lyrebird is one of the world's more spectacular examples of birdlife, with his majestic tail of sixteen fanned, silver feathers that resembles the ancient Greek instrument called a lyre. The bird is dark brown on the top of its body, light brown below, and rufous (reddish) on its throat. The female of the species is smaller and has similar coloring, with a broadly webbed, reddish tail.

The male Albert's lyrebird is less colorful and smaller than the superb species. It possesses the same dramatic fanned tail, but without the outer lyre-shaped feathers. Both sexes are a rich chestnut color.

Adult lyrebirds range from 33 to 38.5 inches (84 to 98 centimeters)—about the size of a rooster—making them one of the biggest passerines (PASS-ur-eenz), perching birds. Male and female lyrebirds have small heads, long legs, tails, and necks, and large feet with powerful claws. Because of their weak, short wings, they seldom fly. Lyrebirds have short, sharp, slightly down-turned bills that they use for picking prey out of leaf litter.

Although they have their own species-specific songs, lyrebirds are natural mimics, much like the American mockingbird. They can copy almost any clear, loud sound, such as chainsaws, horns, guns, crying babies, shouts, trains, alarms, and many bird and animal sounds. The superb lyrebird is generally recognized as the more proficient singer of the two species. Both transmit their songs from generation to generation. Males of both species sing most in the Australian winter months of June and July.

888 Grzimek's Student Animal Life Resource

GEOGRAPHIC RANGE

Both Albert's and the superb lyrebird are native to Australia, where they occur from southern Queensland and northern New South Wales along the Great Dividing Range and south to southwestern Victoria.

HABITAT

Both species of lyrebird live only in Australia's rainforests and mixed temperate forests, although the Albert's specializes in mountainous areas and the superb occupies a broader range of elevations (from foothill to sea-level). Lyrebirds require lush understory vegetation both to feed and to hide from predators, animals that hunt them for food.

DIET

Lyrebirds eat a carnivorous, meat eating, diet of insects and other invertebrates, animals without a backbone.

BEHAVIOR AND REPRODUCTION

The males of both species sing a lot and use their tails to perform an elaborate courtship display for any approaching females, arching their fanned tails over their backs to form a canopy. The males occupy and defend trampled mounds of vegetation, mating with any female who allows them. Females build a messy, dome-shaped nest of sticks near or on a moist patch of ground in which they lay a single, purplish gray, spotted egg. They incubate (keep warm by sitting on) the egg for six weeks without assistance from a male, and the nestling remains in the nest for six to ten weeks.

LYREBIRDS AND PEOPLE

While a source of amusement due to its close mimicry of human-generated sounds, the lyrebird is often regarded as an annoyance as well. Its habit of shuffling through leaf litter for food can be destructive when it occurs in gardens and compost heaps.

CONSERVATION STATUS

Although once nearly extinct due to habitat destruction and overhunting for its exotic tail feathers, the superb lyrebird

A LONG WAIT FOR BEAUTY

Unlike most other bird species, which reach full sexual maturity in a matter of months, young male superb lyrebirds do not grow their fancy, elaborate tails until they reach three or four years of age, and only when they are six do they acquire the extra filamentary feathers that make their appearance so dramatic. Until then, they cluster together and are known as "plain-tails."

is now regarded as common in its native environment. The Albert's lyrebird's Vulnerable status, facing a high risk of extinction, is somewhat more precarious due to its more restricted habitat, but careful protection measures have helped to stabilize its population sizes. Both species remain vulnerable to predation by feral cats and foxes, while increasing human incursion into their environment poses a strong threat.

Albert's lyrebird *(Menura alberti)*

Resident

ALBERT'S LYREBIRD
Menura alberti

SPECIES ACCOUNT

Physical characteristics: The male Albert's lyrebird (also known as Prince Albert's lyrebird) is not as dramatic looking as the superb lyrebird, since its tail lacks the outer lyre-shaped tail feathers of its cousin. The Albert's species is slightly smaller than the superb as well, with adult females measuring 33 inches (84 centimeters) and adult males measuring 35.5 inches (90 centimeters). Both sexes have small heads, long tails, and long, powerful legs and claws. They are virtually flightless, although the birds use their weak, undeveloped wings to help them hop up and down from low branches and other perches, much like a chicken does.

The male Albert's lyrebird performs an elaborate and graceful dance to attract a female bird. Once he has attracted her, he fans his tail over his back before mating with her. (Illustration by Barbara Duperron. Reproduced by permission.)

Albert's lyrebirds are deep chestnut on their upper bodies, with reddish buff throats. The males' tails are glossy black and silver-gray underneath. Both sexes are legendary for their ability to copy almost any sound, natural or mechanical. The male lyrebird's species-specific call is a piercing "craw-cree-craw-craw-wheat," and when alarmed both sexes emit a shrieking "whisk-whisk" cry.

Geographic range: Occupying a smaller range than the superb lyrebird, the Albert's lyrebird is limited to mountainous rainforests between the Mistake Range in southeast Queensland to the Nightcap Range in northeast New South Wales. In all, the bird's territory totals only 580 square miles (1,500 square kilometers), which supports an estimated 3,500 individuals. The highest population densities of Albert's lyrebird have been found at Whian Whian State Forest in the Nightcap Range, but other significant populations exist in the Richmond, Tweed, and McPherson Ranges.

Habitat: Found only in Australian rainforests at about 1,000 feet (300 meters) and above, Albert's lyrebird requires a dense understory that provides deep leaf litter for foraging. The Antarctic poplar is usually present in the lyrebird's environment as well. They bathe daily in still pools or slow-running streams.

Diet: Lyrebirds rely on their strong claws and legs to scratch through leaf litter, fallen branches, and even rocks, uncovering spiders, worms, ants, frogs, lizards, grubs, and snails.

Behavior and reproduction: In optimal conditions, Albert's lyrebirds prefer widely spaced territories, with about five pairs of birds per 0.4 square miles (1 square kilometer). They are sedentary birds, rarely leaving their own territory. Both sexes are shy and difficult to spot, and when threatened will dart and dodge quickly through the underbrush, giving out piercing calls of alarm. Because of their underdeveloped wings, the birds can run much faster than they can fly. Lyrebirds roost in the low branches of trees at night.

During the mating season from May to August, males perform an elaborate and graceful dance atop a low platform of trampled vegetation or in an area of scratched earth. Each male may have as many as ten or fifteen of these display arenas, which he visits in turn. Their vocalizations during this time are complex and penetrating, consisting of a cycle of imitations of various natural and human-made sounds. Known as the "albertcycle," the song is often interspersed with territorial songs, after which the male bird will pause briefly to listen for an answering challenge. Following the pause, he will usually resume his cycle where he left off or he may start all over.

Once the male attracts a female bird, he will fan his tail over his back and prance back and forth over his platform in a rhythmic, dignified manner. The male will mate with as many females as he can entice to his arena.

After mating, the female builds a loosely constructed dome of sticks up several feet (about one meter) off the ground, lining and insulating it with her own feathers, moss, and ferns. She lays one egg in a moist indentation in the center of the structure, incubating it alone and then tending to the nestling without assistance for up to nine months. The young develop slowly, remaining covered with down even at four months old.

Albert's lyrebirds and people: Lyrebirds' extraordinary ability to mimic sounds has amused people for as long as the species have co-existed. One local story from the nineteenth century described how a lyrebird repeatedly caused the evacuation of a logging operation with its imitation of a fire siren until the loggers discovered the culprit. However, other encounters have not been so friendly. Many farmers and gardeners are annoyed by the lyrebirds' habit of shuffling through mulch and leaves, and some conservationists have even suggested that the birds are endangering other ground-dwelling animals and some types of vegetation with their large-scale digging. The bird's shy and elusive nature has thwarted many attempts to study it.

Conservation status: The World Conservation Union (IUCN) categorized Albert's lyrebird as a Vulnerable species in 2003. Part of the reason for the classification is because of the bird's apparent inability to cross over areas of unsuitable habitat to colonize other appropriate environments. Other threats include wild cats, human infringement on rainforest areas, and naturally occurring wildfires that periodically sweep through their environment. ∎

FOR MORE INFORMATION

Books:

Ford, H. A., and D. C. Paton, eds. *The Dynamic Partnership: Birds and Plants in Southern Australia.* South Australia: D. J. Woolman, 1986.

Higgins, P. J., et al., eds. *Handbook of Australian, New Zealand and Antarctic Birds.* Vol. 5, *Tyrant-Flycatchers to Chats.* Melbourne: Oxford University Press, 2001.

Rutgers, Abram. *Birds of Australia.* London: Methuen & Co., 1967.

Schodde, R., and I. J. Mason. *The Directory of Australian Birds—Passerines.* Collingwood, Australia: CSIRO Publishing, 1999.

Smith, L. H. *The Life of the Lyrebird.* Richmond, Australia: William Heinemann Australia, 1988.

Periodicals:

Curtis, H. S. "The Albert Lyrebird in Display." *Emu* 72 (1972): 81–84.

Sibley, C. G. "The Relationship of the Lyrebirds." *Emu* 74 (1974): 65–79.

Web sites:

"Albert's Lyrebird." ARKive: Images of Life on Earth. http://www.arkive.org/species/GES/birds/Menura_alberti/more_info.html (accessed on April 28, 2004).

"Albert's Lyrebird." Birdlife.net. http://www.birdlife.net (accessed on April 28, 2004).

"Lyrebird." Concise Britannica Online. http://concise.britannica.com (accessed on April 28, 2004).

"Lyrebirds." Cornell University Department of Ecology and Evolutionary Biology. http://www.eeb.cornell.edu/winkler/botw/menuridae.html (accessed on April 28, 2004).

"Lyrebirds." National Parks and Wildlife Service Australia. http://www.nationalparks.nsw.gov.au/npws.nsf/Content/Lyrebirds (accessed on April 28, 2004).

"Lyrebird." Wikipedia. http://en.wikipedia.org/wiki/Lyrebird (accessed on April 28, 2004).

SCRUB-BIRDS
Atrichornithidae

Class: Aves
Order: Passeriformes
Family: Atrichornithidae
Number of species: 2 species

PHYSICAL CHARACTERISTICS

Both species of the ancient scrub-bird family, the noisy and the rufous, are 6.5 to 9 inches (16.5 to 23 centimeters) long. Male noisy scrub-birds typically weigh about 1.7 ounces (52 grams), while the smaller male rufous scrub-bird weighs somewhat less. Plainly colored in drab brown with black bars, the birds use their natural camouflage (KAM-uh-flaj) to hide themselves in dense underbrush. The rufous species is reddish brown on top with a buff belly, while the noisy scrub-bird is brown on top and reddish brown on the lower belly, fading to off-white on its breast. Males of both species have distinct black markings on their throats and breasts. Scrub-birds have strong, short legs and rounded, weak wings that render them semi-flightless. Otherwise they are generally stoutly built. Their flat, long foreheads taper to a triangular bill, and they tend to carry their longish tails at an upward angle. Juveniles look similar to adults, but with duller plumage.

GEOGRAPHIC RANGE

Both species of scrub-bird occur only in Australia and only within restricted ranges. The rufous species lives in isolated populations in the Queensland-New South Wales border area. The noisy scrub-bird occupies the far southwestern corner of the country in Two People's Bay Nature Reserve near Albany and, since they were reintroduced there in 1998, the Darling Range of Western Australia, outside the city of Perth.

HABITAT

Scrub-birds require dense, low vegetation in which to hide from predators, animals that hunt them for food, and forage,

search, for food. They are adapted to a thick layer of leaf litter and a moist microclimate, a small, uniformly moist area. The rufous scrub-birds prefer temperate rainforest, whereas the noisy scrub-bird occupies semi-arid areas.

DIET

Both the rufous and noisy scrub-birds eat insects that they find by picking through layers of leaves on the forest floor. Noisy scrub-birds occasionally prey on frogs, geckos, and lizards as well.

BEHAVIOR AND REPRODUCTION

Male scrub-birds are famous for their ear-piercing, metallic calls and ability to imitate other birds' songs as they sing to mark and identify their permanent territories. The noisy scrub-bird has two alarm notes and a three-note call, with a loud, variable song of ten to twenty notes, while the rufous scrub-bird employs a loud, repeated chirp and two alarm notes. Females of both species are much less vocal, and often remain silent or make only quiet squeaks and ticking sounds. Although alert and energetic, both species are shy and highly secretive, moving quickly into dense vegetation when disturbed. Due to their underdeveloped wings, which cannot sustain more than a few yards of flight, scrub-birds prefer to run when threatened. During the mating season (spring for the rufous and winter for the noisy), males of both types prance and display with erect tails, much like their close relatives, the lyrebirds. Scrub-birds generally mate for life, and females occupy areas on the outskirts of the males' territories. Territories are usually widely spaced, with males marking and occupying about 2.5 acres (1 hectare) each. Females take sole responsibility for their clutches of one or two eggs, building a domed nest with a side entrance and partially or completely lined with wood and grass pulp. Nestlings take up to one month to fledge, grow the feathers needed for flying.

SCRUB-BIRDS AND PEOPLE

Both species of scrub-bird are so secretive and sedentary, still, that only the most patient of birdwatchers ever gets to see one. Many people have reported sitting silently for hours near a calling male just to get a glimpse of the creature. The scrub-bird has become a rallying point for Australian conservationists as they have labored to raise the birds' numbers over the past several decades.

CONSERVATION STATUS

The rufous scrub-bird remains one of the rarest birds in the world and has the official conservation status of Near Threatened, in danger of becoming threatened with extinction. Both species were thought to be extinct until the early 1960s, but environmentalists have succeeded in increasing populations of the noisy scrub-bird from fewer than 50 breeding territories in 1961 to nearly 750 in 2002. As a result, the noisy species has been downgraded from Endangered, facing a very high risk of extinction, to Vulnerable, facing a high risk of extinction.

Rufous scrub-bird (*Atrichornis rufescens*)

Resident

RUFOUS SCRUB-BIRD
Atrichornis rufescens

Physical characteristics: The rufous scrub-bird ranges in size from 6.5 inches (16.5 centimeters) for females to 7.1 inches long (18 centimeters) for males. Adults are a dark, reddish-brown with fine black bars on top and a dun-colored belly. Males have black markings in the center of a whitish throat. Both sexes carry their relatively long tails slightly upright. The rufous scrub-bird is perhaps the only species of bird in the world that does not have a wishbone, part of the breast bone, which is one reason it cannot fly very well.

Geographic range: This species exists solely on the central east coast of Australia, at the border between New South Wales and Queensland states. Their isolated populations are concentrated on the high-rainfall Border and Gibraltar Ranges, specifically along the Main Border Track from Mount Bithongable to Mount Howbee.

Habitat: Rufous scrub-birds require a moist microclimate at ground level, a dense layer of ground cover at least 3 feet (0.9 meters) high, and thick leaf litter in which to forage for food. These birds are almost always found at elevations above 2,000 feet (600 meters), although a sighting at about 790 feet (240 meters) was reported in 2000. Their habitat is usually associated with human-created or natural openings in the forest canopy. Most of the birds (an estimated 65 percent) live in wet eucalyptus (yoo-kah-LIP-tus) forests or Antarctic beech forests that are well buffered from fires in nearby rainforests. Mating pairs' territories are spaced far apart, with a maximum of six pairs per 0.4 square miles (1 square kilometer).

The rufous scrub-bird lives on the east coast of Australia, usually at elevations above 2,000 feet (600 meters). (Illustration by Bruce Worden. Reproduced by permission.)

Diet: Rufous scrub-birds use their strong legs and claws to scratch through leaf litter, flushing out invertebrates such as beetles, ants, and spiders.

Behavior and reproduction: Remaining sedentary within well-defined territories for their entire adult lives, rufous scrub-birds dislike disturbance and will run mouse-like into thick foliage at the slightest threat. The species is alert and forages with enthusiasm, but is shy and evasive in general. The female rufous is even more elusive. Because of their underdeveloped wings, rufous scrub-birds run when threatened, instead of flying. During breeding season in September to November (Australia's spring), males use their elevated and fanned tails, lowered wings, and loud, melodious song to woo their partners. They can mimic other birdcalls well, but also use a species-specific "chip" sound. Rufous scrub-birds are typically monogamous (muh-NAH-guh-mus). Females occupy small areas on the outside of their mates' territories. The birds prefer to have widely spaced territories, with males marking and occupying about 2.5 acres (1 hectare) each, ideally. Females take sole responsibility for their clutches of two eggs (one of which is often infertile). They build a domed nest near the ground with a side entrance, completely lining it with a cardboard-like substance made of chewed wood and grass pulp. She attends the chicks for the month it takes them to fledge.

Rufous scrub-birds and people: Avid birdwatchers from all over the world travel to Australia in hopes of seeing one of these rare birds. The species' elusive and secretive nature, in addition to its declining numbers, make it a thrilling experience for many bird lovers.

Conservation status: A 1999 survey of rufous scrub-bird populations suggested an ongoing decline in the bird's presence. Destruction of the species' preferred habitat through logging and burning has caused much of the population decrease, but conservationists are working to educate people, and land clearing no longer appears to be a threat. The rufous scrub-bird, with habitat estimated at only 580 square miles (1,500 square kilometers), has Near Threatened conservation status.   ■

FOR MORE INFORMATION

Books:

Birdlife International. *Threatened Birds of the World.* Barcelona: Lynx Edicions, 2000.

Ferrier, S. "Habitat Requirements of a Rare Species, the Rufous Scrub-bird." In *Birds of Eucalyptus Forests and Woodlands: Ecology, Conservation, and Management.* Sydney: Royal Australian Ornithological Society.

Higgins, P. J., et al., eds. *Handbook of Australian, New Zealand and Antarctic Birds.* Vol. 5, *Tyrant-Flycatchers to Chats.* Melbourne: Oxford University Press, 2001.

Schodde, R., and I. J. Mason. *Australian Birds: Passerines.* Collingwood, Australia: CSIRO, 1999.

Sibley, C. G., and J. E. Alquist. *Phylogeny and Classification of Birds: A Study in Molecular Evolution.* New Haven, CT: Yale University Press, 1990.

Periodicals:

Chisolm, A. H. "The Story of the Scrub-birds." *Emu* 51 (1951): 89–112, 285–297.

Web sites:

"Noisy Scrub-bird Reintroduced to Darling Range." The Nature Base. http://www.calm.wa.gov.au/news/news.cgi?item=923494339 (accessed on May 17, 2004).

"Rufous Scrub-bird *(Atrichornis rufescens).*" Birdlife.net. http://www.birdlife.net/datazone/search/species (accessed on May 17, 2004).

"Rufous Scrub-bird: Lamington National Park." Lamington National Park, Queensland, Australia. http://www.lamington.nrsm.uq.edu.au/Documents/Birds/rufuousscrubbird.htm (accessed on May 17, 2004).

"Scrub-bird." Fact Index. http://www.fact-index.com/s/sc/scrub_bird.html (accessed on May 17, 2004).

"Scrub-birds." Planet Pets. http://www.planet-pets.com/plntsbrd.html (accessed on May 17, 2004).

"Scrub-birds *(Atrichornithidae).*" CREAGRUS@Monterey Bay. http://www.montereybay.com/creagrus/scrub-birds.html (accessed on May 17, 2004).

Class: Aves

Order: Passeriformes

Family: Alaudidae

Number of species: 92 species

family

CHAPTER

phylum

class

subclass

order

monotypic order

suborder

▲ **family**

PHYSICAL CHARACTERISTICS

Although there are numerous species of larks, most of them have in common what is known as a "larkspur," a long, straight claw on the hind toe. These roughly sparrow-sized birds are known for their elaborate, melodious songs and their flamboyant song-display flights during mating season. Because they nest on the ground, larks have evolved into fairly dull-looking birds as protection against predators, animals that hunt them for food. They generally vary in color from brown to pinkish-buff to gray, although some sport more distinguished markings and colors. Usually their upper bodies are heavily streaked or unmarked with a grayish brownish color that closely matches the soil in their specific habitats. Their breasts and underparts are often lighter in color and unmarked. Larks range widely in size from 3.9 to 9 inches (10 to 23 centimeters) and can weigh from just under half an ounce to 2.6 ounces (12 to 73 grams). In most species both sexes look very similar, although the males are often larger than the females.

Some types of larks, most notably the crested lark, have tiny crown feathers that they can raise into a crest, while others, like the horned lark, have small tufts that stand out on the sides of their heads, giving them a horned appearance. In addition, there are almost as many different kinds of bills among larks as there are species. They range in shape from long, thin, and pointed to cone-shaped, short, and thick, depending on the main food source and feeding methods to which a local species has adapted. Most larks have short legs and strong feet for scratching in the dirt, along with a hind toe that is much longer than the front ones. However, some larks, depending on whether they are fast runners or live on hard-packed dirt, have shorter spurs.

After they hatch, baby larks are covered with a thin, fine down. As they mature, they develop a uniformly spotted plumage that conceals them from predators. Unlike other similar birds species, larks grow their mature plumage as soon as they leave the nest and are able to live on their own.

GEOGRAPHIC RANGE

Larks occur all over the world, but many of the species are extremely localized and are either rare or endangered. Most larks live in Africa, but many types also inhabit Asia, Australia, North America, South America, and all of Europe.

HABITAT

All species of lark prefer the open, sparsely vegetated landscapes of grasslands, heaths (shrubby lands), rocky plains, and steppes, but some like more vegetation than others. For instance, the flapped lark and the woodlark rely on the presence of mixed vegetation types such as small bushes and trees for perching and grasses for building nests. Many larks use plowed fields and even wastelands in North America for their breeding grounds, while others find homes on arctic steppes, on high mountain slopes (even up to 15,100 feet [4,600 meters] in the Himalayas), or in the desert.

DIET

Larks eat almost any sort of insect, including venomous spiders, snails, beetles, stink bugs, millipedes, and (rarely) winged bugs taken during flight, as well as seeds, buds, fruits, and green vegetation. All nestlings receive insects to eat. Most larks swallow whole seeds, which are then pulverized by grit in the birds' stomachs. Others use their strong, thick beaks to dehusk seeds or smash them on the ground. Some larks have been observed breaking snail shells on rocks or dropping them from the air. Since water is often unavailable in their environments, many lark species drink dew off leaves or grass, even drinking salty or brackish water when necessary.

BEHAVIOR AND REPRODUCTION

Despite their generally lackluster appearance, larks are energetic and charismatic birds. They are particularly known for their long, beautiful songs, which can last from a few minutes to an hour. Several of the species, especially the Mongolian lark, the crested lark, and the melodious or Lakatoo lark, are capable of imitating dozens of different birds and even human whistling. Most singing comes from male larks during mating season, when they use aerial song-displays to attract mates and defend their territories. Typically the males will ascend from a perch vertically before descending while singing, either gliding back down or closing his wings to plummet in a dive that he stops only by opening his wings at the last moment. Some species of lark, including the Dupont's lark, make rattling sounds with their flight feathers during their ascent, while others, namely the black lark, clap their wings over their back during their song-displays. The flapped lark uses wing sounds exclusively, and some species sing only from perches at the tops of trees, bushes, and rocks instead of during aerial song-displays.

Desert-dwelling species such as the sparrow-lark never settle in one place, their nomadic movements depending on food supply and rainfall. Both migratory and nomadic lark species tend to gather in flocks, and sometimes form male- or female-only flocks in the winter. Many of the seed-eating larks join together in large flocks.

With the exception of mating season, when some species occasionally sing at night, larks are active during the daytime (diurnal) and sleep at night in shallow depressions they carve into the ground with their claws. Like many birds, they bathe in dust or sand rather than water, although they have been seen deliberately letting rain soak their feathers. Larks prefer to scratch their heads on pointed objects such as branches and rocks, rather than using their claws. Strong fliers, they can often be identified by their undulating flight pattern during which they periodically close their wings. However, many species of these birds can walk and run so quickly that they often need not fly. Larks that live in hot, dry climates perch on raised stones and bushes to stay off the hot ground, taking shelter during the heat of the day in lizard burrows or the shade of rocks or plants. Parents shade their nestlings by standing over them with spread wings.

Rainfall, even very erratic precipitation, will trigger breeding behavior in nomadic species of lark. Otherwise, the regular breeding season occurs from March through July or whenever the rainy season begins. As a family, larks are monogamous (muh-NAH-guh-mus) for at least one breeding season and may raise one to three broods together. Males attract a mate on the ground by hopping and prancing around an interested female in an upright posture; presenting an upright tail; drooping, slightly spreading, and sometimes quivering the wings; and raising the feathers on top of the head. Throughout this display, males sing fragments of their characteristic songs, and sometimes offer small pieces of food prior to mounting the female.

The majority of larks build their grass-lined nests in shallow, cup-shaped indentations that they scratch into the ground. If this is impossible for some reason, many larks will surround a small area with pebbles or other small items to delineate the space. Several species build a dome over their nests using plant materials and supported by close-by vegetation. Usually females build their nests alone, but the male of such species as the calandra lark and the Oriental skylark typically assists. Males of other species, including the chestnut-backed sparrow-lark, present ritual gifts of such useful items as spider webs, pebbles, and other nesting material.

Lark eggs are generally light yellow or cream-colored, with an even covering of spots. Females lay one egg per day in the early morning, and in years of abundant rainfall and other beneficial factors will lay a clutch of two to five eggs. Larks that live in harsher climates often have smaller clutches. Once the female has laid all her eggs, she begins to incubate, sit on to warm, them. In some species, including the sparrow-lark, the male might help incubate the clutch as well. However, both sexes of all lark species feed and care for the chicks. While still unable to fly, the young eat food provided by the parents. The male will care for a second brood alone, if it occurs.

LARKS AND PEOPLE

Larks have been a favorite bird of humans because of their long, melodious song (especially that of the skylark), which often evokes thoughts of good fortune and fresh beginnings. The birds' extravagant aerial song-displays no doubt led to the description of a group of larks as an "exaltation," and literature is full of references to the birds as harbingers of spring and bringers of good harvests. Trapping and hunting larks (particularly skylarks) remains a popular pastime in France and the Mediterranean region, where up to ten million are killed annually.

CONSERVATION STATUS

The World Conservation Union (IUCN) has determined that eleven lark species now require special protection. The raso and Rudd's larks of the Cape Verde Islands are Critically Endangered, facing an extremely high risk of extinction; Ash's lark in Somalia and Botha's lark in South Africa are Endangered, facing a very high risk of extinction; and the red lark, Archer's lark, Degodi lark, and Sidamo bushlark are Vulnerable, facing a high risk of extinction. Sclater's lark, the latakoo, or melodius, lark, and Agulhas long-billed lark are Near Threatened, in danger of becoming threatened with extinction.

Many other lark species, but especially those with restricted ranges, small population sizes, or unprotected habitat, are having trouble maintaining their populations due to habitat loss and fragmentation, introduced predators, and illegal hunting.

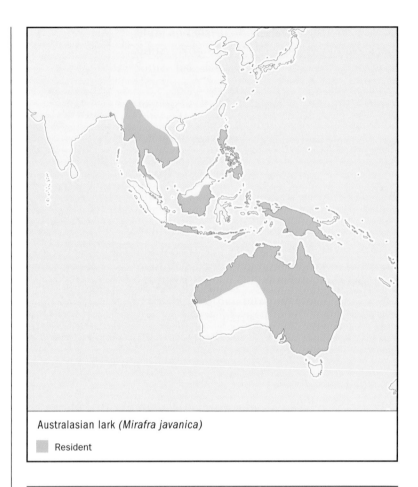

Australasian lark *(Mirafra javanica)*

▇ Resident

AUSTRALASIAN LARK
Mirafra javanica

Physical characteristics: With seventeen subspecies, subgroups of a species in a particular location, the Australasian lark comes in a variety of colors and sizes depending upon its local habitat, although generally the bird weighs about 0.7 ounces (20 grams) and is 4.7 to 5.9 inches (12 to 15 centimeters) long. The Australasian lark has reddish wing patches and inconspicuous coloring. Both sexes of Australasian larks look the same.

Geographic range: As its name indicates, the Australasian lark occupies Australia and nearby Asian countries. It is found in Thailand, the Philippines, Indonesia (Kalimantan, Java, Lesser Sunda Islands,

Bali), New Guinea, and all areas of Australia except the southwest.

Habitat: Australasian larks prefer to live in salty marshes, among scattered bushes in open grassland, and at the edges of plowed fields.

Diet: Like all larks, this species eats seeds and insects.

Behavior and reproduction: Australasian larks are one of the many lark species that regularly perch on wires and trees rather than remaining on or near the ground. The males' song-displays, which can last forty minutes, usually weave in the songs of other birds. This species flocks in small groups outside mating season and is migratory in southern Australia. During mating season, which lasts from November through January, the birds form monogamous pairs and together construct domed nests among low clumps of grass. The female generally lays a clutch of two to four eggs.

The Australasian lark flocks in small groups outside of the mating season and forms monogamous pairs during the mating season. (© H. & J. Eriksen/VIREO. Reproduced by permission.)

Australasian larks and people: The Australasian lark has no special significance to humans.

Conservation status: This species is not threatened. ■

Greater hoopoe-lark (*Alaemon alaudipes*)

Resident

GREATER HOOPOE-LARK
Alaemon alaudipes

Physical characteristics: One of the world's largest larks, the greater hoopoe-lark was so named because of its resemblance to the hoopoe (HUU-puu) bird. In fact, its scientific name means "hoopoe with legs of a lark." They typically measure 7.1 to 7.9 inches (18 to 20 centimeters) long. Males weigh 1.4 to 1.8 ounces (39 to 51 grams), while females, whose bills are also roughly 30 percent shorter, weigh between 1.1 to 1.6 ounces (30 to 47 grams). The hoopoe-lark has a long, slender bill that curves downward slightly. In both sexes, underparts are whitish, upperparts are sand-colored, and breast and throat are black-spotted. The bird has long, broad wings with a bold black-and-white pattern.

Geographic range: The greater hoopoe-lark is an African and Asian bird, occupying patches of habitat in the Cape Verde Islands, in North Africa from Mauritania to Egypt and Sudan, and across the Middle East to India's northwest region.

Greater hoopoe-larks eat mostly insects and snails. They smash snails on rocks or drop them from the air to crack their shells. (Illustration by Emily Damstra. Reproduced by permission.)

Habitat: The greater hoopoe-lark lives in deserts or semideserts and has evolved the ability to survive with little water.

Diet: Hoopoe-larks eat mostly insects and snails, from which they take nutrition as well as water. The birds use their down-curved bills to dig their prey out of hiding places and sandy spots, and have been observed smashing snails on rocks or dropping them from the air to crack their shells.

Behavior and reproduction: Usually seen alone or in pairs, the hoopoe-lark often allows birdwatchers to come within several feet (meters) before it flees. Males of the species defend their territories with a spread-winged posture, and their songs are piercing and loud. The male hoopoe-lark's song-flight, which he may perform continuously for up to an hour, consists of jumping up from a perch as he starts to sing and then flapping vertically to 33 feet (10 meters). He may then perform somersaults to show off his contrasting tail and wing plumage before plummeting to Earth, opening his wings only as he pulls out of the dive and lands.

Greater hoopoe-larks and people: The greater hoopoe-lark has no special significance to humans.

Conservation status: This species is not threatened in general, although in some locations its populations are declining due to conversion of suitable breeding grounds to agricultural, military, or recreational use. ■

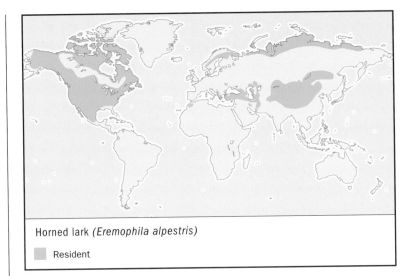

Horned lark (*Eremophila alpestris*)

Resident

HORNED LARK
Eremophila alpestris

Physical characteristics: The horned lark gets its name from the tiny, protruding black feathers on each side of its head, which give the bird a horned appearance. The birds have a softly tawny color on their backs, while their underparts are lighter. They have black bibs, broad black stripes under the eye, and a buttery-yellow or white throat. Tails are mostly black with white outer feathers. Females' "horns" are less apparent and their plumage is more muted overall. Horned larks are generally 5.9 to 6.7 inches (15 to 17 centimeters) long. Males weigh from 1.1 to 1.7 ounces (30 to 48 grams) and females weigh 0.9 to 1.5 ounces (26 to 42 ounces). Wingspan ranges from 12.25 to 14 inches (31 to 35.5 centimeters).

Geographic range: The only member of the lark family native to North America, horned larks nest from Alaska and Canada down to West Virginia, Missouri, North Carolina, coastal Texas, and Kansas, wintering along the Gulf Coast. It also appears throughout northern and southern Europe, where it winters around the North Sea, and in northern and southern Asia. Sightings have also been reported in Morocco, Colombia, Lebanon, and northern Israel.

Habitat: Horned larks prefer to live in large fields and open areas of grassland (including those at airports and in farmland), but also occupy habitats such as arctic tundra and shoreline beaches.

Diet: Horned larks eat mainly insects (especially wasps, ants, caterpillars, grasshoppers, and spiders) during the mating season, but concentrate on seeds in wintertime.

Behavior and reproduction: During its song-display, the male horned lark ascends without singing to heights of 300 to 800 feet (91 to 244 meters), where it begins to circle and sing a high-pitched, tinkling song. When it completes the song, the bird closes it wings and drops headfirst, opening its wings and pulling out of the dive at the last possible second. The male also perches on fence posts, rocks, or bushes to sing its mating song. Horned larks are monogamous for at least one mating season (March through July) and prefer to make their cup-shaped nests on the ground in barren, sandy, or stony areas. Females often surround the nest with a ring of pebbles and line it with down, fine grass, and hair. They commonly lay three to five smooth, glossy, pale greenish white and brown-speckled eggs in a clutch at a rate of one per day. Females begin incubating the eggs once the entire clutch has been laid, sitting on the nest for ten to fourteen days. Nestlings, who receive care from both parents, have brown skin and long, whitish down. They typically leave the nest after nine to twelve days.

The horned lark is particularly known for its preference for walking sedately to travel small distances instead of the more usual hopping, and may often be heard singing its characteristic "tsee-ee" song from any slight elevation. Birders generally regard the species as tough and intrepid because of its tolerance of seemingly inhospitable climates and conditions.

Horned larks and people: The horned lark's jaunty appearance makes it a favorite among birdwatchers.

Conservation status: This species is not officially threatened, although its habitat in a number of areas is jeopardized by development and reforestation of grasslands. As a ground-nester, the horned lark is also heavily preyed upon by cats, skunks, raccoons, coyotes, and other predators. ■

FOR MORE INFORMATION

Books:

Erlich, P., et al. *The Birder's Handbook: A Field Guide to the Natural History of North American Birds.* New York: Simon and Schuster, 1988.

Keith, S., et al., eds. *The Birds of Africa.* Vol. 4. London: Academic Press, 1992.

Sibley, Charles G., and Burt L. Monroe. *Distribution and Taxonomy of Birds of the World.* New Haven, CT: Yale University Press, 1990.

Web sites:

"Australasian Lark." Avibase: The World Bird Database. http://www.bsc-eoc.org/avibase.jsp?pg=summary&lang=EN (accessed on May 17, 2004).

"Hoopoe-Lark." Birding Israel. http://www.birding-israel.com/bird/News/inFocus/hoopoeLark/ (accessed on May 17, 2004).

"An Animal of the High Desert: The Horned Lark." Idaho National Engineering and Environmental Laboratory: Environmental Surveillance, Education, and Research Program. http://www.stoller-eser.com/hornedlark.htm (accessed on May 17, 2004).

"Horned Lark Fact Sheet." State of Connecticut Department of Environmental Protection. http://dep.state.ct.us/burnatr/wildlife/factshts/hlark.htm (accessed on May 17, 2004).

"Lark." Wikipedia. http://en.wikipedia.org/wiki/Alaudidae (accessed on May 17, 2004).

SWALLOWS

Hirundinidae

Class: Aves

Order: Passeriformes

Family: Hirundinidae

Number of species: 88 species

family
CHAPTER

PHYSICAL CHARACTERISTICS

Swallows are distinguishable by their long, sleek tails and wings. Their gaping bill and long tails and wings are built for the long-term flight and maneuverability that enables them to catch their major source of food, flying and water-skimming insects.

Most swallows have black, brown, iridescent blue, or iridescent green plumage on top with a lighter tan, dark orange, or white chest. Their long tails may be forked (like the barn swallow) or straight across (like a cliff swallow), and act as an aerial rudder, or guide.

The legs and feet of the swallow are short and built primarily for perching, not walking. The average size of a swallow ranges from 4.75 to 8 inches (12.0 to 20.3 centimeters) in length, and they weigh from 0.4 to 2.1 ounces (10 to 60 grams).

GEOGRAPHIC RANGE

The majority of swallow species are found in Africa, but one can find swallows on virtually every major continent, except Antarctica and the high Arctic. They are also absent from New Zealand and other oceanic islands.

HABITAT

Swallows seek breeding grounds that have a good supply of flying and/or water-skimming insects, such as areas near lakes, ponds, rivers, streams, and wetlands. The species that build mud nests, such as cave and cliff swallows, also seek areas where mud is plentiful. Other species have specific requirements based

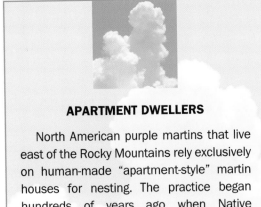

on their nesting habits. During nonbreeding seasons, the majority of North American swallows, like the purple martin, migrate to the warmer climates of Central and South America.

DIET

While tree swallows will eat berries (particularly waxy bayberries) and fruits, most swallow species subsist entirely on flying and water-skimming insects such as beetles and flying ants. Purple martins will eat bigger insects as large as a butterfly, and other species also eat spiders and swarming insects like midges and mosquitoes. Virtually all insects are eaten in flight, and sometimes on the surface of the water. Swallows can even drink in flight by dipping their bills into the water as they fly across a pond or lake.

BEHAVIOR AND REPRODUCTION

Most swallows form monogamous (muh-NAH-guh-mus) pairs. Some species build their nests either in natural or human-made holes, such as tree crevices or nesting boxes. Other species use mud pellets carried by the bill-full to create nests in caves or under human-made overhangs, such as bridges. Migrating species of swallows travel in huge flocks to warmer climates in the winter, and return with the warm weather and hatching insect population.

SWALLOWS AND PEOPLE

Most swallows have a good relationship with their human neighbors. They are attractive birds that adapt well to habitat changes imposed by humans. While some people may consider a mud nest in their eaves or on their front porch a nuisance, the swallows' appetite for flying insects can help keep the pest population down.

CONSERVATION STATUS

There is one Critically Endangered, facing an extremely high risk of extinction, species of swallow, the white-eyed river-martin. There are estimated to be fewer than fifty adults of the species, and the bird, which is native to Thailand, has not been sighted in twenty years and therefore may already be extinct. Their decline has been caused by hunting, habitat destruction, and deforestation.

Four species classified as Vulnerable, facing a high risk of extinction, are also noted by the World Conservation Union (IUCN): the blue swallow, white-tailed swallow, Bahama swallow, and golden swallow. Habitat loss due to deforestation and agricultural land use has been particularly destructive to cavity nesting and grassland-dwelling swallows.

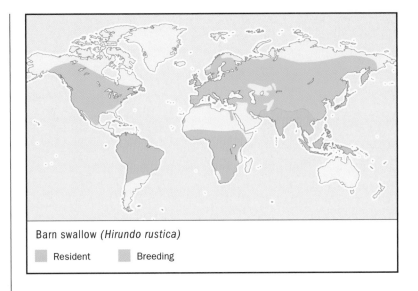

Barn swallow (*Hirundo rustica*)

◼ Resident   ◼ Breeding

BARN SWALLOW
Hirundo rustica

Physical characteristics: The barn swallow has iridescent dark blue plumage on its back, with a dark orange throat and orange to buff breast, although there are some coloring variations among the six subspecies of the bird. It is the only species of swallow that has a long, deeply forked tail. The average size of the barn swallow is 7.5 in (19 cm) long with a weight of .6 oz (17 g).

Geographic range: During the summer months, barn swallows can be found throughout North America. The birds have the most widespread range of any swallow species, and are also found throughout Europe, Asia, Myanmar, Israel, and northern Africa. North American barn swallows winter in Central and South America, while their European and Asian counterparts migrate to central and southern Africa and south and Southeast Asia.

Habitat: During breeding season, barn swallows settle in habitats with abundant insects and some access to wet earth (such as from riverbanks or drainage ditches). They build their cone-shaped, open-topped mud nests in sheltered natural areas, including cliff overhangs and caves. They also quite frequently choose human-made structures to house their families, creating nests in the rafters of barns, the underside of highway overpasses, and the eaves of other buildings.

Because of their abundant insect population, farms make ideal places for barn swallows to live, and the birds can frequently be seen flying close to crops feeding on insects. Along with feathers, the straw and mud that are found in livestock areas also make excellent building materials for a barn-based nest. Barn swallows migrate towards warmer climates in the winter, and can be found in drier climates, such as the desert, when nesting isn't a priority.

Barn swallow nests hold three to six eggs, and both female and male may share incubation and feeding duties. (Dwight Kuhn/ Bruce Coleman Inc. Reproduced by permission.)

Diet: Barn swallows feed on flying insects.

Behavior and reproduction: Barn swallows return to the same area each year to breed, hatch, and fledge, raise until they can fly, their young. Often, they will use the same nest year after year if it remains intact. Building a mud nest may take anywhere from a week to a month, and both male and female work together, using thousands of mud pellets carried one by one in their bills. Straw and grass are also used, and the nests are lined with feathers. Barn swallow nests hold three to six eggs, and both female and male may share incubation duties, sitting on the eggs to keep warm. The birds are colonial, meaning that they often build nests in groups; however, males will defend their nest vigorously from both predators, animals that hunt them for food, and other barn swallows.

Barn swallows and people: Because of their appetite for flying insects that annoy, destroy vegetation, and can carry disease, barn swallows are popular neighbors, particularly to farmers.

Conservation status: Barn swallows are abundant, and not considered threatened. ■

American cliff swallow (Hirundo pyrrhonota)

Resident   Breeding

American cliff swallows build their mud nests not only on the underside of cliffs, but also on the outside of overhanging human-made structures, such as bridges and dams. (© Brenda Tharp/Photo Researchers, Inc. Reproduced by permission.)

AMERICAN CLIFF SWALLOW
Hirundo pyrrhonota

Physical characteristics: American cliff swallows have a long square tail, black to blue back, rust-colored throat and rump, white forehead spot, and white to buff underside. They average 5.1 in (13 cm) in length and 0.8 oz (22.7 g) in weight.

Geographic range: This species breeds throughout North America and migrates to Central and South America in the winter.

Habitat: The cliff swallow builds its mud nest in covered areas such as the underside of cliffs and on the outside of overhanging human-made structures. They are found in a wide variety of biomes where water is available, and even in desert areas near towns and human-made construction. The nests are typically built in colonies, and unlike the barn swallow nest, they are completely enclosed with a small hole for coming and going.

Diet: American cliff swallows feed on insects while the birds are flying.

Behavior and reproduction: Cliff swallows are monogamous, migrating birds. They return to their mud nests annually to lay a clutch of three to six eggs, which they incubate for about two weeks. The brood leaves the nest approximately three weeks after hatching. Some cliff swallows are parasitic, and will lay their eggs in other cliff swallow nests within their colony to be incubated and raised by the other birds.

American cliff swallows and people: Human-made structures like bridges and dams provide an attractive spot for many cliff swallow colonies and in this sense the birds have benefited from development and construction.

Conservation status: American cliff swallows are common and are not considered threatened. ■

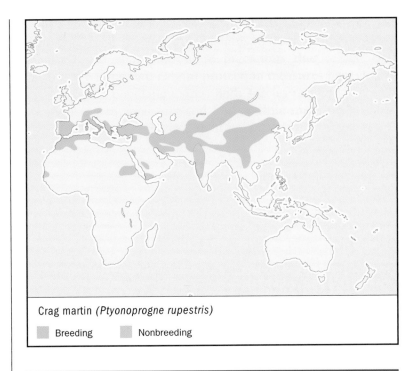

Crag martin (*Ptyonoprogne rupestris*)

Breeding   Nonbreeding

CRAG MARTIN
Ptyonoprogne rupestris

Physical characteristics: Crag martins are an average of 5 in (14 cm) in length. They are brown on top with a dusky color on the throat and belly and dark under the wing. When they fan their squared tails, white spots are visible.

Geographic range: The crag martin breeds in mountainous areas of Europe and Asia, and migrates to the Middle East and Africa. Spain and Portugal have the largest European population, the birds are also found on some Mediterranean islands. Some varieties of crag martin are resident, meaning that they do not migrate.

Habitat: Crag martins prefer to breed in mountainous areas, but like other mud-nest dwelling swallows, can be found in virtually any biome that has a plentiful insect population and offers supplies for nest building during breeding season. Crag martin mud nests are open and are constructed under cliff edges or human-made overhangs.

Diet: The crag martin feeds on flying insects.

Behavior and reproduction: The female crag martin incubates her clutch of three to five eggs. Once the eggs are hatched, both parents feed the chicks.

Crag martins and people: Habitat destruction through development could negatively impact the crag martin, but like other mud-nesters of the swallow family, the species has proven itself very adaptable by building their homes on human-made structures.

Conservation status: Crag martins are plentiful throughout Europe and Asia. ■

FOR MORE INFORMATION

Books:

Alderfer, Jonathan. "Swallows." In *Reference Atlas to the Birds of North America.* Edited by Mel Baughman. Washington, DC: National Geographic Press, 2003.

Sibley, David Allen. *National Audubon Society: The Sibley Guide to Birds.* New York: Alfred A. Knopf, 2000.

Periodicals:

Milius, S. "Birds May Inherit Their Taste for the Town." *Science News* (Dec 23, 2000): 406.

Web sites:

"Barn Swallow." *All About Birds.* Cornell Lab of Ornithology. http://birds.cornell.edu/programs/AllAboutBirds/BirdGuide/Barn_Swallow_dtl.html (accessed on May 28, 2004).

"Swallows: Barn Swallows in Battery Pensacola." National Park Service: Gulf Islands National Seashore. http://www.nps.gov/guis/extended/FLA/Nature/Swallow.htm (accessed on May 28, 2004).

"Attracting and Managing Purple Martins." Purple Martin Conservation Association. http://www.purplemartin.org/main/mgt.html (accessed on May 29, 2004).

While crag martins' natural forest habitat is destroyed by human development, the birds have adapted to build their nests on human-made structures, such as houses and bridges. (Illustration by Brian Cressman. Reproduced by permission.)

Class: Aves

Order: Passeriformes

Family: Motacillidae

Number of species: 54 species

family

C H A P T E R

PHYSICAL CHARACTERISTICS

Birds of the Motacillidae family can be divided into three groups: pipits, longclaws, and wagtails. All members of the family are small to medium sized, ranging in length from 5 to 8.75 inches (12.7 to 22.2 centimeters). Adult wagtails are perhaps the most colorful birds of the group, with their black, white, green, yellow, or gray stripes and patterns. The coloring of pipits, which make up two-thirds of the family, is more subdued, streaked brown to buff, a sand-color, and they have thin, pointy bills and medium to long legs. Pipits, unlike wagtails, do not have different seasonal plumage, feathers. The longclaws often have upper plumage, feathers, designed for camouflage (KAM-uh-flaj; colored to blend in with the surroundings) but brilliantly colored plumage underneath. Adult longclaws have dark, necklace-like plumage next to their throats and chins, which are red, orange, or yellow.

Longclaws are named for their long hind claws, which in several species extend twice as long as the foot, or up to 2 inches (5 centimeters). This hind claw is used for perching on grass clumps and walking.

Pipits, longclaws, and wagtails generally have medium to long tails, which they often pump or wag when walking. They are slender, long-bodied, short-necked, energetic, and quick moving. Pipits and wagtails have very similar body types, causing confusion among birdwatchers, but it is generally agreed that pipits have shorter tails than wagtails and a more upright stance on the ground. Longclaws are the most upright of the group, and are often compared to larks in appearance.

GEOGRAPHIC RANGE

Pipits, longclaws, and wagtails are cosmopolitan, meaning they inhabit all the continents of the world. The species may be found from the Arctic tundra all the way to the Antarctic. Most of the birds are migratory and fly south to spend the winter in Africa and Asia. Wagtails are somewhat rare in Australia, but are otherwise widespread. Pipits are also widespread, although only one species occurs in Australia and one in New Guinea. Longclaws are confined to grassland regions of sub-Saharan Africa.

HABITAT

Most species live in open or semi-open country, and many prefer grassy areas such as fields and rocky meadows. Wagtails particularly favor streams, lake edges, rivers, and wetlands, while pipits search out open grasslands from sea level to as high as 17,400 feet (5,300 meters) in the Himalayas. Longclaws also tend to stick to open grasslands and the edges of wetlands.

DIET

All members of this family primarily eat insects and their eggs, from tiny midges to locusts and dragonflies. Their favorite foods seem to be beetles, grasshoppers, crickets, ants, wasps, praying mantids, and termites. Some species also eat aquatic insects, seeds, berries, plant parts and carrion, dead and decaying meat.

BEHAVIOR AND REPRODUCTION

Pipit, longclaw, and wagtail species are very territorial, and males aggressively defend their breeding areas. Some even attack their reflections in the hubcaps of cars and windows. Some of the species are monogamous (muh-NAH-guh-mus), having only one mate. They perform courtship displays, behaviors that lead to mating. Some species' displays include presenting females with nesting material or food, while others, especially pipits, stage spectacular aerial flights to attract mates and defend their territory.

This family of birds typically builds cup-shaped nests on the ground in a depression or shallow, scraped-out area. Their neatly formed nests are usually made of grass, stems, and other plant parts and lined with hair, feathers, and other soft materials. The female most often constructs the nest, but males are often in attendance and sometimes help. Pipits and wagtails

TREES ARE FOR THE BIRDS

Almost none of the birds in the Motacillidae family like to perch in trees. They would rather stay on the ground, where they feed and nest, and are experts at evading danger by running swiftly to thick vegetation or rocky outcrops.

generally nest in the grass, although wagtails also nest in nooks and cracks in rocks, stream banks, cliffs, and walls, or under bridges and in hollow tree branches and roots. Longclaws also tend to nest in the grass, but prefer to hide in or at the base of a tussock, a clump of grass, or among leafy plants.

Most wagtails and pipits breed from April to August and may have two or three broods, group of chicks that hatch at the same time, per breeding season. Longclaws breed during or shortly after the rainy season. Female longclaws lay a clutch of two to five green, pale blue, or pink eggs. Wagtails lay three to eight eggs and pipits lay two to nine, depending on latitude and environment. Usually the female incubates, sits on, the eggs alone, but sometimes the male helps. Both parents care for the fledglings, young birds that have recently grown the feathers needed for flight, which leave the nest after ten to seventeen days.

Many species migrate in flocks and gather into large groups during the nonbreeding season. Wagtails roost together in reed beds and bush- and scrub-vegetated areas. They will vigorously defend good feeding areas from intruders with a display of head-bobbing and jumping into the air. Wagtails may be identified by the characteristic wagging motion of their longish tails. Pipits also do something similar with their tails, but, with a few exceptions, it is not as noticeable. Both species can run very quickly and prefer to crouch in short vegetation to escape the notice of predators, animals that hunt them for food. They are strong fliers, and usually have an undulating, smooth wave-like, flight pattern. The flight of longclaws, on the other hand, is jerky because of their habit of alternating periods of gliding and flapping. Both pipits and longclaws use song-flights as part of their territorial and mating behaviors; wagtails more often sing their simple, melodious songs from the ground or a perch.

When foraging, searching for food, this family of birds uses numerous techniques, including following the plow as a field is plowed, walking while picking from the ground or water surface, darting after insects, putting their heads underwater, flying or hovering to catch winged prey, and poking into vegetation and leaf litter.

PIPITS, WAGTAILS, LONGCLAWS, AND PEOPLE

People have long been amused by the endearing playfulness of the pipit, which many reports suggest enjoys running in front of people walking on dirt paths and trails and then rising up into the air with a sharp chirp before landing to run again. The family of birds is also beloved by birdwatchers because of their liveliness, energy, and colorfulness. Wagtails especially have special significance for humans, and figure prominently in Japanese, Greek, and African mythology.

CONSERVATION STATUS

With the destruction and degradation of many grassland and wetland, available habitats have decline for Motacillidae populations. As a result, two species have been listed as Endangered, facing a very high risk of extinction, dying out, by the World Conservation Union (IUCN); three species have been designated as Vulnerable, facing a high risk of extinction; and five species are Near Threatened, in danger of becoming threatened with extinction.

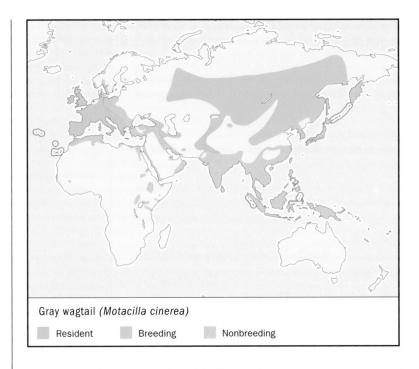

Gray wagtail (*Motacilla cinerea*)

■ Resident ■ Breeding ■ Nonbreeding

GRAY WAGTAIL
Motacilla cinerea

Physical characteristics: Gray wagtails range in size from 7.1 to 7.5 inches (18 to 19 centimeters) and in weight from 0.5 to 0.8 ounces (14 to 22 grams). Their gray upper body is offset by bright yellow on their undersides. In summer the males develop a distinctive face pattern of white stripes and a black bib.

Geographic range: This species inhabits areas of northwest Africa and Europe east to Iran, northeast China and Japan, Pakistan, and New Guinea. They migrate for the winter to western Europe, the Middle East, and Africa south to Malawi.

Habitat: Gray wagtails seek out fast-moving, rocky upland rivers and streams, but many occupy territories near canals and on rock-strewn lakeshores with dense foliage and tree cover. In winter, they can also be seen in lowlands near bodies of water, at the coast, and in estuaries (EST-yoo-air-eez), where freshwater and saltwater mix. Some birds spend the winter in towns.

Diet: Gray wagtails feed mainly on aquatic insects. They also eat small fish and tadpoles. Gray wagtails forage both on the ground and in the water, and occasionally catch airborne insects.

Behavior and reproduction: Gray wagtails are territorial during the breeding season, March through May. Some defend their feeding areas during winter, when they tend to roost in groups. Mating pairs are monogamous, and the male helps to build the nest, usually on a cliff ledge or among tree roots. The female lays three to seven eggs, and both parents then incubate the young for eleven to fourteen days. The young leave the nest within eleven to seventeen days.

Gray wagtails and people: Birdwatchers often confuse this species with the yellow wagtail, but the gray wagtail has a gray, rather than yellowish brown, back; a longer, more strongly patterned black-and-white tail; and a broad, pale wing-bar when in flight.

Conservation status: Gray wagtails are considered Vulnerable due to the destruction of their favored habitats by development and contamination. ■

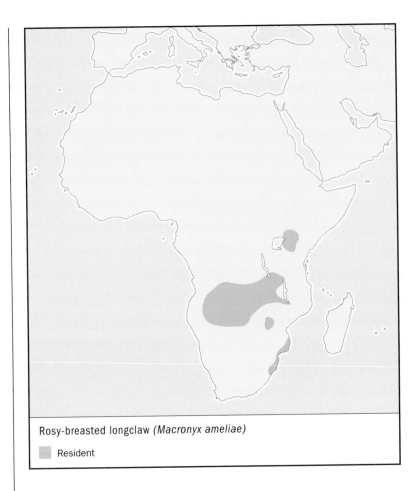

Rosy-breasted longclaw (*Macronyx ameliae*)

Resident

ROSY-BREASTED LONGCLAW
Macronyx ameliae

Physical characteristics: Rosy-breasted longclaws range in length from 7.5 to 8 inches (19 to 20 centimeters) and in weight from 1.1 to 1.4 ounces (30 to 40 grams). Their mottled, speckled, upperparts include an orange-red patch on the throat with a dark band across their lower throat and a pinkish breast. The hind claw on the foot of this bird is extremely long, making up at least half the length of the foot.

Geographic range: This species inhabits southwestern Kenya and north and southwest Tanzania, as well as parts of Angola, Botswana, Zimbabwe, and the east coast of South Africa.

Habitat: Rosy-breasted longclaws live in grass-lands with short bunches of vegetation in areas that are permanently or seasonally moist. They often live near marshes or open bodies of water.

Diet: This species eats mainly insects and sometimes small frogs, but it also forages, searches for food, in grass or on the bare ground and occasionally pursues winged insects into the air.

Behavior and reproduction: This shy longclaw is territorial during the breeding season, when the species tends to gather into pairs or family groups. Males usually sing from the tops of bushes or during song-flights. Mating pairs are monogamous and breed mostly during or after seasonal rains. The female builds a cup-shaped nest of grass within a tuft of grass, and lays two to four eggs. The female incubates them for thirteen to fourteen days, and the fledglings leave the nest after sixteen days.

Rosy-breasted longclaws and people: Rosy-breasted longclaws have no special significance to people.

Conservation status: Rosy-breasted longclaws are listed as Near Threatened in South Africa and Mozambique due to loss of coastal habitat. ■

Rosy-breasted longclaws often live near marshes or open bodies of water, where they feed mainly on insects and sometimes small frogs. (© T. J. Ulrich/VIREO. Reproduced by permission.)

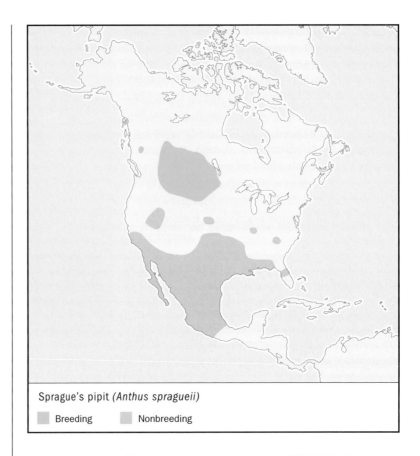

Sprague's pipit *(Anthus spragueii)*

■ Breeding ■ Nonbreeding

SPRAGUE'S PIPIT
Anthus spragueii

Physical characteristics: Sprague's pipit ranges in length from 6.3 to 7 inches (16 to 18 centimeters) and in weight from 0.8 to 1 ounce (22 to 29 grams). Their pale buff face blends into olive-tan upperparts that are streaked with black and buff. Their undersides are whitish or buff with dark streaks and their outer tail feathers are white. This species has a thin, pale-colored bill, dark eyes, and light-colored legs and feet.

Geographic range: Sprague's pipits occupy areas of Canada, including Saskatchewan, Alberta, Manitoba, and British Columbia, and Montana, North Dakota, and South Dakota in the United States. The bird migrates to Mexico and the southern United States in winter.

Habitat: Sprague's pipits inhabit prairies of tall grass and short-grass plains, where their coloring makes them nearly invisible. While migrating, they forage and rest in plowed fields or harvested hay and wheat fields.

Diet: Sprague's pipits eat mainly insects, but sometimes add seeds to their diet.

Behavior and reproduction: This solitary and secretive pipit species is known for flying high into the air when startled. They are also noted for their beautiful, arcing song-flight during mating season in April and May. Mating pairs are monogamous, and build a cup-shaped nest of grass and stems on the ground where tall grass can fall over the structure. The female lays four to seven eggs, and fledglings leave the nest in ten to eleven days.

Sprague's pipits and people: Naturalist and artist James Audubon named this bird after Isaac Sprague, an artist who came with him on a trip up the Missouri River. The first bird of this species was found in 1843.

Conservation status: Sprague's pipits are listed as Vulnerable. Their populations have declined rapidly due to loss of prairie breeding grounds. Prairies have been taken over by agriculture and by the invasion of aggressive plant species. ■

Sprague's pipits breed in tall-grass and short-grass prairies. Their populations have declined rapidly due to loss of prairie breeding grounds to agriculture and the invasion of aggressive plant species. (Illustration by Bruce Worden. Reproduced by permission.)

FOR MORE INFORMATION

Books:

Ali, S., and S. D. Ripley. *Handbook of the Birds of India and Pakistan.* Delhi: Oxford University Press, 1983.

Clements, J. *Birds of the World: A Checklist.* Vista, CA: Ibis Publications, 1991.

Sibley, C. G., and B. L. Monroe. *Distribution and Taxonomy of Birds of the World.* New Haven, CT: Yale University Press, 1990.

Periodicals:

Hall, B. P. "The Taxonomy and Identification of Pipits." *Bulletin of the British Museum of Natural History* 7 (1961): 245–289.

Web sites:

"The Motacillidae." Gordon's Motacillidae Page. http://www.earthlife.net/birds/motacillidae.html (accessed on June 24, 2004).

National Wildlife Federation. "Sprague's Pipit." eNature.com. http://www.enature.com/fieldguide/showSpeciesSH.asp?curGroupID=1&shapeID=961&curPageNum=147&recnum=BD0301 (accessed on June 24, 2004).

Olliver, Narena. "Puhoihoi, the New Zealand Pipit." New Zealand Birds Gallery. http://www.nzbirds.com/NZPipit.html (accessed on June 24, 2004).

"Pipits & wagtails: Motacillidae." Bird Families of the World. http://www.montereybay.com/creagrus/pipits.html (accessed on June 24, 2004).

"Pipits and Wagtails: Grey Wagtail *Motacilla cinerea*." Bird Guides. http://www.birdguides.com/html/vidlib/species/motacilla_cinerea.htm (accessed on June 24, 2004).

"Pipits, wagtails, longclaws." Birds of the World. http://www.eeb.cornell.edu/winkler/botw/motacillidae.html (accessed on June 24, 2004).

"Sprague's Pipit." Patuxent Wildlife Research Center. http://www.mbr-pwrc.usgs.gov/Infocenter/i7000id.html (accessed on June 24, 2004).

CUCKOO-SHRIKES

Campephagidae

Class: Aves

Order: Passeriformes

Family: Campephagidae

Number of species: 74 species

phylum

class

subclass

order

monotypic order

suborder

▲ **family**

PHYSICAL CHARACTERISTICS

Cuckoo-shrikes are small- to medium-sized birds, ranging in length from 5.5 to 14.5 inches (14 to 37 centimeters) and in weight from 0.2 to 6.3 ounces (6 to 180 grams). Some of the seventy-four species are very brightly colored, like the fiery minivet, while others are drab to protect them from predators (animals that hunt them for food), like the Mauritius cuckoo-shrike. Usually the females of this bird family are much less colorful than the males. In general, cuckoo-shrikes have broad-based bills that are slightly hooked and notched, and stiff, bristle-like feathers around their nostrils. Wings are pointed and long, and their tails are fairly long and rounded. Most cuckoo-shrikes have very stiff, erect feathers on their backs and rumps that scientists think may act as a means of defense because they detach easily.

GEOGRAPHIC RANGE

Cuckoo-shrikes are found only in middle and southern Africa, south and Southeast Asia, Australasia, and the western Pacific Islands.

HABITAT

Except for the ground cuckoo-shrike species, cuckoo-shrikes are either mostly or exclusively tree dwellers. In fact, many of the seventy-four species can be found mainly in the canopies, upper layer of a forest, of tall trees. They nest, breed, and forage in a variety of places, but all have trees in common. Their habitats can include swampy, humid, or dry forests, woodlands, savannas, and scrubland. Some species select habitat only in

the interior of forests, but others find homes at the edges of forests, in secondary growth (regrown forests), in gardens of urban or suburban areas, or among coastal vegetation.

DIET

Cuckoo-shrikes mostly eat insects such as caterpillars and some fruit, but some species also eat seeds and plant parts.

BEHAVIOR AND REPRODUCTION

Cuckoo-shrikes are usually monogamous (muh-NAH-guh-mus), have only one mate, and most have permanent territories. Ornithologists, scientists that study birds, know very little about the breeding seasons of cuckoo-shrikes, but they have observed that, except for the white-winged triller and the ground cuckoo-shrike, most species breed during or just after the rainy season and nest solitarily, alone. Males of some of the bigger species use a courtship display, behaviors that lead to mating, in which they alternately lift each wing while calling loudly. In many of the cuckoo-shrike species, male and female together build a small, shallow, cup-shaped nest of small twigs, grasses, moss, lichens (LIE-kenz), roots, and bark. They often bind the nest with spider webs and line it with them as well. The parents typically place the nest on a high horizontal or forked branch of a tree. The female lays a clutch of one to five eggs, but usually two or three. The males of some species help to incubate the eggs, but most often this is the female's duty. Incubation of the eggs takes fourteen to twenty-five days, but in many species the process can take three or more weeks. Both parents care for the young, which leave the nest after thirteen to twenty-four days.

When foraging, cuckoo-shrikes generally poke among the foliage, leaves, of trees and bushes, but some also explore trunks and branches for prey, animals hunted for food. The birds often pursue insects into the air, and occasionally pick insects off the ground.

CUCKOO-SHRIKES AND PEOPLE

Cuckoo-shrikes do not have a special significance to humans.

CONSERVATION STATUS

Four cuckoo-shrike species are listed as Vulnerable, facing a high risk of extinction in the wild, or Endangered, facing a very high risk of extinction. These species include the Ghana cuckoo-shrike, Réunion cuckoo-shrike, Mauritius cuckoo-shrike, and white-winged cuckoo-shrike. However, due to habitat loss and degradation, about a dozen other species have Near Threatened status, in danger of becoming threatened with extinction.

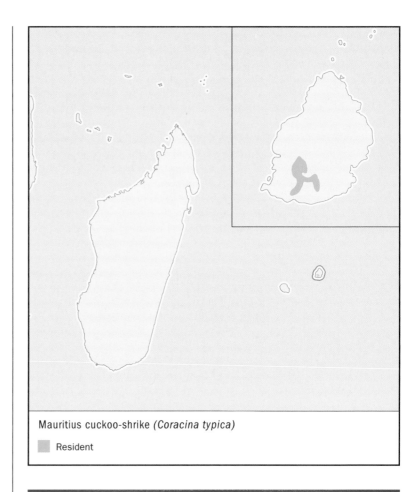

Mauritius cuckoo-shrike (*Coracina typica*)

◼ Resident

MAURITIUS CUCKOO-SHRIKE
Coracina typica

Physical characteristics: Mauritius cuckoo-shrikes measure 8.7 inches (22 centimeters) long and males weigh about 1.5 ounces (43 grams). Males have gray upper bodies, dull white undersides and blackish wings. Females have orange-brown upperparts and reddish orange undersides.

Geographic range: Mauritius cuckoo-shrikes live only in areas of southern Mauritius, an island off the southeast coast of Africa.

Habitat: This species of cuckoo-shrike prefers the canopies of Mauritius's moist tropical evergreen forests, especially at elevations above 1,500 feet (460 meters). However, they will also use nearby forest that has been degraded or altered by humans. Many of the mating pairs may be found in remains of native forests around Black River Gorges and in the Bel Ombre Forest.

Diet: Mauritius cuckoo-shrikes eat mostly large arthropods, invertebrate animals (animals without backbones) with segmented bodies, such as caterpillars, stick bugs, beetles, and praying mantids. They occasionally prey on small reptiles such as geckos and even steal the eggs of other birds, particularly the pink pigeon. The birds find their food mainly by searching through vegetation.

Behavior and reproduction: Generally secretive and solitary birds, Mauritius cuckoo-shrikes live alone or with their mate. Males are territorial even outside of breeding season, which occurs during the rainy period from September to March. Both sexes work together to build a shallow, cup-shaped nest made of fine twigs, lichen, and spider webs, which they place high on a horizontal tree branch. The female lays a clutch of two eggs, which both parents incubate for twenty-four to twenty-five days. Rat predation is a major danger for chicks. Males sing with a melodic trill and have a harsh species-specific call-note.

Generally secretive and solitary birds, Mauritius cuckoo-shrikes live alone or with their mate. Males and females build a nest and incubate their eggs. (Illustration by Emily Damstra. Reproduced by permission.)

Mauritius cuckoo-shrikes and people: Since 1975, many residents of Mauritius have helped to stop the decline of the bird's population through support of programs to restore native ecosystems and habitats.

Conservation status: In 1970, the population of Mauritius cuckoo-shrikes was estimated at about 200 pairs, but by 2000, thanks to conservation efforts, that number had increased to between 300 and 350 pairs. Nevertheless, the species is still considered Vulnerable because of continued habitat loss and destruction in its very small range. ■

Fiery minivet *(Pericrocotus igneus)*

☐ Resident

FIERY MINIVET
Pericrocotus igneus

Physical characteristics: One of the smallest species in the Campephagidae family, the fiery minivet was first recognized as a separate species in 1846 during an expedition to the Moluccas, a group of islands in Indonesia. They range in length from 6 to 6.5 inches (15 to 16.5 centimeters) and typically weigh between 0.5 to 0.6 ounces (14 to 16 grams). Males have black upperparts and throats, with vivid red breast, belly, rump, and outer tail feathers. Females are more subtly colored, with gray upperparts, yellow undersides, orange rumps, and black tails. The bird has a distinct, rising call of "swee-eet."

Geographic range: Fiery minivets are Asian birds, occupying southern Myanmar, southern Thailand, and parts of Malaysia and Brunei, as well as the Indonesian islands of Sumatra and Borneo and the Palawan Province islands of the Philippines.

Habitat: This species typically makes its home in the canopies of forests and along the forest edges, but it will also occupy pine plantations and casuarinas, an Australian evergreen, groves. Many of the birds may be found in lowlands, but it is also commonly sighted in the sub-montane slopes and montane forests of Sumatra at altitudes up to 8,900 feet (2,700 meters). Another favored habitat is coastal mangrove swamps.

Diet: Although little is known about the feeding habits of fiery minivets, ornithologists presume that the species, like birds in the rest of the family, eats primarily insects, particularly moths and caterpillars. They forage in the canopies of trees where they live.

Fiery minivets are frequent participants in what scientists call "mixed-species bird parties," groups that contain a number of bird species. (Illustration by Emily Damstra. Reproduced by permission.)

Behavior and reproduction: Sociable and energetic, fiery minivets are frequent participants in what scientists call "mixed-species bird parties," groups that contain a number of bird species. They are believed to be monogamous, with mated pairs working together to build a cup-shaped nest of fine plant parts, spider webs, and lichens, fungus, that they place high in a tree. This species breeds in Palawan's dry season of December and in Malaysia's rainy season that starts in May. The female usually lays two eggs.

Fiery minivets and people: The species' beautiful coloring makes it a favorite of birdwatchers.

Conservation status: While extensive and ongoing destruction of forests in this region of Asia presents a continuing threat to fiery minivets and many other birds, the species' use of sub-montane slopes and second-growth forests leads scientists to conclude that it is not immediately threatened. Fiery minivets are common in Palawan and Sumatra, although somewhat rare in Thailand. ∎

FOR MORE INFORMATION

Books:

Sibley, C. G., and B. L. Monroe. *Distribution and Taxonomy of Birds of the World.* New Haven, CT: Yale University Press, 1990.

Stattersfield, A. J., and D. R. Capper, eds. *Threatened Birds of the World: The Official Source for Birds on the IUCN Red List.* Cambridge, U.K.: BirdLife International, 2000.

Periodicals:

Ripley, S. D. "Notes on the Genus *Coracina*." *Auk* 58 (1941): 381–395.

Web sites:

"Fiery Minivet." BirdLife International. http://www.birdlife.net/datazone/search/species_search.html?action=SpcHTMDetails.asp&sid=5973&m=0 (accessed on June 13, 2004).

"Cuckoo-shrike." The Encyclopedia Mauritiana. http://www.encyclopedia.mu/Nature/Fauna/Birds/Endemic/Cuckoo-shrike.htm (accessed on June 25, 2004).

"Fiery Minivet." *The Red Data Book: Threatened Birds of Asia.* Online at http://www.rdb.or.id/view_html.php?id=543&op=periigne (accessed on June 25, 2004).

BULBULS

Pycnonotidae

Class: Aves

Order: Passeriformes

Family: Pycnontidae

Number of species: 131 species

family
CHAPTER

PHYSICAL CHARACTERISTICS

Bulbuls have short, concave (curved in) wings. They have long tails for the size of their bodies. Most of them have tails that are square or rounded. Bulbuls have slender, notched bills. Most bulbuls have stiff bristles near the edges of the beak opening. Their nostrils are either oval or long. Bulbuls' toes and legs are weak and short. Some species are noted for their full and showy crest on their head.

Bulbuls are not noted for their bright colors. The basic colors are dull brown, olive green, and gray, though some of the species do have markings such as yellow underparts, or faces with red, yellow, orange, or white plumage. These brighter colors are only on the throat, undertails, head, or ears. The parts on the upper portions are usually the same color or shades of color. In several species the tail is either rust-red or reddish brown. The size of the various species varies, and a bulbul can range from 3.6 to 11.5 inches (9.3 to 29 centimeters). They can weigh between 0.5 and 2 ounces (14 to 57 grams). The male and female birds vary little in appearance, but the female is usually smaller.

GEOGRAPHIC RANGE

Bulbuls can be found throughout tropical southern Asia in the forest and wooded areas of Africa, particularly in Kenya, and on Madagascar, the Indian Ocean islands, India, Sri Lanka, southern China, the Philippines, Indonesia, and Japan. The common bulbul is one of the most common birds of Africa. An estimated fifty-two species reside in Africa, and China has approximately twenty-seven species.

phylum

class

subclass

order

monotypic order

suborder

▲ **family**

The red-whiskered bulbul was introduced to Florida in 1960, and by 1973 there were five hundred birds in an increasing population that expanded southward. By the late 1960s, the same species was established in Los Angeles County, California. The red-whiskered bulbul and the red-vented bulbul were both introduced to Oahu, Hawaii, in the late 1960s. The population of both birds is large there.

HABITAT

Bulbuls are arboreal, living in trees. They live in a variety of areas, including forests, open woodlands, and even gardens created by humans. Some African and Indonesian species live in the interior of the forest. Some like open areas just outside the forest, or forest clearings. Species that have adapted to drier habitats can find homes in cultivated areas. Other bulbuls like to live near water and can be found near rivers or forest streams. The African red-eyed bulbul has adapted to a drier climate and can be found in such areas as savanna (grassland with few trees), semiarid scrub, and bushy hillsides. The common bulbul, also referred to as the African bulbul, is spread throughout Africa, making it the most common of the bulbuls on that continent.

DIET

Bulbuls tend to be omnivores, eating both plants and animals. The diet across the various species ranges from fruits and berries to insects and other arthropods (invertebrates, animals without backbones, with jointed bodies), in addition to small vertebrates, animals with a backbone, including frogs, snakes, and lizards. Some bulbuls have very specific diets; the green-tailed bristle-bill eats only insects in a very specific area, which is made up of a narrow horizontal layer of forest vegetation.

BEHAVIOR AND REPRODUCTION

Bulbuls that are found in forests tend to be secretive. By contrast, those found in garden settings or parks can be bold and gregarious, social. Bulbuls can be very social and are found in groups with their own species and with other species. The spotted greenbul, for instance, is extremely gregarious and travels in a group with other greenbuls in flocks that might have from five to fifty birds. This group never stays too long in one place, even when food is plentiful. Other species that are social, the striated bulbul and the yellow-streaked bulbul, also live in active flocks.

Many bulbuls show aggressive behavior toward members of their own species in addition to those of other species.

Most bulbuls have distinctive singing voices—from chattering to whistles. The chance of hearing a bulbul in a tropical forest is high, and they are usually heard before they are seen. Though few are musical, some bulbuls have beautiful and melodious songs, including the yellow-spotted nicator in West Africa, and the yellow-crowned bulbul, found in Borneo. The greenbul is noted for its constant singing throughout the day, all year long.

Bulbuls as a whole are not migratory, moving to other places seasonally, though some species that are adapted to the cooler climates and temperate zones would be considered partly migratory. The black bulbul, for instance, migrates in flocks of several hundred birds at a time to southern China in the winter months. Brown-eared bulbuls that have been banded and recaptured have been shown to migrate within the Japanese islands. Other bulbuls are sedentary, stay in one place, and might move only a few hundred yards (meters) over a period of several years. Most bulbuls live and travel in pairs, or in family groups, complete with its juvenile members.

Bulbul reproduction can vary. It depends on the climate and region. Breeding can be connected to rainfall, with some species breeding before and after the monsoon, rainy, season. Some species breed year-round, even through the rainy seasons. Most are monogamous (muh-NAH-guh-mus; having only one mating partner) and territorial. Mating rituals vary as well, with some species chasing each other while calling out in a soft tone. In most species, both parents usually work on the nest, though in some species it is only the female. Bulbuls generally have a clutch size (number of eggs in the nest) of two, with three for the yellow-whiskered bulbul and one for the West African nicator. Some of the Asian species can have clutches of four or five. The incubation period, time spent sitting on the nest before hatching, varies for the different species but can last from eleven to fourteen days.

BULBULS AND PEOPLE

People have been listening to the song and chatter of bulbuls for centuries. They are often prized as pet birds due to their singing. Some of these birds have had roles in folk tales where they live. In Ghana, West Africa, for instance, natives refer to the swamp greenbul as the "talky-talky bird." Children will not eat the meat of the bird due to the superstition that they will never stop talking if they do. Due to both abuses and diminishing populations because of capture for the bird market, the government of Thailand has required permits for owning the birds since 1992—owning some of these species is considered a sign of wealth and prestige in Thailand. Some have been used in bird fights. In 2001, five hundred captured bulbuls were found in passage to the south of Thailand.

CONSERVATION STATUS

Two species are considered Endangered, facing a very high risk of extinction, and five have been described as Vulnerable, facing a high risk of extinction. One of these, the streak-breasted bulbul, is native to four different Philippine islands and has lost much of its habitat. Even though it does live in open areas, under some circumstances forests also appear to be necessary for its survival. In addition to protecting habitat, further study of the birds' behavior is necessary so we can fully understand what they need to continue to survive.

Common bulbul *(Pycnonotus barbatus)*

Resident

COMMON BULBUL
Pycnonotus barbatus

Physical characteristics: The common bulbul is normally 3.6 to 4.2 inches (9.1 to 11 centimeters), and can weigh from 0.8 to 2.1 ounces (23 to 60 grams). They tend to be the size of thrushes with a dark crest on the head, dark eye-ring, and a black bill. Upperparts tend to be grayish brown, with a similarly colored breast, a white belly, and a white or yellow undertail. Both sexes are similar in appearance, though the female is slightly smaller. Young birds are duller in color than adults, and have rusty tones.

Geographic range: The common bulbul can be found in Africa south of 20° north latitude, except in the dry southwestern regions

The common bulbul is found in many parts of Africa, in wooded or bush areas, especially those near water. (© W. Tarboton/ VIREO. Reproduced by permission.)

of the continent and near the Cape of Good Hope on Africa's southern tip.

Habitat: The common bulbul thrives in wooded or bush areas, especially those near water.

Diet: Common bulbuls are omnivores, eating various wild and cultivated fruits, flowers, termites, and other insects, in addition to small lizards.

Behavior and reproduction: The common bulbul is monogamous and has been observed to mate for life. Birds pair through a preening ceremony and duet singing. Two to five eggs are laid in a shallow, thin, cup-like nest in a bush or shrub, and the bird lays eggs twice in a season. The incubation period is twelve to fourteen days, most often with only the female sitting on the eggs. Young are cared for by both parents.

Common bulbuls and people: The common bulbul has no particular significance to humans.

Conservation status: This species is not threatened and is plentiful over a wide area. The common bulbul is Kenya's most common bird. ■

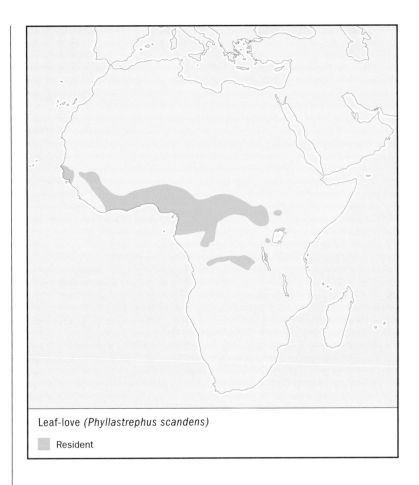

Leaf-love *(Phyllastrephus scandens)*

Resident

LEAF-LOVE
Phyllastrephus scandens

Physical characteristics: The leaf-love species of bulbul generally has a gray head, with a dull gray-olive back, and a bright, rusty tail. The feathers of the tail and rump are full, and the nape of the neck and area near the bill has a light cover of black bristles. The belly of the bird is colored yellow with creamy white undertones. Both sexes are similar. The juvenile bird is also olive-gray with a rusty tone, the chin and the underparts are white, and the undertail is a pale rust.

Leaf-love bulbuls are usually about 5.9 inches (15 centimeters) in length, with a weight range of 1.1 to 1.9 ounces (33 to 53 grams).

Geographic range: Leaf-loves are found in east central Africa, as well as Sudan, western Gambia, Senegal, Guinea, Sierra Leone, Liberia, Mali, Ivory Coast, Ghana, Togo, Nigeria, Cameroon, Gabon, southern Congo, Central African Republic, and Democratic Republic of the Congo.

Habitat: Leaf-love bulbuls live in forests and in the brush and shrub undergrowth, and small trees near water.

Diet: The leaf-love bulbuls are omnivores and scout for food in trees, on the ground, and in any vegetation, feeding on insects and their larvae, small snails, seeds, and berries.

Behavior and reproduction: Leaf-loves are territorial in their habits during breeding season. The nest, which appears as almost being too small, is cup-shaped and suspended in twigs by cobwebs. The female incubates the eggs alone.

Leaf-love bulbuls scout for food in trees, on the ground, and in any vegetation. (Illustration by Brian Cressman. Reproduced by permission.)

Leaf-loves and people: Leaf-loves have no special significance to humans.

Conservation status: The leaf-love bulbul is common throughout its native area, and is not threatened even though its distribution is fragmented. ∎

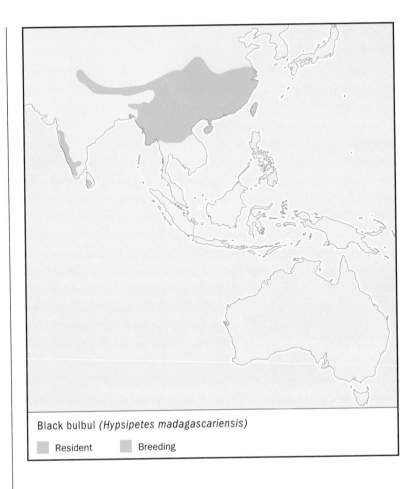

Black bulbul *(Hypsipetes madagascariensis)*

■ Resident ■ Breeding

BLACK BULBUL
Hypsipetes madagascariensis

Physical characteristics: The black bulbul is approximately 7.8 to 10 inches in length (20 to 25.4 centimeters). The bird can be slate gray to shimmering black in color, with a crest that is less than full, but fluffy, and has a forked tail. The black bulbul has bright red legs and feet. Variations among the species include some black bulbuls that have a white head. The birds that live in the western regions of the distribution have plumage that is grayer. Both sexes are similar. The juvenile bird lacks a crest or has one that is not as defined or pronounced, with a white-colored throat and plumage that is grayish brown.

Geographic range: Black bulbuls are native throughout Madagascar (from which they have received their scientific name, *madagascariensis*), the islands of the Indian Ocean, and the mountainous areas of Pakistan, India, Bangladesh, Sri Lanka, India, southern China, Taiwan, Hainan, Myanmar, and Indochina.

Habitat: Black bulbuls prefer tall forests with broad-leaf trees as well as the shade trees of plantations, and tend to live in the mountainous regions of tropical south Asia.

Diet: The black bulbuls are omnivores that feed on seeds and insects.

Black bulbuls are very social, traveling in small or large noisy flocks of up to several hundred birds. (© R. Tipper/VIREO. Reproduced by permission.)

Behavior and reproduction: Black bulbuls are extremely social, often traveling in large, noisy flocks of several hundred; but they are also known to gather in small groups, also noisy and social. They have a variety of screeching noises, are swift in flight, and are one of the few species of bulbuls to migrate.

Black bulbuls breed from March through September, and build their nest high in the trees, and sometimes in the brush. Each clutch has two to four eggs.

Black bulbuls and people: Black bulbuls have no special significance to humans.

Conservation status: The black bulbul shows no signs of extinction and is common in its native areas. ▪

FOR MORE INFORMATION

Books:

Alsop, Fred J. III. *Birds of North America.* Smithsonian Books. London and New York: Dorling Kindersley Publishing, 2001.

Bennun, Leon, and Peter Njoroge. *Important Birds of Kenya.* Bedfordshire, U.K.: Royal Society for the Protection of Birds, 1999.

Campbell, Brude, and Elizabeth Lack, eds. *A Dictionary of Birds.* Vermillion, SD: Buteo Books, 1985.

Lewis, Adrian, and Derek Pomeroy. *A Bird Atlas of Kenya.* Lisse, Netherlands: Swets and Zeitlinger, 1988.

Simpson, Ken, and Nicolas Day. *The Birds of Australia, A Book of Identification.* Dover, NH: Tanager Books, 1984.

Williams, John George, and Norman Arlott. *The Collins Field Guide to the Birds of East Africa.* Brattleboro, VT: Stephen Greene Press, 1992.

Zimmerman, Dale A., Donald A. Turner, and David J. Pearson. *Birds of Kenya and Northern Tanzania.* Princeton, NJ: Princeton University Press, 1999.

Web sites:

"Black Bulbul." Science Daily. http://www.sciencedaily.com (accessed on May 5, 2004).

"Leaf-love." Science Daily. http://www.sciencedaily.com (accessed on May 5, 2004).

"*Pycnonotus barbatus.*" Kenya Birds. http://www.kenyabirds.org.uk (accessed on May 5, 2004).

FAIRY BLUEBIRDS AND LEAFBIRDS
Irenidae

Class: Aves
Order: Passeriformes
Family: Irenidae
Number of species: 14 species

PHYSICAL CHARACTERISTICS

Fairy bluebirds and leafbirds range in length from about 6 to 11 inches (13 to 30 centimeters), and weigh, on average, about 0.5 to 2.8 ounces (13 to 80 grams). Their toes are relatively small for their size, and their ankle bones are short and thick. The birds' bills are fairly heavy. The fairy bluebird adult males are the color of an ultramarine to a turquoise, or cobalt blue, with the color going down over the lower tail. The rest of the bird is the color of black velvet or deep blue. Females are duller in color than the males, as are the juvenile birds. However, the juveniles differ from the females due to their lack of a bright red iris. In leafbirds, both male and female have very bright green plumage, feathers. Fairy bluebirds and leafbirds are similar to bulbuls in that many of their feathers are shed when they are handled.

The four iora species have patterns with various shades of yellow and dull green, and black in some males. All but the great iora have dark wings contrasted with white bars in both males and females. The eyes are pale gray. Their beaks are black, thin, and not curved. Nonbreeding male ioras have dull plumage.

Fairy bluebirds and leafbirds share two characteristics with bulbuls. Those similarities are that the upper tail coverts, feathers at the base of the tail, are long and fluffy, and the patch of hair-like feathers that have no veins on the nape of the neck. They also share the vocal ability that most bulbuls have.

phylum

class

subclass

order

monotypic order

suborder

▲ **family**

GEOGRAPHIC RANGE

Fairy bluebirds and leafbirds can be found throughout Asia, in southern China, Indochina, the Malay Peninsula, the Greater Sundas, and in India. Some species have limited distribution such as the Marshall's iora that is found only in tropical Pakistan and northwestern India, or the yellow-throated leafbird that can be found only on the western Philippine island of Palawan and some its tiny satellite islands. The Philippines mark the eastern boundary for these birds.

HABITAT

None of the fairy bluebirds live on the ground or in the undergrowth, but instead strictly inhabit tree canopies of deciduous or coniferous forests, in the higher branches. Some leafbirds do visit gardens regularly. The ioras have a wider range of dwellings and might be found on beaches or mangrove swamps to secondary forests. They are also found in gardens or orchards.

DIET

In general, the birds of this family are fruit eaters and nectar-feeders, as in the case of the leafbird, though they also eat insects and spiders, as well as eat small fruits such as the oriental mistletoes. Ioras are known to eat fruit, but tend to hunt in pairs for caterpillars, moths, and spiders, moving quickly from branch to branch, and sometimes even hanging upside down in order to find their prey or feed.

BEHAVIOR AND REPRODUCTION

Both ioras and fairy bluebirds roam in flocks. As a rule, they do so with other species. Fairy bluebirds associate with birds that include feeding fruit pigeons and bulbuls. Ioras associate with those of a similar size that are also insect eaters. Leafbirds are also nomadic except during the breeding season, but usually travel in smaller groups or pairs. They are known for their aggression toward other birds and are gifted with the ability to mimic other species.

All three of these groups of birds are monogamous (muh-NAH-guh-mus), meaning that they have only one partner during the breeding season, and also exercise territorial rights during that time. They exhibit differences in the months they breed, varying with location. The common iora nests from May to September, Marshall's iora only breeds from June to August in the drier ranges of Pakistan and northwest India.

Ioras have a mating ritual during which the male becomes a brightly colored vision in contrast to his normal state of being inconspicuous. The male begins by chasing the female, then perches with his wings lowered and proceeds to fluff up his lower back feathers. The male then lifts the tail and gives its call, which consists of hissing sounds. It jumps back and forth above its perch with the white back feathers fluffed, and then goes back to its perch slowly in a spiral while making a sound like a cricket or tree frog.

Fairy bluebirds build their nests at least 16.5 feet (5 meters) up in the forks of trees and the lower canopy. It is a rough sort of platform made of long, thick twigs hidden with a cover of roots and moss, with an open cup formed in the middle for the eggs. The clutch is two or three eggs that are greenish white to olive-gray, with brown splotches, and a grayish purple often coming together into a cap over the wide end of the egg. Observations have indicated that only the female builds the nest, though both male and female parents feed the young.

FAIRY BLUEBIRDS, LEAFBIRDS, AND PEOPLE

Ioras provide humans with a natural form of insect control. Leafbirds pollinate flowering trees, and spread the seeds of the parasitic oriental mistletoe between trees.

Leafbirds are well-represented in art, with the Chinese depicting them since at least the fifteenth century. Many other varieties of this family have been prized as well for their beauty and were shipped commercially in the late nineteenth and early twentieth centuries. Before World War II, India was the largest supplier of these birds. By the 1950s and 1960s, Thailand, and then Indonesia were major sources. By the 1990s, China exported them until a ban was imposed on caged birds in 2001. Indonesia then played the key role in their export. Their tendency to fight with other birds has made them unsuitable for mixed groups of species.

CONSERVATION STATUS

The green iroa, Sumatran blue-masked leafbird, and lesser green leafbird are listed as Near Threatened, in danger of becoming threatened with extinction. The Philippine leafbird is considered Vulnerable, facing a high risk of extinction, due to forest destruction resulting in loss of habitat. In general, many of the species have suffered some loss of habitat, though minimal, and with a wide distribution they are not threatened on a global level.

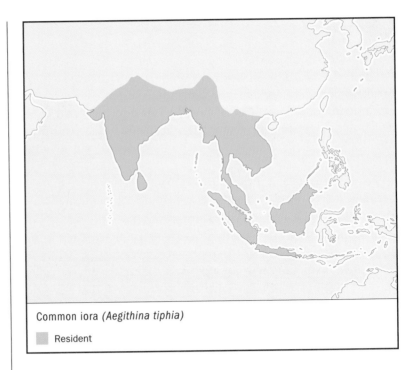

Common iora (*Aegithina tiphia*)

     Resident

COMMON IORA
Aegithina tiphia

Physical characteristics: The common iora ranges in length from 5.5 to 6 inches (13 to 17 centimeters), and has a weight that averages about a 0.5 ounces (13.5 grams). The females are olive-green on their upperparts, with dull yellow underparts, foreheads, and eyebrows, with olive-green crowns. The males have dark green to black upperparts, very bright yellow underparts, black wings with white bars, dark tails, and black crowns.

Geographic range: The common iora can be found throughout almost the entire Indian subcontinent, Sri Lanka, southern Yunnan and southwestern Guanxi in China, all of Myanmar, Indochina, and the Malay Peninsula, Sumatra, Java, Borneo, and Palawan.

Habitat: The common iora dwells in open woodlands, secondary forests, gardens, orchards, mangroves, and beach forests.

Diet: Common ioras are omnivores, but have a diet consisting of arthropods which includes spiders, moths, caterpillars, and other similar insects that can be found on leaves. They also eat some fruit.

Behavior and reproduction: When they are not breeding, common ioras tend to travel in small flocks, or pairs, as they continually hunt for their food. Contact among the birds is made through vocalizing often. Their songs and whistles are both distinctive as well as pleasant.

The common iora is monogamous. The male has specific behaviors for courtship as described in the earlier section on the family of fairy bluebirds, leaping 3.3 to 6.6 feet (1 to 2 meters) above its perch, then gliding down with erect feathers, and taking on the appearance of a sphere-like shape. The nest is deep and cup-shaped, with a clutch of two to four eggs that are white with a pink tint and brown or purple-colored blotches.

The common iora is not threatened, and has likely widened its range due to the creation of gardens and orchards, where it can live. (© M. Strange/VIREO. Reproduced by permission.)

Common ioras and people: The common iora provides insect control in fruit orchards by feeding on caterpillars and other harmful insects.

Conservation status: This species is not threatened. Due to the creation of gardens and orchards, it is most likely that the common iora has widened its habitat range.   ◼

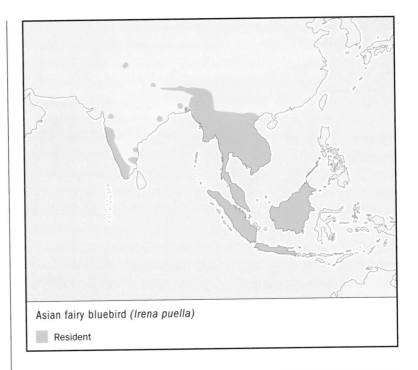

Asian fairy bluebird (*Irena puella*)

■ Resident

ASIAN FAIRY BLUEBIRD
Irena puella

Physical characteristics: The Asian fairy bluebird has a sturdy build, with a length of 10 inches, (25 centimeters), and a weight of 2.5 ounces (75 grams). The male has black under parts, wings, and tail, with ultramarine blue upperparts and feathers under the tail. Females are dark turquoise-blue all over with black flight feathers. Both male and female have red eyes.

Geographic range: The Asian fairy bluebird can be found on the coast of southern India, in the eastern Himalayas, Myanmar, Yunnan, Indochina, Malay Peninsula, Java, Sumatra, Borneo, and the western Philippine island of Palawan.

Habitat: Asian fairy bluebirds can be found living primarily in primary and tall secondary forests.

Diet: Asian fairy bluebirds are omnivores, eating insects and nectar. Their primary source of food is fruit, especially preferring figs.

Behavior and reproduction: These birds can be found in flocks of up to thirty birds, and dwell mostly in the upper parts of the forest. They will bathe in streams, only to return to ascend again, returning to the higher locations. Asian fairy bluebirds are known for their melodious whistle.

Asian fairy bluebirds and people: These birds have no special significance to humans.

Conservation status: Asian fairy bluebirds are not threatened due to their broad distribution. Some populations are at risk, however, because of forest destruction in some areas. ■

FOR MORE INFORMATION

Books:

Campbell, Brude, and Elizabeth Lack, eds. *A Dictionary of Birds.* Vermillion, SD: Buteo Books, 1985.

Web sites:

"Fairy-bluebirds (Irenidae)." Monterey Bay. http://www.montereybay.com/creagrus/fairy-bluebirds.html (accessed on May 5, 2004).

"Fairy Bluebird." Science Daily. http://www.sciencedaily.com (accessed on May 5, 2004).

"Birds of the National Zoo, Fairy Bluebird." Smithsonian National Zoological Park. http://natzoo.si.edu/Animals/Birds/ (accessed on May 5, 2004).

Asian fairy bluebirds can be found in flocks of up to thirty birds, and live mostly in the upper parts of the forest. (© S. Lipschutz/VIREO. Reproduced by permission.)

Class: Aves

Order: Passeriformes

Family: Laniidae

Number of species: 74 species

family

CHAPTER

phylum

class

subclass

order

monotypic order

suborder

▲ **family**

PHYSICAL CHARACTERISTICS

Shrikes range in size from 5.7 to 19.6 inches (14.5 to 50 centimeters) and can weigh anywhere from 0.6 to 3.52 ounces (18 to 100 grams). They are predatory birds, living by feeding on other animals, and they usually have sharply hooked, raptor-like beaks and powerful legs. With so many species in the family, shrikes' coloring varies widely. Some are vividly colored in greens, reds, and yellows, such as the yellow-crowned gonolek and the gray-headed bush shrike, but many others are dramatically patterned with black masks and wing bars, showing pure white underneath and deep black, gray, or russet, a reddish brown, upperparts. The helmet shrikes are known for their bristly feathers on their forehead and, usually, colored wattles, fleshy folds of skin, around their eyes. Except for a few species, including the red-backed shrike, males and females of this family do not look very different. Young shrikes tend to be brown and have many wavy lines and patterns throughout their plumage, feathers.

GEOGRAPHIC RANGE

Shrikes appear throughout the world in Europe, Asia, Africa, North America, Russia, and New Guinea. Virtually all of the bush-shrike species live in Africa, while the helmet-shrikes and the true shrikes live in sub-Saharan Africa. Of the true shrikes, the loggerhead is the only species to occupy North America. The other species are more widespread.

HABITAT

Just as shrikes inhabit many different areas of the world, they also live in many kinds of environments. For instance, many of the larger bush-shrikes occupy lowland and montane woodland up to 9,800 feet (3,000 meters), tending to keep to canopies, upper level of the forest, of trees or their undergrowth. Some shrikes, including the puffbacks, like to live in the tops of high trees in suburban gardens, whereas gonoleks and boubous prefer to look for prey near the ground in thick vegetation and scrub. Except for the marsh tchagra, tchagra shrikes search out dry, semi-open habitat with thick vegetation. Helmet shrikes are common in savannas and open woodlands, and are sometimes even seen in peoples' gardens. The true shrikes, meanwhile, require semi-open habitats with trees for perching so they can look down onto their hunting grounds.

A FULL CUPBOARD IS A TURN ON

With their habit of impaling their prey on thorns and other sharp projections in their environment, loggerheads often create what biologists believe are "larders," or storehouses of food. These serve to both attract mates, who appreciate good providers, and tide the birds over when there is less prey available.

DIET

Shrikes are generally insect eaters, but the larger bush-shrike species and the true shrikes add to their diet with small mammals and other birds' eggs, as well as berries and small fruits.

BEHAVIOR AND REPRODUCTION

Bush-shrikes, which make up the majority of the shrike family, make neat, cup-shaped nests of grass, fine roots, and small twigs, placing them in trees or bushes and sometimes using spider webs to hold them together or snake skins to decorate them. These birds are known to be territorial and monogamous (muh-NAH-guh-mus), having only one mate. After the breeding season, which is usually begins with the start of the rainy season, female bush-shrikes usually lay two or three eggs. Helmet-shrikes, of which very little is known about their breeding behavior, are cooperative breeders, where a dominant mating pair has a number of helpers that assist in feeding and caring for their nestlings, young birds that are unable to leave the nest. These are called "family parties." Helmet-shrikes make small, cup-shaped nests from bits of bark with spider web decorations. The females lay a clutch of two to five eggs. True shrikes also use cooperative breeding. Their nests are cup shaped as well, but sometimes messily constructed. Females lay clutches of three to eight eggs, and their nestlings remain in the nest for fourteen to twenty-one days. Some of the shrike species put on courtship displays, behaviors that lead to mating, such as males and females singing duets, showy flights, and puffing out their back feathers.

Because most shrike species live in heavily vegetated areas and are sedentary, stay in the same area throughout the year, biologists know relatively little about their behavior, because they are hard to find. Bush-shrikes sometimes give their presence away to birdwatchers by their distinctive, piercing whistles and bell-like sounds, especially those that live in dense bush or tropical forests. Helmet-shrikes, like the true shrikes, are more outgoing and visible, gathering and feeding in groups of up to thirty individuals. Twenty-three of the twenty-five true shrike species are extremely territorial and mark out individual areas for themselves that vary in size depending on the species. They generally practice ritual courtship feeding, where the male feeds the female.

Bush-shrikes tend to feed by rummaging through vegetation at different levels of the forest ecosystem. Helmet-shrikes are noisy, sociable hunters that search the woods from tree base to upper branches. The true shrikes depend upon their patience and sharp vision to catch prey, sitting for long periods on perches until something on the ground draws their deadly attention. However, they also jump into the air to catch insects.

SHRIKES AND PEOPLE

Shrikes have only recently overcome their reputation as "harmful" birds, although they are still hunted and either eaten or used as decoys to capture larger birds of prey. Founded in 1991, the International Shrike Working Group, along with numerous bird groups around the world, is working to protect this bird family and learn more about it.

CONSERVATION STATUS

Nine shrike species, including six bush-shrikes, two helmet-shrikes, and one true shrike, are currently on the World Conservation Union (IUCN) Red List, a list of globally threatened animals, those at risk of extinction. All of them are native to sub-Saharan Africa and all live in forest habitats, which are rapidly being cleared to make way for agriculture that use a lot of pesticides. Five other species are listed as Near Threatened, in danger of becoming threatened with extinction, for the same reason.

White helmet-shrike (*Prionops plumatus*)

▨ Resident

WHITE HELMET-SHRIKE
Prionops plumatus

Physical characteristics: Also known as white-crested helmet-shrikes, white helmet-shrikes are distinguished by their helmet-like ruff of stiff white feathers around their bills and foreheads that blend into a long, erect crest. They range in size from 7.4 to 9.8 inches (19 to 25 centimeters) and typically weigh between 0.9 and 1.3 ounces (25 to 37 grams). Males and females look very similar, but the female is slightly larger. The birds' crown, sides of head, and cheeks are gray, with a dark bar on the sides of and around the neck. Otherwise, the upperparts are greenish black, with a narrow white stripe down the wing. Undersides are bright white, including the underside of the tail. The white-crested helmet has a greenish black bill, yellow eyes

surrounded by a yellow wattle, and orange-yellow legs and feet. Young birds are similarly colored, but more subtly.

Geographic range: White helmet-shrikes are native and locally common in sub-Saharan Africa from the western side of the continent east to Eritrea and south along the eastern side of the continent to South Africa. They may also be found in southern Africa from northern Namibia east and south across northern Botswana and South Africa and south into Mozambique and Swaziland.

Habitat: The dominant breeding pairs live in deciduous broad-leaved woodlands, while subordinate, nonbreeding individuals often move farther out during the winter into savannah and cultivated gardens outside cities. This species will rarely breed in eucalyptus (yoo-kah-LIP-tus) plantations.

Diet: Like the majority of the Laniidae family, white helmet-shrikes forage, search for food, in the canopies of trees as well as on their branches and trunks, and on the ground. They also catch insects in the air on occasion. This species spends most of its foraging time in the winter on the ground, and stays in the trees during warmer seasons. White helmet-shrikes especially favor foraging in areas of recent fires. In general, they eat mainly caterpillars, moths, termites, and grasshoppers, but will also eat spiders and lizards.

Behavior and reproduction: White helmet-shrikes are often seen moving among trees in small flocks of three to twenty-four individuals. Their coloring and undulating, wave-like, flight pattern are unmistakable, as is its group chorus, which has been described as sounding like "krawow, krawow, kreee, kreee, kreepkrow, kreepkrow." They are extremely sociable birds, one calling bird will always cause the others in the group to respond. Growls, bill snaps, and squeaks are also used to alert others about prey, intruders, nesting needs, etc. Dominant and subordinate individuals have different calls. The birds are resident, but not sedentary, and leave their breeding territories to wander their local habitats after the young leave the nest.

White helmet-shrikes become sexually mature at two years of age, although the vast majority never get a chance to breed until they are five years old. This is due to the hierarchical (hi-uh-RAAR-kih-kul), rank, structure of their populations, in which there is only one mating pair allowed within a "family party." Other members of the family party are assistants to the dominant pair. The dominant pair chooses the nest site, but all members of the group help build the nest, incubate the clutch, and guard and feed the nestlings.

Dominance is asserted by nudging others away from food and getting prime spots at the roost, but obvious aggression is unusual. These shrikes are extremely social birds and tend to do everything together: preening, attacking intruders, and foraging. Their noisy communications echo through their forest homes as they coordinate activities among themselves. Groups of helmet-shrikes often join with other species of birds as they move around their territory. However, one group of white helmet-shrikes will firmly defend its territory against another group, with displays of bill snapping, calling, and stretching their heads upward. The face-off ends when members of one group fly at the other, hopefully causing the offending group to retreat.

White helmet-shrikes and people: Although many shrikes are still hunted by humans, white helmet-shrikes have no other special significance to people.

Conservation status: White helmet-shrikes are not threatened.   ■

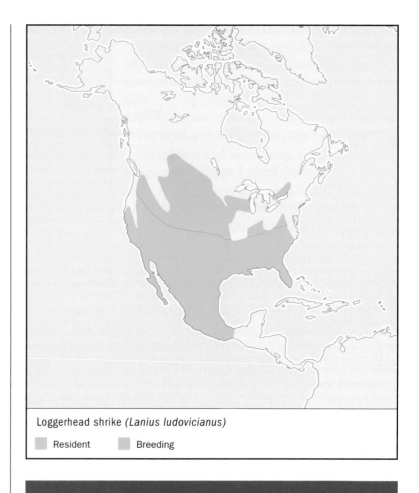

Loggerhead shrike (*Lanius ludovicianus*)

■ Resident ■ Breeding

LOGGERHEAD SHRIKE
Lanius ludovicianus

Physical characteristics: Also known as migrant shrikes and butcherbirds, loggerhead shrikes grow to about 8.2 inches (21 centimeters) long and 1.7 ounces (48 grams) in weight—about as large as a robin. This striking bird is relatively large within the Laniidae family, and has a large head as well, which may be the source of its unusual name. Males and females look similar, with gray, white, and black markings and a black mask that extends to just over the eyes. Their upperparts are gray with white bands at the shoulders, while the bottom half of the wing is black. Undersides are white and sometimes have a barred texture. The loggerhead's appearance varies subtly by region throughout its range.

Geographic range: The only shrike native to North America, the loggerhead also occupies large areas of Mexico, Alaska, and Canada, although its Canadian and Alaskan ranges shrink considerably during winter.

Habitat: Loggerhead shrikes live in many types of semi-open habitats that are dominated by short vegetation. Those native to Illinois, New York, and Maryland frequent pastures, while those endemic to western states prefer sagebrush, desert scrub, and pinyon-juniper woodlands with small shrubby trees. Residential areas with suitable perches often have a number of loggerhead shrikes occupying them, and the birds have been recorded in mountainous areas up to 6,600 feet (2,000 meters) as well.

Diet: Loggerheads eat mainly arthropods, invertebrates (animals without backbones) that have segmented bodies, but seem to prefer beetles and grasshoppers. They feed on small vertebrates, animals with backbones, such as mice, moles, lizards, small birds and snakes, bats, and fish, especially in winter.

Loggerhead shrikes impale their prey on fences or thorned branches to anchor it while they eat. (© Maslowski/Photo Researchers, Inc. Reproduced by permission.)

Behavior and reproduction: Loggerhead shrikes kill their vertebrate prey by quickly breaking their necks and using their sharp, heavy bills, which have a special cutting tooth on the upper part, to sever the spinal cord. The birds carry prey up weighing as much as their own body weight to a fence or thorny bush where they can impale their meal. This technique also allows them to anchor their prey as they dismember and eat them, since their claws are not strong enough for this purpose.

The loggerhead's flight pattern is distinctive, characterized by wing fluttering followed by a glide. When hunting, the birds swoop down from their perch, hover briefly over an area of open ground, and then flap up to another perch.

This species mates in the spring, during which they are most vocal. They do not have a song, but rather a series of sounds more like shrieks or a metallic tapping. Loggerheads are sexually mature at one year, and are usually monogamous, although sometimes a female will mate with a second male and have a second brood during breeding season. Loggerheads sometimes even mate with other species of shrikes. They prefer to mate and raise their young in grassy pastures, shrubs or small trees, on utility wires, or high up in dead trees. Both sexes gather the nest materials, but the female alone makes the structure. The female lays a clutch of five to seven eggs and then begins to incubate them for about sixteen days. The male feeds her during this period. Both parents feed the nestlings, which remain under their care constantly for seventeen to twenty days. The young stay near the nest after fledging, growing the feathers needed for flight, returning at night to be warmed by the female parent, and they receive food from both parents for up to three weeks after leaving the nest. Soon after, the family group breaks up and the individuals begin migration.

Loggerhead shrikes and people: Humans are increasingly appreciative of the loggerhead's ability to control local populations of pest insects and mammals. These birds are also of major interest to conservationists, because their numbers are decreasing for no apparent reason. However, habitat fragmentation and destruction are thought to be major causes.

Conservation status: Loggerhead shrikes are considered endangered, facing a risk of extinction, in Quebec, Canada, but otherwise it is not yet officially on the threatened list. One of its subspecies, the San Clemente loggerhead, is highly endangered, although conservation efforts have improved its outlook. ■

FOR MORE INFORMATION

Books:

Harris, T. *Shrikes and Bush-shrikes.* Princeton, NJ and Oxford, U.K.: Princeton University Press, 2000.

Lefranc, N. *Shrikes: A Guide to the Shrikes of the World.* New Haven, CT and London: Yale University Press, 1997.

Periodicals:

Van Nieuwenhuyse, D. "Global Shrike Conservation: Problems, Methods, and Opportunities." *Aves* 36 (1999): 193–204.

Web sites:

"Birds: Loggerhead Shrike." Hinterland Who's Who. http://www.hww.ca/hww2.asp?pid=1&id=52&cid=7 (accessed on July 2, 2004).

"Helmet-Shrikes *Prionopinae.*" Bird Families of the World http://www.montereybay.com/creagrus/helmet-shrikes.html (accessed on July 2, 2004).

family

PHYSICAL CHARACTERISTICS

Vanga species look so different from one another that only ornithologists, scientists who study birds, and DNA comparisons have been able to find enough similarities among them to realize that they are related species within one family. Males and females of most vanga species have different colors and patterns. Colors among species vary enormously. The three closely related species Lafresnaye's vanga, Van Damm's vanga, and Pollen's vanga, are similar in appearance, both males and females sporting differing patterns of sharply defined black, white, and gray. The head may be entirely black or only partly so, the rest white. Bernier's vanga is simple in design but striking in appearance, with a glossy black body and head, white eye, and blue bill and legs. The female outshines the male, her entire coat being a bright red-brown with narrow, black streaks. Perhaps the most beautiful and memorable of all vanga species is the blue vanga, with its vivid ultramarine blue head, wings, and bill, white underside, white eyes enclosed by a black mask, and a blue and black tail.

As a whole, vangas are small birds. The largest species are the sickle-billed vanga, with a beak-to-tail length of 12.5 inches (32 centimeters) and a body weight of slightly over 4 ounces (114 grams); the helmet vanga, with a length of 12 inches (31 centimeters) and a body weight of 3.8 ounces (108 grams); and the hook-billed vanga, with a length of 11 inches (29 centimeters) and a weight of 2.5 ounces (67 grams). The smallest species are the red-tailed vanga and Chabert's vanga, both 5.5 inches (14 centimeters) long and weighing only 0.5 ounces (14 grams), and the blue vanga, 6 inches (16 centimeters) long and weighing just under 1 ounce (28 grams). Head-and-body lengths for other species run 8 to 10 inches (20 to 25 centimeters).

The original beak of the ancestral vanga species went through some extreme shape changes in descendant species. The helmet vanga sports a big, casque-like (KASK-like) bill reminiscent of the bills of hornbills or toucans. The sickle-billed vanga has a thin, almost needle-like bill, curved downward, that may reach nearly 3 inches (7 centimeters) in length. The bill of the hook-billed vanga is straight, with a small, downturned hook at the end of the upper bill. Van Damm's vanga, Lafresnaye's vanga, and Pollen's vanga share a very unusual bill type. The bill is thick, strong, deep vertically and narrow horizontally, giving it a distinctive chisel shape, and fit for the chisel-like work of prying bark from trees, prior to yanking insects out of the wood.

GEOGRAPHIC RANGE

Vangas occupy varying ranges in the forested parts of Madagascar, a large island off the southeastern coast of Africa. One species, the blue vanga, is the only species found outside of Madagascar, it also lives on the Comoro Islands between Madagascar and Africa.

HABITAT

All vangas are forest species, and are found in all the major forest types of Madagascar, which includes tropical rainforest along the east coast, tropical deciduous forest (with a rainy and a dry, rainless season) along the west coast, and the so-called "spiny forest" (or xeric [ZEHR-ik] forest) in the arid south. Some species also forage in scrub.

DIET

All vanga species are primarily insectivorous, feeding mostly on insects and related creatures like spiders, although some species add small amounts of fruit to their menus, and some spice up their insect diets with frogs, lizards, snails, mouse lemurs, and young birds.

Vangas consume insects and related creatures by means of four methods: gleaning, or plucking insects off leaves, twigs, branches, and bark while the bird is perching; sally gleaning, or gleaning while flying tight loops about the feeding site; flycatching, in which a bird on the wing snags and eats flying insects; and probing, in which the bird uses its bill to poke under and tear off strips of tree bark to reach insects. A vanga species may use one of these feeding methods, or various combinations.

When handling relatively large prey, too large to be downed in a single gulp, some vanga species engage in "clamping" or "grasping." When clamping, a perching vanga, having caught the prey with its bill, transfers it to one of the perching feet, which holds the prey against the branch. When grasping, a vanga holds the prey in an outstretched foot that is not grasping a branch. In either case, the vanga then tears apart and eats its prey.

Vangas may forage together in mixed-species flocks of two or more vanga species and sometimes including insectivorous bird species of other families, for protection in numbers and for helping one another find food.

BEHAVIOR AND REPRODUCTION

Little is known about reproductive behavior. Mating and raising of chicks for most species takes place from October through January, although breeding times are not known for all vanga species. Two exceptions are the nuthatch vanga and Bernier's vanga, which nest through August and September.

A female lays from one to four eggs. The eggs are variously colored among species. The nests so far observed have been bowl-shaped and built on branches or in forks of branches. The nests are woven from various types of plant materials, such as leaf stalks, twigs, moss, and rootlets. Several vanga species reinforce the weaving with spider webs.

VANGAS AND PEOPLE

No vangas are pest species, since they are confined to forested areas away from agricultural land and have little interaction with humans. In Madagascar's growing ecotourism industry, vangas play a starring role as symbols of the uniqueness of Madagascar's animal life.

CONSERVATION STATUS

The World Conservation Union (IUCN) lists three vanga species as Vulnerable, facing a high risk of extinction, and one as Endangered, facing a very high risk of extinction. The species listed as Vulnerable are the red-shouldered vanga, due to restricted territory and a small population; Bernier's vanga, because of its small population and deforestation; and the helmet vanga, because of limited territory and deforestation. Van Dam's vanga is listed as Endangered due to its very small range and fragmented populations.

Rufous vanga (*Schetba rufa*)

Resident

RUFOUS VANGA
Schetba rufa

Physical characteristics: Bill-to-tail length is 8 inches (20 centimeters). The male has a black head, neck, and chest, with blue highlights. The bill is blue-gray, the eyes are dark red, the upperparts are reddish brown and the belly is white. The wings are red-brown and brown. The female is similarly colored, the differences being white cheeks, chin, and throat on the otherwise black head, and a gray collar.

Geographic range: The rufous vanga lives in Madagascar, in rainforest along most of the east coast, and in tropical deciduous forest in the northwest.

Habitat: The rufous vanga prefers undisturbed rainforest from sea level to 5,400 feet (1,800 meters) above sea level, and undisturbed or slightly disturbed tropical deciduous forest.

Diet: The rufous vanga feeds mainly on insects and occasionally on small lizards.

Behavior and reproduction: The rufous vanga picks insects and lizards from branches and tree trunks or flushes them from ground litter. Of the various vanga species, this vanga spends the most time foraging on the ground. Often an individual sits on a low branch for long periods of time, watching for moving prey. The rufous vanga sometimes follows another bird, the white-breasted mesite (family Mesitornithidae). The mesite runs through ground litter, flushing out insects and other small animals for its own feeding, the vanga helping itself to some. It is not a mutually beneficial relationship; the vanga merely takes advantage of the mesite's feeding tactic.

Rufous vangas live in groups of four to eight, and may join in mixed-species feeding flocks with other vangas or with bird species other than vangas. (© T. Schulenberg/VIREO. Reproduced by permission.)

Rufous vangas live in groups of four to eight, and may join in mixed-species feeding flocks with other vangas or with bird species other than vangas. Their voice is melodious, and pairs may sing duets, often punctuated by clacking their bills.

The rufous vanga is one of the few vanga species whose reproductive biology is even partly known. The breeding period runs October through December, and chicks are born November through January. A female lays one to four eggs. A noteworthy aspect of reproduction in this species, seen in other bird families, is "helping behavior." During the breeding season, a nesting site may be occupied by one or two extra individuals in addition to the nesting pair. These "helpers" will fill in for the parents, sitting on the eggs and even feeding and guarding the chicks while the parents are out feeding. Some of the helpers are immature males, recognized as such by their spotted necks.

Rufous vangas and people: Rufous vangas do not interact with humans in any significant way.

Conservation status: A widespead species in Madagascar, the rufous vanga has no special conservation status. ■

FOR MORE INFORMATION

Books:

Goodman, Steven M., and Jonathan P. Benstead. *The Natural History of Madagascar.* Chicago: University of Chicago Press, 2003.

Langrand, O. *Guide to the Birds of Madagascar.* New Haven, CT: Yale University Press, 1990.

Morris, P., and Hawkins, F. *Birds of Madagascar: A Photographic Guide.* New Haven, CT: Yale University Press, 1998.

Periodicals:

Goodman, S. M., A. F. A. Hawkins, and C. A. Domergue. "A New Species of Vanga (Vangidae) from Southwestern Madagascar." *Bulletin of the British Ornithological Society* 117 (1997): 5–10.

Graetz, J. "Nest Observations of the Helmet Vanga, *Euryceros prevostii.*" *Newsletter of the Working Group on Madagascar Birds* 1, no. 2 (1991).

Safford, Roger. "The Helmet Vanga, *Euryceros prevostii.*" *Bulletin of the African Bird Club* 7, no. 1 (March 2000).

Yamagishi, S., et al. "Extreme Endemic Radiation of the Malagasy Vangas (Aves: Passeriformes)." *Journal of Molecular Evolution* 53, no. 1 (July 2001): 39–46.

Web sites:

Birdlife International. http://www.birdlife.net (accessed on June 20, 2004).

family

CHAPTER

PHYSICAL CHARACTERISTICS

Birds of the Bombycillidae family range in size from about 5.9 to 9.4 inches (15 to 24 centimeters) long and can weigh from 1 to 2.1 ounces (30 to 60 grams). They are sleek, elegantly marked songbirds, with short bills, crested heads, and plump bodies. Waxwings generally have buff-gray bodies with black eye and chin masks. Their contrasting wings have white, yellow, or vivid red patches. Except for the Japanese waxwing, their common name refers to the distinctive red appendages on their secondary flight feathers, which look like drops of wax. Biologists do not know if the spots have a purpose, but they are absent in juveniles. The birds' tail bands are usually yellow, but sometimes orange. Waxwings have very high-pitched chatters, whistles, and warbles that many human ears can miss. Silky flycatchers have longer tails, and their crests look more bristly. These birds are generally brown, black, or gray, and some of the four species have yellow or white patches. The gray hypocolius is a gray bird with a black mask and tail band. Ornithologists, scientists who study birds, continue to debate whether the hypocolius makes up a separate family of birds unrelated to the flycatchers and waxwings.

GEOGRAPHIC RANGE

Each of the three groups has a different range. Waxwings are present across temperate regions of North America, Europe, and Asia, while the cedar waxwing winters as far south as Guatemala. Silky flycatchers occupy habitat from the southern United States into Central America, and the gray hypocolius lives in the Middle East and the Indian subcontinent.

phylum

class

subclass

order

monotypic order

suborder

▲ **family**

HABITAT

Waxwings have become increasingly common in suburban neighborhoods, where they feast on fruits and berry-producing bushes. However, they prefer rows of bushes, shrubs, or trees, and open woodlands. Silky flycatchers and the hypocolius live in dry scrub, characterized by straggly, stunted tree and shrub growth, and desert.

DIET

The staple foods for this family are fruit and berries. Cedar waxwings have a special part of their esophagus in which they store these foods, probably to make the most of the materials they can digest while foraging, searching for food. These birds also eat insects, and will fly after them, pick them off leaves or bark, or dive after them from high perches.

BEHAVIOR AND REPRODUCTION

Birds from the Bombycillidae family are generally outgoing and energetic. Waxwings travel in flocks that can reach into the thousands searching for fruit sources. They are not territorial. Silky flycatchers are more territorial, and nest in casual colonies. Phainopeplas migrate laterally to find wetter habitats after their breeding season ends.

Waxwings are monogamous (muh-NAH-guh-mus), having just one mating partner for the breeding season. The breeding habits of the silky flycatchers and hypocolius are not well known. All of the Bombycillidae species make a small, cup-shaped nest, usually in the strong fork of a tree. Waxwings lay four to six eggs, and silky flycatchers lay two to four. The young birds have no feathers when they hatch, and both parents feed them.

WAXWINGS, SILKY FLYCATCHERS, AND PEOPLE

Because they tend to move suddenly and in large numbers into human areas in search of food, people sometimes view the arrival of these birds as an invasion. Waxwings especially, which tend to fly into windows in suburban areas and to gorge on any berry-producing bushes, are occasionally considered pests.

CONSERVATION STATUS

None of the birds in this family are listed as endangered or threatened. In fact, in North America, populations of cedar waxwings have increased.

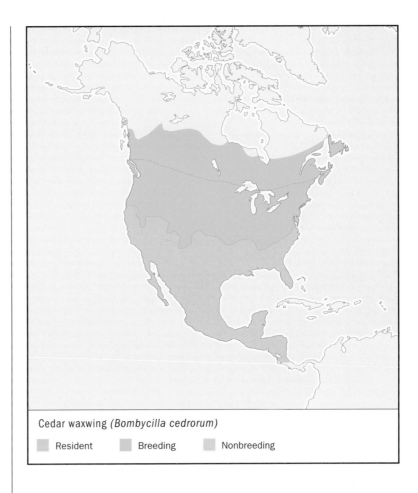

Cedar waxwing (*Bombycilla cedrorum*)

☐ Resident ☐ Breeding ☐ Nonbreeding

CEDAR WAXWING
Bombycilla cedrorum

Physical characteristics: Sleek and elegant birds, cedar waxwings have plumage, feathers, with a silky texture. Weighing in at about 1.2 ounces (32 grams), adult waxwings are usually about 6 inches (15 centimeters) long. They are colored in pale shades of gray and brown, with pale yellow on their breast and belly. The inner feathers of its wings, the secondary flight feathers, end in what look like drops of red wax, and a white-edged black mask covers the eye area at a downward angle, giving them a serious appearance. The average life span of the cedar waxwing is one to five years, but occasionally they live up to seven years.

Geographic range: Found only in North America during most times of the year, cedar waxwings breed mainly in Canada and winter in the southern United States and Mexico. They are common in the central and northeastern United States and Pacific Northwest.

Habitat: Cedar waxwings prefer to stay out of forest interiors, but hang around areas on the outskirts to find food and perching sites. They mainly inhabit abandoned fields and open woodland, as well as grasslands, farms, pine tree plantations, orchards, and suburban gardens, especially when these areas are near streams or rivers.

Diet: This species feeds mainly on fleshy fruits while hanging from branches of trees. They particularly favor cedar or juniper berries during the winter, but will also eat insects. During spring, these waxwings seek out the sweet sap of maple trees, hanging from branches to lick up the drops. Biologists have noted that cedar waxwings occasionally become intoxicated by alcohol in overripe fruit, and have observed the birds falling to the ground, flying into windows, or being hit by cars as they sit dazed in the street.

Behavior and reproduction: Cedar waxwings are very social birds and flock together all year. They rarely do anything on the ground, preferring to preen, to smooth and clean their feathers, and look for insects from high, exposed places. Although they are not territorial, parents may show aggressive behavior at their nest, including mouth opening, crest raising, feather ruffling. Their flight pattern consists of short, direct flights from bush to bush using steady wing beats. They have two basic calls: a high-pitched, quickly repeated buzz or trill and a hiss-like whistle.

This species is monogamous within a breeding season, from June through August. They are one of the last bird species in North America to nest because they rely on the ripening of summer fruit as their cue to breed. Males court their mates by performing a hopping dance and delivering an insect or bit of fruit to her. If the female joins the male in the hopping dance, the pair mates for the season and the female begins choosing the nest site.

Female waxwings often have two broods, groups of young birds that hatch together, per season. Females lay a clutch, a group of eggs, of two to six speckled pale blue-gray eggs in a cup-shaped nest woven of grasses and fine twigs. Females incubate, sit on, the eggs for twelve to fifteen days, after which both parents feed and care for the nestlings, young birds unable to leave the nest. The young fledge, grow the feathers needed for flight, after fourteen to seventeen days and usually go off to join another flock. The young will not begin breeding until the following summer. Occasionally, brown cowbirds lay their eggs in the waxwings' nests to trick the waxwings into taking on their parental duties for them.

Cedar waxwings and people: Many people are first acquainted with these beautiful birds after one smashes into their garden-facing windows. Some people consider them pests because of their greedy consumption of berries and fruits. However they are also very helpful in controlling the insect population.

Conservation status: Populations of this species have increased greatly since the pesticide DDT was banned in the 1970s. They are not a threatened species. ∎

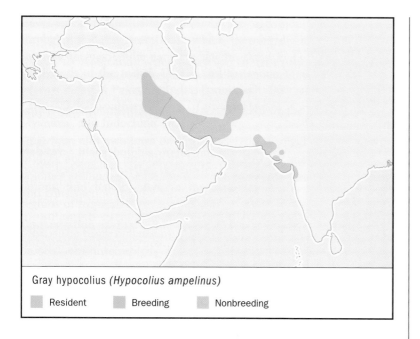

Gray hypocolius (*Hypocolius ampelinus*)

■ Resident   ■ Breeding   ■ Nonbreeding

GRAY HYPOCOLIUS
Hypocolius ampelinus

Physical characteristics: Also known as gray flycatchers, gray hypocoliuses are unique in the family. Adults are generally about 9 inches (23 centimeters) long and weigh about 1.3 to 2 ounces (28 to 55 grams). Gray hypocoliuses are long-tailed birds with a distinctive crest and white markings on their wings. Males are a uniform gray color with a black mask that goes around their heads and a bold black triangular band on their tails. Females are a sandy-brown color with a creamy throat and no mask. Their tail ends are dark. Juveniles are colored like the female.

Geographic range: Gray hypocoliuses are birds of the Middle East and Indian subcontinent, wintering in Saudi Arabia and breeding throughout Iran, Iraq, Turkmenistan, and Pakistan.

Habitat: This species occupies tropical and subtropical areas, especially areas with more dense vegetation and arid, dry, lowlands. They are most often found in river valleys near desert or semidesert, and forage through small tree groupings, irrigated and cultivated areas, palm groves, and broad-leaf scrub.

The gray hypocolius is difficult to study, partly because it is a skittish and shy bird, not easy to find, and flies immediately to dense vegetation when it's disturbed. (Illustration by Jacqueline Mahannah. Reproduced by permission.)

Diet: Gray hypocoliuses eat mostly fruit, but sometimes insects as well. They rarely go to the ground, instead looking through foliage, leaves, for food. They are known for their careful and deliberate feeding behavior, using their long tails as a lever to balance as they extend their bodies to reach fruit and berries. When eating fruit, the bird chews the pulp and spits out pits, larger seeds, and skin.

Behavior and reproduction: Skittish and shy birds unless accustomed to the presence of humans, gray hypocoliuses are not easy to find and fly immediately to dense vegetation when disturbed. This bird, like its cousins, is outgoing and social, and in winter forms flocks of up to twenty individuals that live in loose colonies. This species has a soft, gentle, cat-like call: "tre-tur-tur" or "whee-oo." Their flight pattern is strong and direct, with quick wing beats and occasional undulating, wave-like, glides.

Gray hypocoliuses breed from May to June, locating the nest within a dense bush or low tree up to 12 feet (4 meters) from the ground. The cup-shaped nest sits atop a base of twigs, and is made of grass and plant down and lined with wool, hair, and more down. The female lays three or four oval-shaped, smooth, glossy eggs that are white to pale gray. Both parents take turns incubating the clutch for fourteen to fifteen days.

Gray hypocoliuses and people: Many devoted birdwatchers wait a lifetime to add a sighting of this bird to their list. Their residence in the politically charged countries of the Middle East makes them particularly difficult to observe.

Conservation status: Gray hypocoliuses are not believed to be threatened, although biologists encounter many political difficulties when attempting to visit the bird's home countries to study it. ■

FOR MORE INFORMATION

Books:

Baicich, Paul. *A Guide to the Nests, Eggs, and Nestlings of North American Birds.* Princeton, NJ: Princeton University Press, 1997.

Grimmet, Richard, Carol Inskipp, and Tim Inskipp. *Birds of the Indian Subcontinent.* London: Christopher Helm Ltd, 1998.

Sibley, C. G., and B. L. Monroe. *Distribution and Taxonomy of Birds of the World.* New Haven, CT: Yale University Press, 1991.

Zim, Herbert Spencer, Ira Noel Gabrielson, and James Gordon Irving. *Birds: A Guide to Familiar Birds of North America.* New York: St. Martin's Press, 2001.

Periodicals:

Witmer, M. C. "Consequences of an Alien Shrub on the Plumage, Coloration, and Ecology of Cedar Waxwings." *Auk* 113 (1996): 735–743.

Web sites:

"*Bombacilla cedrorum* (Cedar Waxwing)." Animal Diversity Web. http://animaldiversity.ummz.umich.edu/site/accounts/information/Bombycilla_cedrorum.html (accessed on July 3, 2004).

"Grey Hypocolius." Stamps of Israeli Birds. http://my.ort.org.il/holon/birds/ba2.html (accessed on July 3, 2004).

"HYPOCOLIUS: Hypocoliidae." Bird Families of the World. http://www.montereybay.com/creagrus/hypocolius.html (accessed on July 3, 2004).

"WAXWINGS: Bombycillidae." Bird Families of the World. http://www.montereybay.com/creagrus/waxwings.html (accessed on July 3, 2004).

Class: Aves

Order: Passeriformes

Family: Dulidae

One species: Palmchat (*Dulus dominicus*)

family

CHAPTER

phylum

class

subclass

order

monotypic order

suborder

▲ **family**

PHYSICAL CHARACTERISTICS

The only member of its family, the palmchat was first described in 1766. The bird is typically 7.5 to 8 inches (19 to 20 centimeters) long and has a fairly long tail. Its upper parts are olive brown, with a dark yellow-green area across its rump and on the edges of its primary wing feathers. Its under parts are creamy white with heavy brown streaks, while its strong bill is yellow and its eyes are russet. Adult males and females look very similar, but immature birds have darker throats. Although it is distantly related to the North American waxwings, its plumage is not soft and velvety. It is a vocal bird, and may be recognized by its cheerful gurgles and "cheep" calls. It does not have a song, but rather blurts out noises and single notes.

GEOGRAPHIC RANGE

The palmchat is one of only two birds native to the Caribbean (the other is the Jamaican tody). It is native to the West Indian island of Hispaniola, which is split into Haiti and the Dominican Republic, including the Saona and Gonave islands.

HABITAT

Palmchats forage and breed almost exclusively in savannas, flat grasslands, dotted with royal palms and in valleys, and tend to stay at elevations between sea level and 4,900 feet (1,500 meters). It is also happy to live in city parks and other areas heavily trafficked by humans as long as food trees are present.

DIET

This species eats mainly fruit, including berries from palm trees and gumbo-limbo trees. They also eat blossoms and buds, particularly of orchid tree blooms, but are not considered harmful to the trees.

BEHAVIOR AND REPRODUCTION

Palmchats are very social birds and congregate in small flocks that have a communal nest where they meet and rest. These little bands usually consist of several pairs. The birds show great affection for each other, preferring to snuggle close together on branches even in their tropical climate. Palmchats' reputation for alertness and energy may come partly from their continuously erect posture, with tails pointed straight down. The flocks are noisy, especially near their group nest, where they rest at night and during daytime breaks in activity. When not looking for food, palmchats sit on palm fronds or the upward-pointing ends of pruned fronds. They emerge from their nests in the early morning to preen and dry in the sun.

Palmchats eat mainly berries and other fruit. (© Doug Wechsler/VIREO. Reproduced by permission.)

These birds breed mostly between March and June, but occasionally some pairs will breed at other times. Several pairs of palmchats build a nest together, each with its own chamber and entrance. The large, messy nest is built around the crown of a palm, supported by its lower fronds. In areas lacking palms, the birds will build their nests on top of telephone poles, in the dense foliage of a broad-leafed tree, or in pine trees. Their main building material is twigs, which they intertwine loosely to create the 3- to 6.5-foot-diameter (1- to 2-meter) structure. Some of the twigs can be as long as 10 to 18 inches (25 to 45 centimeters) long. The females lay two to four grayish purple eggs that are thickly spotted at the wide end.

PALMCHATS AND PEOPLE

These lively birds are a familiar sight in most towns on Hispaniola and its environs, but they do not have any particular significance to humans.

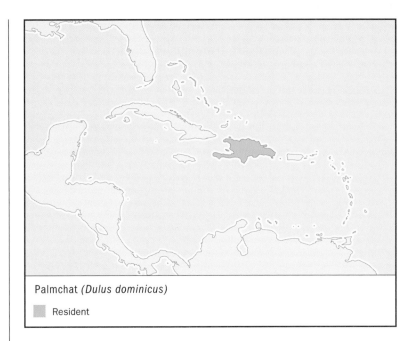

Palmchat *(Dulus dominicus)*

▪ Resident

CONSERVATION STATUS

The palmchat is not threatened.

FOR MORE INFORMATION

Books:

Bird, David M. *The Bird Almanac: A Guide to the Essential Facts and Figures of the World's Birds.* Buffalo, NY: Firefly Books Ltd., 2004.

Gill, Frank B. *Ornithology.* New York: W. H. Freeman and Company, 1994.

Raffaele, Herbert A. *A Guide to the Birds of the West Indies.* Princeton, NJ: Princeton University Press, 1998.

Sibley, David A. *The Sibley Guide to Birdlife and Behavior.* New York: Alfred A. Knopf, 2001.

Wauer, Roland H. *A Birder's West Indies: An Island-by-Island Tour.* Houston, TX: University of Texas Press, 1996.

Web sites:

"Dulus dominicus—Palmchat." InfoNatura. http://www.natureserve.org (accessed on June 21, 2004).

"Dulidae." CREAGRUS@Monterey Bay.http://www.montereybay.com/creagrus (accessed on June 21, 2004).

phylum

class

subclass

order

monotypic order

suborder

▲ **family**

HEDGE SPARROWS
Prunellidae

Class: Aves

Order: Passeriformes

Family: Prunellidae

Number of species: 13 species

PHYSICAL CHARACTERISTICS

These birds, also known as "accentors," are small and sparrow-like in appearance but not related to sparrows. The bill of a hedge sparrow is slender and more pointed than the sparrow. They range in size from 5 to 7 inches (13 to 18 centimeters), with a weight of 0.5 to 1.4 ounces (18 to 40 grams). The differences between the male and female are slight, though the male has longer wings, with ten functional primary feathers that can be rounded or pointed at the tip. The male is heavier than the female. The legs and feet of the bird are very strong. In general, the anatomy of the birds is strong and muscular, a feature that has been adapted due to their diet.

In color, a hedge sparrow tends to be brown-toned gray or a rusty brown. Males are slightly brighter than females, but are otherwise similar in appearance.

GEOGRAPHIC RANGE

Hedge sparrows are known to be widely distributed throughout the Palearctic region that includes the area from western Europe to Japan, in Asia north of the Himalayan mountains, and in Africa, north of the Sahara desert.

HABITAT

Hedge sparrows tend to live in the thick undergrowth of shrubs, and in alpine meadows rather than in the trees themselves. Habitats can vary slightly among the species.

The robin accentor can be found at high altitudes in central Asia, and prefers to live in dwarf rhododendrons and other scrub, or among the willows of damp meadows.

DIET

Accentors gather food by hunting or foraging on the ground, preferring invertebrates that crawl, particularly insects such as beetles, flies, aphids, ants, spiders, and worms. They feed primarily on seeds and berries in the winter and forage together in flocks.

BEHAVIOR AND REPRODUCTION

Accentors tend to have a very developed social system even though they are also known to be quiet and unobtrusive. Most of their activity occurs on the ground, or close to it, moving through running and hopping with small flicks of the wings and tail. When they are in flight, they exhibit rapid and undulating moves.

Female accentors tend to be exclusive. The male of some species, such as the dunnock, might set up song territories in order to compete for and monopolize females. The result can be a male with two or three females, called polygyny (puh-LIH-juh-nee), or it can be a female with two or three males, called polyandry (PAH-lee-an-dree); or several males associated with several females, known as polygamy (puh-LIH-guh-mee). Polyandry is considered to be unusual even though it does occur. In such a situation, the breeding territory would be larger than for a single male-female pairing, providing for more protection against a greater number of predators. The Himalayan accentor can breed at altitudes as high as 16,400 feet (5,000 meters) into the mountains.

Breeding season for accentors runs from late March to August, with variations among the species depending on location and latitude. They lay a clutch of three to six eggs that are light blue-green to blue. Two clutches are generally bred and hatched every year, with an incubation period of eleven to fifteen days, with the nestlings raised another twelve to fourteen days before they leave the nest, or become fledglings. Both male and female take care of the young together.

HEDGE SPARROWS AND PEOPLE

Accentors have an impact on people primarily in regard to ecotourism and the economic benefits from visitors focused on following birds in their natural habitats.

CONSERVATION STATUS

The Yemen accentor has been listed as Near Threatened, in danger of becoming threatened with extinction. Due to grazing animals, in addition to human behavior, the shrubland habitat on which the bird relies has been degraded. Other species have also declined but are not considered at risk. During the 1980s, the dunnocks that breed in England declined, but are maintaining themselves against further loss into the twenty-first century.

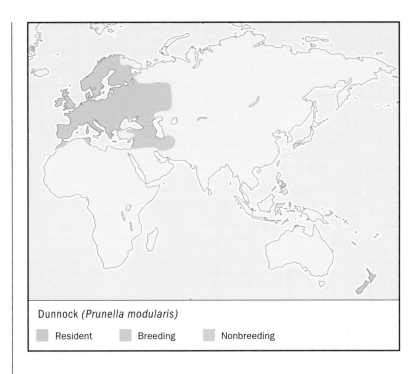

Dunnock (*Prunella modularis*)

■ Resident   ■ Breeding   ■ Nonbreeding

DUNNOCK
Prunella modularis

Physical characteristics: The dunnock is a relatively small bird that has an average length of 6 inches (15 centimeters), and weighs about 0.7 ounces (19 grams). Like other accentors, its beak is pointed and slender and its feet and legs are sturdy. The dunnock can have a blue-gray head and breast, and a light and dark brown back with streaks, brown-streaked flanks, and pink legs. The under parts of the dunnock tend to be uniformly gray with apricot markings.

Geographic range: The dunnock can be found throughout Europe, as far east as the western regions of Russia. In the northern regions, the dunnock is migratory. Those living in the southern parts of France and Spain tend to reside there on a continual basis. Between 1860 and 1880, the dunnock was introduced to New Zealand and remains there, as well.

Habitat: The dunnock resides in woods that have an ample amount of undergrowth, as well as in the hedges and shrubbery at the edges

of forests. They also thrive in farm areas that have a lot of vegetation, and in the gardens of the United Kingdom and New Zealand.

Diet: Dunnocks are omnivores, eating various invertebrates such as insects, spiders, and worms during warm months. In the winter they survive on seeds and berries, some of the various kind of seeds are in feeders meant for songbirds in gardens and backyards.

Behavior and reproduction: Dunnocks are known for their secretive behavior and tend to be shy in their habits. Most of the populations are migratory. During breeding season, they are seen either as individuals or in pairs. During the winter they tend to gather in large flocks in order to forage for food—with a good food source, a hundred or more might gather. The bird's voice is heard in a short but complex song that is composed of a succession of rapid and even notes and trills.

Breeding season for dunnocks runs approximately from the beginning of April to the end of July, generally raising two broods a year. The incubation period lasts from twelve to fourteen days, and the young are ready to fly about eleven to thirteen days after they are hatched. Both male and female parents care for the young. Dunnocks are sometimes polyandrous breeders, with a female mating with several males within the breeding territory. In that case, it is usual for all of the parties involved to raise the young.

Dunnocks and people: Dunnocks provide an economic benefit due to the numbers of people who engage in bird watching and the travel that sometimes accompanies it. The dunnock is also well known in the English countryside. In 2001, the ticks that live on dunnocks and other migratory birds were linked to the spread of a bacterial pathogen known as *Ehrlichia phagocytophila,* which causes the rare human disease of ehrlichiosis. This disease has been compared to Rocky Mountain spotted fever and emerges about twelve days following the bite of a tick. Though cases have occurred in the United States, the illness tends to be centered in the Far East and Southeast Asia, with most cases reported in western Japan.

Conservation status: The dunnock is not a threatened species, although its population in Britain did experience a decline by 45 to 60 percent between 1975 and 2001. Since 1986 the population remained steady. The cause was unknown. The decline was not experienced throughout the British Isles and Wales actually enjoyed a population increase. ■

FOR MORE INFORMATION

Books:

Alsop, Fred J. III. *Birds of North America.* Smithsonian Books. London and New York: Dorling Kindersley Publishing, 2001.

Campbell, Bruce, and Elizabeth Lack, eds. *A Dictionary of Birds.* Vermillion, SD: Buteo Books, 1985.

Elphick, Chris, John B. Dunning Jr., and David Allen Sibley, eds. *The Sibley Guide to Bird Life & Behavior.* New York: Alfred A. Knopf, Inc., 2001.

Fisher, James, and Roger Tory Peterson. *The World of Birds.* Garden City, NJ: Doubleday & Company, Inc., 1964.

Web sites:

"Dunnock." Bird Diary. http://www.birddiary.co.uk (accessed on May 5, 2004).

"Dunnock." British Garden Birds. http://www.garden7ndash;birds.co.uk/dunnock.htm (accessed on May 5, 2004).

"Breeding Birds in the Wider Countryside." Joint Nature Conservation Committee. http://www.bto.org/birdtrends/wcrdunno.htm (accessed on May 5, 2004).

"Dunnock." New Zealand Birds. http://www.nzbirds.com/Dunnock.html (accessed on May 5, 2004).

family
CHAPTER

PHYSICAL CHARACTERISTICS

Mimids, members of the Mimidae family, average in length from 8.2 to 12.2 inches (20.5 to 30.5 centimeters). Their plumage, feathers, is not bright or colorful. Most species are shades of gray or brown and gray with some black or whitish markings. Many have long, curved bills used for foraging for prey on the ground or in trees.

GEOGRAPHIC RANGE

Mimids are found throughout North and South America, and on a number of islands, including the Falklands, West Indies, Bermuda, the Galápagos, and some islands in the Caribbean.

HABITAT

Mimid habitats are varied. Many species prefer low and dense vegetation that provides a protective cover for nests. Those that are forest dwellers usually prefer the edge of a forest for this reason. Several species are endemic to small islands.

DIET

Because of the diversity of species in the Mimidae family, the birds eat anything from insects to animal flesh. Fruit, berries, and seeds are a common dietary staple. Some of the larger thrasher species will also eat small fish and lizards.

BEHAVIOR AND REPRODUCTION

Mimid behavior ranges from the loud and outgoing to the shy and secretive, depending on the species. The mimids, particularly

THE MOCKINGBIRD SONG

An amazing mimic, the mockingbird is able to imitate the songs of dozens of other bird species and incorporate them into his own call. They also mimic natural sounds around them, such as the croak of a frog or the chirp of a cricket. And mockingbirds kept as pets can repeat human and household noises, such as the ringing of a phone. The birds were popular pets in the nineteenth century. President Thomas Jefferson had one that he reportedly let fly around the White House on occasion.

the mockingbird species, are known for their song. Most are monogamous (muh-NAH-guh-mus) during the breeding season, and very defensive. Thrasher males are unique in that they share incubation (sitting on the eggs) duties with their mate.

THRASHERS, MOCKINGBIRDS, AND PEOPLE

Because of their interesting and often melodic songs and ability to mimic the calls of other birds and other environmental noises, many people enjoy having mimids nearby. However, The birds are very territorial and defend their nestlings vigorously. Some mockingbirds and gray catbirds have been known to attack people when threatened.

CONSERVATION STATUS

The Cozumel thrasher and the Socorro mockingbird, both residents of Mexico, are on the Critically Endangered list, facing an extremely high risk of extinction. The Socorro mockingbird lives on a small island off the coast of Mexico, where the birds' numbers are dwindling due to predatory cats and grazing sheep overtaking their habitat. The Charles mockingbird, another island-dweller, is classified as Endangered, facing a very high risk of extinction, due to predators, as is the white-breasted thrasher. The population of the white-breasted thrasher is also declining due to habitat loss along with the black catbird, which is considered Near Threatened, in danger of becoming threatened with extinction. Finally, the Hood mockingbird is classified as Vulnerable, facing a high risk of extinction, due to its small population and limited range.

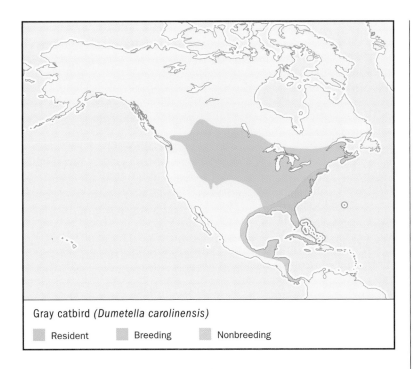

Gray catbird (*Dumetella carolinensis*)

■ Resident   ■ Breeding   ■ Nonbreeding

GRAY CATBIRD
Dumetella carolinensis

Physical characteristics: True to its name, the gray catbird is almost entirely slate gray, with a small patch of black on the top of its head, a black tail, black legs, and rust-colored undertail feathers. Their bill is short, straight, and black. Average size is 8.5 inches (21.5 centimeters) long with a weight of 1.3 ounces (36.8 grams). Both the males and the females of the species are similar in appearance.

Geographic range: The gray catbird can be found in southern Canada (from British Columbia to Nova Scotia) and the central and eastern United States (extending south from Canada down to northeastern Arizona in the West and to northern Florida in the East) during breeding season. This species winters on the east coast, from southern New England down through Florida and along the Gulf Coast into Central America. The gray catbird is also found in the Bahamas, Cuba, and Jamaica.

Habitat: The gray catbird is not a sociable bird, preferring to stay hidden and nest within its preferred habitat, which is dense and

Gray catbirds build their cup-shaped nests in well concealed areas. (© F. Truslow/VIREO. Reproduced by permission.)

shrubby vegetation. Some favorite nesting areas include scrub, abandoned orchards and farmland, the periphery of forests, alongside streams and roads, under cactus pads (leaves), and occasionally within dense shrubbery in residential areas.

Diet: In the spring breeding months gray catbirds are primarily insect eaters, feeding on caterpillars, millipedes, grasshoppers, ants, spiders, and beetles. Starting with summer and into the fall, they start to incorporate more fruit into their diet, preferring grapes and other small fruits. When not foraging under the cover of vegetation, they can be seen walking along the ground using their bills to find insects.

Behavior and reproduction: Gray catbirds build nests under dense cover of scrub or thickets. Their cup-shaped nests are well concealed and woven from vines, twigs, straw, grasses, and occasional bits of paper or plastic. Soft hair and grass lines the inside. The male may help in nest construction, but it is usually the female that does most of the work. She lays a clutch of up to six blue-green eggs, which are incubated for about two weeks. Both male and female feed the hatchlings, who leave the nest about eight to twelve days after they hatch.

Gray catbirds and people: Gray catbirds tend to avoid people and are not considered an agricultural or residential pest.

Conservation status: Gray catbirds are common throughout North and South America. ■

Hood mockingbird *(Nesomimus macdonaldi)*

▨ Resident

HOOD MOCKINGBIRD
Nesomimus macdonaldi

Physical characteristics: Hood mockingbirds are dull white on the chest and belly and streaked or spotted gray to brown coloring on the top. The dark wing feathers appear edged off-white. They may also have darker spots on the chest. The Hood mockingbird sports a black streak across its yellow-to-brown eyes, and has a black bill and legs.

Geographic range: The Hood mockingbird is found primarily on a small island in the Galápagos known as Hood Island (also known as Espantildeola).

The Hood mockingbird uses its long, curved beak to crack open seabird eggs, such as waved albatross eggs, in order to eat their contents. (© George Holton/Photo Researchers, Inc. Reproduced by permission.)

Habitat: Hood Island is a low-lying, flat-topped island with primarily rocky terrain and sand and pebble beaches. The available vegetation is primarily scrub. Fresh water is scarce.

Diet: The Hood mockingbird is an omnivore, which means it eats animals as well as vegetation. The bird uses its long, curved beak to crack open seabird eggs in order to eat their contents. It will also drink blood from the wounds of other living or dead animals, and scavenge carrion (decaying animal carcasses).

Behavior and reproduction: During nonbreeding season, Hood mockingbirds travel in large groups of around forty to forage and defend their territories. In the months of March and April when nesting time occurs, they split off into smaller groups. The species are cooperative breeders, meaning many birds will share feeding duties for the young in a group, not just the parent birds. The typically breeding group is approximately five adult males and two or three adult females.

Hood mockingbirds and people: Because of their remote location, Hood mockingbirds don't encounter people except in the form of ecotourists and researchers. When they do come in contact with humans, they are said to be unafraid and will readily approach them and scavenge for food and fresh water if accessible.

Conservation status: The Hood mockingbird is classified as a Vulnerable species because of its limited range and the risk that dangerous weather pattern changes could affect its population. ■

FOR MORE INFORMATION

Books:

George, Phillip Brandt. "Thrashers, Bulbuls, Starlings." In *Reference Atlas to the Birds of North America,* edited by Mel Baughman. Washington, DC: National Geographic Press, 2003.

Sibley, David Allen. *National Audubon Society: The Sibley Guide to Birds.* New York: Alfred A. Knopf, 2000.

Periodicals:

Clark, Gary. "A Singer and a Song; Mockingbird's Arrival is Among Area's Signs of Spring." *Houston Chronicle* (Feb 21, 2003): 3.

Web sites:

"BirdLife's Online World Bird Database: The Site for Bird Conservation. Version 2.0." BirdLife International. http://www.birdlife.org (accessed on May 25, 2004).

"Gray Catbird." All About Birds. Cornell Lab of Ornithology. http://birds.cornell.edu/programs/AllAboutBirds/BirdGuide/Gray_Catbird_dtl.html (accessed on May 28, 2004).

DIPPERS
Cinclidae

Class: Aves

Order: Passeriformes

Family: Cinclidae

Number of species: 5 species

phylum

class

subclass

order

monotypic order

suborder

▲ **family**

PHYSICAL CHARACTERISTICS

Of all Passeriformes, or perching birds, dippers are the only true aquatic songbirds. They have plump bodies with short tails, strong legs, and powerful feet. Their preen, or oil, glands are larger than those found in most perching birds and help keep their feathers waterproof. This is essential because dippers spend most of their lives in or near rivers and streams. Their eyes have nictating membranes, or inner eyelids, that allow the birds to see underwater.

Most species are uniformly gray or brown, but some species have white heads or underbellies. All dippers have white eyelids and short, hard bills.

GEOGRAPHIC RANGE

Dippers can be found in Europe, Asia, North Africa, and the western regions of North and South America. Though conditions are suitable for dippers to nest in other areas, they have not done so.

HABITAT

Dippers make their nests above shallow mountain rivers and streams, behind waterfalls, and sometimes on rocky ledges beside mountain lakes. The water must be fast moving to keep it rich in oxygen and free of sediment and pollutants. Dippers will migrate south or to lower elevations when these water sources freeze in winter. The undersides of bridges over waterways and human-made nesting boxes have also become appropriate homes for dippers.

DIET

The main source of food for dippers is insect larvae (LAR-vee), small fish such as minnows, and fish roe, or eggs.

BEHAVIOR AND REPRODUCTION

These birds are called dippers because of the way they dip or bow when they become agitated, mate, or defend territory. They also blink their eyes rapidly, displaying their white eyelids.

Dippers are unique because they spend most of their lives in water, often submerged, searching for food. Their waterproof feathers and the swimming motions of their rounded wings allow them to stay underwater. Their feet often grasp pebbles to anchor them to the river bottom. They will dive into water to escape predators.

The songs of both sexes, sharp "zit-zit" sounds, can be heard over the roar of rushing water.

Generally, dippers mate for life and either remain in a familiar nesting area or return to it yearly. Their nests are rounded with a wide entrance in the side. Both sexes build the outer nest with moss, grasses, and leaves, but the female creates the interior of softer grasses. Because the nests are build near water, the exteriors are usually moist and may stay green.

Dippers can have two broods, or groups of offspring, hatch at the same time each year. They usually lay two white eggs in the tropics and as many as seven in other climates. Females incubate their eggs, keep them warm for hatching, for sixteen days. They are then fed by both parents for up to twenty-two days.

DIPPERS AND PEOPLE

Dippers serve as an indicator species, a bird or animal whose presence reveals a specific characteristic, for good water quality.

CONSERVATION STATUS

Mining, pollution, and even the presence of evergreen trees can dump chemicals, acids, and wastes into waterways that can

ANTING BEHAVIOR

Though other birds interact with ants, American dippers participate in active anting, or placing ants, one at a time, into their feathers. Scientists think that ants help control parasites such as mites by spraying formic acid into the bird's feathers.

reduce dipper food supplies and eventually decrease their populations. Currently, these birds are not threatened, though their numbers fluctuate in response to pollution. However, one subspecies of Eurasian dipper is extinct, or died out, and several other groups are Vulnerable, facing a high risk of extinction.

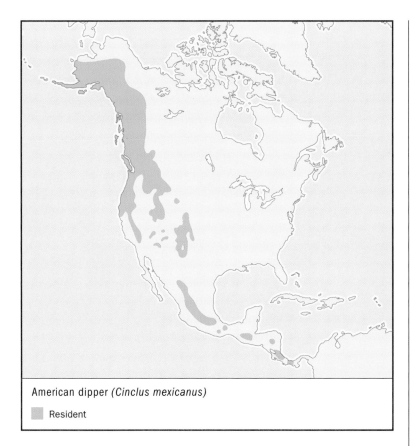

American dipper (*Cinclus mexicanus*)

■ Resident

AMERICAN DIPPER
Cinclus mexicanus

Physical characteristics: The American dipper is also called the Mexican dipper, the water ouzel, and the waterthrush. It is 6 to 7 inches (15 to 17.5 centimeters) long. The male weighs 2 to 2.4 ounces (57 to 66 grams), and the female weighs 1.5 to 2.3 ounces (43 to 65 grams). Its body is slate gray with a paler throat. A flap covers their nostrils to keep water out.

Geographic range: They are found along the western coast of North America from the Arctic Circle, through Canada and into Oregon, Washington, and California, as well as in central Mexico and Central America. It is also found in Arizona, Nevada, Colorado, South Dakota, and Wyoming.

The female American dipper incubates her eggs for fourteen to seventeen days. The young fledglings are fed by both parents for twenty-four to twenty-six days. (Jeff Foott/Bruce Coleman Inc. Reproduced by permission.)

Habitat: The American dipper prefers cool climates and high altitudes, up to 11,000 feet (3,500 meters) in the United States. One group even endures the severe winters of Alaska and South Dakota, which can drop to 40° below zero F (−40°C).

Diet: American dippers walk along the bottoms of stream beds, totally submerged, hunting for insect larvae, worms, and snails. Sometimes, these birds will fly along the surface of the waterway, scooping up flies and other insects. They will also weed out sluggish insects from snowbanks and seaweed cast upon the shore.

Behavior and reproduction: This species of bird behaves like most other dippers. Its song is melodious, with a sharp "dzik-dzik" call that occurs anytime, not just to attract a mate.

Mating occurs from May to July. American dipper nests are spherical, about a foot in diameter with the usual side entrance. North American birds lay four to five white eggs, but Costa Rican birds will lay only two to four. Incubation by the female takes fourteen to seventeen days. The young fledglings are fed by both parents for twenty-four to twenty-six days.

American dippers and people: This species has been accused of causing damage to fish hatcheries, though no evidence has been found.

Conservation status: American dippers are not threatened or at risk of dying out. They are very sensitive to the water quality of the rivers and streams near their nests and will abandon them if they become polluted. Mining has contributed to water pollution in regions where American dippers nest. Bird populations are often supported and may even increase in numbers by the introduction of nest boxes placed near streams by humans and by American dippers using the undersides of bridges over waterways as nesting sites.

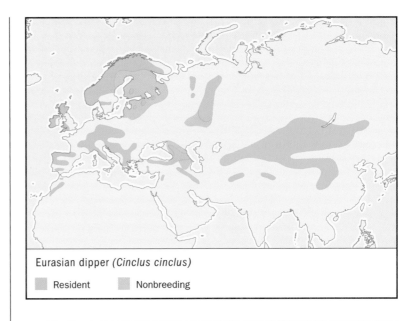

Eurasian dipper (*Cinclus cinclus*)

■ Resident   ■ Nonbreeding

EURASIAN DIPPER
Cinclus cinclus

Physical characteristics: Eurasian dippers, also known as English dippers or white-throated dippers, are small round-bodied birds with short tails. They are only 6.7 to 7.9 inches (17 to 20 centimeters) long. Males weigh between 1.9 and 2.7 ounces (53 to 76 grams), and females weigh 1.6 to 2.5 ounces (46 to 72 grams). Most of them have dark brown feathers on their heads, backs, and bellies, with white chests and throats. Some birds have blackish feathers on their backs with chestnut brown on their undersides and only white on their breasts and chins. The black-bellied dipper has no brown on its belly, while a subspecies in Asia has a white underside.

Geographic range: Eurasian dippers can be found in Great Britain, Norway, Spain, Italy, Greece, and France, as well as western Europe, Turkey, North Africa, and Asia from the Himalayas to China. In winter, birds in Scandinavia will move south into Poland and Russia.

Habitat: Like other dippers, Eurasian dippers nest near swift-moving mountain streams. Sometimes, this species can be found near the rocky shores of lakes.

Diet: Eurasian dippers usually feed on the larvae of aquatic insects like caddis worms and beetles. They also like freshwater mollusks, water fleas, newly hatched fish, and roe.

Behavior and reproduction: Eurasian dippers behave as other dippers, and feed underwater. Both sexes sing and have a "zil-zil" call. Males change their call to "clink-clink" when they are seeking the attention of females during mating.

This species generally mates for life and will often have two or three broods. They will separate after the young are on their own and will return to their home nests in the spring.

Both sexes help build their oval nests above rushing streams or rivers, usually in rock faces or in the support pieces of bridges. One to seven white eggs are laid and incubated by the female for twelve to eighteen days. Both parents feed the young birds for twenty to twenty-four days.

Eurasian dippers and people: This species, like most dippers, has no special significance to humans.

Conservation status: Though the Eurasian dipper is not threatened, most populations have shown declines due to water pollution and increased acids caused by runoff from planting evergreen trees. If the water quality improves, the birds return to their former nesting sites. ■

Eurasian dippers nest near swift-moving mountain streams, where they search for their food. (© J. Peltomaki/VIREO. Reproduced by permission.)

FOR MORE INFORMATION

Books:

Brewer, David, and Barry Kent Mackay. *Wrens, Dippers, and Thrashers: A Guide to the Wrens, Dippers, and Thrashers of the World.* New Haven, CT: Yale University Press, 2001.

Robbins, Michael. *Birds (Fandex Family Field Guides).* New York: Workman Publishing Company, 1998.

Tyler, Stephanie J. *Dippers.* San Diego, CA: Elsevier Science & Technology, 1994.

Weidensaul, Scott. *Birds (National Audubon Society First Field Guides).* New York: Scholastic Trade, 1998.

Periodicals:

Barber, Robert E. "Joy-bird." *American Forests* (Spring 1996): 34–35.

Osborn, Sophie A. H. "Anting by an American Dipper (*Cinclus mexicanus*)." *Wilson Bulletin* (September 1998): 423–425.

Turbak, Gary. "The Bird That Files Through Water: Scientists Continue to Marvel at the American Dipper. A Species Remarkably Adapted for Life Near Raging Rivers." *National Wildlife* (June–July 2000).

THRUSHES AND CHATS
Turdidae

Class: Aves
Order: Passeriformes
Family: Turdidae
Number of species: 331 species

PHYSICAL CHARACTERISTICS

Thrushes have a varied appearance among their vast number of species, though some basic characteristics are common to all. They average in size from about 5 to 13 inches (12 to 33 centimeters) and are categorized as small to medium in size. The smaller species are known as chats.

Birds of this family are known for their upright posture and bills that tend to be thin and have no curves with a very slight hook. Their wings are rounded, except for in the species that are true migrants, which have longer and more pointed wingtips out of necessity for their long flights. The outermost wings are usually very short. Their tails are generally not very long and often short with square tips.

Some adult species show no marked differences between the male and female. Others vary significantly. For example, blackbirds include males that are jet-black and females that are pale brown. On the other hand, male and female song thrushes are identical in appearance. Thrushes in general are woodland songbirds that do not have any pronounced ornamentation in terms of crests, ruffs, or other feathered features. The variety of colors among the species is often stunning with marked but subtle tones. The color can range from muted brown on top with a paler shade on the spotted underside, to those with red heads, gray rears and cheeks, to those with a variable blue and blue-gray with a deep orange to rusty-red underneath and on the tail. Some tropical varieties might be electric blue and white, as well as others that are a mixture of deep colors of orange,

phylum
class
subclass
order
monotypic order
suborder
▲ **family**

black, white, and gray with varying patterns that include spots and streaks of colors.

GEOGRAPHIC RANGE

Thrushes and chats are widely distributed throughout the world except in desert regions or those far northern regions that are not woodland areas. They can be found in the new and old worlds, in the islands of the Pacific, Atlantic, and Indian oceans, in North America and through Europe and Asia to the tips of South America, Africa, and Australia.

HABITAT

Thrushes live primarily in forests, or in cultivated areas where trees are plentiful. The habitat range of the different species can vary widely, from very specific requirements to very broad. The American robin, for instance, is very adaptable and lives in parks, forests, gardens, backyards, and in farm areas. Other species might live in high-altitude mountainsides, or areas that have been recently burned. One species, the nightingale in Europe, requires the specific habitat of dense thicket. In general, the populations of thrushes and chats are known throughout the world for their adaptable living conditions.

DIET

Thrushes in general are omnivores eating a wide variety of both plants and animals. Their diet includes earthworms and larvae (LAR-vee), beetles or other insects, berries, and fruit. One species, the rock thrush, feeds entirely on animals. This family of birds tends to forage, search, on the ground or in bushes for their food. In winter they gather food together in large flocks. A typical thrush feeding habit is their movement across the ground in continuing short and bouncy hops, as they pause to listen and look for signs of worms under the surface. As they tilt their heads from side to side in determining this, once discovered, they then swing forward to pick up their prey with their bills.

BEHAVIOR AND REPRODUCTION

In addition to their feeding on the ground, thrushes usually remain close to the ground most of the time, staying under the cover of forest or scrub. In order to find invertebrates, animals without a backbone, to eat, they scratch with their feet and turn over dead leaves and other debris with their bills. Thrushes and chats tend to be territorial birds during breeding, using their song to attract mates and to warn off any males that might be intending to interfere in their territory. In winter and for migration, some species form into large flocks. Thrushes prefer the shelter of warm and dry spots at night. Non-breeding birds might roost alone; many roost in communes; and still others are known to roost in groups of hundreds. The fieldfare has been observed roosting in flocks of 20,000—a mixed-thrush group found roosting in France one winter held 200,000 birds. Such roosts for all of these birds tend to be in dense thickets with temperatures even both inside and out, with minimum exposure to wind or other elements. The rock thrushes do roost alone in rock crevices or in high tree branches, and sometimes even inside the roofs of old, secluded buildings. Ring ouzels also roost alone, but among rocks and boulders.

Breeding begins when the birds are one year old, and these birds tend to remain monogamous (muh-NAH-guh-mus; having only one mate) for the mating season. On occasion, both male and female might mate with others. The males sing during the breeding season, usually perched in a visible spot or in the tree canopy.

The typical nest is shaped as an open cup that has been lined with grassy material and sticks. Sometimes mud is used to hold it together better. Some nests are placed in trees or other objects—American robins are known to place nests in the rafters of old buildings, or even into the secure roofs of porches and doorways, including such unusual places as traffic lights, or in boats or cars that are in regular use so they can access the nest freely. Some species build their nest on the ground or in tree cavities. The female is almost entirely responsible for building the nest, and it is usually preserved for a second brood of birds. The clutch can number from two to ten eggs, though it is usually four to five. One female incubates (warms enough for hatching) the birds for ten to seventeen days. Many species have two broods per year, and some have three or more. Survival of the chicks can often be at risk. All but one or two of a large brood might survive, with the others dying through disease, predators, starvation, or accident.

THRUSHES, CHATS, AND PEOPLE

Throughout much of southern and Mediterranean Europe, especially in Spain, Italy, and Greece, these birds are prized as food delicacies. They are caught and killed in large numbers and offered on restaurant menus and sold in supermarkets, either bottled or as thrush paté. The practice has been going on for centuries. While no exact determination has been made regarding the threat this might be to the species, none are in short supply. Elsewhere in Western Europe, people prize such features as the song of the nightingale and have honored the birds through song and poetry. Many of these birds are among the best-loved garden birds throughout the world.

CONSERVATION STATUS

Many species of thrushes are plentiful and show no signs of becoming extinct (dying out). Certain others continue to be studied, particularly the song thrush in Britain, due to a serious decline in their numbers in the decades at the end of the twentieth century. The decline involves the problems of survival of the young chicks, as well as the ability for some birds to produce a second brood. Some habitats have been compromised through extensive farming, and in Britain through development. No such apparent threat existed in the rest of Europe, where the numbers remained high in the early years of the twenty-first century. Some species have been on the brink of extinction due to the introduction of predators, or change of habitat. In the Seychelles (islands off of Africa in the Indian Ocean), for instance, coconut plantations have replaced the natural forest habitat of the magpie-robin, and the introduction of such predators as cats and rats brought danger to the bird populations. Some recovery was made possible through the very intense efforts of conservationists.

Eastern bluebird (*Sialia sialis*)

■ Resident ■ Breeding ■ Nonbreeding

EASTERN BLUEBIRD
Sialia sialis

Physical characteristics: Eastern bluebirds have a length of 5.4 to 7.1 inches (13.9 to 17.8 centimeters). The adult male has a bright blue head and upperparts. Its throat, the sides of its neck, and its breast and flanks are colored orange, with a white belly. Females are duller blue with a crown and back that is gray in tone. Its eyes have white rings around them. Also in the female, the throat, breast, and sides are browner in color compared to the male's orange. Young birds tend to have gray-brown upperparts with white spotting on the back, as well as a brown chest with white scalloping, wings and tail that are blue in tint, with a white belly and undertail feathers.

Eastern bluebirds nest in tree cavities. If a female has a second set of chicks during the breeding season, the male takes care of the first set until they're ready to leave the nest. (Laura Riley/Bruce Coleman Inc. Reproduced by permission.)

Geographic range: The Eastern bluebird can be found in eastern North America, as far north as Hudson Bay, as far west as Arizona and the Rocky Mountains, and south to Bermuda, Florida, and central Mexico.

Habitat: The Eastern bluebird prefers the comforts of forest edges, open woodlands, farmland edges, or meadows, avoiding densely wooded or highly populated areas.

Diet: Eastern bluebirds are omnivores. In winter they eat fruit, particularly berries. Throughout the rest of the year they prefer eating insects, earthworms, snails, and other invertebrates.

Behavior and reproduction: Eastern bluebirds tend to group in pairs of families, and perch upright on exposed branches or at the tops of trees. In the winter they tend to be very sociable and form large flocks, roosting communally. They look for food on the ground, in foliage, or even in the air.

Eastern bluebirds tend to be monogamous, usually having two broods a year, and sometimes three. They nest in tree cavities, or holes—sometimes it might be in a cavity abandoned by a woodpecker. The female constructs the nest from dry grasses and weeds or pine needles, lining it with grass and sometimes with hair or fur. She lays three to six eggs that are mostly pale blue, though they can also be white. The female incubates the eggs for twelve to fourteen days. When the young are hatched, they are helpless, naked, and blind, and must stay in the nest where they are nourished and cared for by both parents. They grow their flight feathers about fifteen to twenty days after hatching, and remain in the nest for a few weeks after. If the female is preparing for the second brood, the male will take over the care of the young fledglings. In the case of the second brood, the young from the first also join in their care as well.

Eastern bluebirds and people: Eastern bluebirds tend to stay away from densely populated areas, and have no specific connection with humans.

Conservation status: Though no longer threatened as a species, some numbers were declining at the end of the twentieth century—up to 90 percent—due to the loss of nesting cavities, possibly due to the removal of dead trees and branches by humans, or in competition for nesting spots with house sparrows and European starlings. Efforts to stop the eastern bluebirds' decline, such as the introduction of nesting boxes, have helped significantly in many areas. ■

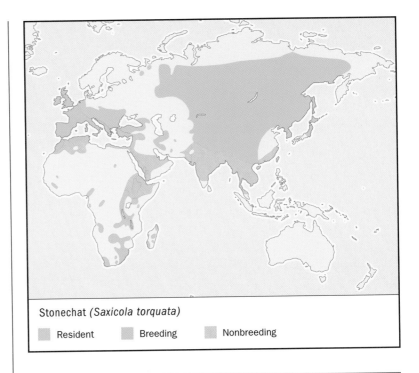

Stonechat (*Saxicola torquata*)

■ Resident   ■ Breeding   ■ Nonbreeding

STONECHAT
Saxicola torquata

Physical characteristics: The stonechat has a length of 4.9 inches (12.5 centimeters) with a weight of 0.46 to 0.6 ounces (13 to 17 grams). The males have black heads with orange breasts, and white patches on the sides of the neck that cover a large area. The females and young birds are similar in appearance, and have brown heads as well as less pronounced shades of orange and white.

Geographic range: The stonechat can be found throughout Britain and Ireland; in Europe from Denmark south to the Iberian peninsula and east to the Black Sea; in the Middle East; in certain local areas of Arabia; in Japan and China; and scattered throughout the southern parts of Africa. Some have been spotted in spring and summer as far north as Alaska.

Habitat: Stonechats prefer to live in rough grassland with thorny scrub, as well as in recently cultivated areas, forest clearings with bushy undergrowth, and along open coastal areas above rocky shores and cliffs.

Diet: Stonechats tend to be carnivores, feeding on insects and other small invertebrates.

Behavior and reproduction: Stonechats live in pairs or family groups, perching on open bush tops or on the stems of tall grasses, as well as on overhead wires. They are known for their frequent and harsh calls that sound like scoldings. In breeding, they are monogamous and territorial. They build their nests close to the ground in dense growth, and keep them hidden and sheltered from the sun. Their nests are built from grass stems with an entrance tunnel. The female lays four to six eggs, incubating them for thirteen to fourteen days. Newly hatched young grow their flight feathers after thirteen days.

Stonechats and people: Stonechats have no special significance to humans.

Conservation status: Stonechats are not considered threatened. ■

Stonechats live in pairs or family groups, and build their nests close to the ground in dense growth, to keep them hidden and sheltered from the sun. (Illustration by Barbara Duperron. Reproduced by permission.)

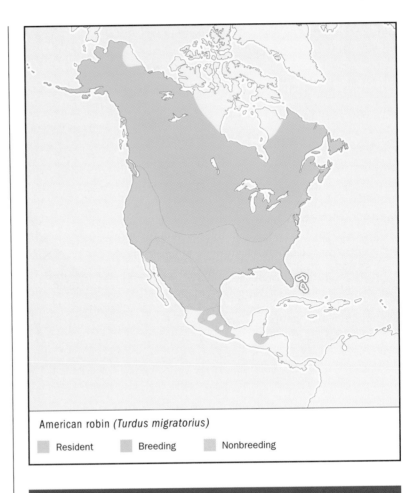

American robin (*Turdus migratorius*)

▮ Resident ▮ Breeding ▮ Nonbreeding

AMERICAN ROBIN
Turdus migratorius

Physical characteristics: The American robin has a range in length of 9.8 to 11 inches (25 to 28 centimeters). Males weigh an average of 2.1 to 3.2 ounces (59 to 91 grams); females weigh between 2.5 to 3.3 ounces (72 to 94 grams), and thus are usually larger than males. Both males and females have dark, brownish gray upperparts. Males have black heads and females have heads that are black and brownish gray. Eye rings are white; bills are yellow; and breasts are brick red in the male and chestnut-orange in the female. The lower belly and undertail feathers are white. The tail is dark with white outer corners. Young birds look similar to adults but have white markings on their backs and shoulders, and heavy spotting on their underparts.

Geographic range: The American robin can be found throughout Canada, Alaska, the United States, and Mexico. It winters south of its breeding range, usually in the Bahamas and Guatemala.

Habitat: The American robin prefers to inhabit damp forests and woodlands throughout its territorial range, from the tundra to gardens, parks, in local shrubs, throughout farmland with hedges, and in scattered woods.

Diet: The American robin is an omnivore, feeding on fruits, berries, grass seeds, and many invertebrates including beetles, caterpillars, grasshoppers, snails, spiders, and earthworms.

Behavior and reproduction: This bird is frequently seen feeding on the ground. Outside of breeding season, the birds create large roosts and flocks in winter. They breed between April and August, with their nests often being large and messy. Nests are made of grass, twigs, stems, and string, and lined with mud and fine grass. The female lays three to four bright blue eggs that are incubated for eleven to fourteen days. She has two broods during the season.

The American robin is a well recognized bird in North America. The female lays bright blue eggs that she incubates for eleven to fourteen days. (© T. Fink/VIREO. Reproduced by permission.)

American robins and people: The American robin is a very common and easily recognized bird, often seen pulling earthworms up from lawns and gardens. It is significant to North American people as a popular sign of spring, and was once hunted for meat in the southern United States.

Conservation status: This species is not considered to be threatened.   ■

FOR MORE INFORMATION

Books:

Alsop, Fred J. III. *Birds of North America.* Smithsonian Books. London and New York: Dorling Kindersley Publishing, 2001.

Campbell, Brude, and Elizabeth Lack, eds. *A Dictionary of Birds.* Vermillion, SD: Buteo Books, 1985.

Fisher, James, and Roger Tory Peterson. *The World of Birds.* Garden City, NJ: Doubleday & Company, Inc., 1964.

Web sites:

"All Taxa Biodiversity Inventory, Eastern Bluebird." Discover Life in America. http://www.dlia.org/atbi/species/animals/vertebrates/birds (accessed on May 11, 2004).

"Family Turdidae (Thrushes)." Animal Diversity Web. http://animaldiversity.ummz.umich.edu/site/accounts/classification/Turdidae.html (accessed on June 13, 2004).

Roberson, Don. "Thrushes, Turdidae." CREAGRUS@Monterey Bay. http://www.montereybay.com/creagrus/thrushes.html (accessed on May 11, 2004).

"Thrushes, Robins." Birds of the World. http://www.eeb.cornel.edu/winkler/botw/turdidae.html (accessed on May 11, 2004).

BABBLERS
Timaliidae

Class: Aves

Order: Passeriformes

Family: Timaliidae

Number of species: About 280 species

PHYSICAL CHARACTERISTICS

Scientists have disagreed about what birds to include in this family. The group now includes birds having ten primary feathers (strong feathers at the tip of the wing), twelve retrices (RET-rihs-uhs), or tail feathers, and large, powerful legs and feet, which limit flight and restrict these birds to small foraging and nesting ranges. Babblers are diverse in coloring, size, habitat, and behavior. Though their colors are dull, some have vivid patterns. All of these birds have distinctive songs.

There are more than thirty tropical species; a dozen scimitar (SIH-muh-tur) babblers that have long curved bills, twenty wren-babblers, some parrotbills, and a few picathartes or rockfowl.

GEOGRAPHIC RANGE

With the exception of the picathartes, which evolved in Africa, most members of this family originated in Asia. Babblers can be found in regions of China, Southeast Asia, Malaysia, Australia and New Guinea, Japan and the Philippines, India, Nepal, and Sri Lanka. The only American species traces its roots to Asia as well.

HABITAT

Most babblers live in forested regions. A few adapted to desert and savanna (grassland) areas, and one species is semi-aquatic in a marsh environment.

DIET

Babblers feed mainly on insects, though some species will eat fruit, seeds, frogs, and reptiles, depending on their specific habitats and the season of the year. The Arabian babbler, which lives in the desert where food is scarce, will eat almost anything.

BEHAVIOR AND REPRODUCTION

Babblers sing loudly and almost constantly, making babbler an apt name. Most of them hop about in small groups in the underbrush, looking for food.

Most forest-dwelling babblers socialize in flocks, but pair up during mating season and raise one or two broods, or groups of young hatched at the same time. Species in other habitats have developed different social systems and mating patterns. The bearded reedling lays four to eight eggs and can produce up to four broods in a season, with birds from the first brood being able to mate during the same season in which they were born. This adaptation is a response to living in unstable habitats and is a way to produce enough offspring so that the species survives.

The Arabian babbler and related species use cooperative breeding, where a social group defends its territory so that a few birds can mate. Usually a dominant male and female mate, and other birds wait for the opportunity to find a willing mate. Some members wait up to seven years for their chance to breed.

Nests for most babblers are cup-shaped or spherical (ball-shaped), made from bark, twigs, and grasses, built in shrubs or bushes. Babbler eggs can be pure white, solid colored, speckled, or streaked.

BABBLERS AND PEOPLE

Babblers, popular with zoos and exotic bird collectors, were once heavily trapped. Ecotourism, an industry based on attracting tourists to view birds, animals, and natural habitats, can help protect babbler populations in their natural environments by allowing people to see the birds there, instead of in zoos.

Chinese farmers have complained that the laughing thrush causes crop damage, but the bird helps with insect control in agricultural fields.

CONSERVATION STATUS

As of 2002, five species in the Philippines, India, Nigeria, Cameroon, and Vietnam are listed as Endangered, facing a very high risk of extinction, dying out, due to deforestation, or the cutting down of forests.

Twenty-two species are listed as Vulnerable, facing a high risk of extinction. Most of them are suffering from habitat destruction, and three have had their numbers seriously depleted by collectors.

Another thirty-nine species are classified as Near Threatened, in danger of becoming threatened with extinction. These birds are also suffering from habitat destruction in Sumatra, Borneo, the Malay Peninsula, and the Philippines.

Two species no longer exist, or are extinct. Astley's leiothrix was overtrapped by collectors, and the bearded reedling in southern Turkey died out because of the destruction of its wetland habitat.

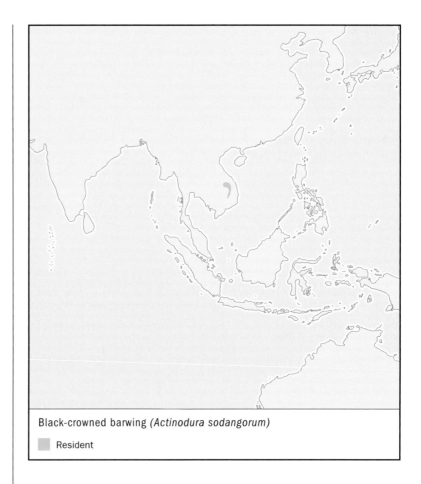

Black-crowned barwing *(Actinodura sodangorum)*

Resident

BLACK-CROWNED BARWING
Actinodura sodangorum

Physical characteristics: This babbler is 9.6 inches (24 centimeters) from tip to tail, but its weight is unknown. Both sexes have small brown bodies with reddish brown underbellies and long tails with thin white stripes ringing the black feathers. Black-crowned barwings have a small black crest on their heads and black stripes on their throat.

Geographic range: This species was discovered in 1996 in the western highlands of Vietnam. This was thought to be their exclusive habitat until they were found in six other places in the same province and along the Dakchung plateau in Laos.

Habitat: The black-crowned barwing prefers evergreen and pine forests where there are plenty of insects. It will also take what food it needs from bushes in grasslands and along the edges of cultivated fields.

Diet: The black-crowned barwing eats a diet of insects it plucks from leaves in the high branches of trees or bushes.

Behavior and reproduction: This bird is non-social, preferring to feed alone or with another bird. It mates for life and sings duets with its partner, taking turns singing the melody line. Neither its reproductive cycle nor its nest have been observed in the wild.

Black-crowned barwings and people: These birds have bright coloring, and may be attractive to birdwatchers.

Conservation status: The black-crowned barwing is Vulnerable to extinction because more of its habitat is being used for farmland. ■

The black-crowned barwing was just discovered in 1996, and so scientists still have much to learn about the bird. (Illustration by Bruce Worden. Reproduced by permission.)

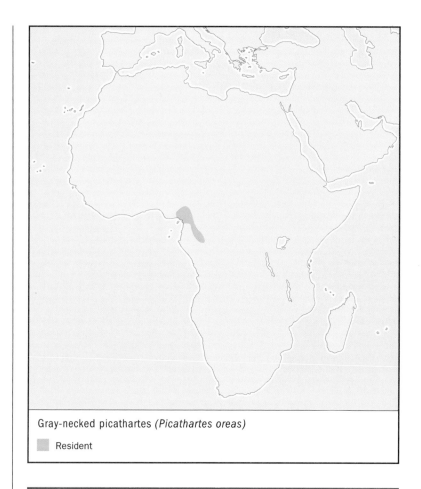

Gray-necked picathartes *(Picathartes oreas)*

▣ Resident

GRAY-NECKED PICATHARTES
Picathartes oreas

Physical characteristics: The gray-necked picathartes is also known as the red-headed rockfowl, the blue-headed picathartes, and the gray-necked bald crow. It is a medium-sized bird about 14 inches (35 centimeters) long and weighs 7.7 ounces (220 grams). Its head is brightly colored in red, blue, and black, against a gray body with a pale yellow underbelly. Black bristles on the top of its head and a ruff at the back of its neck can be raised when the bird is agitated.

Geographic range: This species is found primarily in West Africa in Cameroon, Nigeria, Gabon, and the island of Bioko in the Gulf of Guinea.

Habitat: Gray-necked picathartes nest in rainforest regions near rock formations or inside caves.

Diet: This bird searches for prey by looking through litter on the rainforest floor. Its favorite foods are crabs, frogs, lizards, snails, worms, and army ants.

Behavior and reproduction: A social bird, the gray-necked picathartes forages on the ground in pairs or in small groups of up to ten birds. They roost at night in trees in large numbers.

The gray-necked picathartes keeps the same mate throughout life. Both mates build cup-shaped nests with thick walls made of mud and plant matter, resulting in pottery-like structures. Fixed to rock faces in dense rainforests or wedged into crevices in cave walls, these nests may take up to a year to build. The female lays two multi-colored speckled eggs, and both parents incubate, or sit on the eggs, for twenty-four days.

Gray-necked picathartes and people: These birds have unusual markings, and may be attractive to birdwatchers. They were once imported heavily for exhibition in zoos, but that was stopped in 1973. This species is not frightened by people who enter its nesting areas and shows curiosity about human visitors.

Conservation status: This species is Vulnerable because it depends on the diminishing rainforest for shelter and food.   ■

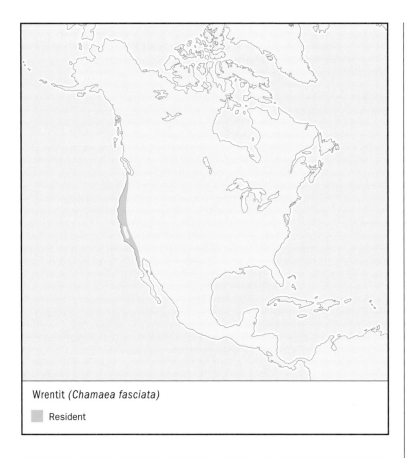

Wrentit (*Chamaea fasciata*)

■ Resident

WRENTIT
Chamaea fasciata

Physical characteristics: The tiny wrentit is 6.3 inches long (16 cm) and weighs only a half ounce (14 grams). Its coloring varies from brown in northern regions to gray in the south. The bird has a sharp bill and a long tail that is usually tilted upright.

Geographic range: The wrentit is considered to be the only babbler in the New World (North, Central, and South America) and may have arrived by crossing the Bering Strait in prehistoric times. It is found along a narrow strip of the West Coast of the United States from Oregon to Baja California.

Habitat: Wrentits live in dense brush, preferring to nest in bushes, whether in the natural setting or in landscaping. They live and die

The wrentit is a small bird, and the only babbler in the New World. (Illustration by Bruce Worden. Reproduced by permission.)

within the 1 to 2.5 acres (0.4 to 1 hectare) surrounding the nest from which they hatched. They are reluctant to fly over open spaces of even 30 to 40 feet (9 to 12 meters), which keeps them from expanding their nesting territory.

Diet: The wrentit eats mainly insects and spiders. Young birds feed exclusively on insects, but adults also eat fruit and berries in the fall and winter when insects are scarce.

Behavior and reproduction: Secretive birds, wrentits live in mated pairs for their entire lives. Both sexes build long, cup-like nests, hidden deep in the inner branches of bushes. The outer structure is made of bark, twigs, hair, and feathers, and then lined with spider webs. Sometimes, the birds cover the outside of their nests with lichen. The female lays three to five pale, greenish blue eggs. Both parents feed the young birds until thirty to thirty-five days after hatching.

The wrentit's continuous song is a series of accelerating high notes, often bouncing back and forth between birds. They will not sing when Bewick's wrens are singing near them and will wait several minutes to begin their own songs after the wrens have left the wrentit's territory.

Wrentits and people: Wrentits are favorites of birdwatchers.

Conservation status: Though the wrentit habitat is being developed by humans, it is not yet threatened with extinction. ■

FOR MORE INFORMATION

Books:

Bird, D. M., J. Berry, and Steve Kress. *Birds: An Explore Your World Handbook (Discovery Channel).* New York: Random House, 1999.

Buff, Shelia. *Birding for Beginners.* New York: Lyons Press, 1993.

MacKinnon, J. R., K. Phillipps, and P. Andrews. *A Field Guide to the Birds of Borneo, Sumatra, Java, and Bali.* New York: Oxford University Press, 1993.

MacKinnon, J. R., K. Phillipps, and Fen-Qi He. *A Field Guide to the Birds of China.* New York: Oxford University Press, 2000.

Robbins, Michael. *Birds (Fandex Family Field Guides).* New York: Workman Publishing Company, 1998.

Weidensaul, Scott. *Birds (National Audubon Society First Field Guides)*. New York: Scholastic Trade, 1998.

Periodicals:

Cibois, Alice. "Mitochondrial DNA Phylogeny of Babblers (Timaliidae)." *The Auk* (January 2003): 35–55.

WRENS

Troglodytidae

Class: Aves

Order: Passeriformes

Family: Troglodytidae

Number of species: 76 species

family

phylum

class

subclass

order

monotypic order

suborder

▲ family

PHYSICAL CHARACTERISTICS

Wrens range in length from 3.5 to 9 inches (9 to 22 centimeters) and weigh between 0.3 and 2 ounces (8 and 57 grams). This songbird of the undergrowth and scrub has feathers that are generally brown or gray-brown. Its wings are short and rounded. They carry their tails in an upright position. Some of them have prominent bars or spotting on the underparts as well as barring on their tails. Both the male and female look alike. They do not have different colors during breeding. Their bills tend to be thin, long, and curved.

GEOGRAPHIC RANGE

Wrens are an American family of birds that can be found throughout North and South America, as far north as Alaska and northern Canada and as far south as Tierra del Fuego in Argentina (the southern tip of South America). One species lives in Europe, North Africa, and Asia. The greatest diversity of species can be found in Central and South America.

HABITAT

The many species and subspecies of wrens live in a large range of habitats depending on their location. They include grasslands, deep forests, forest edges, marshland vegetation such as reeds and cattails, some wetland forests, abandoned farmland, and suburban gardens.

DIET

The eating habits of the majority of wrens remain unknown. The wrens whose eating habits are known—particularly the ten

North American species that have been well studied—are primarily carnivores, eating insects. Cactus wrens are one of the known exceptions, eating large quantities of vegetable matter, such as cactus seeds. Other exceptions are the Carolina wren and Bewick's wren, which feed on berries and plant seeds in the winter.

Some species' diets might also include small frogs or lizards. Wrens usually look for food from their perch rather than catching it in midair. Some species gather their food from whatever is scattered over the forest floor. Most of the other species (whose habits have been observed) feed in the bottom areas of tangled vegetation, with some hunting at slightly higher levels. Some tropical species will follow ant swarms, but none do it on a regular basis.

BEHAVIOR AND REPRODUCTION

Wrens are often known to be secretive in their habits, though this characteristic does not include all members of the family. Some species, such as the cactus wrens, are very much the opposite of secretive—they are noisy birds who make their presence known. Still, most wrens do like to live quiet lives and spend their days in the lower levels of dense undergrowth. They disappear when they notice the least noise or activity that is outside of their own. The nightingale wren is a prime example of this sort of disappearance. Because of this, the nightingale wren is also very hard to observe.

The wrens' vocalizations are what make them noticeable. They sing very loudly, usually way out of proportion for their size. Some species sing not simply in spring or summer but throughout the year. Wrens can have as few as three songs to as many as 219, which is the number of songs recorded from the western marsh wren. Vocalization is used as territorial protection and defense during and outside of breeding seasons.

Wrens have three breeding habits that are unique. They build multiple nests, have multiple partners, and have cooperative nesting, meaning other birds help care for the nest of a breeding pair. Egg destruction of both their own and other species' eggs is also common. Observers have suggested that this could be a way of reducing competition for food sources. In fact, the population decline for some wrens, such as Bewick's wren in eastern North America, has been directly linked to the rise of population in the house wren, due probably to its habit of attacking nests.

The nests that wrens build for breeding are sturdier than those built just for roosting. Wrens like to have a quick getaway when disturbances are nearby, and this led observers to believe that the flimsy roosting nests makes that quick getaway easier. Other species, like the cactus wrens, roost in their nests year-round. Most of the nests are domed with side entrances. Some species, like the northern house wren, do not build nests with a roof over them. Also, many other species build beautiful and elaborate nests, sometimes with two chambers. In the case of the song wren, the opposite is true—their nests are very messy.

North American wrens lay three to ten eggs at a time. The eggs are various colors, with some white to cream, tan, or pink, and often having a brownish mottling on them that can be very pale to very bold in color. The female of the smaller species incubates the eggs (warms them for hatching) for twelve to fifteen days; in larger species, the incubation might average up to sixteen days. The young are hatched helpless, blind, and naked, and are fed by both parents until they become fledglings (grow their flight feathers). This occurs when they are ten to seventeen days old in the smaller species, and an average of twenty-one days in the larger. After fledging, the parents continue to feed the young for about two weeks, unless the female begins produce another group of young. In that case it is usually the male that takes the responsibility for feeding. In many of the species, the young continue to return to the breeding nest to roost for an extended period of time. While some species breed at one year of age, others continue to stay with their parents for years and help raise their siblings. This is called cooperative breeding.

WRENS AND PEOPLE

Wrens do not seem to have much of an impact on agriculture or farming. They have been significant to humans throughout the centuries in legend and poetry, and as hunted birds. In Celtic myth, the wren was the king of the oak tree, symbolizing the old year. The robin (part of the thrushes and chats family) was the symbol for the new year. That is suggested as the cause for the practice of some Celtics in the British Isles, including parts of Ireland, to hunt the wren at the end of the year on St. Stephen's Day (December 26) in order to pave the way for the robin's eventual arrival. In Native American culture, the wren symbolizes the "busybody" probably due to its continual singing, and was expected to be present at labor, rejoicing the birth of a girl, and lamenting the birth of a boy.

CONSERVATION STATUS

Most species are in no known danger of extinction (no longer existing). Some populations have actually increased, while others have declined or become separated due to the loss of forests. Human activities and intervention have actually helped in the case of the northern and southern house wrens, birds known for their easy adaptation to suburban gardens and backyards. Some species, however, are in danger. Two species, Apolinar's wren and the zapata wren, are considered Endangered, facing a very high risk of extinction. Niceforo's wren is Critically Endangered, facing an extremely high risk of extinction. Cobb's wren and the clarion wren are Vulnerable, facing a high risk of extinction, and three other wren species are listed as Near Threatened, in danger of becoming threatened with extinction.

Cactus wren *(Campylorhynchus brunneicapillus)*

▨ Resident

CACTUS WREN
Campylorhynchus brunneicapillus

Physical characteristics: The cactus wren measures in length from about 7.2 to 8.5 inches (18 to 21.6 centimeters) and is the largest species of wren in North America. In color, the bird is a chocolate brown on top with a plain cap. Its back is streaked very prominently in black and white, and the wings, which can spread to a length of 10.7 inches (over 27 centimeters), are barred with buff and black tones. The tail feathers vary between having blackish brown and gray-brown bars. The outer tail feathers are very noticeably barred black and white. The underparts of the bird are buff-white and are spotted heavily with black, especially on the chest. Eyes are reddish brown with a dull black bill that has a paler base. Its legs are a pinkish brown.

Both sexes are similar in appearance. The juvenile bird has spots and streaks that are not as defined as the adult, and its eyes are muddy gray-brown.

Geographic range: Cactus wrens can be found from southeast California to southwest Nevada, and into southern Arizona and New Mexico, as well as southwest Texas through central Mexico. Cactus wrens are also throughout the Baja California peninsula.

Habitat: Cactus wrens inhabit areas that are desert or semi-desert; they also live along arid hillsides and locales that provide them with vegetation such as spiny cacti (KACK-tie, or KACK-tee) and cholla, which is used for nesting.

Diet: Cactus wrens are primarily carnivores (meat eaters), eating invertebrates, animals without a backbone, such as ants, wasps, spiders, and caterpillars, as well as small frogs and lizards. The vegetable matter they consume includes cactus seeds and fruit. They will visit bird feeders and eat pieces of bread and slices of potato or raw apple. They do not need to drink but will if water is available. They tend to be ground feeders, overturning ground litter and stones in order to find their prey.

Behavior and reproduction: Cactus wrens live in pairs or small family groups. When the bird is disturbed, it will run on the ground like a thrasher rather than fly. These birds are often unruly and noisy, with a song that is a loud, harsh series of "jar-jar-jar" notes, usually delivered from the top of a cactus or other perch.

The cactus wren is monogamous (muh-NAH-guh-mus). The breeding nest is an oval-like ball with a side entrance hole that is made of dry grasses and fibers lined with feathers. They are usually located right in spiny cacti and no effort is made to hide them. The female usually lays three to five eggs, though the number can range from two to seven, and they are light brown or pinkish in color with tiny speckles of reddish brown. The female alone incubates the eggs in a period that can last sixteen days. The newly hatched and young birds are fed by both sexes for nineteen to twenty-three days. The cactus wren might attempt up to six broods a year, though usually only three of those are successfully reared.

Cactus wrens and people: The cactus wren is a popular bird for observation due to human familiarity in its habitat. It has been recognized as the state bird of Arizona.

Conservation status: The cactus wren is not a threatened species, and in the most favorable habitats is one of the most common. This adaptable bird seems to need only spiny cactus in order to thrive.   ■

House wren (Troglodytes aedon)

■ Resident   ■ Breeding   ▨ Nonbreeding

HOUSE WREN
Troglodytes aedon

Physical characteristics: The house wren can range in length from 4.6 to 5 inches (11.5 to 12.5 centimeters) with a weight of 0.3 to 0.4 ounces (8 to 11 grams). The bird is plain, mostly gray-brown on its upperparts. It has pale gray underparts, narrow black bars on the sides and lower belly, with wings and tail that have a narrow black barring. Its brown eyes have a pale streak above them, and a narrow pale eye ring. The bill is thin and slightly curved downward. Both sexes are similar, and the young have a dusky mottling on their breasts.

Geographic range: The house wren can be found across North America from the Canadian province of New Brunswick all the way

The house wren is found throughout North America, in northern areas during the breeding season and farther south during the winter. (Joe McDonald/Bruce Coleman Inc. Reproduced by permission.)

south to California and west to central Alberta and southern British Columbia. It migrates in winter south of its breeding grounds to areas that include South Carolina west to southern Arizona and south to the Mexican state of Oaxaca (wah-HAH-kah).

Habitat: The house wren prefers to dwell in open country with brushy areas, and among abandoned farmland, forest edges, and in well-vegetated suburban areas, as well as open deciduous and coniferous forests in the western part of North America.

Diet: The house wren forages in tangled vegetation and is primarily a carnivore, eating invertebrates that include spiders, caterpillars, and other bugs; it also eats small amounts of vegetation.

Behavior and reproduction: House wrens are either found by themselves or in pairs. They are loud and obvious in their behavior, easily noticeable. They can be bold. When males are beginning to mate, they create "dummy" nests as a part of the courtship ritual. The female eventually joins him, inspecting the nests and making the decision about which one is best for the breeding nest. The bird is a cavity nester, mostly building their nests in such places as abandoned woodpecker holes or tree cavities, or even hornets' nests that are no longer being used. They have also adapted to human-made nest boxes and other artificial nesting sites. The female lays four to eight eggs, which are whitish with small reddish brown spots. Eggs are incubated for thirteen to fifteen days, and done by the female. The young are born helpless, blind, and naked, and stay in the nest for twelve to eighteen days after hatching. The house wren has two to three broods a year.

Cactus wrens and people: This common bird is popular with humans due to being so familiar and so adaptable to artificial nests; as a result it is one of the best-studied birds in America.

Conservation status: These wrens are not threatened. ■

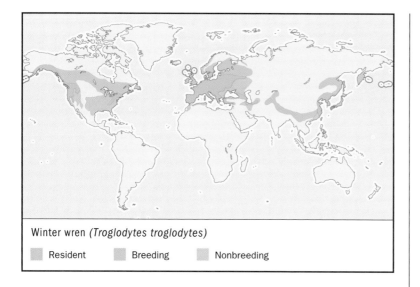

Winter wren *(Troglodytes troglodytes)*

Resident   Breeding   Nonbreeding

WINTER WREN
Troglodytes troglodytes

Physical characteristics: The winter wren averages 3.6 to 4 inches (9 to 10 centimeters) in length, with an average weight of 0.3 to 0.4 ounces (8 to 11 grams). It is a very small, short-tailed wren marked heavily by bars. Its upperparts are a warm dark brown, with pronounced markings of narrow dark bars on the wing and tail feathers. Its chin and throat are a grayish brown with a descending color that becomes more reddish. Its flanks are also a deep reddish brown with darker bars. The eyes, bill, and legs are brown. Both sexes are similar. The juvenile bird has faint spotting on its chest, and flank bars that are even less distinct.

Geographic range: The winter wren is found across four continents, including North America from Alaska southward to the mountains of California, and eastward across Canada to Newfoundland and south to the mountains of Georgia; wintering all the way south to northern Mexico. It can be found in the Old World from Iceland to Scandinavia, south to Spain, Morocco, Algeria, and Libya; eastward to Russia, Caucasus, Turkey, and Iran; and in central Asia from Afghanistan to eastern Siberia, Japan, China, and Taiwan, including many offshore islands in Europe and east Asia.

Winter wrens are common throughout their range in North America, Europe, Asia, and northern Africa. (Illustration by Barbara Duperron. Reproduced by permission.)

Habitat: The winter wren can be found in enormously varied habitats, from the forested areas of North America to the European and Asian bush and woodland areas, as well as in suburban areas and treeless offshore islands with low scrubby vegetation. In fact, it is the only member of the wren family that can be found in Europe.

Diet: The winter wren is primarily an insectivore, or insect-eater, but it is occasionally known to eat spiders and rarely known to eat juniper berries. These birds feed on the forest floor and sometimes along stream banks, scurrying through leaves and brush in a mouse-like manner.

Behavior and reproduction: Winter wrens are protective of their territories during the breeding season, but will sometimes roost communally during the winter with several dozen birds. These birds spend most of their time down in vegetation, hopping through the dense tangles. Flights are always short and low, from cover to cover. Their song is loud and abrasive, with a long series of trills and clear notes.

Winter wrens and people: These birds are both familiar to and popular with humans, and a common subject of folklore in many countries. It is so well known in England that it was given the name of "Jenny Wren."

Conservation status: Winter wrens are not considered to be threatened, and are a generally abundant species throughout their geographic range. ■

Black-capped donacobius *(Donacobius atricapillus)*

Resident

BLACK-CAPPED DONACOBIUS
Donacobius atricapillus

Physical characteristics: The black-capped donacobius wren averages in length from 8.5 to 9 inches (21 to 22 centimeters), with a weight of 1.1 to 1.5 ounces (31 to 42 grams). Its appearance makes the bird unique and unmistakable with a head and shoulders that are glossy black, a back that is more of a brown, and a rump that is olive-brown. Its tail feathers are black with noticeable white tips. Its wings are blackish with an obvious white flash at the bottom. The bird has underparts that are a warm yellow with black bars on its side. Its eyes

are a bright yellow, and its legs are a dusky green. The black-capped donacobius also has a yellow cheek pouch that can puff out.

Geographic range: The black-capped donacobius can be found from Panama to coastal Brazil and into northern Argentina.

Habitat: The black-capped donacobius can be found in the brushy vegetation over slow-moving rivers and ponds, at sea level and rarely up to 2,000 feet (750 meters), usually lower.

Diet: The black-capped donacobius's diet and feeding habits are unknown.

Behavior and reproduction: The black-capped donacobius is noisy and expressive, with pairs taking part in loud, ritualized displays, and spreading their wings. Their song is a series of loud whistles. The female's song is lower and has a more grating quality than the male, and the birds often join in a chorus.

The black-capped donacobius breeds cooperatively, meaning that the nesting pair usually gets help raising their new hatchlings. This comes from up to two additional birds—usually their own young from the previous year or two. When a pair has no assistants, they raise only one bird. Help increases the brood to two. The nest is an open cup and is most often built near or over the water. Eggs are a purplish white covered with reddish or purplish spots and blotches. The female alone incubates the eggs for sixteen to eighteen days, with both sexes and the helpers feeding the young. The birds gain their flight feathers at seventeen to eighteen days. Adult birds keep their young cool by wetting their body feathers in water. The black-capped donacobius only has one brood each breeding season.

Black-capped donacobius and people: The black-capped donacobius has no significant connection to humans.

Conservation status: Not threatened, probably due to their adaptability throughout their breeding distribution. ■

FOR MORE INFORMATION

Books:

Alsop, Fred J. III. *Birds of North America.* Smithsonian Books. London and New York: Dorling Kindersley Publishing, 2001.

Campbell, Brude, and Elizabeth Lack, eds. *A Dictionary of Birds.* Vermillion, SD: Buteo Books, 1985.

Sibley, David Allen, Chris Elphik, and John B. Dunning, eds. *The Sibley Guide to Bird Life and Behavior.* New York: Knopf Publishing Group, 2001.

Web sites:

"Everything About Wrens." About Birds. http://birding.about.com/od/birdswrens/ (accessed on June 16, 2004).

"Wrens." BirdWeb. http://www.birdweb.org/birdweb/family_EZ.asp?famname=Troglodytidae (accessed on June 16, 2004).

family
CHAPTER

PHYSICAL CHARACTERISTICS

Old World warblers encompass a variety of different species, as small as 3.1 inches (8 centimeters) long to as large as 9.8 inches (25 centimeters), weighing from 0.1 to 2 ounces (4 to 56 grams). Many species live eight to twelve years.

All Old World warblers have bristles at the base of thin, pointed bills that help them catch flying insects. The wings of species that migrate are long and pointed, whereas the wings of birds that remain within permanent territories are round and short.

Most of the birds in this family are dully colored in greens, yellows, grays, and browns.

GEOGRAPHIC RANGE

These birds have a wide distribution, including the subarctic, Europe, Asia, Africa, North and South America, Australia, and Pacific islands.

HABITAT

Old World warblers occupy a variety of habitats from arid scrubland to islands in the ocean, and every habitable niche in between, ranging from sea level to as high as several thousand feet (meters). Many species occupy specific levels within a habitat, with one species claiming the higher portions, as in the forest canopy, and others claiming lower regions such as bushes or the forest floor.

DIET

Generally, this family of birds lives on insects and spiders. Some species eat snails and small crustaceans. Others, such as the golden-crowned kinglet and some African species, feed on nectar and sap. Some large reed warblers eat fish and frogs. Young hatchlings eat insects and occasionally berries. Migratory birds change their diets to berries and fruit in order to have enough stored fat for flying long distances.

BEHAVIOR AND REPRODUCTION

Many members of this bird family mate for a single nesting or a season, with some mating for life. Males of some species keep two or more females, maintaining separate nests and young. Serial monogamy (muh-NAH-guh-mee), or mating for a single nesting then finding another mate or mates for other nestings, is quite common. Some males have as many as eleven nestings in a season.

MIXED FLOCK MIGRATION

The blue-gray gnatcatcher migrates in large mixed flocks of many different species of birds. Though different species, they all prefer forested regions. They stop over in forest edge habitats where there is an abundant variety of food for the diverse flock and adequate protection from predators.

Courtship behavior is equally diverse among Old World warblers. Some males will sing elaborate songs. Others will dance, displaying a variety of postures. Still others build nests for show and bring objects as gifts to females.

Old World warblers create nearly every shape and type of nest imaginable. There are cup-shaped nests, domed nests, and round balls that are built from all kinds of plant materials, including moss, lichen, twigs, and grasses. Some nests are built on the ground, some in bushes, and others in trees as high as 80 feet (26 meters). Nests are wedged into the forks of branches or tucked into crevices in walls. Some are hung from vines or leaves. Tailorbirds actually sew their nests. The female punctures leaves with her bill and threads grasses through the holes, even knotting the ends so the nests don't unravel. Both sexes of some species build nests. Females alone will build nests among species whose males have more than one mate.

Females lay one to twelve eggs and incubate them, or sit on them until they are hatched, alone. Males of a few species share this duty. The eggs remain in the nest for ten to twenty-one days and are fed by their parents for one to four more weeks. The young have no feathers at birth.

Some Old World warblers forage with many different species in large groups. Others will only feed with their own family group or with their mates.

Some species spy insects from a perch and swoop down on them. Other species stand on the ground and scoop up insects. A few species will either scratch through the litter on the forest floor or use their wings to move the leaves about. Kemp's longbill will poke its bill into dead wood found on the ground.

Old World warblers are a vocally diverse family. Nearly all of them have developed song patterns that range from strictly unmusical repetitions to beautiful, complex melodies. Songs are used to mark territory, attract mates, and communicate with family groups. Duets are songs between bonded mates.

OLD WORLD WARBLERS AND PEOPLE

Since Old World warblers are insect eaters, they hold the potential to be effective pest control for farmers and timber producers. Some nectar-eating species may also act as pollinators for cultivated plants.

CONSERVATION STATUS

Several species are threatened, or at high risk of becoming extinct, or dying out. Fifteen species of marsh warbler are at high risk of becoming extinct. These species are experiencing population declines due to their isolation on oceanic islands where their habitats are being reduced.

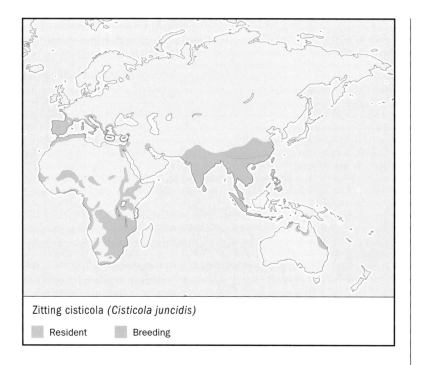

Zitting cisticola *(Cisticola juncidis)*

Resident   Breeding

ZITTING CISTICOLA
Cisticola juncidis

Physical characteristics: Also called the fantailed warbler, the fantailed cisticola, and the streaked cisticola, this bird is 3.9 to 4.7 inches (10 to 12 centimeters) long and weighs 0.3 to 0.4 ounces (8 to 12 grams). It has a brown body streaked with black, reddish sides and rump, and a black and white spotted belly. It has a small thin bill, short round wings, and a small tail.

Geographic range: These birds can be found in Spain, North Africa, sub-Saharan Africa, the Mediterranean, India, Southeast Asia, Indonesia, and the north coast of Australia.

Habitat: The zitting cisticola prefers grassy wetlands as well as some cultivated areas, like sugar cane and grain fields.

Diet: This species eats insect larvae (LAR-vee), spiders, and insects, especially grasshoppers and beetles.

Behavior and reproduction: The zitting cisticola takes insects and insect larvae on the ground. It stays in permanent territories but will

Male zitting cisticolas build a "show" nest to attract a female, and the female builds the "real" nest, where she lays her eggs. (Illustration by Barbara Duperron. Reproduced by permission.)

move away from the nesting regions after the young can fly. Mediterranean populations are migratory.

The song of the zitting cisticola is a string of a sharp "zit" notes emitted in half-second to one-second intervals.

The males of this species are serially monogamous. Males can mate with one to eleven females in a year. Sometimes, some males will mate with many females at the same time.

Male zitting cisticolas build show nests close to the ground and signal to females by singing. The female builds the real nest, a pear-shaped bag, constructed by weaving and sewing plant fibers and spider webs. She lays two to six eggs and incubates them for eleven to fifteen days. The female feeds the young for ten to twenty days until they leave the nest.

Zitting cisticolas and people: There is no special significance to humans.

Conservation status: This species is not considered to be threatened. ■

Blue-gray gnatcatcher (*Polioptila caerulea*)

Resident   Breeding   Nonbreeding

BLUE-GRAY GNATCATCHER
Polioptila caerulea

Physical characteristics: The blue-gray gnatcatcher measures 4 to 4.5 inches (10.2 to 11.4 centimeters) long and weighs 0.18 to 0.25 ounces (5 to 7 grams). Bearing a long, thin bill, it has a blue-gray back, a white underbelly with buff sides, a buff colored face, and a long upright tail that is white on the outer edges and black on the inside. When the male breeds, it has a black eye ring; otherwise, it is white.

Geographic range: These birds breed throughout the United States except in the Great Plains, and many will winter in the southern United States, Mexico, Honduras, and Cuba. Some permanent populations exist in Mexico and the Bahamas.

Blue-gray gnatcatcher chicks leave the nest ten to fifteen days after hatching. (© R.and S. Day/ VIREO. Reproduced by permission.)

Habitat: The blue-gray gnatcatcher lives in the swampy underbrush and thickets of pine and leafy forests. In the western United States, these birds are found in arid scrub and stands of pinyon-juniper. In humid tropical areas, the birds will occupy the vine tangle of rainforest as well as thorn forests, scrub, and clearings.

Diet: This species eats insects and spiders. The blue-gray gnatcatcher finds insects by diving for them from the air to the forest floor or catching them in the air. Sometimes, they will forage while sitting on a perch.

Behavior and reproduction: These birds live alone or in pairs. Among migratory populations, males will stake out territory, singing loudly, well before the females arrive. Their calls are a thin whine. The male's is a series of notes, chips, and whistles.

Birds of this species mate for life. The male brings his mate to a nest that they both build, made in a cup shape from grasses and spider webs, covered with lichen, and situated on high branches of trees or shrubs. The female lays four to five pale blue eggs flecked with brown that are incubated for eleven to fifteen days by both the male and female. When the eggs hatch, only the female feeds them, but both parents will feed them when they leave the nest, usually in ten to fifteen days.

Blue-gray gnatcatchers and people: Blue-gray gnatcatchers have no special significance to humans.

Conservation status: This species is not considered to be threatened. ■

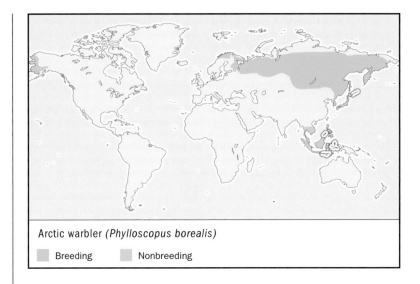

Arctic warbler (*Phylloscopus borealis*)

▮ Breeding   ▮ Nonbreeding

ARCTIC WARBLER
Phylloscopus borealis

Physical characteristics: The Arctic warbler is 4.1 to 5.1 inches long (10.4 to 13 centimeters) and weighs 0.3 to 0.5 ounces (8 to 15 grams). It has an olive-green back, yellowish white belly, a dark eye line, and straw-colored legs. Its wings are long with two white bars on them.

Geographic range: This species is found in Alaska, Scandinavia, Japan, and the northern regions of Europe and Asia. It winters in Southeast Asia.

Habitat: Arctic warblers live mainly in deciduous forests in the North and in taiga, or subarctic wet evergreen forests. They will winter in rainforest, gardens, woodlands, and mangroves.

Diet: These birds eat insects, especially mosquitoes, and larvae.

Behavior and reproduction: The Arctic warbler finds insects and larvae in leaves, high above the ground. A very active bird, it darts among trees and will flick its wings and tail when it perches.

These birds prefer to live alone or with a mate. Sometimes, they will gather in small family groups. The male will defend his territory through song and wing twitching displays.

Arctic warblers mate for life. The female builds a dome-shaped nest of dry grasses and hair, with a side entrance on the forest floor. The female then lays five to seven pink-speckled white eggs and incubates them for eleven to thirteen days. Hatchlings stay in the nest for thirteen to fourteen days and are fed by both parents.

Arctic warblers and people: There is no known significance to humans.

Conservation status: This species is not considered to be threatened. ■

The male arctic warbler defends his territory through song and wing twitching displays. (© Doug Wechsler/VIREO. Reproduced by permission.)

FOR MORE INFORMATION

Books:

Baker, Kevin. *Warblers of Europe.* Princeton, NJ: Princeton University Press, 1997.

BirdLife International. *Threatened Birds of the World.* Barcelona and Cambridge, U.K.: Lynx Edicions and BirdLife International, 2000.

Perrins, Christopher. *Firefly Encyclopedia of Birds.* Richmond Hill, Canada: Firefly Books, 2003.

Shirihai, Hadoram, Gabriel Gargallo, and Andreas J. Helbig. *Sylvia Warblers.* Princeton, NJ: Princeton University Press, 2001.

Weidensaul, Scott. *Birds (National Audubon Society First Field Guides).* New York: Scholastic Trade, 1998.

Periodicals:

Rodewald, P. G., and Margaret C. Brittingham. "Habitat Use and Behavior of Mixed Species Landbird Flocks during Fall Migration." *Wilson Bulletin* (March 2002): 87–99.

family

CHAPTER

PHYSICAL CHARACTERISTICS

Old World flycatchers are divided into two groups, the typical Old World flycatchers, and the African flycatchers. The typical flycatchers are small to medium sized, ranging from 3 to 9 inches (7.6 to 2.3 centimeters) long. Their coloring varies from black and white to browns to vivid blues and reds. Both males and females are colored similarly, though males have brighter colors than females in some species. Because these birds look for food by perching and flying in complex maneuvers to catch flying insects, they have short legs and small feet. They also have bristles on their beaks that help them catch their prey.

African flycatcher species are also small to medium sized. They have short flattened bills with a slightly hooked tip and bristles like the typical flycatchers. Their feet and legs vary according to the species. Their most striking feature is an area of bare skin, usually in white or buff, around the eye that is most visible when they are excited. Males have glossy black and white feathers, and the females are brown and reddish.

GEOGRAPHIC RANGE

Old World flycatchers can be found in Europe, Asia, Africa, India, Micronesia, and Australia and New Guinea. The greatest concentration of species lives in tropical regions of Africa and Asia. African flycatchers are found only in Africa.

HABITAT

Some Old World flycatchers live in dry forests, grasslands, and savanna, while others prefer wetlands and moist forests.

Still others make their homes in pastures, orchards, gardens, and residential landscaping.

DIET

Members of this family are all insect eaters, and some eat spiders.

BEHAVIOR AND REPRODUCTION

Many Old World flycatchers hunt for food by sitting on a high perch and waiting for insects to fly by, then they swoop down and eat them in flight. Others find insects on leaves, bark, branches, and even spider webs. Some even dive to the forest floor to pick up spiders.

These birds defend their nests during mating season by singing and fighting with other birds of their species. They build cup-shaped nests, made of grass and bark, in small openings in trees, stumps, and rock ledges, or in the forks of tree branches. Females lay two to seven spotted or speckled eggs. Both parents of some species build the nest, whereas only the female does the nest building in other species. Both parents feed hatchlings and young birds after they leave the nest. In some species such as the African flycatcher, young birds from a previous mating help feed the newly hatched young.

Tropical and subtropical species of Old World flycatchers remain in their territories permanently, though they may move to a different altitude during the year. Northern species breed in the temperate, not too hot or too cold, and sub-arctic areas and then move to the warmer tropic or subtropical regions in the winter. Old World flycatchers are strong fliers and are capable of traveling long distances.

These birds are rather shy and stay within their family groupings of a mate and immature offspring.

OLD WORLD FLYCATCHERS AND PEOPLE

Because of the beauty of their coloring and song, Old World flycatchers contribute to ecotourism, travel for the purpose of observing wildlife and learning about the environment without interfering.

EGG RECOGNITION

Spotted flycatchers are very skilled at identifying their own eggs and will remove or ignore eggs placed in their nests by opportunistic birds, such as the common cuckoo or the cowbird. Opportunistic birds are birds that put their eggs in other birds' nests for them to raise. This egg recognition skill is the result of past exploitation by the cuckoo.

CONSERVATION STATUS

Eighteen species of true Old World flycatchers are at risk of extinction, or dying out. Nineteen other species are listed as Near Threatened, in danger of becoming threatened with extinction. Habitat destruction is the main reason that populations are declining. Some rare species have not been studied enough to determine their conservation status. At-risk species include, the Nimba flycatcher and the red-tailed newtonia, which are listed as Vulnerable, facing a high risk of extinction in the wild. Banded wattle-eyes are Endangered, facing a very high risk of extinction in the wild.

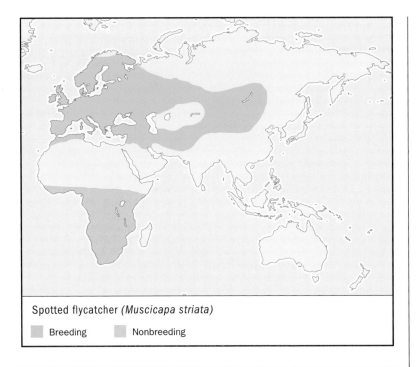

Spotted flycatcher (*Muscicapa striata*)

■ Breeding   ▨ Nonbreeding

SPOTTED FLYCATCHER
Muscicapa striata

Physical characteristics: Both sexes of spotted flycatchers have brownish gray bodies and white undersides, with long tails and long wings. Some have gray streaks along their throats. The birds have black bills and short, black legs. Young birds have brown bodies and spotted undersides. This is where the species gets its name. They are 5 inches (12.7 centimeters) long.

Geographic range: Spotted flycatchers can be found in Europe, Russia, western Asia, and North Africa. They spend the winter in southwestern Asia and Africa.

Habitat: Spotted flycatchers prefer forests with deciduous trees, trees that lose their leaves in winter. These forested areas can be natural or cultivated as in orchards, parks, and gardens. Because they feed from high perches, they often hunt in cleared areas between trees.

Diet: Spotted flycatchers eat flying insects.

Spotted flycatchers swoop down from perches where they watch for prey, and capture flying insects while they are in the air. (Illustration by Barbara Duperron. Reproduced by permission.)

Behavior and reproduction: Spotted flycatchers swoop down from perches where they watch for flying insects, capturing them while in the air. They frequently return to the same perch to wait for more prey.

These birds build an open nest in a recess, hollowed out area, usually in a wall, a crotch of a tree, or a tree hollow. They will also nest in open-fronted nest boxes. Females lay four to six greenish eggs with rust colored spots.

Members of this family winter in Africa and southwestern Asia as single birds. They return to their territories as the season changes.

The song of the spotted flycatcher is a series of six squeaky notes.

Spotted flycatchers and people: This species has no special importance to humans, except to be appreciated by birdwatchers.

Conservation status: The population of spotted flycatchers is declining in parts of their territory but they are not threatened. ■

Little slaty flycatcher (Ficedula basilanica)

▨ Resident

LITTLE SLATY FLYCATCHER
Ficedula basilanica

Physical characteristics: Little slaty flycatchers are small, only 5 inches (12.7 centimeters), with heavy bills and short tails. Males have slate gray heads, backs, and tails, with a white underside, a grey breast band and sides, brown wings, and pink feet. They also have white circles around their eyes that are exposed when they sing. Females have reddish brown heads and wings, with brighter color on their tails, and white undersides with a reddish wash on the breast and sides. They also have a buff ring around their eyes.

Geographic range: This species is native to the Philippines, occurring on the islands of Samar, Leyte, Dinagat, Basilan, and Mindanao.

Little slaty flycatchers are quite shy and are best found by listening to their song or call. (Illustration by Barbara Duperron. Reproduced by permission.)

Habitat: Little slaty flycatchers live in the dense understory, the smaller trees in a forest, from sea level to 3,900 feet (1,200 meters). Sometimes, these birds can be found as high as 394 feet (120 meters) up in the trees.

Diet: Little slaty flycatchers eat insects.

Behavior and reproduction: The species has a high-pitched, three-note call with a beautiful, warbling song. Little slaty flycatchers are quite shy and are best found by listening to their song or call.

Like other Old World flycatchers they build cup-shaped nests. Little slaty flycatchers live in permanent territories.

Little slaty flycatchers and people: There is some economic potential for ecotourism for communities where little slaty flycatchers live.

Conservation status: Populations have decreased due to lowland forest loss from logging and other land clearing for mining and recreational development, making this species Vulnerable. There are between 2,500 and 10,000 little slaty flycatchers in the world. ■

Cape batis (*Batis capensis*)

░ Resident

CAPE BATIS
Batis capensis

Physical characteristics: Cape batises belong to a group called wattle-eyes. All thirty-one wattle-eyes live in Africa. They are called wattle-eyes because they have bright flesh colored circles around their eyes. This group of birds is being reconsidered as an Old World flycatcher and has been granted its own family grouping by some taxonomists, scientists who classify animals according to specific traits.

Also called cape puffbacks, cape batises have large heads relative to their small bodies. They weigh 5.1 ounces (13 grams) and are 6 inches (15 centimeters) long. They have short tails, round wings, and orange eyes. Males have dark blue-gray backs and tails, black

Cape batises build a small cup-shaped nest of dry grasses, held together with spider webs. The nest is built low in thick brush in the fork of a branch and holds one to three eggs.
(© W. Tarboton/VIREO. Reproduced by permission.)

heads, white throats and bellies edged in reddish brown, and a black breast band. Females have brown heads, a brownish wash over the breast, and no breast band.

Geographic range: Cape batises live along the coast of South Africa and deep into the escarpments, steep slopes or cliffs, of Swaziland and Zimbabwe.

Habitat: Cape batises make their home in forests, scrub, and planted gardens in southern Africa. Their range is from sea level to 7,050 feet (2,150 meters).

Diet: Like other flycatchers, cape batises eat insects.

Behavior and reproduction: This species lives in permanent territories with a mate, either alone or in small groups, though some populations will gather in large flocks of ten to thirty birds. Sometimes, cape batises will forage for food with other bird species. Some populations migrate to different elevations as the seasons change.

Cape batises actively seek insects throughout the forest canopy by flushing, frightening, them from their places of cover, hiding. The birds then capture their prey as it flies.

This species mates from September to December, building a small cup-shaped nest of dry grasses, held together with spider webs. The nest is built low in thick brush in the fork of a branch and holds one to three eggs. The female incubates, sits on and warms, the eggs for seventeen to twenty-one days. Mating pairs stay together for life.

Cape batises have a monotonous, unchanging, call of repeating "tu" syllables and a simple whistle.

Cape batises and people: This species has the potential to contribute to ecotourism, an industry based on attracting tourists to view birds and other animals in their environments.

Conservation status: Cape batises are not threatened with extinction. ■

FOR MORE INFORMATION

Books:

Perrins, Christopher. *Firefly Encyclopedia of Birds.* Richmond Hill, Canada: Firefly Books, 2003.

Robbins, Michael. *Birds: Fandex Family Field Guides.* New York: Workman Publishing Company, 1998.

Stattersfield, A. J., David R. Capper, and Guy C. L. Dutson. *Threatened Birds of the World.* Barcelona and Cambridge, U.K.: Lynx Edicions and BirdLife International, 2000.

Weidensaul, Scott. *Birds: National Audubon Society First Field Guides.* New York: Scholastic Trade, 1998.

Class: Aves

Order: Passeriformes

Family: Maluridae

Number of species: 30 species

family

phylum

class

subclass

order

monotypic order

suborder

▲ **family**

PHYSICAL CHARACTERISTICS

These birds range in length from 5.5 to 8.6 inches (14 to 22 centimeters) and weigh from 0.27 to 1.2 ounces (7.6 to 34.1 grams). Grasswrens are colored brown and tan with black and white markings. Only faint shades mark the differences between the sexes in grasswrens. Female undersides tend to be more russet, reddish, in color than male. Breeding male fairy-wrens display colors of bright blues, violets, purples, and russets. Some have cheek patches of bright turquoise—these cheek patches can be blown out to form a face fan during territorial contests or courting displays. Emu-wrens have long tails that are filament-like, or thread-like.

GEOGRAPHIC RANGE

Fairy-wrens can be found throughout Australia and New Guinea. Some species are found only in a limited area, while others are distributed over the entire continent. Emu-wrens and grasswrens only inhabit Australia. Fairy-wrens are found in New Guinea as well as Australia.

HABITAT

The various species of Australian fairy-wrens can be found in different habitats. Grasswrens find homes in grasslands of the dry interior lands of the continent with a very limited geographic distribution. Emu-wrens inhabit many different kinds of environments such as swampland, and the thickets of the southern Australian plains along the coastal belts. Others inhabit the arid, dry, interior. Fairy-wrens also live in many different kinds of habitats, from tropical grasslands to wet forests and woodlands, and the semi-arid interior. Yet other species have adapted to humans and inhabit parks and suburban gardens.

DIET

Australian fairy-wrens are omnivores, eating both plants and animals. They forage, search for food, on the ground for wide range of invertebrates, animals with backbones and also harvest foliage, twigs, and bark, and sometimes catch flying insects from the air. Some species are more specific in their foraging, as in the case of the purple-crowned fairy-wren that forages in pandanus plants along the edges of tropical streams, rivers, and ponds.

BEHAVIOR AND REPRODUCTION

Most members of the Australian fairy-wrens live in family groups. They are usually territorial and sedentary, do not migrate. They communicate with other group members with a wide variety of melodious calls. They keep busy foraging for food, climbing through the thick undergrowth, and hopping over open areas of ground with their tails cocked.

Most species of the family are cooperative breeders, meaning that they have help with the care of the young from the offspring of previous years. The adults studied have a high rate of survival, and breed extensively. Their nests are domed balls of woven grass with side entrances. Clutches have two to four red-spotted, white eggs. The female usually incubates the eggs for a period of ten to fourteen days. Young birds are fed for four to six weeks.

A team of scientists from Cambridge University and Bristol University, England, led by a professor from the Australian National University, reported in 2003 that superb Australian fairy-wrens have found a way to combat predatory habits of cuckoos—in this case, the Australian Horsfield's bronze-cuckoo. The cuckoo kills any host young by kicking them out of their nest, and then lays an egg that resembles the fairy-wren's egg, and so the superb Australian fairy-wren does not remove the egg. Within forty-eight hours of hatching, the cuckoo kicks out the host's chick from the nest. But the host fairy-wrens, at least approximately 40 percent of those studied, abandoned the nest two days later, and the cuckoo chick starves to death while the fairy-wrens nest again.

AUSTRALIAN FAIRY-WRENS AND PEOPLE

There is no specific connection to humans other than through observation that has named the family as among the most beautiful of birds. They continue to be studied as a "recently" discovered separate family, only identified in 1975. DNA research in the late 1990s finally discovered their distinct identity.

CONSERVATION STATUS

Australian fairy-wrens are not currently threatened, though overgrazing and the changes in the land that come from agriculture and timber production do provide a potential threat.

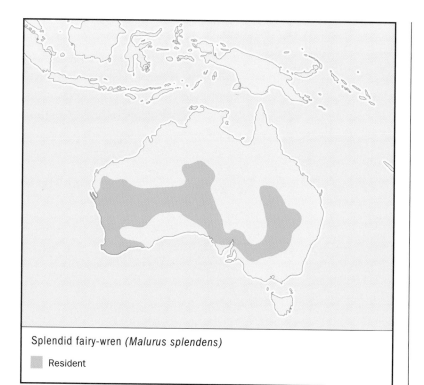

Splendid fairy-wren (*Malurus splendens*)

■ Resident

SPLENDID FAIRY-WREN
Malurus splendens

Physical characteristics: Splendid fairy-wrens are 5.5 inches (14 centimeters) in length. The male and female differ in weight, with the male weighing about 0.28 to 0.39 ounces (7.9 to 11.1 grams), and the female weighing about 0.27 to 0.36 ounces (7.6 to 10.2 grams). While in breeding plumage the male is a very bright, deep blue with turquoise cheek patches and crown, black breast, face, and back markings. Females, nonbreeding males, and juveniles are drab olive on top with blue tails and wings.

Geographic range: Splendid fairy-wren populations are scattered throughout Australia, including the western coastal areas, the interior, and some in the east.

Males and females both mate with a number of other birds during the breeding season. (© Wayne Lawler/Photo Researchers, Inc. Reproduced by permission.)

Habitat: Splendid fairy-wrens mostly inhabit the drier acacia (uh-KAY-shah) woodlands and scrublands.

Diet: Splendid fairy-wrens are primarily carnivores, meat-eaters, foraging on the ground for insects such as ants, grasshoppers, spiders, and insect larvae (LAR-vee), but they also eat foliage up to canopy height. They forage for food doing a hop-search, pouncing on their prey, and may catch flying insects in the air.

Behavior and reproduction: Splendid fairy-wrens are stronger fliers than other fairy-wrens, and also forage in a variety of ways. The bird is a territorial breeder, and is usually found in small groups. Its voice is a loud series of trills.

Splendid fairy-wrens are promiscuous breeders, meaning both males and females mate with a number of other birds. The male is the father of less than half of the offspring in his territory. Clutches have two to four, red-spotted white eggs. Females incubate the eggs for about two weeks, and fledging takes place in ten to thirteen days.

Splendid fairy-wrens and people: No known significance to humans, other than extensive research and observation by scientists.

Conservation status: Splendid fairy-wrens are not threatened, but they may be threatened in the future by loss of habitat for agriculture and overgrazing. ■

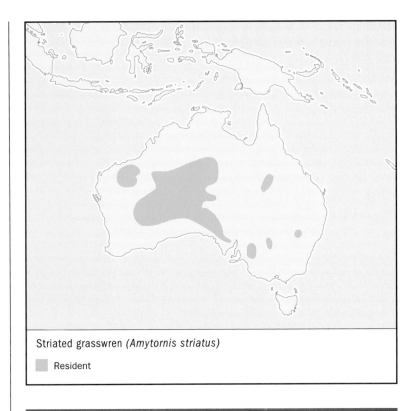

Striated grasswren (*Amytornis striatus*)

☐ Resident

STRIATED GRASSWREN
Amytornis striatus

Physical characteristics: Striated grasswrens average 5.7 to 6.9 inches (14.5 to 17.5 centimeters) in length. The male weighs between 0.56 and 0.78 ounces (16 and 22 grams). Both males and females are similar in appearance, with russet brown and paler shades of brown and tan on the upperparts and with buff-whitish undersides. They also have russet, reddish, splashes on the sides and a bill that has black whisker marks. The female has chestnut flakes.

Geographic range: Striated grasswrens have populations scattered across Australia, including areas from New South Wales to Western Australia, with a small central area of Queensland for one of its subspecies.

Habitat: Striated grasswrens can be found on sand plains and rocky hills, and throughout the shrubby vegetation of the dry interior land.

Diet: Striated grasswren forage for food on the ground, eating insects, particularly ants and beetles, and seeds. They also have been observed eating cactus flowers and foraging at midnight.

Behavior and reproduction: By nature, the striated grasswren is secretive in its behavior. The birds are poor fliers, hopping instead over open ground with their tails cocked, or with it horizontal when they are traveling through vegetation that is very thick. Striated grasswrens can be found alone, or in small family groups. Their song is melodious with trills and whistles.

Due to the difficulty of observing this bird, their breeding habits have been difficult to define. A clutch has two or three red-spotted, white eggs. Cooperative breeding or help with the nest has not been observed.

Striated grasswrens and people: There is no special significance between striated grasswrens and people. Since this bird is often distributed in areas that can be difficult to travel into, the bird can be difficult to observe.

Conservation status: By the early twenty-first century the striated grasswren had been listed by the New South Wales National Park as Near Threatened, in danger of becoming threatened. Their population and distribution has been severely reduced due destruction of favorable habitat by overgrazing, the introduction of herbivores, as well as predatory cats and foxes, and extensive fires.

The striated grasswren is secretive in its behavior, and is a difficult bird to study. (Illustration by Joseph E. Trumpey. Reproduced by permission.)

FOR MORE INFORMATION

Books:

Campbell, Brude, and, Lack, Elizabeth, eds. *A Dictionary of Birds.* Vermillion, SD: Buteo Books, 1985.

Fisher, James, and Roger Tory Peterson. *The World of Birds.* Garden City, NJ: Doubleday & Company, Inc., 1964.

Lewis, Adrian, and Derek Pomeroy. *A Bird Atlas of Kenya.* Lisse, Netherlands: Swets and Zeitlinger, 1988.

Simpson, Ken, and Nicolas Day. *The Birds of Australia, A Book of Identification.* Dover, NH: Tanager Books, 1984.

Web sites:

Ehrlich , Paul R., David Dobkin, and Darryl Wheye. "Birds, DNA, and Evolutionary Convergence." Stanford Alumni Organization. http://www.stanfordalumni.org/birdsite/text/essays/Birds,_DNA.html (accessed on June 9, 2004).

"Fairywrens & Grasswrens." Monterey Bay. http://www.montereybay.com/creagrus/fairywrens.html (accessed on June 9, 2004).

"Striated Grasswrens." Gluepot's Biological Treasures and Threatened Birds. http://birdsaustralia.com.au/gluepot/threatened.html (accessed on June 9, 2004).

"Striated Grasswrens." Michael Morcombe's Field Guide to Australian Birds. http://www.michaelmorcombe.com.au/striatedgrasswre.html (accessed on June 9, 2004).

Class: Aves

Order: Passeriformes

Family: Acanthizidae

Number of species: 63 to 68 species

family
CHAPTER

PHYSICAL CHARACTERISTICS

Australian warblers tend to be small- to medium- sized birds, with an average length of 3.5 to 10 inches (9 to 27 centimeters) and a weight range of 0.25 to 2.5 ounces (7 to 70 grams). Most of the species are olive-green, somewhat drab-colored birds, but with distinctive markings on the head and face, such as light eyebrows, spots, and streaks. Some species have yellow or reddish rumps. Some of the thornbills and gerygones have yellow undersides, while the pilotbird and rockwarbler have reddish brown underside. This family of birds has slender bills. The tails of some species are cocked, tilted, regularly. Males and females are similar in appearance.

GEOGRAPHIC RANGE

Australian warblers are distributed throughout Australia, New Guinea, and New Zealand, including the Chatham Islands. They are also found in Indonesia and South East Asia.

HABITAT

Australian warblers occur in many different habitats throughout their distribution area including, mangroves, rainforests, eucalyptus (yoo-kah-LIP-tus) forests and woodlands, shrub lands, and desert.

DIET

Most of this family captures small invertebrates, animals without backbones, from the foliage, twigs, branches, and trunks,

phylum

class

subclass

order

monotypic order

suborder

▲ **family**

picking their prey with their long and slender bills. They eat primarily small insects, but occasionally some species eat seeds and fruits.

BEHAVIOR AND REPRODUCTION

The Australian warbler family of birds is a very active group, hopping over the ground and through the foliage of the trees or bushes. Some species can be very mysterious in their behavior. Most species tend to be sedentary and tend to stay in the same area throughout the year with only local movement. However, one species, the white-throated gerygone does migrate into southeastern Australia in the spring. All other species are weak fliers. In song and vocalization, most species are melodious, loud, and have distinctive voices. Some are even gifted mimics, able to copy or imitate other species' calls. Others have only buzzing, trilling or rattling notes with short quiet songs. Certain species like the bristlebirds have whistling calls that are carried far in order to announce their presence.

Some species are cooperative breeders, where nonbreeding birds assist the parents with the care and protection of chicks, while in other species only parents raise their chicks. The breeding season lasts from late winter to early summer. Several breeding attempts occur each season. Nests are domed, usually placed in trees or shrubs, with some in crevices and hollows, or even on the ground. Clutches commonly include two eggs, but have been observed with as many as five. The color of the eggs comes in many forms including white, white with sparse spotting, cream or buff with widespread spotting, and chocolate. The eggs that are incubated only by the female are laid at forty-eight-hour intervals. Incubation and the independence of fledglings are both accomplished over a long period of time. Both parents, and sometimes the helpers, feed the young. Many nests succumb to predators. Bronze-cuckoos lay their eggs in some nests and kick out the young warblers. Adult survival each year is as high as 80 percent—a high percentage for birds that are so small.

AUSTRALIAN WARBLERS AND PEOPLE

Humans do not often take notice of this small, drab bird, though the songs of some species are definitely well-known. With many exhibiting such cryptic behavior, bird watching can be difficult, which is one reason that it has taken so long to identify so many of the species.

CONSERVATION STATUS

One species of gerygone, the Lord Howe gerygone was already Extinct, no longer existing, by the beginning of the twenty-first century. The Biak gerygone is Endangered, facing a very high risk of extinction in the wild; and the Norfolk Island gerygone is Vulnerable, facing a high risk of extinction in the wild. These populations have been hurt by habitat loss as well as from the introduction of predatory mammals. In 2000, the Action Plan for Australian Birds listed a large number of this family as Threatened, in danger of extinction, or Almost Threatened, close to becoming threatened. Other threats to these populations have been extensive fires and grazing from the introduced mammals. Only the Coorong subspecies remained categorized as secure on the Australian list.

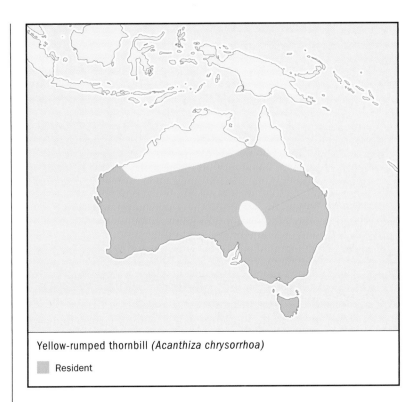

Yellow-rumped thornbill (*Acanthiza chrysorrhoa*)

▢ Resident

YELLOW-RUMPED THORNBILL
Acanthiza chrysorrhoa

Physical characteristics: Yellow-rumped thornbills average 4 inches (10 centimeters) in length, with a weight of 0.32 ounces (9 grams). They are known for their bright yellow rump—from which they derived their common name—and their black crown with white spots, and white brow.

Geographic range: Yellow-rumped thornbills can be found throughout central and southern Australia, including Tasmania, an island off the southern coast of Australia.

Habitat: Yellow-rumped thornbills inhabit open woodland areas and edges, farmland, grassland that has trees or bushes sparsely located throughout the area, parks, and gardens.

Diet: Yellow-rumped thornbills are omnivores, eating both animals and plants. They eat primarily insects and other invertebrates, and

occasionally, seeds. The birds forage the ground for the most part, but will sometimes forage on shrubs and low trees.

Behavior and reproduction: Yellow-rumped thornbills live in family groups or small flocks with others thornbills. They tend to be active, noisy, and sing with twittering melodies and calls. Their yellow rumps are easy to spot while in flight but they virtually disappear when the birds land. Generally they only move locally, and tend to be non-migratory, sedentary.

The breeding season is from July to December, and sometimes goes later. The nest is domed, built in a bush or sapling, and is made of grass, lichen, and other plant fibers. The side entrance is concealed by a hood. A false cup-shaped nest is put on the top, probably to confuse predators or cuckoos. Both males and females build the nest. Each clutch has two to four lightly speckled, pink eggs. Only the female incubates the eggs, which is a period of eighteen to twenty days. The fledging period lasts seventeen to nineteen days. The parents often have the assistance of helpers. Many nests do not survive predators or the parasites of the bronze-cuckoos.

Yellow-rumped thornbills and people: People are well-acquainted with this colorful bird, and it is particularly familiar to those who live in the country.

Conservation status: This species is not threatened with extinction. ∎

Yellowhead (*Mohua ochrocephala*)

▨ Resident

YELLOWHEAD
Mohua ochrocephala

Physical characteristics: Yellowheads measure 6 inches (15 centimeters) in length, and weigh 0.7 ounces (20 grams). Their uppersides are olive with a bright yellow head and yellow breast.

Geographic range: Yellowheads can be found on South Island of New Zealand, including Marlborough, Nelson, Westland, western Otago, Southland, and near Dunedin.

Habitat: Yellowheads inhabit forest areas, especially those that are dominated by beech trees.

Diet: Yellowheads forage throughout the day in the shaded canopy, the upper layer of the forest, or upper subcanopy, layer just below the canopy. They are primarily insectivores, insect eaters, picking insects from the foliage, branches, and trunks, and sometimes even dead wood. Yellowheads prefer larvae, the newly hatched, wingless forms of insects. They sometimes eat fruit, flowers, and fungi.

Behavior and reproduction: During the non-breeding season, yellowheads form large flocks, and are joined by other bird species. During the breeding season, yellowheads live in pairs or trios and are distributed over a large home range. Their mechanical-like call is varied, with six to eight notes repeated rapidly.

The yellowhead engages in cooperative breeding, and is possibly polygamous (puh-LIH-guh-mus), having more than one mate. They breed from October to February. They build cup-shaped nests in holes. Clutch sizes are typically three to four eggs that are pinkish with reddish brown blotches. They are incubated only by the female for a period of eighteen to twenty-one days. The young fledge at twenty-one days. Two or three adults continue to feed them after fledging for up to fifty-five more days.

During the breeding season, yellowheads live in pairs or trios and are distributed over a large home range. (Illustration by Amanda Humphrey. Reproduced by permission.)

Yellowheads and people: There is no known significance between people and yellowheads.

Conservation status: Yellowheads have been declared Vulnerable. Their population has declined significantly due to loss of forest, and their habit of avoiding edges, stunted, and regrowth forests. They are not as vulnerable to nest predators as many New Zealand birds because they nest in holes, but the young birds that are newly fledged often face risk from predators.   ■

FOR MORE INFORMATION

Books:

Campbell, Brude, and Elizabeth Lack, eds. *A Dictionary of Birds*. Vermillion, SD: Buteo Books, 1985.

Higgins, P. J., and J. M. Peter, eds. *Handbook of Australian, New Zealand & Antarctic Birds*. Vol. 6, *Pardalotes to Shrike-Thrushes*. Melbourne: Oxford, 2002.

Hvass, Hans. *Birds of the World, in Color*. New York: E. P. Dutton & Company, Inc., 1964.

Simpson, Ken, and Nicolas Day. *The Birds of Australia, A Book of Identification*. Dover, NH: Tanager Books, 1984.

Web sites:

"Australo-Papuan Warblers, Acanthizidae." Bird Families of the World. http://www.montereybay.com/creagrus/auz_warblers.html (accessed on June 17, 2004).

AUSTRALIAN CHATS
Epthianuridae

Class: Aves
Order: Passeriformes
Family: Epthianuridae
Number of species: 5 species

PHYSICAL CHARACTERISTICS

Australian chats are small birds that range in length from 4.3 to 5.5 inches (11 to 14 centimeters), and weigh between 0.3 and 0.6 ounces (9 and 18 grams). These birds have long and delicate legs. Some species have bills that are decurved, curve downward. The bills of all species are fine, or smooth. Like their relatives, the honeyeaters, their tongues are brush-tipped, which allows some species to eat nectar.

Male Australian chats are very brightly colored, especially during breeding season, with yellow, orange, or red undersides. Females, juvenile, immature birds, and some species of non-breeding male chats have plumage, feathers, which is colored but not very bright. The male white-fronted chat is black, white, and gray.

GEOGRAPHIC RANGE

Australian chats can be found all over Australia, except in the tree-covered north and east coasts, or in southwestern Tasmania, an island off the southeastern coast of Australia. The different species of chats tend to live in different areas of their range. The orange chat and the crimson chat tend to live throughout the center of the continent from the west coast to the western slopes of the Great Dividing Range, and from the south coast to the tropics. They prefer the more arid land, dry, and are seldom found in the wetter areas. White-fronted chats can be found across southern Australia. They are also the only species that inhabit Tasmania. Gibberbirds live in the stony deserts of central Australia.

phylum

class

subclass

order

monotypic order

suborder

▲ **family**

HABITAT

Australian chats are usually linked to various kinds of shrublands. They also live in the nearby semi-arid woodland areas full of acacias (uh-KAY-shahz). Gibberbirds live in areas that have come to be known as "Gibber plains" and are stony deserts, with a light grass and saltbush cover. Yellow chats prefer the low vegetation that grows close to swamps, floodplains, and bore drains.

DIET

Australian chats are primarily insectivores, eating insects and spiders that they grab on the ground or from low shrubs. White-fronted chats sometimes eat snails, other invertebrates (animals without backbones), and seeds—grabbing their prey from either dry or wet ground, or from shallow water. They sometimes run after aerial prey, but almost never capture flying insects. Gibberbirds eat a lot of seeds on a regular basis. Crimson chats will consume nectar, just like their honeyeater relatives.

BEHAVIOR AND REPRODUCTION

Australian chats tend to gather in small flocks. During breeding season they pair off and some species defend breeding territories. Observations have suggested that white-fronted chat males are more likely to defend their mate than a territory. The birds show off while on perches, or in flight, dipping their tails and raising the colorful feathers on their heads or back ends. Orange and crimson chats tend to be nomadic, with a north-south seasonal migration, travel, and also in response to local rainfall. When it is dry, the birds move toward the coasts.

The calls of the Australian chats are simple and metallic. Their songs are pretty with a twittering or piping sound. When they sense danger, they issue a harsh churring call.

White-fronted and crimson chats have been observed more than the other species when breeding. White-fronted chats have long breeding seasons, peaking in late winter and spring, August to November, and breeding again after the rainy season in later summer and fall, March to April. They are known to make up to five attempts at raising young during each season. Their cup-shaped nests are made from grass, rushes, twigs, and plant fiber, and sometimes mammal hair or fur and feathers. Nests are placed 1 to 4 feet (0.3 to 1.2 meters) from the ground in small bushes and sometimes on the ground. Clutches have two to four eggs, with at most five eggs, that are fleshy or pinkish white with small reddish spots at the larger end. Both male and female incubate, sit on, the eggs, hatching after thirteen to fourteen days. Both parents protect and feed the young. Each parent averages seven visits per hour. White-fronted chats fledge, grow the feathers necessary for flight, after about fourteen days; a couple of days earlier for the orange and crimson. About 30 percent of nests succeed. Most fail due to predators such as cats, foxes, snakes, and ravens. The infamous Horsefield's bronze cuckoo parasitize a small portion of the nests. Cuckoos lay their eggs in other birds' nests, a host nest, and when cuckoo chicks hatch host parents care for the cuckoo chick, sometimes neglecting their own smaller chicks.

AUSTRALIAN CHATS AND PEOPLE

Desert travelers and bird watchers enjoy the colorful orange and crimson chats.

CONSERVATION STATUS

Two subspecies of yellow chats are Endangered, facing a very high risk of extinction, dying out, in the wild, and one species is Critically Endangered, facing an extremely high risk of extinction in the wild. They are at risk due to the loss and degradation of their habitats.

Crimson chat (*Epthianura tricolor*)

▮ Resident

CRIMSON CHAT
Epthianura tricolor

Physical characteristics: Crimson chats average about 4.7 inches (12 centimeters) in length, and 0.4 ounces (11 grams) in weight. Males have dark brown backs, with a white throat and white center belly, and white undertail coverts, small feathers that cover the base of longer tail and wing feathers. Their eyes are a creamy white, and they display a vivid crimson, red, crown and undersides. Females have light brown upperparts and head, with a white throat and belly, and pale red and buff patches on the breast, flanks, and rump. Juveniles look like females except that they do not have any red on their breast.

Geographic range: Crimson chats can be found throughout the inland, western, and southern coasts of Australia, and occasionally in southeastern and eastern Australia.

Habitat: Crimson chats tend to prefer to live in arid and semi-arid shrubland. They sometimes can be found in grassland or farmland.

Diet: Crimson chats are omnivores, eat animals and plants, primarily eating insects and other invertebrates, animals without backbones, off the ground and from low shrubs, and sometimes from the air. They also eat seeds and probe flowers for nectar.

Behavior and reproduction: Crimson chats tend to be nomadic in nonbreeding season. They call with a metallic, harsh deep tone, whistling and twittering call. Because they usually come out and breed after rains, their breeding range can differ greatly from one year to the next.

Crimson chats form seasonal breeding pairs. Their cup-like nests can be found in low shrubs no higher than 3 feet (0.9 meters). They have clutches with two to five eggs. Both male and female incubate the eggs for ten to fourteen days, with fledges at ten days. Both parents also protect and feed the young, and show distraction displays that draw predators away from the young.

Male and female crimson chats both incubate their eggs and care for the young after they hatch. (© Peter Slater/Photo Researchers, Inc. Reproduced by permission.)

Crimson chats and people: Desert visitors enjoy observing the colorful bird.

Conservation status: Crimson chats are common in Australia, and are not threatened. Their numbers in various locations may differ. ■

FOR MORE INFORMATION

Books:

Blakers, M., S. J. J. F. Davies, and P. N. Reilly. *The Atlas of Australian Birds.* Carlton, Australia: Melbourne University Press, 1984.

Campbell, Bruce, and Elizabeth Lack, eds. *A Dictionary of Birds.* Vermillion, SD: Buteo Books, 1985.

Simpson, Ken, and Nicolas Day. *The Birds of Australia.* Dover, NH: Tanager Books, 1984.

Web sites:

"Australian Chat, Epthianuridae." Bird Families of the World. http://montereybay.com/creagrus/Australian_chats.html (accessed on June 18, 2004).

"Australian Chats." World Bird Guide. http://www.mangoverde.com/birdsound (accessed on June 18, 2004).

"Bird Checklist of the World—Australia (continental including Tasmania)." Avibase—The World Bird Database. http://www.bsc-eoc.org/avibase/avibase.jsp?region=auct&pg=checklist&list=clements (accessed on June 18, 2004).

family

CHAPTER

phylum

class

subclass

order

monotypic order

suborder

▲ **family**

PHYSICAL CHARACTERISTICS

The three species of this family of Passeriformes, or perching birds, are very similar in appearance. The largest, the chowchilla, is about 12 inches (30 centimeters) long. The two species of logrunners are only 7.3 to 8.4 inches (18.5 to 21 centimeters) long. They are stocky birds, with powerful legs and claws. Their specialized tails bear sharp spines on the stiff shafts of all ten tail feathers. This trait led this family of birds to also be called spine-tailed logrunners.

Male logrunners and chowchillas have white breasts, and females have reddish orange breasts. Chowchillas have unmarked black and white feathers. Logrunners, however, have patterns of brown, black, gray, white, and dull red.

GEOGRAPHIC RANGE

Logrunners and chowchillas are found only in Australia and New Guinea. The southern logrunner is restricted to the eastern coastal forests of Australia. The chowchilla is found in northeastern Australia in the Atherton Tableland region above 1,475 feet (450 meters). The New Guinea logrunner occupies territory in the central highlands of New Guinea from 6,500 to 9,300 feet (1,980 to 2,840 meters). Some subspecies of the New Guinea logrunner live in regions as far up as 11,300 feet (3,450 meters) and in lower areas near 3,900 feet (1,200 meters).

HABITAT

Logrunners and chowchillas live on the litter-strewn floor of dense rainforests and wet sclerophyll (SKLARE-uh-fill) forests.

Sclerophyll forests have plants with hard leaves that have adapted, changed, to low levels of phosphorous, a chemical that encourages plant growth. Logrunners and chowchillas will move into nearby vegetation if it is dense enough. These adjacent territories may include non-native plants have been introduced into the wild.

DIET

Logrunners and chowchillas eat adult insects, larvae (LAR-vee), the newly hatched form of insects, and worms. Sometimes they also forage for berries.

BEHAVIOR AND REPRODUCTION

Logrunners and chowchillas never leave their permanent ranges of 1.7 to 9.8 acres (0.7 to 4 hectares), though they will defend a much larger territory. They live with a mate or in small groups of two to five birds.

Logrunners and chowchillas have different mating patterns. Logrunners begin nesting in the winter months as early as April and last until November. The chowchilla nests anytime, but July through December is most common. Females of all three species build dome-shaped nests made of twigs, which are topped with dry leaves and moss, and include a roof overhang that keeps the interior nest dry during rainstorms. Chowchilla nests are larger to accommodate their bigger size.

Female southern logrunners lay two white eggs. Chowchillas and the New Guinea logrunner lay only one, although only 75 percent of the eggs hatch. Eggs hatch after twenty-one to twenty-five days and chicks remain in the nest for sixteen to eighteen days for the northern logrunner and twenty-two to twenty-seven days for the chowchilla. Females incubate, or sit on the eggs until they hatch. Males bring food to the female, but only she feeds the young. More than one chowchilla male will bring food to the female for the hatchlings. After the fledglings, birds that have grown the feathers needed for flight, leave the nest, they are still fed by both parents.

Chowchillas and logrunners have loud calls that can be heard at dawn before the birds begin foraging, searching for food, and at dusk when they are settling down for the night. If they encounter other birds, they will call out as if to remind others of their territory boundaries.

These birds are shy and will shriek if startled, but have been known to ignore humans when they feed, walking right over a person's foot as they forage.

LOGRUNNERS, CHOWCHILLAS, AND PEOPLE

Because these birds are relatively shy and their habitats are restricted, they are unknown to most people except one native group. The Dyirbal Aboriginal people named the chowchilla after its call, which is: "chow chowchilla chowry chook chook."

CONSERVATION STATUS

Southern logrunners, although not threatened with extinction, dying out, are decreasing in population due to the clearing of rainforest for pasture and farmland. They are adapting by moving into places where exotic plants have been introduced and have spread into zones between cleared land and the remains of rainforests. Chowchillas, on the other hand, have not been affected by the loss of sections of their habitat through deforestation, the cutting down of trees. New Guinea logrunners are considered rare but this is most likely due to their shy nature and the remoteness of their territory.

SCLEROPHYLL FORESTS

Sclerophyll (SKLARE-uh-fill) forests, where logrunners live, are unique to Australia. These forests evolved, changed, in response to low levels of phosphorous, a chemical that encourages plant growth. Sclerophyll plants have hard leaves that contain lignin, a substance that prevents them from wilting. Dry sclerophyll forests have eucalyptus trees that are 32.8 to 98.4 feet (10 to 30 meters) tall with smaller sclerophyllic plants underneath. Eucalyptus (yoo-kah-LIP-tus) in wet forests are taller, over 98.4 feet (30 meters), and contain plants with softer leaves such as tree ferns.

Southern logrunner *(Orthonyx temminckii)*

■ Resident

SOUTHERN LOGRUNNER
Orthonyx temminckii

Physical characteristics: Southern logrunners, also known as spine-tailed logrunners, are 7.3 to 8.3 inches (18.5 to 21 centimeters) long. Males weigh 2.08 to 2.4 ounces (58 to 70 grams), and females weigh 1.6 to 2.08 ounces (46 to 58 grams). This species has tan and grey feathers with a black stripe on its wings. The female has an orange throat, while the throat of the male is white.

Geographic range: These birds live in a narrow strip forest on the eastern coast of Australia from New South Wales in the north to Queensland in the south.

Habitat: Southern logrunners thrive in the heavy vegetation on the rainforest or wet sclerophyll forest floor. They will range into nearby underbrush if it is sufficiently dense.

Diet: Southern logrunners eat insects, worms, and other invertebrates, animals without backbones, that they find in the soil.

Behavior and reproduction: Southern logrunners use their tails to help them find food. Spreading their tails, they anchor the sharp tips into the ground. This allows them to rake their feet through the litter on the forest floor, and scratch the ground to uncover larvae and insects. They can pivot on their tails, clearing an 8-inch (20-centimeter) circle. Yellow-throated scrubwrens and eastern whipbirds often follow behind logrunners and chowchillas and pick up insects and grubs the other birds ignored.

When southern logrunners are startled or in danger, their piercing "keek" call can be heard for some distance. (Illustration by Michelle Meneghini. Reproduced by permission.)

Southern logrunners stay within their territory throughout the year. They mate for life and will form small family groupings within their territory. The bird usually breeds from May to August, but have been observed mating as early as April and as late as October, producing one or two broods, groups of offspring hatched at the same time.

Only the female builds the nest, which is a dome-shaped structure, made of sticks and grasses, built against a tree trunk or bush low to the ground. The entrance is placed on the side and a flap of moss covers the entryway, protecting the interior from rain.

Only two white eggs are laid by the female. The female incubates the eggs for twenty-one to twenty-five days. When hatched, the young birds remain in the nest for sixteen to eighteen days, fed by their parents.

Although shy, they will ignore humans. But when startled or in danger, their piercing "keek" call can be heard for some distance. Their normal song is an equally loud series of "weet" sounds.

Southern logrunners and people: There is no known significance between southern logrunners and people.

Conservation status: Southern logrunners are not threatened with extinction. Their population in the northern part of their range is large enough for the species to be considered common. Their numbers in the south are decreasing, and they are quite rare in the southernmost part of their range, due to the cutting down of the southern rainforests. Southern logrunners survive in pockets of rainforest in the south by moving into areas where exotic plants like blackberry bushes and lantana have been planted and quickly moved into cleared land. ■

FOR MORE INFORMATION

Books:

Higgins, P. J., and J. M. Peter, eds. *Handbook of Australian New Zealand and Antarctic Birds: Pardalotes to Shrike-thrushes.* Melbourne: Oxford University Press, 2003.

Perrins, Christopher. *Firefly Encyclopedia of Birds.* Richmond Hill, Canada: Firefly Books, 2003.

Robbins, Michael. *Birds: Fandex Family Field Guides.* New York: Workman Publishing Company, 1998.

Schodde, R. *Directory of Australian Birds: Passerines.* Collingwood, Australia: CSIRO Publishing, 1999.

Simpson, K., and N. Day. *A Field Guide to the Birds of Australia.* Ringwood, Australia: Penguin Books Australia Ltd., 1996.

Weidensaul, Scott. *Birds: National Audubon Society First Field Guides.* New York: Scholastic Trade, 1998.

QUAIL THRUSHES AND WHIPBIRDS

Eupetidae

Class: Aves

Order: Passeriformes

Family: Eupetidae

Number of species: 16 to 19 species

phylum

class

subclass

order

monotypic order

suborder

▲ **family**

PHYSICAL CHARACTERISTICS

Quail thrushes range in length from 6.7 to 12.2 inches (17 to 31 centimeters), and weigh 1 to 7 ounces (30 to 205 grams). The majority of the species have strong legs with long ankle bones. The bill tends to be short, and their tails are mostly long and wide. Their feathers are thick and fluffy. Quail thrushes are striking with patterns of black, white, brown, and orange—a color normally found only on the undersides. The top parts of the birds look like the ground cover.

Three or four of the jewel-babblers are similar in appearance to quail thrushes, only with large patches of blue in the plumage, feathers. Rail-babblers—often considered a part of this inclusive group although their true ancestry continues to remain questionable—have long necks and tails, and plumage that is chestnut-colored, with a blue streak running along the side of their neck. The species of Australian whipbirds and wedgebills are slim, dull in their color, and have long tails. Their crest is short but is pointed. The Papuan whipbird looks somewhat like a smaller version of those birds, but only superficially. This bird has no crest. Melampittas have long legs, noticeably short tails, and black plumage. The small bird, ifrit, has a medium-short tail and rusty brown plumage and a bright blue cap.

GEOGRAPHIC RANGE

All of the species except the rail-babbler are found exclusively in Australia and New Guinea. The rail-babbler lives in the lowland peninsular areas of Thailand, Malaysia, Sumatra, and Borneo.

HABITAT

Australian quail thrushes, with the exception of the spotted quail thrush, prefer arid habitats, particularly dry woodland areas, stony plains, sandhills and shrub steppe, a plain with few trees. The rail-babbler and the species of New Guinea live in the rainforest and in many different types of closed forest-type areas. The greater melampitta can be found only in the forest of karst, environments that are characterized by heavy limestone deposits with deep ground fissures, cracks, and sinkholes, and often sitting over underground streams and caves. The eastern whipbird is also found in the rainforest, eucalyptus forests that are wet, and other areas with a low density of vegetation. The western whipbird is found in areas with dense vegetation that is thick and dry. Wedgebills are at home in dry woodlands, steppes, a semi-arid grass covered plain, and heathlands.

DIET

Australian quail thrushes tend to be ground feeders, slowly moving around and eating prey by picking it with their bills. These birds shuffle through the leaves and other ground litter with their legs. They are, for the large part, insectivores, eating insects and other invertebrates, animals without backbones, and sometimes small vertebrates, animals with backbones. They are also known to eat seeds. The only one of the family that differs from this routine is the ifrit. Ifrits gather food in the forest at varying elevations, stalking through trunks and branches and probing in the bark and moss for their prey.

BEHAVIOR AND REPRODUCTION

Quail thrushes tend to be shy and secretive, except for the ifrit. Those that live in the rainforest hide themselves in the thick vegetation. Quail thrushes will either freeze or break into flight when they are disturbed. When they land, they will either stop and freeze, or run away quickly on foot. Whipbirds and melampittas will often approach any non-obtrusive observer, cautious but curious. As a whole, the birds are usually heard but not seen. They indicate their presence with vocalizations that can range from thin whistles to loud and booming notes. Both male and female eastern whipbirds take part in antiphonal, answering, duets in a way that gave birth to their name. The male whistles loudly, sounding like a whip has passed through the air with the female following right away with two loud cracks.

Quail thrushes make their nests of dry vegetation and put them in small depressions on the ground. The ifrit will build a much bulkier nest with thick walls about 10 feet (3 meters) off the ground. Most of the nests are cup-shaped; but the melampitta will build a domed nest with a side entrance and put it up the side of tree fern trunk. Quail thrushes, jewel-babblers, and the rail-babbler have clutches of two eggs, and the other species, have only one egg. The eggs have dark spots and blotches all over them, with a pale background underneath the markings. Australian whipbirds and wedgebills have eggs that are light blue with black scribbles very boldly marking them. Due to the problems of observing these secretive birds, the male and female roles in incubation and brooding, as well as the time of the nesting periods remain unknown.

AUSTRALIAN CHATS AND PEOPLE

Due to their secretive behavior and habits, quail thrushes and whipbirds are unknown to the average person, with the exception of the eastern whipbird. The eastern whipbird's call is known throughout the Australian bush, with its distinctive sound—though more people have heard this species than have seen it. Ifrits carry a variety of poisons in their tissues, especially in the feathers. The poison's true purpose has not yet been determined, but it does seem to be connected to the bird's diet. Another species of New Guinea birds known to have similar toxins is the pitohius of the Pachycephalidae (whistler) family.

CONSERVATION STATUS

Rail-babblers and western whipbirds are Near Threatened, in danger of becoming threatened with extinction, because of habitat loss. The western whipbird population in southwest Australia has been threatened by fires that have decreased the distribution and the numbers of this species. In the 1960s the population was down to seventeen pairs or less, and has recovered through conservation. With restricted burning, captive breeding, and the transfer of individual birds, the population climbed to over 500 individuals. A subspecies of the spotted quail-thrush inhabiting the Mount Lofty Ranges of South Australia has almost disappeared from that area due to habitat loss.

Spotted quail-thrush (*Cinclosoma punctatum*)

▪ Resident

SPOTTED QUAIL-THRUSH
Cinclosoma punctatum

Physical characteristics: Spotted quail-thrushes range in length from 10.2 to 11 inches (26 to 28 centimeters), and weigh between 2.4 and 3.1 ounces (67 and 87 grams). Their plumage is a mottled blend of white, buff, rust or reddish brown, brown, and black. They have light brown heads with a white brow stripe. Their throats are black with a white patch, and their breasts are a pinkish tone.

Geographic range: The spotted quail-thrush can be found in southeast Australia, Tasmania, and in the Mount Lofty Ranges, in south-central Australia.

Spotted quail-thrushes prefer living on the ground, and are sedentary, secretive, and shy. (Illustration by John Megahan. Reproduced by permission.)

Habitat: Spotted quail-thrushes live in eucalyptus forest with a littered, open floor, and prefer areas on rocky hillsides.

Diet: Spotted quail-thrushes tend to be insectivores, eating insects and other invertebrates, but they also eat small vertebrates and seeds at times. They pick their prey from the ground which they hunt in a slow, meandering fashion.

Behavior and reproduction: Spotted quail-thrushes prefer living on the ground, and are sedentary, stay in one place, secretive, and shy. If they are frightened they will take flight in a way similar to a quail. When they land, the spotted quail-thrushes will run off quickly, or freeze in position.

Their vocalizations are a repeated, double-note song, as well as a high thin contact call, inaudible to the average person.

Spotted quail-thrushes have a breeding season from late July-August to December. The female builds the cup-like nest of dry vegetation and puts the nest into a depression in the ground near the base of a tree, shrub, rock, or clump of grass. The female also incubates, sits on and warms, the clutch of two spotted eggs, but the male helps to feed the chicks during and after the nineteen day fledging period, when chicks grow the feathers needed for flight. In any breeding season, one to three broods may be raised.

Spotted quail-thrushes and people: There is no known significance between spotted quail-thrushes and people.

Conservation status: Spotted quail-thrushes are locally common, but are sparsely populated. Those in the Mt. Lofty Ranges, South Australia, are Critically Endangered, facing an extremely high risk of extinction in the wild, and may already be extinct. They are threatened by loss of habitat due to clearance and fragmentation. ■

FOR MORE INFORMATION

Books:

Blakers, M., S. J. J. F. Davies, and P. N. Reilly. *The Atlas of Australian Birds.* Carlton, Australia: Melbourne University Press, 1984.

Campbell, Bruce, and Elizabeth Lack, eds. *A Dictionary of Birds.* Vermillion, SD: Buteo Books, 1985.

Coates, Brian J. "Passerines." In *The Birds of Papua New Guinea.* Vol. 2. Alderley, Australia: Dove Publications, 1993.

Simpson, Ken, and Nicolas Day. *The Birds of Australia.* Dover, NH: Tanager Books, 1984.

Web sites:

"Crowdy Bay National Park Fauna." Crowdy Bay National Park. http://www.harringtoncrowdy.com/HarringtonCrowdyBayNPFaunaList. html (accessed on June 19, 2004).

Dettmann, Belinda. "Number 24." Flightline. http://www.deh.gov.au/ biodiversity/science/abbbs/pubs/jan-2000.pdf (accessed on June 19, 2004).

FANTAILS

Rhipiduridae

Class: Aves

Order: Passeriformes

Family: Rhipiduridae

Number of species: 42 species

family

C H A P T E R

PHYSICAL CHARACTERISTICS

Fantails, also known as "wagtail flycatchers," vary in length from 5.5 to 8.5 inches (14 to 21.5 centimeters), with weights between 0.2 to 0.9 ounces (6 to 25 grams). These small birds get their name from their long, rounded, fan-shaped tail, often encompassing as much as 50 percent of the bird's total length. Their characteristic flat, triangular bill is common to most flying insectivores, insect eaters. Wide bristles surround the bill in an unusual arrangement of double rows. Most fantails have small feet, except for those more terrestrial, land-dwelling, species. Wings are somewhat rounded, causing the fantails to fly slower but making it easier to maneuver.

Fantails do not usually have bright plumage, feathers, with brown, rust, white, gray, black, or a combination of these, dominating the color scheme. Two species that inhabit the northwestern and western boundaries of the family's distribution area are the exception. The black-cinnamon fantail with its bold, contrasting colors also proves to be an exception. Most males and females are alike in their plumage, though the black fantail of New Guinea has black males and rust-colored females. Another New Guinea species, the dimorphic fantail also shows two colors: one phase is dark, with the black and rust tail; the other shows a light gray tail. Little difference exists between adults and juveniles except that the juveniles' colors are more faded with rusty edges to some of their feathers, especially the wing coverts, feathers that cover the primary flight feathers. Overall, there is a wide variety of color spread throughout the species that are found over a number of islands.

phylum

class

subclass

order

monotypic order

suborder

▲ **family**

GEOGRAPHIC RANGE

Fantails are generally found in the Australasian countries, Australia and surrounding islands, but can also be seen well outside of these areas. They generally inhabit regions of eastern Pakistan, India, Sri Lanka, the Himalayas, southern China, Southeast Asia, the Philippines, Indonesia, New Guinea, Australia, New Zealand, and the islands of the southwestern Pacific, east of Samoa and north to Micronesia. Several species are known to coexist in the same areas of New Guinea, with up to seven found in the very same locale. Some species such as the white-throated fantail inhabiting areas from eastern Pakistan through south and southeast Asia to Borneo, as well as others, are found to be widely distributed. Some species are restricted to only one small island, such as the case of the Ponapé fantail and the Matthias fantail are endemic to Ponapé, Micronesia, and to Mussau, in the Bismarck Archipelago, respectively.

HABITAT

Most species of fantails are found in the rainforest most of the time. Yet there is a wide range of habitats where various species also prefer to inhabit. The mangrove fantail is restricted to mangroves. The rufous fantail of Australia lives mostly in the rainforest and wet sclerophyll (SKLARE-uh-fill) forest, Australian forests populated by plants with hard, short, spiky leaves, during breeding and nonbreeding seasons; but during migration, they are known to land in more open areas, even city centers. The willie wagtail enjoys the greatest diversity of habitats, preferring open areas, but found in deserts and city parks, as well. The only areas they do not live are the dense rainforests. Varying species might live in the same area, but prefer different elevations in the forest areas where they live. For instance, the sooty-thicket fantail lives in the low, dense thickets. Willie wagtails spend most of their time on the ground hunting for food.

DIET

Fantails are primarily insectivores, eating insects and other small invertebrates. Only the larger species, such as the willie wagtail are strong enough to capture and handle larger prey. In the case of larger prey such as moths, they must be hammered on a branch in order to subdue them and make them ready to be eaten. Willie wagtails might capture small lizards and eat them also. Most prey are caught while the bird is air-borne. The gray fantail is known to be stunning to watch while flying in pursuit of its prey. They whirl in rapid loops, characterized by sudden changes in direction that sometimes appear to endanger the bird. When the bird moves through the leaves, its tail is cocked. Some observers think this helps the bird to flush out insects. Some fantails also have been known to deliberately divide their environments among species inhabiting the same locality, as they utilize different foraging, hunting for food, methods at differing elevations. Willie wagtails remain within 10 feet (3 meters) of the ground.

BEHAVIOR AND REPRODUCTION

Fantails are known for holding their tail cocked, tilted to one side, alternately fanning and closing it, and swinging it from side to side while a bird is perched or moving around in the foliage, plant leaves. They also use this tail posture when in flight, performing highly aerobatic, looping flights in order to catch their insect prey. Viewed sometimes as "hysterical," the fantails tend to be restless, and rarely perch for long. Some species are more sedate, calmer.

Several fantail species are tame and easily approach humans while engaged in capturing insects, flushed out by a moving observer. They use other harmless larger animals in a similar way, willie wagtails often use domestic cattle both as a perch and to flush out insects. When an animal is perceived as predator, however, fantails can become extremely aggressive, even toward larger birds, attacking them and landing on their backs. Willie wagtails signal their aggression by giving a rasping, scolding call and expanding their white eyebrow. Territorial disputes that result in defeat will render the losing bird's white eyebrow invisible after it shrinks. Some fantails such as the thicket-fantails are shy and hard to see in the dense undergrowth they inhabit.

Tropical populations of fantails are sedentary, they do not migrate and live in the same area all year long. In some southern temperate, not too hot or cold, regions, and at the higher elevations, the fantails often travel considerable distances with the seasons. The rufous fantail of Australia moves north and south along the east coast on a regular basis. The southeastern populations of grey fantails travel long distances north and northwest during the winter. Such species as the white-throated and yellow-bellied fantails, spend the summer in the Himalayas and move to lower altitudes at the end of the summer.

Fantails are not noted for their songs, but have relatively pleasant voices. The calls are simple, and the voices tend to sound very delicate. When they do sing, the song tends to be rapid and full of enthusiasm. The gray fantail's song has been compared to the notes of a violin. The willie wagtail, again an exception, has a scolding call and strong song, with the ability to be heard at some distance.

The fantail breeding habits are virtually unknown in the rarer species, but widely studied in the more common. Most have similar breeding habits with both sexes building a nest that is a small, neat cup of fine grass stems bound by a thick external coating of cobwebs. They place their nest in a horizontal fork, or some other human-made structure or other suitable site, at a height of 3 to 50 feet (1 to 15 meters) off the ground, though usually within 10 feet (3 meters) of the ground. Fantails have been observed attaching a "tail" underneath the nest made of the nesting material. A clutch includes two to four eggs that are pale or cream colored and marked with brown or gray blotches and spots that form a wreath at the larger end of the egg or around its middle. Yellow-bellied fantails have cream or pinkish cream eggs with a cap on the larger end and pinkish brown flecks or small spots on the cap. Both parents incubate, sit on, the eggs over a time period of twelve to fourteen days. After they hatch the chicks stay in the nest for thirteen to fifteen more days, with both parents taking care of them.

Nests are not concealed and so are easy prey for larger birds. In an experiment, researchers constructed artificial nests with eggs made from modeling clay. The team observed that more than ten bird species and several small mammals attempted to steal the eggs. This was evident due to the bite marks found on the eggs. The eggs' major predator was the pied currawong, which conducted more than half of the raids. Nest parasitism from the cuckoo is also common. Cuckoo parents lay their eggs in the nest of other bird species, such as the fantail When the cuckoo chicks hatch, they push the other eggs from the nest and are raised by the host parents. The rufous fantail can be host to the begging young pallid cuckoo, which weighs more than eight times the size of the fantail.

FANTAILS AND PEOPLE

Some fantails are common and active in certain areas making them well-known to people. Because of their tame and friendly way with humans, they are a favorite of birdwatchers and the public in general. In certain areas of New Guinea, the willie wagtail is believed to be the ghost of a paternal relative. Superstition surrounds the legend that a singing bird hanging out near a garden that has just been planted is good luck, and the crops will grow well. In other places, it is known as a gossip, so people discussing important matters do not do so when the bird is nearby.

CONSERVATION STATUS

The many species of fantail that live on large land masses are not threatened with extinction. However, several of the island populations are Vulnerable, facing a high risk of extinction in the wild. These include the Malaita fantail on Malaita in the Solomon Islands of the Pacific, whose population is known to be small. What is causing this low population remains uncertain. The Manus fantail from the Admiralty Islands of Papua New Guinea was once common on Manus Island, though no records of them exist since 1934. They are still found on neighboring islands, but no reason has been determined for the decline in population.

The five species that are considered Near Threatened, in danger of becoming threatened with extinction, include the cinnamon-tailed fantail and long-tailed fantail, both of the Tanimbar Islands; Cockerell's fantail of the Solomon Islands; dusky fantail of San Christobal, Solomon Islands; and Matthias fantail of the Mussau, Bismarck Archipelago. The possible cause is the high number of logging operations throughout these species' range. The threat to the rarer, harder-to-observe species in remote locations remains difficult to determine. Small populations may be threatened by introduced species or the alteration of their habitat.

White-throated fantail (*Rhipidura albicollis*)

▪ Resident

WHITE-THROATED FANTAIL
Rhipidura albicollis

Physical characteristics: White-throated fantails have lengths that range from 6.9 to 8.1 inches (17.5 to 20.5 centimeters), with weights between 0.3 to 0.45 ounces (9 to 13 grams). They are primarily gray with a white throat, brow, and on the tip of their tail.

Geographic range: White-throated fantails can be found throughout northeastern Pakistan, India, southeastern Tibet, southern China, Myanmar, Thailand, Peninsular Malaysia, Sumatra, Borneo, in the foothills and adjacent plains up to 10,000 feet (3,000 meters).

Habitat: White-throated fantails generally prefer broad-leaved evergreen forests and are also comfortable living in areas that have been modified by humans, such as bamboo, in parks, secondary regrowth, and in wooded gardens.

White-throated fantails are primarily insectivores, feeding along branches and also outside of foliage. They hunt for food either by themselves, in pairs, or in mixed hunting parties. (Illustration by Jacqueline Mahannah. Reproduced by permission.)

Diet: White-throated fantails are primarily insectivores, feeding along branches and also outside of foliage. They hunt for food either by themselves, in pairs, or in mixed hunting parties.

Behavior and reproduction: White-tailed fantails are typical of other birds of the family. They continually fan their tail as a part of their restless, showy behavior. They live in the undergrowth and middle growth of the forest. In the winter they move from higher elevations to the foothills and plains below their habitat the rest of the year. Their song is made up of thin, high-pitched notes.

The breeding season varies throughout the population distribution, averaging from February through May, to March through August. During the season up to two broods might be raised. Both males and females build the nest, and incubate the eggs that are spotted and in clutches of three eggs. The nest is cup-shaped, and made of fine grass stems held together by cobwebs around its exterior, with a dangling "tail" of grasses hanging underneath. The incubation period is from twelve to thirteen days, with fledging, growing of flight feathers, occurring at thirteen to fifteen days.

White-throated fantails and people: There is no special relationship between white-throated fantails and people.

Conservation status: White-throated fantails are not threatened. ■

Willie wagtail (Rhipidura leucophrys)

▨ Resident

WILLIE WAGTAIL
Rhipidura leucophrys

Physical characteristics: Willie wagtails are larger than the average fantail, with a length of 7.1 to 8.7 inches (18 to 22 centimeters), and an average weight of 0.6 to 0.8 ounces (17 to 24 grams). They have black plumage and a white brow and breast.

Geographic range: Depending on the particular population of willie wagtail, they can be found throughout Moluccas, New Guinea and the surrounding islands. One population can be found on the Bismarck Archipelago, Solomon Islands, and northern Australia. The other population can be found in southwest, southern, central, and southeast Australia.

Habitat: Willie wagtails prefer open areas and can live in a variety of diverse environments such as the desert, open grasslands, and in city parks, but they are not found in dense rainforest or eucalyptus forest.

Diet: Willie wagtails are carnivores, meat eaters, eating primarily insects and small lizards. They get their food by hawking, diving and grasping their prey, from perches. They grab insects out of the air or grab them from the ground after a short run.

Behavior and reproduction: This bird is primarily terrestrial, and runs, walks, or hops along the ground foraging for its prey. While in motion, their tails are usually lifted but not fanned out. When they pause, their tails swing back and forth, and up and down. Willie wagtails always have a mate nearby, but are usually alone when observed. They are noisy, active birds, often confronting or attacking larger animals that are known predators, or that enter their territory during breeding. They show aggression by puffing out their white eyebrows. In Australia the birds are considered primarily sedentary. However, in New Guinea they are known to leave certain areas during the dry season and return during the rainy season in order to breed. When willie wagtails are upset, they can be heard as giving a harsh scolding sound.

Both willie wagtail parents build the nest, incubate, and care for the young. (© Peter Slater/Photo Researchers, Inc. Reproduced by permission.)

Willie wagtails breed mostly from July through February in Australia, but can nest in any month depending on suitable conditions. They can have up to four or more broods in any season. Both parents build the nest, incubate, and care for the young. Their nests are made of grass and fine bark, then covered with a spider web. However, the nests do not have the characteristic "tail" dangling underneath. The nest is placed on a horizontal fork or in a human-made structure or other suitable site, no higher than 16.5 feet (5 meters) above the ground. The eggs are cream colored with brown and gray speckles that form a wreath at the larger end. The incubation period lasts fourteen to fifteen days, with fledging after fourteen days.

Willie wagtails and people: Willie wagtails are popular in Australia. In parts of New Guinea legend says that they are the ghost of a paternal relative and thought to bring good luck. They are also considered to be a gossip so people avoid telling secrets when the birds are around.

Conservation status: Willie wagtails are common and are not a threatened species. ■

FOR MORE INFORMATION

Books:

Campbell, Brude, and Elizabeth Lack, eds. *A Dictionary of Birds.* Vermillion, SD: Buteo Books, 1985.

Coates, Brian J. "The Birds of Papua New Guinea." In *Passerines.* Vol. 2. Alderley, Australia: Dove Publications, 1993.

Hvass, Hans. *Birds of the World, in Color.* New York: E. P. Dutton & Company, Inc., 1964.

Web sites:

"Fantails and Allies." Personal Museum of Natural History. http://www.planktonik.com/museum/en/birds (accessed on June 17, 2004).

"Fantails of the World." World Bird Gallery. http://www.camacdonald.com/birding/Sampler6_Crows%28Fantails%29.htm (accessed on June 17, 2004).

"Fantails: Rhipiduridae." Bird Families of the World. http://www.montereybay.com/creagrus/fantails.html (accessed on June 17, 2004).

Species List by Biome

CONIFEROUS FOREST
African broadbill
African pitta
American cliff swallow
American goldfinch
American robin
Anna's hummingbird
Barn swallow
Barred eagle-owl
Belted kingfisher
Black-and-red broadbill
Black-and-white warbler
Black-capped chickadee
Black-capped vireo
Black-crowned barwing
Blue-gray gnatcatcher
Bornean bristlehead
Brown creeper
Brown kiwi
Cedar waxwing
Chaffinch
Chimney swift
Crag martin
Cuban tody
Dollarbird
Dunnock
Dusky woodswallow
Eastern bluebird
Eastern screech-owl
Emu

Fan-tailed berrypecker
Fiery minivet
Fire-breasted flowerpecker
Gray butcherbird
Gray nightjar
Gray parrot
Gray potoo
Green magpie
House sparrow
House wren
Ivory-billed woodpecker
Japanese white-eye
Kirtland's warbler
Kokako
Laughing kookaburra
Little slaty flycatcher
Malaysian honeyguide
Northern bobwhite quail
Northern wryneck
Nuthatch
Oilbird
Orange-breasted trogon
Osprey
Palmchat
Peregrine falcon
Red crossbill
Red-breasted nuthatch
Red-cockaded woodpecker
Resplendent quetzal
Rifleman

Rose-throated becard
Rufous treecreeper
Rufous-browed peppershrike
Rufous-capped nunlet
Rufous-tailed jacamar
Satyr tragopan
Scarlet macaw
Sparkling violet-ear
Spotted nutcracker
Striated pardalote
Whip-poor-will
White-necked puffbird
White-throated fantail
Winter wren
Wrentit
Yellow-bellied sapsucker
Yellow-breasted chat

CONTINENTAL MARGIN
Blue-footed booby
Brown pelican
Great cormorant
Northern gannet

DECIDUOUS FOREST
African broadbill
African pitta
American cliff swallow
American goldfinch

American robin
Anna's hummingbird
Arctic warbler
Asian fairy-bluebird
Australian magpie-lark
Baltimore oriole
Bar-breasted mousebird
Barn owl
Barn swallow
Baywing
Black bulbul
Black guan
Black-and-white warbler
Black-capped chickadee
Black-capped vireo
Blue jay
Blue-crowned motmot
Blue-gray gnatcatcher
Brown creeper
Brown kiwi
Bushtit
Cedar waxwing
Chaffinch
Chimney swift
Coppersmith barbet
Crag martin
Crested tree swift
Cuban tody
Dollarbird
Dunnock
Dusky woodswallow
Eastern bluebird
Eastern screech-owl
Emu
Eurasian golden oriole
European bee-eater
European roller
Fire-breasted flowerpecker
Gray catbird
Gray nightjar
Gray-crowned babbler
Great tit
House sparrow
House wren
Ivory-billed woodpecker
Jacky winter

Japanese white-eye
Leaf-love
Northern wryneck
Nuthatch
Orange-breasted trogon
Osprey
Painted buttonquail
Peregrine falcon
Peruvian plantcutter
Plain chachalaca
Red-breasted nuthatch
Red-cockaded woodpecker
Rifleman
Rose-ringed parakeet
Rufous scrub-bird
Rufous vanga
Rufous-capped nunlet
Rufous-tailed jacamar
Satyr tragopan
Scarlet macaw
Southern scrub robin
Spotted flycatcher
Striated pardalote
Tawny frogmouth
Toucan barbet
Whip-poor-will
White-breasted mesite
White-helmet shrike
White-necked puffbird
Wild turkey
Willie wagtail
Willow ptarmigan
Winter wren
Wood duck
Yellow-bellied sapsucker
Yellow-breasted chat
Yellow-fronted tinkerbird
Yellowhead
Yellow-rumped thornbill

DESERT

American cliff swallow
American mourning dove
Barn swallow
Cactus wren

California condor
Collared pratincole
Crab plover
Crested caracara
Crimson chat
Egyptian vulture
Emu
Gray catbird
Gray hypocolius
Greater hoopoe-lark
Greater roadrunner
Harris's hawk
House sparrow
Malleefowl
Namaqua sandgrouse
Northern lapwing
Ostrich
Pallas's sandgrouse
Peregrine falcon
Peruvian plantcutter
Rock pigeon
Snow finch
Splendid fairy-wren
Striated grasswren
Verdin
Western scrub-jay
Willie wagtail

GRASSLAND

African broadbill
African palm swift
African paradise-flycatcher
American cliff swallow
American mourning dove
American robin
Anna's hummingbird
Arctic skua
Australasian lark
Australian magpie-lark
Australian pratincole
Bar-breasted mousebird
Barn owl
Barn swallow
Baya weaver
Baywing

Black rail
Black-capped chickadee
Black-capped vireo
Black-crowned barwing
Black-faced sheathbill
Blue bustard
Blue jay
Blue-black grassquit
California condor
Cape sugarbird
Cattle egret
Cedar waxwing
Collared pratincole
Common cuckoo
Common myna
Common waxbill
Corncrake
Crag martin
Crested caracara
Crimson chat
Dollarbird
Eastern phoebe
Eclectus parrot
Egyptian vulture
Emu
Eurasian bittern
European bee-eater
European roller
European starling
European white stork
Fan-tailed berrypecker
Golden-winged sunbird
Gray go-away-bird
Gray hypocolius
Gray potoo
Gray woodpecker
Gray-crowned crane
Great blue heron
Great bustard
Great kiskadee
Green woodhoopoe
Gyrfalcon
Hammerhead
Harris's hawk
Helmeted guineafowl
Hoopoe

Horned lark
House sparrow
Jacky winter
Killdeer
King vulture
Laysan finch
Lesser rhea
Loggerhead shrike
Long-billed curlew
Malleefowl
Northern bobwhite quail
Northern lapwing
Northern raven
Northern wryneck
Ostrich
Painted buttonquail
Pallas's sandgrouse
Palmchat
Peregrine falcon
Peruvian plantcutter
Purple sunbird
Rainbow lorikeet
Red-billed oxpecker
Red-legged seriema
Red-winged blackbird
Rock pigeon
Roseate spoonbill
Rose-ringed parakeet
Rosy-breasted longclaw
Rufous-capped nunlet
Sacred ibis
Sandhill crane
Savanna sparrow
Secretary bird
Shoebill
Small buttonquail
Snowy owl
Song sparrow
Southern ground-hornbill
Southern red bishop
Southern scrub robin
Spotted munia
Sprague's pipit
Stonechat
Tawny frogmouth
Village weaver

White-helmet shrike
White-necked puffbird
Wild turkey
Wrentit
Yellow-fronted tinkerbird
Yellow-rumped thornbill
Zebra finch

LAKE AND POND
African jacana
American anhinga
American cliff swallow
American white pelican
Australian magpie-lark
Barn swallow
Baya weaver
Belted kingfisher
Black tern
Black-and-red broadbill
Black-capped donacobius
Canada goose
Chaffinch
Common iora
Common loon
Crag martin
Eurasian bittern
Gray wagtail
Great blue heron
Great cormorant
Great crested grebe
Greater flamingo
Greater thornbird
Hammerhead
Hoatzin
Mallard
Mute swan
Northern wryneck
Osprey
Peregrine falcon
Pheasant-tailed jacana
Red-throated loon
Roseate spoonbill
Rosy-breasted longclaw
Rufous hornero
Sacred ibis

Shoebill
Song sparrow
Sunbittern
Sungrebe
Village weaver
Western grebe
Wood duck
Yellow-breasted chat
Zebra finch

OCEAN
Arctic skua
Blue-footed booby
Chatham mollymawk
Common diving-petrel
Common iora
Common loon
Common murre
Emperor penguin
Great auk
King eider
Laysan albatross
Laysan finch
Macaroni penguin
Magellanic penguin
Magnificent frigatebird
Manx shearwater
Northern fulmar
Northern gannet
Puffin
Red-throated loon
White-tailed tropicbird
Wilson's storm-petrel

RAINFOREST
African paradise-flycatcher
African pitta
Albert's lyrebird
Amazonian umbrellabird
American cliff swallow
Apapane
Arctic warbler
Asian fairy-bluebird
Australasian figbird
Baltimore oriole

Barn owl
Barn swallow
Barred antshrike
Bishop's oo
Black-naped monarch
Blue-crowned motmot
Bornean bristlehead
Buff-spotted flufftail
Cape batis
Common bulbul
Common cuckoo
Common iora
Common sunbird-asity
Common trumpeter
Coppery-chested jacamar
Crag martin
Cuban tody
Dodo
Eclectus parrot
Fan-tailed berrypecker
Feline owlet-nightjar
Fiery minivet
Golden whistler
Golden-winged sunbird
Gray antbird
Gray nightjar
Gray potoo
Gray-breasted mountain-
  toucan
Gray-necked picathartes
Great blue turaco
Greater racket-tailed drongo
Greater thornbird
Guianan cock-of-the-rock
Hairy hermit
Helmeted hornbill
Highland tinamou
Hooded pitta
House sparrow
Kagu
King bird of paradise
King vulture
Kokako
Little slaty flycatcher
Long-tailed manakin
Luzon bleeding heart

Lyre-tailed honeyguide
Malaysian honeyguide
Maleo
Mauritius cuckoo-shrike
Osprey
Peregrine falcon
Purple sunbird
Purple-bearded bee-eater
Rainbow lorikeet
Red-billed scythebill
Ribbon-tailed astrapia
Roseate spoonbill
Rose-ringed parakeet
Ruby-cheeked sunbird
Rufous scrub-bird
Rufous vanga
Rufous-collared kingfisher
Rusty-belted tapaculo
Satin bowerbird
Sharpbill
Southern cassowary
Southern logrunner
Spangled cotinga
Spotted quail-thrush
Square-tailed drongo
Striated pardalote
Stripe-headed rhabdornis
Sulawesi red-knobbed
  hornbill
Sunbittern
Toco toucan
Toucan barbet
Variable pitohui
Victoria's riflebird
Wattled curassow
White-breasted mesite
Willie wagtail
Wire-tailed manakin

RIVER AND STREAM
African broadbill
African pitta
American anhinga
American cliff swallow
American dipper
American white pelican

Australian magpie-lark
Baltimore oriole
Barn swallow
Baya weaver
Black-and-red broadbill
Black-capped donacobius
Canada goose
Cedar waxwing
Chaffinch
Common loon
Crag martin
Crested caracara
Cuban tody
Dusky woodswallow
Eurasian dipper
European bee-eater
European roller
Gray catbird
Gray hypocolius
Gray wagtail
Gray woodpecker
Great blue heron
Great cormorant
Great crested grebe
Green woodhoopoe
Gyrfalcon
Hoatzin
Mute swan
Northern wryneck
Peregrine falcon
Red-breasted nuthatch
Red-throated loon
Roseate spoonbill
Rosy-breasted longclaw
Rufous-capped nunlet
Rufous hornero
Rufous-tailed jacamar
Sacred ibis
Shoebill
Snow bunting
Song sparrow
Southern red bishop
Spotted bowerbird
Striped honeyeater
Sunbittern
Sungrebe

Village weaver
Wood duck
Yellow-breasted chat
Yellow-fronted tinkerbird

SEASHORE
American cliff swallow
American white pelican
Arctic warbler
Australian magpie-lark
Barn swallow
Beach thick-knee
Belted kingfisher
Black tern
Black-faced sheathbill
Blue-footed booby
Brown pelican
Cactus wren
California condor
Collared pratincole
Common iora
Common murre
Crab plover
Crag martin
Cuban tody
Fiery minivet
Golden whistler
Gray wagtail
Great auk
Great blue heron
Great cormorant
Greater flamingo
Gyrfalcon
Hood mockingbird
Horned lark
Magnificent frigatebird
Northern gannet
Osprey
Peregrine falcon
Puffin
Roseate spoonbill
Ruddy turnstone
Sacred ibis
Saunder's gull
Snow bunting

Song sparrow
Splendid fairy-wren
Stonechat
Variable oystercatcher
Victoria's riflebird
White-tailed tropicbird

TUNDRA
American robin
Arctic skua
Arctic warbler
Canada goose
Common loon
Gyrfalcon
Horned lark
Northern raven
Peregrine falcon
Red-throated loon
Ruddy turnstone
Savanna sparrow
Snow bunting
Snowy owl
Willow ptarmigan

WETLAND
African jacana
African snipe
American anhinga
American avocet
American cliff swallow
American white pelican
Australasian lark
Australian magpie-lark
Baltimore oriole
Barn swallow
Black rail
Black tern
Black-faced sheathbill
Black-winged stilt
Canada goose
Cattle egret
Common bulbul
Common iora
Crag martin
Crested caracara

Eurasian bittern
European white stork
Gray wagtail
Gray-crowned crane
Great blue heron
Great cormorant
Greater flamingo
Greater painted snipe
Hairy hermit
Hammerhead
Harris's hawk
Horned screamer
House sparrow
Killdeer

King eider
Leaf-love
Limpkin
Long-billed curlew
Mallard
Mute swan
Northern lapwing
Osprey
Peregrine falcon
Pheasant-tailed jacana
Red-crowned crane
Red-winged blackbird
Roseate spoonbill
Rosy-breasted longclaw

Ruddy turnstone
Rufous-bellied seedsnipe
Sacred ibis
Sandhill crane
Saunder's gull
Shoebill
Sunbittern
Village weaver
Wood duck
Wood stork
Yellow-breasted chat
Zebra finch
Zitting cisticola

Species List by
Geographic Range

AFGHANISTAN
Barn swallow
Chaffinch
Common myna
Crag martin
Egyptian vulture
Eurasian golden oriole
European bee-eater
European roller
European starling
Gray hypocolius
Great cormorant
Great crested grebe
Great tit
Greater hoopoe-lark
Hoopoe
House sparrow
Mute swan
Northern lapwing
Northern raven
Peregrine falcon
Rock pigeon
Snow finch
Spotted flycatcher
Spotted nutcracker
Winter wren

ALBANIA
Barn swallow
Chaffinch

Common cuckoo
Corncrake
Crag martin
Dunnock
Egyptian vulture
Eurasian dipper
Eurasian golden oriole
European bee-eater
European roller
European starling
Gray wagtail
Great cormorant
Great crested grebe
Great tit
Hoopoe
Horned lark
House sparrow
Mallard
Northern gannet
Northern lapwing
Northern raven
Northern wryneck
Nuthatch
Peregrine falcon
Red crossbill
Rock pigmeon
Snow bunting
Spotted flycatcher
Stonechat
Winter wren

Zitting cisticola

ALGERIA
Barn swallow
Black-winged stilt
Chaffinch
Common bulbul
Common cuckoo
Common murre
Corncrake
Crag martin
Dunnock
Egyptian vulture
Eurasian bittern
Eurasian golden oriole
European bee-eater
European roller
European starling
Gray wagtail
Great cormorant
Great crested grebe
Greater hoopoe-lark
Hoopoe
House sparrow
Mallard
Northern gannet
Northern lapwing
Northern raven
Northern wryneck
Peregrine falcon

Rock pigeon
Ruddy turnstone
Small buttonquail
Spotted flycatcher
Stonechat
Winter wren
Zitting cisticola

ANDORRA

Great cormorant
Peregrine falcon

ANGOLA

African jacana
African palm swift
African paradise-flycatcher
African snipe
Bar-breasted mousebird
Barn swallow
Black tern
Black-winged stilt
Buff-spotted flufftail
Cattle egret
Collared pratincole
Common bulbul
Common cuckoo
Common waxbill
Eurasian golden oriole
European bee-eater
European roller
European white stork
Gray go-away-bird
Great cormorant
Greater painted snipe
Green woodhoopoe
Hammerhead
Helmeted guineafowl
Hoopoe
House sparrow
Lyre-tailed honeyguide
Namaqua sandgrouse
Osprey
Ostrich
Peregrine falcon
Red-billed oxpecker

Rock pigeon
Rosy-breasted longclaw
Ruddy turnstone
Sacred ibis
Secretary bird
Small buttonquail
Southern ground-hornbill
Southern red bishop
Spotted flycatcher
Square-tailed drongo
Stonechat
Village weaver
White-helmet shrike
Wilson's storm-petrel
Yellow-fronted tinkerbird
Zitting cisticola

ANTARCTICA

Black-faced sheathbill
Emperor penguin
Macaroni penguin
Wilson's storm-petrel

ARGENTINA

American anhinga
American cliff swallow
Arctic skua
Barn owl
Barn swallow
Barred antshrike
Baywing
Black rail
Black-capped donacobius
Black-winged stilt
Blue-black grassquit
Cattle egret
Common diving-petrel
Crested caracara
Emperor penguin
Gray potoo
Great kiskadee
Greater thornbird
Harris's hawk
House sparrow
King vulture
Lesser rhea

Limpkin
Macaroni penguin
Magellanic penguin
Manx shearwater
Peregrine falcon
Red-billed scythebill
Red-legged seriema
Rock pigeon
Roseate spoonbill
Ruddy turnstone
Rufous hornero
Rufous-bellied seedsnipe
Rufous-browed peppershrike
Rufous-tailed jacamar
Sharpbill
Sparkling violet-ear
Sungrebe
Toco toucan
Wilson's storm-petrel
Wood stork

ARMENIA

Barn swallow
Chaffinch
Common cuckoo
Dunnock
Egyptian vulture
Eurasian dipper
Eurasian golden oriole
European bee-eater
European roller
European starling
Great cormorant
Great crested grebe
Great tit
Hoopoe
Horned lark
House sparrow
Northern lapwing
Northern raven
Nuthatch
Peregrine falcon
Red crossbill
Rock pigeon
Snow finch
Stonechat

Winter wren

ASCENSION
White-tailed tropicbird

AUSTRALIA
Albert's lyrebird
Arctic skua
Australasian figbird
Australasian lark
Australian magpie-lark
Australian pratincole
Beach thick-knee
Black-winged stilt
Cattle egret
Common diving-petrel
Crimson chat
Dollarbird
Dusky woodswallow
Eclectus parrot
Emu
European starling
Golden whistler
Gray butcherbird
Gray-crowned babbler
Great cormorant
Great crested grebe
Greater painted snipe
House sparrow
Jacky winter
Laughing kookaburra
Mallard
Malleefowl
Mute swan
Osprey
Painted buttonquail
Peregrine falcon
Rainbow lorikeet
Rock pigeon
Ruddy turnstone
Rufous scrub-bird
Rufous treecreeper
Satin bowerbird
Southern cassowary
Southern logrunner
Southern scrub robin

Splendid fairy-wren
Spotted bowerbird
Spotted quail-thrush
Striated grasswren
Striated pardalote
Striped honeyeater
Tawny frogmouth
Victoria's riflebird
Willie wagtail
Wilson's storm-petrel
Yellow-rumped thornbill
Zebra finch
Zitting cisticola

AUSTRIA
Barn swallow
Black tern
Chaffinch
Collared pratincole
Common cuckoo
Corncrake
Crag martin
Dunnock
Eurasian golden oriole
European bee-eater
European roller
European starling
European white stork
Gray wagtail
Great cormorant
Great crested grebe
Great tit
Hoopoe
House sparrow
Mallard
Mute swan
Northern lapwing
Northern raven
Northern wryneck
Nuthatch
Peregrine falcon
Red crossbill
Rock pigeon
Snow bunting
Snow finch
Spotted flycatcher

Spotted nutcracker
Stonechat
Winter wren

AZERBAIJAN
Barn swallow
Cattle egret
Chaffinch
Common cuckoo
Dunnock
Egyptian vulture
Eurasian dipper
Eurasian golden oriole
European bee-eater
European roller
European starling
European white stork
Great cormorant
Great crested grebe
Great tit
Hoopoe
Horned lark
House sparrow
Mallard
Northern lapwing
Northern raven
Nuthatch
Peregrine falcon
Red crossbill
Red-throated loon
Rock pigeon
Snow finch
Spotted flycatcher
Winter wren

BAHAMAS
American avocet
American mourning dove
American robin
Barn owl
Belted kingfisher
Black-and-white warbler
Black-winged stilt
Blue-gray gnatcatcher
Brown pelican
Cattle egret

Crested caracara
European starling
Gray catbird
House sparrow
Killdeer
Kirtland's warbler
Osprey
Peregrine falcon
Rock pigeon
Ruddy turnstone
White-tailed tropicbird
Wood stork
Yellow-bellied sapsucker

BANGLADESH
Barn swallow
Baya weaver
Black bulbul
Black-naped monarch
Black-winged stilt
Cattle egret
Common cuckoo
Common iora
Common myna
Coppersmith barbet
Crested tree swift
Dollarbird
Eurasian bittern
European white stork
Gray nightjar
Gray wagtail
Great cormorant
Great crested grebe
Great tit
Greater painted snipe
Greater racket-tailed drongo
Green magpie
Hooded pitta
Hoopoe
House sparrow
Mallard
Northern wryneck
Osprey
Peregrine falcon
Pheasant-tailed jacana
Purple sunbird

Rock pigeon
Rose-ringed parakeet
Ruby-cheeked sunbird
Ruddy turnstone
Small buttonquail
Spotted munia
Stonechat
White-throated fantail
Zitting cisticola

BELARUS
Barn swallow
Black tern
Chaffinch
Common cuckoo
Corncrake
Dunnock
Eurasian bittern
Eurasian golden oriole
European roller
European starling
European white stork
Great cormorant
Great crested grebe
Great tit
Hoopoe
House sparrow
Mallard
Northern lapwing
Northern raven
Northern wryneck
Nuthatch
Peregrine falcon
Red crossbill
Rock pigeon
Spotted flycatcher
Spotted nutcracker
Winter wren

BELGIUM
Barn swallow
Black tern
Chaffinch
Common cuckoo
Common murre
Corncrake

Dunnock
Eurasian golden oriole
European roller
European starling
European white stork
Gray wagtail
Great auk
Great cormorant
Great crested grebe
Great tit
Hoopoe
House sparrow
Mallard
Manx shearwater
Mute swan
Northern fulmar
Northern gannet
Northern lapwing
Northern wryneck
Nuthatch
Peregrine falcon
Puffin
Red-throated loon
Rock pigeon
Ruddy turnstone
Spotted flycatcher
Stonechat
Winter wren

BELIZE
American anhinga
American mourning dove
Baltimore oriole
Barn owl
Barred antshrike
Belted kingfisher
Black rail
Black-and-white warbler
Black-winged stilt
Blue-black grassquit
Blue-crowned motmot
Blue-gray gnatcatcher
Brown pelican
Cattle egret
Cedar waxwing
Crested caracara

Gray catbird
Great blue heron
Great kiskadee
Harris's hawk
House sparrow
Killdeer
King vulture
Limpkin
Magnificent frigatebird
Northern raven
Osprey
Peregrine falcon
Plain chachalaca
Rock pigeon
Rose-throated becard
Ruddy turnstone
Rufous-browed peppershrike
Rufous-tailed jacamar
Savanna sparrow
Scarlet macaw
Sungrebe
Whip-poor-will
White-necked puffbird
Wood stork
Yellow-bellied sapsucker
Yellow-breasted chat

BENIN

African jacana
African palm swift
African paradise-flycatcher
Barn swallow
Black tern
Black-winged stilt
Cattle egret
Collared pratincole
Common bulbul
Eurasian bittern
European bee-eater
European roller
Gray parrot
Gray woodpecker
Great blue turaco
Greater painted snipe
Green woodhoopoe
Hammerhead

Helmeted guineafowl
Hoopoe
Leaf-love
Northern wryneck
Osprey
Peregrine falcon
Rose-ringed parakeet
Ruddy turnstone
Sacred ibis
Secretary bird
Small buttonquail
Spotted flycatcher
Square-tailed drongo
Village weaver
White-helmet shrike
Wilson's storm-petrel
Yellow-fronted tinkerbird
Zitting cisticola

BERMUDA

European starling
Gray catbird
House sparrow
White-tailed tropicbird

BHUTAN

Asian fairy-bluebird
Barn swallow
Black-naped monarch
Cattle egret
Common cuckoo
Coppersmith barbet
Crested tree swift
Dollarbird
Eurasian bittern
European white stork
Fire-breasted flowerpecker
Gray nightjar
Great cormorant
Great crested grebe
Greater painted snipe
Hooded pitta
Hoopoe
House sparrow
Northern wryneck
Osprey

Pheasant-tailed jacana
Purple sunbird
Rock pigeon
Rose-ringed parakeet
Satyr tragopan
Small buttonquail
Snow finch
Spotted munia
Spotted nutcracker
Stonechat
White-throated fantail
Zitting cisticola

BOLIVIA

Amazonian umbrellabird
American anhinga
Barn owl
Barn swallow
Barred antshrike
Baywing
Black-capped donacobius
Black-winged stilt
Blue-black grassquit
Blue-crowned motmot
Cattle egret
Chimney swift
Crested caracara
Gray antbird
Gray potoo
Great kiskadee
Greater thornbird
Hairy hermit
Harris's hawk
Horned screamer
House sparrow
Killdeer
King vulture
Lesser rhea
Limpkin
Oilbird
Peregrine falcon
Red-billed scythebill
Red-legged seriema
Roseate spoonbill
Rufous hornero
Rufous-bellied seedsnipe

Rufous-browed peppershrike
Rufous-capped nunlet
Rufous-tailed jacamar
Scarlet macaw
Sharpbill
Spangled cotinga
Sparkling violet-ear
Sunbittern
Sungrebe
Toco toucan
Wattled curassow
White-necked puffbird
Wood stork

BOSNIA AND HERZEGOVINA
Barn swallow
Chaffinch
Common cuckoo
Corncrake
Dunnock
Eurasian dipper
Eurasian golden oriole
European bee-eater
European roller
European starling
European white stork
Gray wagtail
Great cormorant
Great crested grebe
Great tit
Hoopoe
House sparrow
Mallard
Northern lapwing
Northern raven
Northern wryneck
Nuthatch
Peregrine falcon
Red crossbill
Rock pigeon
Snow bunting
Snow finch
Spotted flycatcher
Stonechat
Winter wren

Zitting cisticola

BOTSWANA
African jacana
African palm swift
African paradise-flycatcher
African snipe
Bar-breasted mousebird
Barn swallow
Black-winged stilt
Cattle egret
Common bulbul
Common waxbill
Corncrake
Eurasian golden oriole
European roller
European white stork
Gray go-away-bird
Great cormorant
Greater painted snipe
Green woodhoopoe
Hammerhead
Helmeted guineafowl
Hoopoe
House sparrow
Namaqua sandgrouse
Osprey
Ostrich
Peregrine falcon
Red-billed oxpecker
Rock pigeon
Rosy-breasted longclaw
Sacred ibis
Secretary bird
Small buttonquail
Southern ground-hornbill
Southern red bishop
Spotted flycatcher
Stonechat
Village weaver
White-helmet shrike
Yellow-fronted tinkerbird
Zitting cisticola

BRAZIL
Amazonian umbrellabird

American anhinga
American cliff swallow
Barn owl
Barn swallow
Barred antshrike
Baywing
Black-capped donacobius
Black-winged stilt
Blue-black grassquit
Blue-crowned motmot
Brown pelican
Cattle egret
Chimney swift
Common trumpeter
Coppery-chested jacamar
Crested caracara
Gray antbird
Gray potoo
Great kiskadee
Greater thornbird
Guianan cock-of-the-rock
Hairy hermit
Harris's hawk
Hoatzin
Horned screamer
House sparrow
King vulture
Limpkin
Magellanic penguin
Magnificent frigatebird
Manx shearwater
Oilbird
Osprey
Peregrine falcon
Red-billed scythebill
Red-legged seriema
Rock pigeon
Roseate spoonbill
Ruddy turnstone
Rufous hornero
Rufous-browed peppershrike
Rufous-capped nunlet
Rufous-tailed jacamar
Rusty-belted tapaculo
Scarlet macaw

Sharpbill
Spangled cotinga
Sparkling violet-ear
Sunbittern
Sungrebe
Toco toucan
Wattled curassow
White-necked puffbird
Wilson's storm-petrel
Wire-tailed manakin
Wood stork

BULGARIA

Barn swallow
Black-winged stilt
Chaffinch
Common cuckoo
Corncrake
Dunnock
Egyptian vulture
Eurasian bittern
Eurasian golden oriole
European bee-eater
European roller
European starling
European white stork
Gray wagtail
Great cormorant
Great crested grebe
Great tit
Hoopoe
House sparrow
Mallard
Mute swan
Northern lapwing
Northern raven
Northern wryneck
Nuthatch
Peregrine falcon
Red crossbill
Red-throated loon
Rock pigeon
Snow bunting
Spotted flycatcher
Stonechat
Winter wren

Zitting cisticola

BURKINA FASO

African jacana
African palm swift
Barn swallow
Black-winged stilt
Cattle egret
Collared pratincole
Common bulbul
Egyptian vulture
Eurasian bittern
European bee-eater
European roller
European white stork
Gray woodpecker
Greater painted snipe
Green woodhoopoe
Hammerhead
Helmeted guineafowl
Hoopoe
Northern wryneck
Osprey
Peregrine falcon
Rose-ringed parakeet
Sacred ibis
Secretary bird
Small buttonquail
Village weaver
White-helmet shrike
Yellow-fronted tinkerbird

BURUNDI

African jacana
African palm swift
African paradise-flycatcher
African pitta
African snipe
Bar-breasted mousebird
Barn swallow
Black-winged stilt
Buff-spotted flufftail
Cattle egret
Collared pratincole
Common bulbul
Common cuckoo

Common waxbill
Corncrake
Eurasian golden oriole
European bee-eater
European roller
European white stork
Gray parrot
Gray-crowned crane
Great blue turaco
Great cormorant
Great crested grebe
Green woodhoopoe
Hammerhead
Helmeted guineafowl
Hoopoe
Osprey
Ostrich
Peregrine falcon
Red-billed oxpecker
Sacred ibis
Small buttonquail
Southern ground-hornbill
Southern red bishop
Spotted flycatcher
Stonechat
Village weaver
Yellow-fronted tinkerbird
Zitting cisticola

CAMBODIA

Arctic warbler
Asian fairy-bluebird
Australasian lark
Barn swallow
Baya weaver
Black-naped monarch
Black-winged stilt
Cattle egret
Common cuckoo
Common iora
Common myna
Coppersmith barbet
Crested tree swift
Dollarbird
Fire-breasted flowerpecker
Gray nightjar

Gray wagtail
Great cormorant
Great tit
Greater painted snipe
Greater racket-tailed drongo
Green magpie
Hoopoe
Northern wryneck
Orange-breasted trogon
Osprey
Peregrine falcon
Pheasant-tailed jacana
Purple sunbird
Rock pigeon
Ruby-cheeked sunbird
Ruddy turnstone
Small buttonquail
Spotted munia
Stonechat
White-throated fantail
Zitting cisticola

CAMEROON
African broadbill
African jacana
African palm swift
African paradise-flycatcher
African pitta
Bar-breasted mousebird
Barn swallow
Black tern
Black-winged stilt
Buff-spotted flufftail
Cattle egret
Collared pratincole
Common bulbul
Common waxbill
Eurasian bittern
Eurasian golden oriole
European roller
European white stork
Gray parrot
Gray woodpecker
Gray-necked picathartes
Great blue turaco
Great cormorant

Green woodhoopoe
Hammerhead
Helmeted guineafowl
Hoopoe
Leaf-love
Lyre-tailed honeyguide
Northern wryneck
Osprey
Peregrine falcon
Rose-ringed parakeet
Ruddy turnstone
Sacred ibis
Secretary bird
Small buttonquail
Spotted flycatcher
Square-tailed drongo
Stonechat
Village weaver
White-helmet shrike
Wilson's storm-petrel
Yellow-fronted tinkerbird
Zitting cisticola

CANADA
American cliff swallow
American dipper
American goldfinch
American mourning dove
American robin
American white pelican
Anna's hummingbird
Arctic skua
Baltimore oriole
Barn owl
Barn swallow
Belted kingfisher
Black tern
Black-and-white warbler
Black-capped chickadee
Blue jay
Brown creeper
Bushtit
Canada goose
Cattle egret
Cedar waxwing
Chimney swift

Common loon
Common murre
Eastern bluebird
Eastern phoebe
Eastern screech-owl
European starling
Gray catbird
Great auk
Great blue heron
Great cormorant
Gyrfalcon
Horned lark
House sparrow
House wren
Killdeer
King eider
Loggerhead shrike
Long-billed curlew
Mallard
Manx shearwater
Northern fulmar
Northern gannet
Northern raven
Osprey
Peregrine falcon
Puffin
Red crossbill
Red-breasted nuthatch
Red-throated loon
Red-winged blackbird
Rock pigeon
Ruddy turnstone
Sandhill crane
Savanna sparrow
Snow bunting
Snowy owl
Song sparrow
Sprague's pipit
Western grebe
Whip-poor-will
Willow ptarmigan
Wilson's storm-petrel
Winter wren
Wood duck
Yellow-bellied sapsucker
Yellow-breasted chat

CENTRAL AFRICAN REPUBLIC

African broadbill
African jacana
African palm swift
African paradise-flycatcher
Bar-breasted mousebird
Barn swallow
Black-winged stilt
Buff-spotted flufftail
Cattle egret
Collared pratincole
Common bulbul
Common waxbill
Eurasian bittern
Eurasian golden oriole
European white stork
Gray parrot
Gray woodpecker
Great blue turaco
Great cormorant
Green woodhoopoe
Hammerhead
Helmeted guineafowl
Hoopoe
Leaf-love
Lyre-tailed honeyguide
Northern wryneck
Osprey
Ostrich
Peregrine falcon
Red-billed oxpecker
Rose-ringed parakeet
Sacred ibis
Secretary bird
Shoebill
Small buttonquail
Spotted flycatcher
Square-tailed drongo
Village weaver
White-helmet shrike
Yellow-fronted tinkerbird

CHAD

African jacana
African palm swift

African paradise-flycatcher
Barn swallow
Black-winged stilt
Cattle egret
Collared pratincole
Common bulbul
Egyptian vulture
Eurasian bittern
European white stork
Gray woodpecker
Great cormorant
Green woodhoopoe
Hammerhead
Helmeted guineafowl
Hoopoe
Northern wryneck
Osprey
Ostrich
Peregrine falcon
Rock pigeon
Rose-ringed parakeet
Sacred ibis
Secretary bird
Small buttonquail
Square-tailed drongo
Village weaver
White-helmet shrike
Yellow-fronted tinkerbird

CHILE

Arctic skua
Barn owl
Barn swallow
Black rail
Black-winged stilt
Blue-black grassquit
Brown pelican
Cattle egret
Chimney swift
Common diving-petrel
Crested caracara
Emperor penguin
Harris's hawk
House sparrow
Killdeer

Lesser rhea
Macaroni penguin
Magellanic penguin
Osprey
Peregrine falcon
Rock pigeon
Ruddy turnstone
Rufous-bellied seedsnipe
Sparkling violet-ear
Wilson's storm-petrel

CHINA

Arctic warbler
Asian fairy-bluebird
Barn swallow
Baya weaver
Black bulbul
Black tern
Black-naped monarch
Black-winged stilt
Cattle egret
Chaffinch
Common cuckoo
Common iora
Common murre
Common myna
Coppersmith barbet
Crag martin
Crested tree swift
Dollarbird
Eurasian bittern
Eurasian dipper
Eurasian golden oriole
European roller
European starling
Fire-breasted flowerpecker
Gray nightjar
Gray wagtail
Great bustard
Great cormorant
Great crested grebe
Great tit
Greater painted snipe
Greater racket-tailed drongo
Green magpie

Hooded pitta
Hoopoe
Horned lark
House sparrow
Japanese white-eye
Mallard
Mute swan
Northern lapwing
Northern raven
Northern wryneck
Nuthatch
Orange-breasted trogon
Osprey
Pallas's sandgrouse
Peregrine falcon
Pheasant-tailed jacana
Purple sunbird
Red crossbill
Red-crowned crane
Red-throated loon
Rock pigeon
Rose-ringed parakeet
Ruby-cheeked sunbird
Ruddy turnstone
Satyr tragopan
Saunder's gull
Small buttonquail
Snow bunting
Snow finch
Spotted flycatcher
Spotted munia
Spotted nutcracker
Stonechat
White-throated fantail
Willow ptarmigan
Winter wren
Zitting cisticola

COLOMBIA
Amazonian umbrellabird
American anhinga
Baltimore oriole
Barn owl
Barn swallow
Barred antshrike

Belted kingfisher
Black tern
Black-and-white warbler
Black-capped donacobius
Black-winged stilt
Blue-black grassquit
Blue-crowned motmot
Blue-footed booby
Brown pelican
Cattle egret
Common trumpeter
Coppery-chested jacamar
Crested caracara
Gray antbird
Gray potoo
Gray-breasted mountain-
 toucan
Great blue heron
Great kiskadee
Greater flamingo
Guianan cock-of-the-rock
Hairy hermit
Harris's hawk
Highland tinamou
Hoatzin
Horned lark
Horned screamer
House sparrow
Killdeer
King vulture
Limpkin
Magnificent frigatebird
Oilbird
Osprey
Peregrine falcon
Red-billed scythebill
Roseate spoonbill
Ruddy turnstone
Rufous-browed peppershrike
Rufous-tailed jacamar
Rusty-belted tapaculo
Scarlet macaw
Spangled cotinga
Sparkling violet-ear
Sunbittern
Sungrebe

Toucan barbet
Wattled curassow
White-necked puffbird
Wilson's storm-petrel
Wire-tailed manakin
Wood stork

COMOROS
White-tailed tropicbird

CONGO
African jacana
African palm swift
African paradise-flycatcher
African pitta
Bar-breasted mousebird
Barn swallow
Black tern
Black-winged stilt
Buff-spotted flufftail
Cattle egret
Collared pratincole
Common bulbul
Common cuckoo
Common waxbill
Eurasian golden oriole
Gray parrot
Great blue turaco
Great cormorant
Greater painted snipe
Hammerhead
Helmeted guineafowl
Hoopoe
Leaf-love
Lyre-tailed honeyguide
Osprey
Peregrine falcon
Ruddy turnstone
Sacred ibis
Small buttonquail
Spotted flycatcher
Square-tailed drongo
Stonechat
Village weaver
Zitting cisticola

COSTA RICA

American anhinga
American dipper
American mourning dove
Baltimore oriole
Barn owl
Barn swallow
Barred antshrike
Belted kingfisher
Black guan
Black rail
Black tern
Black-and-white warbler
Black-winged stilt
Blue-black grassquit
Blue-crowned motmot
Blue-footed booby
Brown pelican
Cattle egret
Cedar waxwing
Crested caracara
Gray catbird
Gray potoo
Great blue heron
Great kiskadee
Harris's hawk
Highland tinamou
House sparrow
Killdeer
King vulture
Limpkin
Long-tailed manakin
Magnificent frigatebird
Oilbird
Osprey
Peregrine falcon
Plain chachalaca
Resplendent quetzal
Rock pigeon
Roseate spoonbill
Rose-throated becard
Ruddy turnstone
Rufous-browed peppershrike
Rufous-tailed jacamar
Scarlet macaw
Sharpbill
Sunbittern
Sungrebe
White-necked puffbird
Wood stork
Yellow-bellied sapsucker
Yellow-breasted chat

CROATIA

Barn swallow
Chaffinch
Collared pratincole
Common cuckoo
Corncrake
Dunnock
Eurasian bittern
Eurasian dipper
Eurasian golden oriole
European bee-eater
European roller
European starling
European white stork
Gray wagtail
Great cormorant
Great crested grebe
Great tit
Hoopoe
House sparrow
Mallard
Northern lapwing
Northern raven
Northern wryneck
Nuthatch
Peregrine falcon
Red crossbill
Red-throated loon
Rock pigeon
Snow bunting
Snow finch
Spotted flycatcher
Stonechat
Winter wren
Zitting cisticola

CUBA

American avocet
American mourning dove
Barn owl
Belted kingfisher
Black rail
Black-and-white warbler
Black-winged stilt
Blue-gray gnatcatcher
Brown pelican
Crested caracara
Cuban tody
Gray catbird
Greater flamingo
House sparrow
Ivory-billed woodpecker
Killdeer
Limpkin
Magnificent frigatebird
Northern bobwhite quail
Osprey
Peregrine falcon
Rock pigeon
Roseate spoonbill
Ruddy turnstone
Whip-poor-will
White-tailed tropicbird
Wood duck
Wood stork
Yellow-bellied sapsucker

CYPRUS

European roller
Great cormorant
Northern gannet
Peregrine falcon
Zitting cisticola

CZECH REPUBLIC

Barn swallow
Black tern
Chaffinch
Common cuckoo
Corncrake
Dunnock
Eurasian dipper
Eurasian golden oriole
European roller
European starling

European white stork
Gray wagtail
Great cormorant
Great crested grebe
Great tit
Hoopoe
House sparrow
Mallard
Mute swan
Northern lapwing
Northern raven
Northern wryneck
Nuthatch
Peregrine falcon
Red crossbill
Rock pigeon
Snow bunting
Spotted flycatcher
Spotted nutcracker
Stonechat
Winter wren

DEMOCRATIC REPUBLIC OF THE CONGO

African broadbill
African jacana
African palm swift
African paradise-flycatcher
African pitta
African snipe
Barn swallow
Black tern
Black-winged stilt
Buff-spotted flufftail
Cattle egret
Collared pratincole
Common bulbul
Common cuckoo
Common waxbill
Corncrake
Egyptian vulture
Eurasian bittern
Eurasian golden oriole
European bee-eater
European roller

European white stork
Golden-winged sunbird
Gray go-away-bird
Gray parrot
Gray woodpecker
Gray-crowned crane
Great blue turaco
Great cormorant
Great crested grebe
Greater painted snipe
Green woodhoopoe
Hammerhead
Helmeted guineafowl
Hoopoe
House sparrow
Leaf-love
Lyre-tailed honeyguide
Northern wryneck
Osprey
Peregrine falcon
Red-billed oxpecker
Ruddy turnstone
Sacred ibis
Secretary bird
Shoebill
Small buttonquail
Southern ground-hornbill
Southern red bishop
Spotted flycatcher
Square-tailed drongo
Stonechat
Village weaver
White-helmet shrike
Yellow-fronted tinkerbird
Zitting cisticola

DENMARK

Barn swallow
Canada goose
Chaffinch
Common cuckoo
Common murre
Corncrake
Dunnock
Eurasian bittern
European roller

European starling
Great auk
Great cormorant
Great crested grebe
Great tit
House sparrow
Mallard
Manx shearwater
Mute swan
Northern fulmar
Northern gannet
Northern lapwing
Northern wryneck
Nuthatch
Peregrine falcon
Puffin
Red crossbill
Red-throated loon
Rock pigeon
Snow bunting
Spotted flycatcher
Stonechat
Winter wren

DJIBOUTI

African paradise-flycatcher
African snipe
Bar-breasted mousebird
Cattle egret
Collared pratincole
Common bulbul
Corncrake
Crab plovers
Egyptian vulture
European roller
Great cormorant
Greater flamingo
Greater hoopoe-lark
Green woodhoopoe
Hammerhead
Hoopoe
Osprey
Ostrich
Peregrine falcon
Red-billed oxpecker
Ruddy turnstone

Sacred ibis
Secretary bird
Small buttonquail
Stonechat
Wilson's storm-petrel

DOMINICAN REPUBLIC
American mourning dove
Barn owl
Belted kingfisher
Black rail
Black-and-white warbler
Black-winged stilt
Brown pelican
Cattle egret
Crested caracara
Greater flamingo
House sparrow
Killdeer
Limpkin
Magnificent frigatebird
Osprey
Palmchat
Peregrine falcon
Rock pigeon
Roseate spoonbill
Ruddy turnstone
White-tailed tropicbird
Wilson's storm-petrel
Wood stork
Yellow-bellied sapsucker

ECUADOR
Amazonian umbrellabird
American anhinga
Barn owl
Barn swallow
Barred antshrike
Black tern
Black-winged stilt
Blue-black grassquit
Blue-crowned motmot
Blue-footed booby
Brown pelican
Cattle egret
Chimney swift

Common trumpeter
Coppery-chested jacamar
Crested caracara
Gray antbird
Gray potoo
Gray-breasted mountain-
  toucan
Great kiskadee
Greater flamingo
Harris's hawk
Highland tinamou
Hood mockingbird
Horned screamer
House sparrow
Killdeer
King vulture
Limpkin
Magnificent frigatebird
Oilbird
Osprey
Peregrine falcon
Red-billed scythebill
Roseate spoonbill
Ruddy turnstone
Rufous-bellied seedsnipe
Rufous-browed peppershrike
Rufous-tailed jacamar
Rusty-belted tapaculo
Scarlet macaw
Sharpbill
Spangled cotinga
Sparkling violet-ear
Sunbittern
Sungrebe
Toucan barbet
White-necked puffbird
Wilson's storm-petrel
Wire-tailed manakin

EGYPT
Barn swallow
Black tern
Black-winged stilt
Cattle egret
Common bulbul
Corncrake

Egyptian vulture
Eurasian bittern
European roller
Gray wagtail
Great cormorant
Great crested grebe
Greater flamingo
Greater hoopoe-lark
Greater painted snipe
Hoopoe
House sparrow
Mallard
Northern gannet
Northern lapwing
Northern raven
Osprey
Peregrine falcon
Rock pigeon
Ruddy turnstone
Stonechat
Zitting cisticola

EL SALVADOR
American anhinga
American mourning dove
Baltimore oriole
Barn owl
Barred antshrike
Belted kingfisher
Black rail
Black tern
Black-and-white warbler
Black-winged stilt
Blue-black grassquit
Blue-crowned motmot
Blue-footed booby
Blue-gray gnatcatcher
Brown creeper
Brown pelican
Cattle egret
Cedar waxwing
Crested caracara
Great blue heron
Great kiskadee
Harris's hawk
House sparrow

Killdeer
King vulture
Limpkin
Long-tailed manakin
Magnificent frigatebird
Northern raven
Osprey
Peregrine falcon
Rock pigeon
Roseate spoonbill
Rose-throated becard
Ruddy turnstone
Rufous-browed peppershrike
Rufous-tailed jacamar
Sunbittern
Sungrebe
Whip-poor-will
White-necked puffbird
Wood stork
Yellow-bellied sapsucker
Yellow-breasted chat

EQUATORIAL GUINEA
African jacana
African palm swift
African paradise-flycatcher
African pitta
Barn swallow
Black tern
Black-winged stilt
Cattle egret
Collared pratincole
Common bulbul
Common waxbill
Gray parrot
Gray-necked picathartes
Great blue turaco
Great cormorant
Great crested grebe
Hammerhead
Helmeted guineafowl
Leaf-love
Lyre-tailed honeyguide
Osprey
Peregrine falcon
Ruddy turnstone

Sacred ibis
Spotted flycatcher
Village weaver
Wilson's storm-petrel
Zitting cisticola

ERITREA
African paradise-flycatcher
African snipe
Bar-breasted mousebird
Cattle egret
Collared pratincole
Common bulbul
Corncrake
Crab plovers
Egyptian vulture
Eurasian bittern
European roller
European white stork
Gray woodpecker
Greater flamingo
Greater hoopoe-lark
Greater painted snipe
Green woodhoopoe
Hammerhead
Helmeted guineafowl
Hoopoe
Osprey
Ostrich
Peregrine falcon
Red-billed oxpecker
Rock pigeon
Rose-ringed parakeet
Ruddy turnstone
Sacred ibis
Secretary bird
Small buttonquail
Stonechat
White-helmet shrike
Wilson's storm-petrel
Zitting cisticola

ESTONIA
Barn swallow
Black tern
Chaffinch

Common cuckoo
Common murre
Corncrake
Dunnock
Eurasian bittern
Eurasian dipper
Eurasian golden oriole
European roller
European starling
European white stork
Great cormorant
Great crested grebe
Great tit
Hoopoe
House sparrow
Mallard
Northern fulmar
Northern gannet
Northern lapwing
Northern raven
Northern wryneck
Nuthatch
Osprey
Red crossbill
Rock pigeon
Spotted flycatcher
Willow ptarmigan
Winter wren

ETHIOPIA
African jacana
African palm swift
African paradise-flycatcher
African snipe
Bar-breasted mousebird
Barn swallow
Black-winged stilt
Buff-spotted flufftail
Cattle egret
Collared pratincole
Common bulbul
Common waxbill
Corncrake
Egyptian vulture
Eurasian bittern
European roller

European white stork
Gray wagtail
Gray woodpecker
Great cormorant
Great crested grebe
Greater painted snipe
Green woodhoopoe
Hammerhead
Helmeted guineafowl
Hoopoe
Northern wryneck
Osprey
Ostrich
Peregrine falcon
Red-billed oxpecker
Rose-ringed parakeet
Sacred ibis
Secretary bird
Small buttonquail
Stonechat
Village weaver
White-helmet shrike
Yellow-fronted tinkerbird
Zitting cisticola

FALKLAND ISLANDS
Arctic skua
Crested caracara
Emperor penguin
House sparrow
Macaroni penguin
Magellanic penguin
Peregrine falcon

FIJI
European starling
Golden whistler
White-tailed tropicbird

FINLAND
Arctic warbler
Barn swallow
Chaffinch
Common cuckoo
Common murre

Corncrake
Dunnock
Eurasian bittern
Eurasian dipper
European roller
European starling
Gray wagtail
Great cormorant
Great crested grebe
Great tit
Gyrfalcon
Horned lark
House sparrow
Mute swan
Northern fulmar
Northern gannet
Northern lapwing
Northern raven
Northern wryneck
Osprey
Peregrine falcon
Puffin
Red crossbill
Red-throated loon
Rock pigeon
Ruddy turnstone
Spotted flycatcher
Spotted nutcracker
Willow ptarmigan
Winter wren

FRANCE
Barn swallow
Black tern
Black-winged stilt
Cattle egret
Chaffinch
Common cuckoo
Common loon
Common murre
Corncrake
Dunnock
Eurasian bittern
Eurasian dipper
Eurasian golden oriole
European bee-eater

European roller
European starling
European white stork
Gray wagtail
Great auk
Great cormorant
Great crested grebe
Great tit
Greater flamingo
Hoopoe
House sparrow
Mallard
Manx shearwater
Mute swan
Northern fulmar
Northern gannet
Northern lapwing
Northern raven
Northern wryneck
Nuthatch
Osprey
Peregrine falcon
Puffin
Red crossbill
Red-throated loon
Rock pigeon
Ruddy turnstone
Snow finch
Spotted flycatcher
Stonechat
Wilson's storm-petrel
Winter wren
Zitting cisticola

FRENCH GUIANA
American anhinga
Barn owl
Barn swallow
Barred antshrike
Black tern
Black-capped donacobius
Black-winged stilt
Blue-black grassquit
Blue-crowned motmot
Brown pelican
Cattle egret

Common trumpeter
Crested caracara
Gray antbird
Gray potoo
Great kiskadee
Guianan cock-of-the-rock
Hairy hermit
Hoatzin
King vulture
Limpkin
Magnificent frigatebird
Osprey
Peregrine falcon
Roseate spoonbill
Ruddy turnstone
Rufous-browed peppershrike
Rufous-tailed jacamar
Scarlet macaw
Spangled cotinga
Sunbittern
Sungrebe
White-necked puffbird
Wilson's storm-petrel
Wood stork

GABON
African broadbill
African jacana
African palm swift
African paradise-flycatcher
African pitta
Bar-breasted mousebird
Barn swallow
Black tern
Black-winged stilt
Buff-spotted flufftail
Cattle egret
Collared pratincole
Common bulbul
Common cuckoo
Common waxbill
Eurasian golden oriole
Gray parrot
Gray-necked picathartes
Great blue turaco
Great cormorant

Greater painted snipe
Hammerhead
Helmeted guineafowl
Hoopoe
Leaf-love
Lyre-tailed honeyguide
Osprey
Peregrine falcon
Ruddy turnstone
Sacred ibis
Small buttonquail
Spotted flycatcher
Square-tailed drongo
Stonechat
Village weaver
Wilson's storm-petrel
Zitting cisticola

GAMBIA
African palm swift
African paradise-flycatcher
Black tern
Black-winged stilt
Cattle egret
Collared pratincole
Common bulbul
Egyptian vulture
Eurasian bittern
Gray woodpecker
Greater flamingo
Green woodhoopoe
Hammerhead
Helmeted guineafowl
Hoopoe
Leaf-love
Magnificent frigatebird
Northern wryneck
Osprey
Peregrine falcon
Rose-ringed parakeet
Ruddy turnstone
Sacred ibis
Secretary bird
Small buttonquail
Village weaver
White-helmet shrike

Wilson's storm-petrel
Yellow-fronted tinkerbird

GEORGIA
Barn swallow
Chaffinch
Common cuckoo
Corncrake
Dunnock
Egyptian vulture
Eurasian dipper
Eurasian golden oriole
European bee-eater
European roller
European starling
Gray wagtail
Great cormorant
Great crested grebe
Great tit
Hoopoe
Horned lark
House sparrow
Northern raven
Northern wryneck
Nuthatch
Peregrine falcon
Red crossbill
Rock pigeon
Snow finch
Spotted flycatcher
Stonechat
Winter wren

GERMANY
Barn swallow
Black tern
Canada goose
Chaffinch
Common cuckoo
Common murre
Corncrake
Dunnock
Eurasian bittern
Eurasian dipper
Eurasian golden oriole

European roller
European starling
European white stork
Gray wagtail
Great auk
Great bustard
Great cormorant
Great crested grebe
Great tit
Hoopoe
House sparrow
Mallard
Manx shearwater
Mute swan
Northern fulmar
Northern gannet
Northern lapwing
Northern raven
Northern wryneck
Nuthatch
Peregrine falcon
Puffin
Red crossbill
Red-throated loon
Rock pigeon
Ruddy turnstone
Snow bunting
Snow finch
Spotted flycatcher
Spotted nutcracker
Stonechat
Winter wren

GHANA
African broadbill
African jacana
African palm swift
African paradise-flycatcher
African pitta
Barn swallow
Black tern
Black-winged stilt
Cattle egret
Collared pratincole
Common bulbul
Eurasian bittern

European bee-eater
European roller
Gray parrot
Gray woodpecker
Great blue turaco
Greater painted snipe
Green woodhoopoe
Hammerhead
Helmeted guineafowl
Hoopoe
Leaf-love
Northern wryneck
Osprey
Peregrine falcon
Rose-ringed parakeet
Ruddy turnstone
Sacred ibis
Secretary bird
Small buttonquail
Spotted flycatcher
Square-tailed drongo
Village weaver
White-helmet shrike
Wilson's storm-petrel
Yellow-fronted tinkerbird
Zitting cisticola

GREECE
Barn swallow
Chaffinch
Common cuckoo
Corncrake
Crag martin
Dunnock
Egyptian vulture
Eurasian bittern
Eurasian dipper
Eurasian golden oriole
European bee-eater
European roller
European starling
Gray wagtail
Great cormorant
Great crested grebe
Great tit
Hoopoe

Horned lark
House sparrow
Mallard
Mute swan
Northern gannet
Northern lapwing
Northern raven
Northern wryneck
Peregrine falcon
Red crossbill
Rock pigeon
Spotted flycatcher
Stonechat
Winter wren
Zitting cisticola

GREENLAND
Arctic skua
Common loon
Common murre
Great auk
Great cormorant
Gyrfalcon
King eider
Mallard
Manx shearwater
Northern fulmar
Northern gannet
Northern raven
Peregrine falcon
Puffin
Red-throated loon
Ruddy turnstone
Snow bunting
Snowy owl

GUATEMALA
American anhinga
American dipper
American mourning dove
American robin
Baltimore oriole
Barn owl
Barred antshrike
Belted kingfisher
Black rail

Black tern
Black-and-white warbler
Black-capped vireo
Black-winged stilt
Blue-black grassquit
Blue-crowned motmot
Blue-footed booby
Blue-gray gnatcatcher
Brown creeper
Brown pelican
Cattle egret
Cedar waxwing
Crested caracara
Gray catbird
Great blue heron
Great kiskadee
Harris's hawk
House sparrow
Killdeer
King vulture
Limpkin
Long-tailed manakin
Magnificent frigatebird
Northern raven
Osprey
Peregrine falcon
Plain chachalaca
Resplendent quetzal
Rock pigeon
Roseate spoonbill
Rose-throated becard
Ruddy turnstone
Rufous-browed peppershrike
Rufous-tailed jacamar
Savanna sparrow
Scarlet macaw
Sunbittern
Sungrebe
Whip-poor-will
White-necked puffbird
Wood stork
Yellow-bellied sapsucker
Yellow-breasted chat

GUINEA
African palm swift

African paradise-flycatcher
Barn swallow
Black tern
Black-winged stilt
Buff-spotted flufftail
Cattle egret
Collared pratincole
Common bulbul
Common waxbill
Eurasian bittern
European bee-eater
European roller
Gray parrot
Gray woodpecker
Great blue turaco
Green woodhoopoe
Hammerhead
Helmeted guineafowl
Hoopoe
Leaf-love
Northern wryneck
Osprey
Peregrine falcon
Rock pigeon
Rose-ringed parakeet
Ruddy turnstone
Sacred ibis
Small buttonquail
Square-tailed drongo
Stonechat
Village weaver
White-helmet shrike
Wilson's storm-petrel
Yellow-fronted tinkerbird

GUINEA-BISSAU
African palm swift
African paradise-flycatcher
Barn swallow
Black tern
Black-winged stilt
Cattle egret
Collared pratincole
Common bulbul
Common waxbill
Egyptian vulture

Eurasian bittern
Gray parrot
Gray woodpecker
Green woodhoopoe
Hammerhead
Helmeted guineafowl
Hoopoe
Leaf-love
Magnificent frigatebird
Northern wryneck
Osprey
Peregrine falcon
Rose-ringed parakeet
Ruddy turnstone
Sacred ibis
Small buttonquail
Square-tailed drongo
Village weaver
Wilson's storm-petrel

GUYANA
American anhinga
Barn owl
Barn swallow
Barred antshrike
Belted kingfisher
Black tern
Black-capped donacobius
Black-winged stilt
Blue-black grassquit
Blue-crowned motmot
Brown pelican
Cattle egret
Common trumpeter
Crested caracara
Gray antbird
Gray potoo
Great kiskadee
Greater flamingo
Guianan cock-of-the-rock
Hairy hermit
Hoatzin
King vulture
Limpkin
Magnificent frigatebird
Oilbird

Osprey
Peregrine falcon
Roseate spoonbill
Ruddy turnstone
Rufous-browed peppershrike
Rufous-tailed jacamar
Scarlet macaw
Sharpbill
Spangled cotinga
Sparkling violet-ear
Sunbittern
Sungrebe
White-necked puffbird
Wilson's storm-petrel
Wood stork

HAITI

American mourning dove
Barn owl
Belted kingfisher
Black-and-white warbler
Black-winged stilt
Brown pelican
Cattle egret
Crested caracara
Greater flamingo
House sparrow
Killdeer
Limpkin
Magnificent frigatebird
Osprey
Palmchat
Peregrine falcon
Rock pigeon
Roseate spoonbill
Ruddy turnstone
White-tailed tropicbird
Wood stork
Yellow-bellied sapsucker

HONDURAS

American anhinga
American mourning dove
Baltimore oriole
Barn owl
Barred antshrike

Belted kingfisher
Black tern
Black-and-white warbler
Black-winged stilt
Blue-black grassquit
Blue-crowned motmot
Blue-footed booby
Blue-gray gnatcatcher
Brown creeper
Brown pelican
Cattle egret
Cedar waxwing
Crested caracara
Gray catbird
Great blue heron
Great kiskadee
Harris's hawk
House sparrow
Killdeer
King vulture
Limpkin
Long-tailed manakin
Magnificent frigatebird
Northern raven
Osprey
Peregrine falcon
Plain chachalaca
Resplendent quetzal
Rock pigeon
Roseate spoonbill
Rose-throated becard
Ruddy turnstone
Rufous-browed peppershrike
Rufous-tailed jacamar
Scarlet macaw
Sunbittern
Sungrebe
Whip-poor-will
White-necked puffbird
Wood stork
Yellow-bellied sapsucker
Yellow-breasted chat

HUNGARY

Barn swallow
Black tern

Chaffinch
Collared pratincole
Common cuckoo
Corncrake
Dunnock
Eurasian golden oriole
European bee-eater
European roller
European starling
European white stork
Gray wagtail
Great bustard
Great cormorant
Great crested grebe
Great tit
Hoopoe
House sparrow
Mallard
Northern lapwing
Northern raven
Northern wryneck
Nuthatch
Peregrine falcon
Red crossbill
Rock pigeon
Snow bunting
Spotted flycatcher
Stonechat
Winter wren

ICELAND

Arctic skua
Common loon
Common murre
European starling
Great auk
Great cormorant
Gyrfalcon
King eider
Mallard
Manx shearwater
Northern fulmar
Northern gannet
Northern raven
Puffin
Red-throated loon

Snow bunting

INDIA
Asian fairy-bluebird
Barn swallow
Baya weaver
Black bulbul
Black-naped monarch
Black-winged stilt
Cattle egret
Chaffinch
Collared pratincole
Common cuckoo
Common iora
Common myna
Coppersmith barbet
Crab plovers
Crag martin
Crested tree swift
Dollarbird
Egyptian vulture
Eurasian bittern
Eurasian golden oriole
European bee-eater
European roller
European starling
European white stork
Fire-breasted flowerpecker
Gray hypocolius
Gray nightjar
Gray wagtail
Great cormorant
Great crested grebe
Great tit
Greater flamingo
Greater painted snipe
Greater racket-tailed drongo
Green magpie
Hooded pitta
Hoopoe
House sparrow
Mallard
Northern lapwing
Northern raven
Northern wryneck
Osprey

Peregrine falcon
Pheasant-tailed jacana
Purple sunbird
Rock pigeon
Rose-ringed parakeet
Ruby-cheeked sunbird
Ruddy turnstone
Satyr tragopan
Small buttonquail
Spotted munia
Spotted nutcracker
Stonechat
White-throated fantail
Wilson's storm-petrel
Zitting cisticola

INDONESIA
Arctic warbler
Asian fairy-bluebird
Australasian figbird
Australasian lark
Australian magpie-lark
Australian pratincole
Barn swallow
Barred eagle-owl
Baya weaver
Beach thick-knee
Black-and-red broadbill
Black-naped monarch
Black-winged stilt
Bornean bristlehead
Cattle egret
Common iora
Coppersmith barbet
Dollarbird
Eclectus parrot
Fan-tailed berrypecker
Feline owlet-nightjar
Fiery minivet
Fire-breasted flowerpecker
Golden whistler
Gray nightjar
Gray wagtail
Gray-crowned babbler
Great cormorant
Great tit

Greater painted snipe
Greater racket-tailed drongo
Green magpie
Helmeted hornbill
Hooded pitta
King bird of paradise
Malaysian honeyguide
Maleo
Orange-breasted trogon
Osprey
Peregrine falcon
Pheasant-tailed jacana
Purple-bearded bee-eater
Rainbow lorikeet
Rock pigeon
Ruby-cheeked sunbird
Ruddy turnstone
Rufous-collared kingfisher
Small buttonquail
Southern cassowary
Spotted munia
Sulawesi red-knobbed
  hornbill
Variable pitohui
White-throated fantail
Willie wagtail
Wilson's storm-petrel
Zebra finch
Zitting cisticola

IRAN
Barn swallow
Black-winged stilt
Cattle egret
Chaffinch
Common cuckoo
Common myna
Corncrake
Crab plovers
Crag martin
Dunnock
Egyptian vulture
Eurasian dipper
Eurasian golden oriole
European bee-eater
European roller

European starling
European white stork
Gray hypocolius
Gray wagtail
Great bustard
Great cormorant
Great crested grebe
Great tit
Greater flamingo
Greater hoopoe-lark
Hoopoe
Horned lark
House sparrow
Mallard
Mute swan
Northern lapwing
Northern raven
Nuthatch
Osprey
Peregrine falcon
Purple sunbird
Red-throated loon
Rock pigeon
Ruddy turnstone
Snow finch
Spotted flycatcher
Stonechat
Wilson's storm-petrel
Winter wren

IRAQ
Black-winged stilt
Cattle egret
Chaffinch
Collared pratincole
Corncrake
Dunnock
Egyptian vulture
Eurasian bittern
European bee-eater
European roller
European starling
Gray hypocolius
Gray wagtail
Great cormorant
Great crested grebe

Greater hoopoe-lark
Hoopoe
House sparrow
Mallard
Northern lapwing
Nuthatch
Osprey
Peregrine falcon
Rock pigeon
Spotted flycatcher
Stonechat

IRELAND
Barn owl
Barn swallow
Canada goose
Chaffinch
Common cuckoo
Common loon
Common murre
Corncrake
Dunnock
Eurasian dipper
European starling
Gray wagtail
Great auk
Great cormorant
Great crested grebe
Great tit
House sparrow
Mallard
Manx shearwater
Mute swan
Northern gannet
Northern lapwing
Northern raven
Peregrine falcon
Puffin
Red-throated loon
Rock pigeon
Ruddy turnstone
Spotted flycatcher
Stonechat
Willow ptarmigan
Winter wren

ISRAEL
Black-winged stilt
Cattle egret
Collared pratincole
Common cuckoo
Egyptian vulture
European bee-eater
European roller
Great cormorant
Greater flamingo
Hoopoe
Horned lark
House sparrow
Mallard
Northern gannet
Northern lapwing
Peregrine falcon
Rock pigeon
Stonechat
Winter wren
Zitting cisticola

ITALY
Barn swallow
Black tern
Black-winged stilt
Cattle egret
Chaffinch
Common cuckoo
Corncrake
Crag martin
Dunnock
Egyptian vulture
Eurasian dipper
Eurasian golden oriole
European bee-eater
European roller
European starling
Gray wagtail
Great cormorant
Great crested grebe
Great tit
Greater flamingo
Hoopoe
House sparrow
Mallard

Mute swan
Northern gannet
Northern lapwing
Northern raven
Northern wryneck
Nuthatch
Peregrine falcon
Red crossbill
Rock pigeon
Snow finch
Spotted flycatcher
Stonechat
Winter wren
Zitting cisticola

IVORY COAST
African broadbill
African jacana
African palm swift
African paradise-flycatcher
African pitta
Barn swallow
Black tern
Black-winged stilt
Cattle egret
Collared pratincole
Common bulbul
Common waxbill
Eurasian bittern
European bee-eater
European roller
Gray parrot
Gray woodpecker
Great blue turaco
Green woodhoopoe
Hammerhead
Hoopoe
Leaf-love
Lyre-tailed honeyguide
Northern wryneck
Osprey
Peregrine falcon
Rose-ringed parakeet
Ruddy turnstone
Sacred ibis
Small buttonquail

Spotted flycatcher
Square-tailed drongo
Village weaver
White-helmet shrike
Wilson's storm-petrel
Yellow-fronted tinkerbird
Zitting cisticola

JAMAICA
American mourning dove
Barn owl
Belted kingfisher
Black rail
Black-and-white warbler
Brown pelican
Cattle egret
Crested caracara
European starling
Gray catbird
House sparrow
Killdeer
Magnificent frigatebird
Osprey
Peregrine falcon
Rock pigeon
Ruddy turnstone
White-tailed tropicbird
Wood stork

JAPAN
Arctic warbler
Barn swallow
Cattle egret
Common murre
Dollarbird
Eurasian bittern
Gray nightjar
Gray wagtail
Great cormorant
Great tit
Greater painted snipe
Hoopoe
Japanese white-eye
Laysan albatross
Mallard
Mute swan

Northern fulmar
Northern lapwing
Northern raven
Nuthatch
Osprey
Peregrine falcon
Red crossbill
Red-crowned crane
Red-throated loon
Rock pigeon
Saunder's gull
Spotted nutcracker
Stonechat
Willow ptarmigan
Winter wren

JORDAN
Black-winged stilt
Cattle egret
Collared pratincole
Common bulbul
Egyptian vulture
European bee-eater
European roller
Gray wagtail
Great cormorant
Hoopoe
House sparrow
Northern gannet
Northern lapwing
Peregrine falcon
Rock pigeon
Stonechat
Winter wren

KAZAKHSTAN
Barn swallow
Black tern
Black-winged stilt
Chaffinch
Collared pratincole
Common cuckoo
Common myna
Corncrake
Egyptian vulture
Eurasian bittern

Eurasian golden oriole
European bee-eater
European roller
European starling
European white stork
Great cormorant
Great crested grebe
Great tit
Greater flamingo
Hoopoe
Horned lark
House sparrow
Mallard
Mute swan
Northern raven
Pallas's sandgrouse
Peregrine falcon
Red crossbill
Red-throated loon
Rock pigeon
Snow bunting
Spotted flycatcher
Spotted nutcracker
Stonechat
Willow ptarmigan
Winter wren

KENYA

African broadbill
African jacana
African palm swift
African paradise-flycatcher
African snipe
Bar-breasted mousebird
Barn swallow
Black-winged stilt
Buff-spotted flufftail
Cattle egret
Collared pratincole
Common bulbul
Common cuckoo
Common waxbill
Corncrake
Crab plovers
Egyptian vulture
Eurasian golden oriole

European bee-eater
European roller
European white stork
Golden-winged sunbird
Gray parrot
Gray wagtail
Gray woodpecker
Gray-crowned crane
Great blue turaco
Great cormorant
Great crested grebe
Greater flamingo
Greater painted snipe
Green woodhoopoe
Hammerhead
Helmeted guineafowl
Hoopoe
Northern wryneck
Osprey
Ostrich
Peregrine falcon
Red-billed oxpecker
Rock pigeon
Rosy-breasted longclaw
Ruddy turnstone
Sacred ibis
Secretary bird
Shoebill
Small buttonquail
Southern ground-hornbill
Southern red bishop
Spotted flycatcher
Square-tailed drongo
Stonechat
Village weaver
White-helmet shrike
Wilson's storm-petrel
Zitting cisticola

KUWAIT

Black-winged stilt
Cattle egret
Chaffinch
Collared pratincole
Crab plovers
Eurasian bittern

European roller
Gray wagtail
Great cormorant
Great crested grebe
Greater hoopoe-lark
House sparrow
Mallard
Northern lapwing
Nuthatch
Osprey
Peregrine falcon
Rock pigeon
Ruddy turnstone
Spotted flycatcher
Wilson's storm-petrel
Zitting cisticola

KYRGYZSTAN

Barn swallow
Chaffinch
Common cuckoo
Crag martin
Egyptian vulture
Eurasian bittern
Eurasian golden oriole
European roller
European starling
Gray wagtail
Great cormorant
Great crested grebe
Great tit
Hoopoe
House sparrow
Mallard
Northern raven
Pallas's sandgrouse
Peregrine falcon
Rock pigeon
Snow finch
Spotted flycatcher
Stonechat
Winter wren

LAOS

Asian fairy-bluebird
Australasian lark

Barn swallow
Baya weaver
Black bulbul
Black-and-red broadbill
Black-crowned barwing
Black-naped monarch
Black-winged stilt
Cattle egret
Common cuckoo
Common iora
Common myna
Coppersmith barbet
Crested tree swift
Dollarbird
Eurasian bittern
Fire-breasted flowerpecker
Gray nightjar
Gray wagtail
Great cormorant
Greater painted snipe
Greater racket-tailed drongo
Green magpie
Hoopoe
Northern wryneck
Orange-breasted trogon
Peregrine falcon
Pheasant-tailed jacana
Purple sunbird
Rock pigeon
Ruby-cheeked sunbird
Small buttonquail
Spotted munia
Stonechat
White-throated fantail
Zitting cisticola

LATVIA
Barn swallow
Black tern
Chaffinch
Common cuckoo
Common murre
Corncrake
Dunnock
Eurasian bittern
Eurasian dipper

Eurasian golden oriole
European roller
European starling
European white stork
Great cormorant
Great crested grebe
Great tit
Hoopoe
House sparrow
Mallard
Northern fulmar
Northern gannet
Northern lapwing
Northern raven
Northern wryneck
Nuthatch
Red crossbill
Rock pigeon
Spotted flycatcher
Spotted nutcracker
Willow ptarmigan
Winter wren

LEBANON
Black-winged stilt
Cattle egret
Collared pratincole
Common bulbul
Common cuckoo
Dunnock
Egyptian vulture
European bee-eater
European roller
Great cormorant
Greater flamingo
Hoopoe
Horned lark
House sparrow
Mallard
Northern gannet
Northern lapwing
Nuthatch
Peregrine falcon
Rock pigeon
Spotted flycatcher
Stonechat

Winter wren

LESOTHO
African jacana
African snipe
Barn swallow
Black-winged stilt
Blue bustard
Cattle egret
Common cuckoo
Common waxbill
Corncrake
European roller
European white stork
Great cormorant
Great crested grebe
Greater painted snipe
Green woodhoopoe
Hammerhead
Helmeted guineafowl
Hoopoe
House sparrow
Osprey
Peregrine falcon
Sacred ibis
Secretary bird
Small buttonquail
Southern red bishop
Spotted flycatcher
Stonechat
Village weaver
Zitting cisticola

LESSER ANTILLES
Barn owl
Belted kingfisher
Brown pelican
Cattle egret
Crested caracara
Greater flamingo
House sparrow
Killdeer
Magnificent frigatebird
Osprey
Peregrine falcon
Rock pigeon

Ruddy turnstone
White-tailed tropicbird
Wood stork

LIBERIA
African broadbill
African palm swift
African paradise-flycatcher
African pitta
Barn swallow
Black tern
Black-winged stilt
Buff-spotted flufftail
Cattle egret
Collared pratincole
Common bulbul
Common waxbill
Eurasian bittern
Gray parrot
Gray woodpecker
Great blue turaco
Hammerhead
Leaf-love
Lyre-tailed honeyguide
Northern wryneck
Osprey
Peregrine falcon
Ruddy turnstone
Sacred ibis
Small buttonquail
Spotted flycatcher
Village weaver
Wilson's storm-petrel

LIBYA
Barn swallow
Black-winged stilt
Common bulbul
Crag martin
Egyptian vulture
Eurasian bittern
Gray wagtail
Greater hoopoe-lark
House sparrow
Mallard
Northern gannet

Northern lapwing
Northern raven
Peregrine falcon
Rock pigeon
Ruddy turnstone
Stonechat
Winter wren

LIECHTENSTEIN
Barn swallow
Black tern
Chaffinch
Common cuckoo
Corncrake
Dunnock
Eurasian golden oriole
European roller
European starling
Gray wagtail
Great cormorant
Great crested grebe
Great tit
Hoopoe
House sparrow
Mallard
Mute swan
Northern lapwing
Northern raven
Northern wryneck
Nuthatch
Peregrine falcon
Red crossbill
Rock pigeon
Snow finch
Spotted flycatcher
Stonechat
Winter wren

LITHUANIA
Barn swallow
Black tern
Chaffinch
Common cuckoo
Common murre
Corncrake
Dunnock

Eurasian bittern
Eurasian dipper
Eurasian golden oriole
European roller
European starling
European white stork
Great cormorant
Great crested grebe
Great tit
Hoopoe
House sparrow
Mallard
Northern fulmar
Northern gannet
Northern lapwing
Northern raven
Northern wryneck
Nuthatch
Red crossbill
Rock pigeon
Spotted flycatcher
Spotted nutcracker
Winter wren

LUXEMBOURG
Barn swallow
Black tern
Chaffinch
Common cuckoo
Corncrake
Dunnock
Eurasian golden oriole
European roller
European starling
European white stork
Gray wagtail
Great cormorant
Great crested grebe
Great tit
Hoopoe
House sparrow
Mallard
Mute swan
Northern lapwing
Northern raven
Northern wryneck

Nuthatch
Peregrine falcon
Red crossbill
Rock pigeon
Spotted flycatcher
Stonechat
Winter wren

MACEDONIA
Barn swallow
Chaffinch
Common cuckoo
Corncrake
Crag martin
Dunnock
Egyptian vulture
Eurasian dipper
Eurasian golden oriole
European bee-eater
European roller
European starling
European white stork
Gray wagtail
Great cormorant
Great crested grebe
Great tit
Hoopoe
Horned lark
House sparrow
Mallard
Northern lapwing
Northern raven
Northern wryneck
Nuthatch
Peregrine falcon
Red crossbill
Rock pigeon
Snow bunting
Spotted flycatcher
Stonechat
Winter wren

MADAGASCAR
African palm swift
Black-winged stilt
Cattle egret

Common sunbird-asity
Crab plovers
Greater flamingo
Greater painted snipe
Hammerhead
Hoopoe
Peregrine falcon
Ruddy turnstone
Rufous vanga
Sacred ibis
Stonechat
White-breasted mesite
Wilson's storm-petrel

MALAWI
African broadbill
African jacana
African palm swift
African paradise-flycatcher
African pitta
African snipe
Bar-breasted mousebird
Barn swallow
Black-winged stilt
Buff-spotted flufftail
Cape batis
Cattle egret
Collared pratincole
Common bulbul
Common cuckoo
Common waxbill
Corncrake
Eurasian golden oriole
European bee-eater
European roller
European white stork
Gray go-away-bird
Gray-crowned crane
Great cormorant
Greater painted snipe
Green woodhoopoe
Hammerhead
Helmeted guineafowl
Hoopoe
House sparrow
Osprey

Peregrine falcon
Red-billed oxpecker
Rock pigeon
Sacred ibis
Secretary bird
Small buttonquail
Southern ground-hornbill
Southern red bishop
Spotted flycatcher
Square-tailed drongo
Stonechat
Village weaver
White-helmet shrike
Yellow-fronted tinkerbird
Zitting cisticola

MALAYSIA
Arctic warbler
Asian fairy-bluebird
Barn swallow
Barred eagle-owl
Baya weaver
Black-and-red broadbill
Black-naped monarch
Black-winged stilt
Common iora
Common myna
Coppersmith barbet
Dollarbird
Fiery minivet
Fire-breasted flowerpecker
Gray nightjar
Gray wagtail
Great cormorant
Greater painted snipe
Greater racket-tailed drongo
Green magpie
Helmeted hornbill
Hooded pitta
Malaysian honeyguide
Orange-breasted trogon
Osprey
Peregrine falcon
Pheasant-tailed jacana
Rock pigeon
Ruby-cheeked sunbird

Ruddy turnstone
Rufous-collared kingfisher
Spotted munia
White-throated fantail
Zitting cisticola

MALI

African jacana
African palm swift
African paradise-flycatcher
Barn swallow
Black-winged stilt
Cattle egret
Collared pratincole
Common bulbul
Egyptian vulture
Eurasian bittern
European bee-eater
European roller
European white stork
Gray wagtail
Gray woodpecker
Greater hoopoe-lark
Greater painted snipe
Green woodhoopoe
Hammerhead
Helmeted guineafowl
Hoopoe
Leaf-love
Northern wryneck
Osprey
Ostrich
Peregrine falcon
Rock pigeon
Rose-ringed parakeet
Sacred ibis
Secretary bird
Small buttonquail
Stonechat
Village weaver
White-helmet shrike
Yellow-fronted tinkerbird
Zitting cisticola

MAURITANIA

Barn swallow

Black-winged stilt
Cattle egret
Collared pratincole
Common bulbul
Crag martin
Egyptian vulture
Eurasian bittern
European roller
European white stork
Gray woodpecker
Greater flamingo
Greater hoopoe-lark
Greater painted snipe
Green woodhoopoe
Hammerhead
Helmeted guineafowl
Hoopoe
Magnificent frigatebird
Manx shearwater
Northern gannet
Osprey
Ostrich
Peregrine falcon
Rock pigeon
Rose-ringed parakeet
Ruddy turnstone
Secretary bird
Small buttonquail
Wilson's storm-petrel
Zitting cisticola

MAURITIUS

Dodo
Mauritius cuckoo-shrike

MEXICO

American anhinga
American avocet
American cliff swallow
American dipper
American goldfinch
American mourning dove
American robin
American white pelican
Anna's hummingbird
Baltimore oriole

Barn owl
Barn swallow
Barred antshrike
Belted kingfisher
Black rail
Black tern
Black-and-white warbler
Black-capped vireo
Black-winged stilt
Blue jay
Blue-black grassquit
Blue-crowned motmot
Blue-footed booby
Blue-gray gnatcatcher
Brown creeper
Brown pelican
Bushtit
Cactus wren
Canada goose
Cattle egret
Cedar waxwing
Common loon
Crested caracara
Eastern bluebird
Eastern phoebe
Eastern screech-owl
European starling
Gray catbird
Great blue heron
Great kiskadee
Greater roadrunner
Harris's hawk
Horned lark
House sparrow
House wren
Killdeer
King vulture
Limpkin
Loggerhead shrike
Long-billed curlew
Long-tailed manakin
Magnificent frigatebird
Mallard
Northern bobwhite quail
Northern gannet
Northern raven

Osprey
Peregrine falcon
Plain chachalaca
Red-throated loon
Red-winged blackbird
Resplendent quetzal
Rock pigeon
Roseate spoonbill
Rose-throated becard
Ruddy turnstone
Rufous-browed peppershrike
Rufous-tailed jacamar
Sandhill crane
Savanna sparrow
Scarlet macaw
Song sparrow
Sprague's pipit
Sungrebe
Verdin
Western grebe
Western scrub-jay
Whip-poor-will
White-necked puffbird
Wild turkey
Wilson's storm-petrel
Winter wren
Wood duck
Wood stork
Wrentit
Yellow-bellied sapsucker
Yellow-breasted chat

MOLDOVA

Barn swallow
Black tern
Chaffinch
Collared pratincole
Common cuckoo
Corncrake
Dunnock
Eurasian bittern
Eurasian golden oriole
European bee-eater
European roller
European starling
European white stork

Great cormorant
Great crested grebe
Great tit
Hoopoe
House sparrow
Mallard
Northern lapwing
Northern raven
Northern wryneck
Nuthatch
Peregrine falcon
Rock pigeon
Snow bunting
Spotted flycatcher
Stonechat
Winter wren

MONACO

Greater flamingo
Northern gannet

MONGOLIA

Barn swallow
Black tern
Black-winged stilt
Common cuckoo
Crag martin
Eurasian bittern
Gray wagtail
Great bustard
Great cormorant
Great crested grebe
Hoopoe
Horned lark
House sparrow
Mallard
Mute swan
Northern raven
Northern wryneck
Nuthatch
Pallas's sandgrouse
Peregrine falcon
Red crossbill
Rock pigeon
Snow bunting
Snow finch

Spotted flycatcher
Spotted nutcracker
Stonechat

MOROCCO

Barn swallow
Black-winged stilt
Cattle egret
Chaffinch
Collared pratincole
Common bulbul
Common cuckoo
Common murre
Corncrake
Crag martin
Dunnock
Egyptian vulture
Eurasian dipper
Eurasian golden oriole
European bee-eater
European roller
European starling
Gray wagtail
Great bustard
Great cormorant
Great crested grebe
Greater flamingo
Greater hoopoe-lark
Hoopoe
Horned lark
House sparrow
Magnificent frigatebird
Mallard
Manx shearwater
Northern gannet
Northern raven
Ostrich
Peregrine falcon
Rock pigeon
Ruddy turnstone
Small buttonquail
Spotted flycatcher
Stonechat
Wilson's storm-petrel
Winter wren
Zitting cisticola

MOZAMBIQUE

African broadbill
African jacana
African palm swift
African paradise-flycatcher
African pitta
African snipe
Bar-breasted mousebird
Barn swallow
Black-winged stilt
Buff-spotted flufftail
Cape batis
Cattle egret
Collared pratincole
Common bulbul
Common cuckoo
Common waxbill
Corncrake
Crab plovers
Eurasian golden oriole
European bee-eater
European roller
European white stork
Gray go-away-bird
Gray-crowned crane
Great cormorant
Greater painted snipe
Green woodhoopoe
Hammerhead
Helmeted guineafowl
Hoopoe
House sparrow
Osprey
Ostrich
Peregrine falcon
Rock pigeon
Rosy-breasted longclaw
Ruddy turnstone
Sacred ibis
Secretary bird
Small buttonquail
Southern ground-hornbill
Southern red bishop
Spotted flycatcher
Square-tailed drongo
Stonechat

Village weaver
White-helmet shrike
Wilson's storm-petrel
Yellow-fronted tinkerbird
Zitting cisticola

MYANMAR

Asian fairy-bluebird
Australasian lark
Barn swallow
Barred eagle-owl
Baya weaver
Black bulbul
Black-and-red broadbill
Black-naped monarch
Black-winged stilt
Cattle egret
Common cuckoo
Common iora
Common myna
Coppersmith barbet
Crested tree swift
Dollarbird
Fiery minivet
Fire-breasted flowerpecker
Gray nightjar
Gray wagtail
Great cormorant
Great crested grebe
Great tit
Greater painted snipe
Greater racket-tailed drongo
Green magpie
Helmeted hornbill
Hooded pitta
Hoopoe
House sparrow
Mallard
Northern wryneck
Orange-breasted trogon
Osprey
Peregrine falcon
Pheasant-tailed jacana
Purple sunbird
Rock pigeon
Rose-ringed parakeet

Rose-ringed parakeet
Ruby-cheeked sunbird
Ruddy turnstone
Rufous-collared kingfisher
Small buttonquail
Spotted munia
Stonechat
White-throated fantail
Winter wren
Zitting cisticola

NAMIBIA

African jacana
African palm swift
African paradise-flycatcher
Arctic skua
Barn swallow
Black tern
Black-winged stilt
Cattle egret
Common cuckoo
Common waxbill
Egyptian vulture
Eurasian golden oriole
European roller
European white stork
Gray go-away-bird
Great cormorant
Great crested grebe
Greater painted snipe
Green woodhoopoe
Hammerhead
Helmeted guineafowl
Hoopoe
House sparrow
Namaqua sandgrouse
Osprey
Ostrich
Peregrine falcon
Rock pigeon
Ruddy turnstone
Sacred ibis
Secretary bird
Small buttonquail
Southern ground-hornbill
Southern red bishop

Spotted flycatcher
White-helmet shrike
Wilson's storm-petrel
Yellow-fronted tinkerbird
Zitting cisticola

NEPAL
Asian fairy-bluebird
Barn swallow
Black-naped monarch
Cattle egret
Common cuckoo
Coppersmith barbet
Crested tree swift
Dollarbird
Egyptian vulture
Eurasian bittern
Eurasian golden oriole
European roller
European white stork
Fire-breasted flowerpecker
Gray nightjar
Gray wagtail
Great cormorant
Great crested grebe
Greater painted snipe
Hooded pitta
Hoopoe
House sparrow
Northern wryneck
Osprey
Peregrine falcon
Pheasant-tailed jacana
Purple sunbird
Rock pigeon
Rose-ringed parakeet
Ruby-cheeked sunbird
Satyr tragopan
Small buttonquail
Snow finch
Spotted munia
Spotted nutcracker
Stonechat
White-throated fantail
Winter wren

Zitting cisticola

NETHERLANDS
Barn swallow
Black tern
Chaffinch
Common cuckoo
Common murre
Corncrake
Dunnock
Eurasian golden oriole
European roller
European starling
European white stork
Great auk
Great cormorant
Great crested grebe
Great tit
House sparrow
Mallard
Manx shearwater
Mute swan
Northern fulmar
Northern gannet
Northern lapwing
Northern wryneck
Nuthatch
Peregrine falcon
Puffin
Red-throated loon
Rock pigeon
Ruddy turnstone
Spotted flycatcher
Stonechat
Winter wren

NEW CALEDONIA
Beach thick-knee
Black-winged stilt
House sparrow
Kagu
Osprey
Painted buttonquail
Peregrine falcon
Rainbow lorikeet

White-tailed tropicbird

NEW ZEALAND
Arctic skua
Black-winged stilt
Brown kiwi
Canada goose
Cattle egret
Chatham mollymawk
Common diving-petrel
Emperor penguin
European starling
Great cormorant
Great crested grebe
House sparrow
Kokako
Laughing kookaburra
Mallard
Mute swan
Rifleman
Rock pigeon
Ruddy turnstone
Variable oystercatcher
Wilson's storm-petrel
Yellowhead

NICARAGUA
American anhinga
American dipper
American mourning dove
Baltimore oriole
Barn owl
Barred antshrike
Belted kingfisher
Black tern
Black-and-white warbler
Black-winged stilt
Blue-black grassquit
Blue-crowned motmot
Blue-footed booby
Brown creeper
Brown pelican
Cattle egret
Cedar waxwing
Crested caracara

Gray catbird
Gray potoo
Great blue heron
Great kiskadee
Harris's hawk
House sparrow
Killdeer
King vulture
Limpkin
Long-tailed manakin
Magnificent frigatebird
Northern raven
Osprey
Peregrine falcon
Plain chachalaca
Resplendent quetzal
Rock pigeon
Roseate spoonbill
Rose-throated becard
Ruddy turnstone
Rufous-browed peppershrike
Rufous-tailed jacamar
Scarlet macaw
Sunbittern
Sungrebe
White-necked puffbird
Wood stork
Yellow-bellied sapsucker
Yellow-breasted chat

NIGER

African jacana
African palm swift
African paradise-flycatcher
Barn swallow
Black-winged stilt
Cattle egret
Collared pratincole
Common bulbul
Egyptian vulture
Eurasian bittern
European white stork
Gray woodpecker
Greater hoopoe-lark
Greater painted snipe
Green woodhoopoe

Hammerhead
Helmeted guineafowl
Hoopoe
Northern wryneck
Osprey
Ostrich
Peregrine falcon
Rock pigeon
Rose-ringed parakeet
Sacred ibis
Secretary bird
Small buttonquail
Village weaver
Yellow-fronted tinkerbird
Zitting cisticola

NIGERIA

African jacana
African palm swift
African paradise-flycatcher
African pitta
Bar-breasted mousebird
Barn swallow
Black tern
Black-winged stilt
Buff-spotted flufftail
Cattle egret
Collared pratincole
Common bulbul
Common waxbill
Eurasian bittern
European roller
European white stork
Gray parrot
Gray woodpecker
Gray-necked picathartes
Great blue turaco
Greater painted snipe
Green woodhoopoe
Hammerhead
Helmeted guineafowl
Hoopoe
Leaf-love
Lyre-tailed honeyguide
Northern wryneck
Osprey

Peregrine falcon
Rose-ringed parakeet
Ruddy turnstone
Sacred ibis
Secretary bird
Small buttonquail
Spotted flycatcher
Square-tailed drongo
White-helmet shrike
Wilson's storm-petrel
Yellow-fronted tinkerbird
Zitting cisticola

NORTH KOREA

Arctic warbler
Barn swallow
Common cuckoo
Common murre
Dollarbird
Eurasian bittern
Gray nightjar
Gray wagtail
Great bustard
Great cormorant
Great tit
Greater painted snipe
Hoopoe
Mute swan
Nuthatch
Red crossbill
Red-crowned crane
Red-throated loon
Rock pigeon
Saunder's gull
Stonechat
Winter wren

NORWAY

Arctic skua
Arctic warbler
Barn swallow
Chaffinch
Common cuckoo
Common loon
Common murre

Corncrake
Dunnock
Eurasian dipper
European starling
Gray wagtail
Great auk
Great cormorant
Great crested grebe
Great tit
Gyrfalcon
Horned lark
House sparrow
King eider
Manx shearwater
Northern fulmar
Northern gannet
Northern lapwing
Northern raven
Northern wryneck
Nuthatch
Osprey
Peregrine falcon
Puffin
Red crossbill
Red-throated loon
Rock pigeon
Ruddy turnstone
Snow bunting
Snowy owl
Spotted flycatcher
Spotted nutcracker
Willow ptarmigan
Winter wren

OMAN
Crab plovers
Egyptian vulture
European roller
Gray wagtail
Greater hoopoe-lark
Hoopoe
House sparrow
Osprey
Peregrine falcon
Purple sunbird
Rock pigeon

Ruddy turnstone
Wilson's storm-petrel

PAKISTAN
Barn swallow
Baya weaver
Black bulbul
Black-winged stilt
Cattle egret
Chaffinch
Collared pratincole
Common cuckoo
Common myna
Coppersmith barbet
Crab plovers
Crag martin
Egyptian vulture
Eurasian bittern
Eurasian golden oriole
European bee-eater
European roller
European starling
European white stork
Gray hypocolius
Gray wagtail
Great cormorant
Great crested grebe
Great tit
Greater flamingo
Greater hoopoe-lark
Greater painted snipe
Hoopoe
House sparrow
Mallard
Mute swan
Northern lapwing
Northern raven
Osprey
Peregrine falcon
Pheasant-tailed jacana
Purple sunbird
Rock pigeon
Rose-ringed parakeet
Ruddy turnstone
Small buttonquail
Snow finch

Spotted flycatcher
Spotted nutcracker
Stonechat
White-throated fantail
Wilson's storm-petrel

PANAMA
American anhinga
American dipper
American mourning dove
Baltimore oriole
Barn owl
Barn swallow
Barred antshrike
Belted kingfisher
Black guan
Black rail
Black tern
Black-and-white warbler
Black-capped donacobius
Black-winged stilt
Blue-black grassquit
Blue-crowned motmot
Blue-footed booby
Brown pelican
Cattle egret
Crested caracara
Gray catbird
Gray potoo
Great blue heron
Great kiskadee
Hairy hermit
Harris's hawk
Highland tinamou
House sparrow
Killdeer
King vulture
Limpkin
Magnificent frigatebird
Oilbird
Osprey
Peregrine falcon
Red-billed scythebill
Resplendent quetzal
Rock pigeon
Roseate spoonbill

Rose-throated becard
Ruddy turnstone
Rufous-browed peppershrike
Rufous-tailed jacamar
Scarlet macaw
Sharpbill
Sunbittern
Sungrebe
White-necked puffbird
Wood stork
Yellow-bellied sapsucker

PAPUA NEW GUINEA
Australasian figbird
Australasian lark
Australian magpie-lark
Australian pratincole
Barn swallow
Beach thick-knee
Black-winged stilt
Cattle egret
Dollarbird
Eclectus parrot
Fan-tailed berrypecker
Feline owlet-nightjar
Golden whistler
Gray wagtail
Gray-crowned babbler
Hooded pitta
Jacky winter
King bird of paradise
Osprey
Peregrine falcon
Rainbow lorikeet
Ribbon-tailed astrapia
Ruddy turnstone
Southern cassowary
Variable pitohui
White-tailed tropicbird
Willie wagtail
Wilson's storm-petrel
Zitting cisticola

PARAGUAY
American anhinga
American cliff swallow

Barn owl
Barn swallow
Barred antshrike
Baywing
Black-capped donacobius
Black-winged stilt
Blue-black grassquit
Blue-crowned motmot
Cattle egret
Crested caracara
Gray potoo
Great kiskadee
Greater thornbird
Hairy hermit
Harris's hawk
House sparrow
King vulture
Limpkin
Peregrine falcon
Red-billed scythebill
Red-legged seriema
Roseate spoonbill
Rufous hornero
Rufous-browed peppershrike
Rufous-tailed jacamar
Sharpbill
Sungrebe
Toco toucan
Wood stork

PERU
Amazonian umbrellabird
American anhinga
Arctic skua
Barn owl
Barn swallow
Barred antshrike
Black rail
Black tern
Black-capped donacobius
Black-winged stilt
Blue-black grassquit
Blue-crowned motmot
Blue-footed booby
Brown pelican
Cattle egret

Chimney swift
Common trumpeter
Coppery-chested jacamar
Crested caracara
Gray antbird
Gray potoo
Gray-breasted mountain-
   toucan
Great kiskadee
Hairy hermit
Harris's hawk
Highland tinamou
Hoatzin
Horned screamer
House sparrow
Killdeer
King vulture
Lesser rhea
Limpkin
Magellanic penguin
Oilbird
Osprey
Peregrine falcon
Peruvian plantcutter
Red-billed scythebill
Rock pigeon
Roseate spoonbill
Ruddy turnstone
Rufous-bellied seedsnipe
Rufous-browed peppershrike
Rufous-capped nunlet
Rufous-tailed jacamar
Rusty-belted tapaculo
Scarlet macaw
Sharpbill
Spangled cotinga
Sparkling violet-ear
Sunbittern
Sungrebe
Wattled curassow
White-necked puffbird
Wilson's storm-petrel
Wire-tailed manakin
Wood stork

PHILIPPINES
Arctic warbler

Asian fairy-bluebird
Australasian lark
Barn swallow
Beach thick-knee
Black-naped monarch
Black-winged stilt
Cattle egret
Coppersmith barbet
Dollarbird
Fiery minivet
Fire-breasted flowerpecker
Gray nightjar
Gray wagtail
Greater painted snipe
Hooded pitta
Japanese white-eye
Little slaty flycatcher
Luzon bleeding heart
Osprey
Peregrine falcon
Pheasant-tailed jacana
Rock pigeon
Ruddy turnstone
Small buttonquail
Spotted munia
Stripe-headed rhabdornis
Zitting cisticola

POLAND
Barn swallow
Black tern
Chaffinch
Common cuckoo
Common murre
Corncrake
Dunnock
Eurasian bittern
Eurasian dipper
Eurasian golden oriole
European roller
European starling
European white stork
Gray wagtail
Great cormorant
Great crested grebe
Great tit

Hoopoe
House sparrow
Mallard
Northern fulmar
Northern gannet
Northern lapwing
Northern raven
Northern wryneck
Nuthatch
Osprey
Peregrine falcon
Puffin
Red crossbill
Rock pigeon
Snow bunting
Snow finch
Spotted flycatcher
Spotted nutcracker
Winter wren

PORTUGAL
Barn swallow
Black-winged stilt
Chaffinch
Collared pratincole
Common cuckoo
Common loon
Common murre
Crag martin
Dunnock
Egyptian vulture
Eurasian dipper
Eurasian golden oriole
European bee-eater
European roller
European white stork
Gray wagtail
Great bustard
Great cormorant
Great crested grebe
Great tit
Hoopoe
House sparrow
Mallard
Manx shearwater
Northern gannet

Northern lapwing
Northern raven
Northern wryneck
Nuthatch
Osprey
Peregrine falcon
Red crossbill
Red-throated loon
Rock pigeon
Ruddy turnstone
Spotted flycatcher
Stonechat
Wilson's storm-petrel
Winter wren
Zitting cisticola

PUERTO RICO
American mourning dove
Barn owl
Belted kingfisher
Brown pelican
Cattle egret
Crested caracara
European starling
Greater flamingo
House sparrow
Killdeer
Magnificent frigatebird
Osprey
Peregrine falcon
Rock pigeon
Ruddy turnstone
White-tailed tropicbird
Wood stork
Yellow-bellied sapsucker

QATAR
European roller
Greater hoopoe-lark
Hoopoe
House sparrow
Stonechat

ROMANIA
Barn swallow

Black tern
Black-winged stilt
Chaffinch
Collared pratincole
Common cuckoo
Corncrake
Dunnock
Egyptian vulture
Eurasian bittern
Eurasian dipper
Eurasian golden oriole
European bee-eater
European roller
European starling
European white stork
Gray wagtail
Great cormorant
Great crested grebe
Great tit
Hoopoe
House sparrow
Mallard
Northern lapwing
Northern raven
Northern wryneck
Nuthatch
Peregrine falcon
Red crossbill
Red-throated loon
Rock pigeon
Snow bunting
Spotted flycatcher
Stonechat
Winter wren

RUSSIA
Arctic skua
Arctic warbler
Barn swallow
Black tern
Black-winged stilt
Cattle egret
Chaffinch
Collared pratincole
Common cuckoo

Common murre
Corncrake
Crag martin
Dollarbird
Dunnock
Eurasian bittern
Eurasian dipper
Eurasian golden oriole
European bee-eater
European starling
European white stork
Gray nightjar
Gray wagtail
Great bustard
Great cormorant
Great crested grebe
Great tit
Greater painted snipe
Gyrfalcon
Hoopoe
Horned lark
House sparrow
King eider
Mallard
Mute swan
Northern fulmar
Northern gannet
Northern lapwing
Northern raven
Northern wryneck
Nuthatch
Osprey
Pallas's sandgrouse
Peregrine falcon
Puffin
Red crossbill
Red-crowned crane
Red-throated loon
Rock pigeon
Ruddy turnstone
Sandhill crane
Snow bunting
Snow finch
Snowy owl
Spotted flycatcher
Spotted nutcracker

Stonechat
Willow ptarmigan
Winter wren

RWANDA
African jacana
African palm swift
African paradise-flycatcher
African pitta
African snipe
Bar-breasted mousebird
Barn swallow
Black-winged stilt
Buff-spotted flufftail
Cattle egret
Collared pratincole
Common bulbul
Common cuckoo
Common waxbill
Corncrake
Eurasian golden oriole
European bee-eater
European roller
European white stork
Gray parrot
Gray woodpecker
Gray-crowned crane
Great blue turaco
Great cormorant
Great crested grebe
Green woodhoopoe
Hammerhead
Helmeted guineafowl
Hoopoe
Osprey
Ostrich
Peregrine falcon
Red-billed oxpecker
Sacred ibis
Shoebill
Small buttonquail
Southern red bishop
Spotted flycatcher
Stonechat
Village weaver

Yellow-fronted tinkerbird
Zitting cisticola

SÃO TOMÉ AND PRÍNCIPE
White-tailed tropicbird

SAUDI ARABIA
African palm swift
Black-winged stilt
Cattle egret
Crab plovers
Crag martin
Egyptian vulture
European roller
Gray hypocolius
Gray wagtail
Great cormorant
Greater hoopoe-lark
Hammerhead
Hoopoe
House sparrow
Mallard
Northern lapwing
Osprey
Peregrine falcon
Rock pigeon
Ruddy turnstone
Stonechat
Wilson's storm-petrel

SENEGAL
African palm swift
African paradise-flycatcher
Black tern
Black-winged stilt
Cattle egret
Collared pratincole
Common bulbul
Common waxbill
Egyptian vulture
Eurasian bittern
European roller
European white stork
Gray wagtail

Gray woodpecker
Greater flamingo
Greater hoopoe-lark
Greater painted snipe
Green woodhoopoe
Hammerhead
Helmeted guineafowl
Hoopoe
Leaf-love
Magnificent frigatebird
Northern wryneck
Osprey
Peregrine falcon
Rose-ringed parakeet
Ruddy turnstone
Sacred ibis
Secretary bird
Small buttonquail
Village weaver
White-helmet shrike
Wilson's storm-petrel
Yellow-fronted tinkerbird
Zitting cisticola

SEYCHELLES
White-tailed tropicbird

SIERRA LEONE
African broadbill
African palm swift
African paradise-flycatcher
African pitta
Barn swallow
Black tern
Black-winged stilt
Buff-spotted flufftail
Cattle egret
Collared pratincole
Common bulbul
Common waxbill
Eurasian bittern
Gray parrot
Gray woodpecker
Great blue turaco
Hammerhead
Leaf-love

Lyre-tailed honeyguide
Northern wryneck
Osprey
Peregrine falcon
Rose-ringed parakeet
Ruddy turnstone
Sacred ibis
Small buttonquail
Spotted flycatcher
Square-tailed drongo
Village weaver
Wilson's storm-petrel

SINGAPORE
Baya weaver

SLOVAKIA
Barn swallow
Black tern
Chaffinch
Collared pratincole
Common cuckoo
Corncrake
Dunnock
Eurasian golden oriole
European bee-eater
European roller
European starling
European white stork
Gray wagtail
Great cormorant
Great crested grebe
Great tit
Hoopoe
House sparrow
Mallard
Northern lapwing
Northern raven
Northern wryneck
Nuthatch
Peregrine falcon
Red crossbill
Rock pigeon
Snow bunting
Snow finch
Spotted flycatcher

Stonechat
Winter wren

SLOVENIA
Barn swallow
Black tern
Chaffinch
Collared pratincole
Common cuckoo
Corncrake
Dunnock
Eurasian dipper
Eurasian golden oriole
European bee-eater
European roller
European starling
Gray wagtail
Great cormorant
Great crested grebe
Great tit
Hoopoe
House sparrow
Mallard
Northern lapwing
Northern raven
Northern wryneck
Nuthatch
Peregrine falcon
Rock pigeon
Snow bunting
Snow finch
Spotted flycatcher
Stonechat
Winter wren
Zitting cisticola

SOMALIA
African jacana
African palm swift
African paradise-flycatcher
Bar-breasted mousebird
Barn swallow
Black-winged stilt
Cattle egret
Collared pratincole
Common bulbul

Corncrake
Crab plovers
Egyptian vulture
European roller
European white stork
Gray wagtail
Great cormorant
Greater hoopoe-lark
Green woodhoopoe
Hammerhead
Hoopoe
Ostrich
Peregrine falcon
Red-billed oxpecker
Rose-ringed parakeet
Ruddy turnstone
Sacred ibis
Small buttonquail
Spotted flycatcher
Square-tailed drongo
Stonechat
White-helmet shrike
Wilson's storm-petrel

SOUTH AFRICA
African jacana
African palm swift
African paradise-flycatcher
African snipe
Arctic skua
Bar-breasted mousebird
Barn swallow
Black tern
Black-winged stilt
Blue bustard
Buff-spotted flufftail
Cape batis
Cape sugarbird
Cattle egret
Collared pratincole
Common bulbul
Common cuckoo
Common waxbill
Corncrake
Crab plovers
Eurasian golden oriole

European bee-eater
European roller
European starling
European white stork
Gray-crowned crane
Great cormorant
Great crested grebe
Greater flamingo
Greater painted snipe
Green woodhoopoe
Hammerhead
Helmeted guineafowl
Hoopoe
House sparrow
Manx shearwater
Mute swan
Namaqua sandgrouse
Osprey
Ostrich
Peregrine falcon
Red-billed oxpecker
Rock pigeon
Rosy-breasted longclaw
Ruddy turnstone
Sacred ibis
Secretary bird
Small buttonquail
Southern ground-hornbill
Southern red bishop
Spotted flycatcher
Square-tailed drongo
Stonechat
Village weaver
White-helmet shrike
Wilson's storm-petrel
Yellow-fronted tinkerbird
Zitting cisticola

SOUTH KOREA
Arctic warbler
Barn swallow
Cattle egret
Common cuckoo
Common murre
Dollarbird
Eurasian bittern

Gray nightjar
Gray wagtail
Great cormorant
Great tit
Greater painted snipe
Japanese white-eye
Mallard
Mute swan
Northern lapwing
Nuthatch
Red crossbill
Red-throated loon
Rock pigeon
Saunder's gull
Stonechat
Winter wren

SPAIN

Barn swallow
Black-winged stilt
Chaffinch
Collared pratincole
Common cuckoo
Common loon
Common murre
Corncrake
Crag martin
Dunnock
Egyptian vulture
Eurasian bittern
Eurasian dipper
Eurasian golden oriole
European bee-eater
European roller
European white stork
Gray wagtail
Great auk
Great bustard
Great cormorant
Great crested grebe
Great tit
Greater flamingo
Hoopoe
House sparrow
Mallard
Manx shearwater

Northern fulmar
Northern gannet
Northern lapwing
Northern raven
Northern wryneck
Nuthatch
Peregrine falcon
Red crossbill
Red-throated loon
Rock pigeon
Ruddy turnstone
Small buttonquail
Snow finch
Spotted flycatcher
Stonechat
Wilson's storm-petrel
Winter wren
Zitting cisticola

SRI LANKA

Baya weaver
Black bulbul
Common iora
Common myna
Coppersmith barbet
Crested tree swift
Dollarbird
Eurasian golden oriole
Gray nightjar
Great tit
Greater racket-tailed drongo
House sparrow
Pheasant-tailed jacana
Purple sunbird
Rose-ringed parakeet
Spotted munia
White-throated fantail
Wilson's storm-petrel

SUDAN

African jacana
African palm swift
African paradise-flycatcher
Bar-breasted mousebird
Barn swallow

Black tern
Black-winged stilt
Buff-spotted flufftail
Cattle egret
Collared pratincole
Common bulbul
Common waxbill
Corncrake
Crab plovers
Crag martin
Egyptian vulture
Eurasian bittern
European roller
European white stork
Gray wagtail
Gray woodpecker
Great blue turaco
Great cormorant
Greater flamingo
Greater hoopoe-lark
Greater painted snipe
Green woodhoopoe
Hammerhead
Helmeted guineafowl
Hoopoe
Leaf-love
Northern wryneck
Osprey
Ostrich
Peregrine falcon
Red-billed oxpecker
Rock pigeon
Rose-ringed parakeet
Ruddy turnstone
Sacred ibis
Secretary bird
Shoebill
Small buttonquail
Spotted flycatcher
Square-tailed drongo
Stonechat
Village weaver
White-helmet shrike
Wilson's storm-petrel
Yellow-fronted tinkerbird
Zitting cisticola

SURINAME

American anhinga
Barn owl
Barn swallow
Barred antshrike
Black tern
Black-capped donacobius
Black-winged stilt
Blue-black grassquit
Blue-crowned motmot
Brown pelican
Cattle egret
Common trumpeter
Crested caracara
Gray antbird
Gray potoo
Great kiskadee
Guianan cock-of-the-rock
Hairy hermit
Hoatzin
King vulture
Limpkin
Magnificent frigatebird
Osprey
Peregrine falcon
Roseate spoonbill
Ruddy turnstone
Rufous-browed peppershrike
Scarlet macaw
Sharpbill
Spangled cotinga
Sunbittern
Sungrebe
White-necked puffbird
Wilson's storm-petrel
Wood stork

SWAZILAND

African jacana
African palm swift
African paradise-flycatcher
African snipe
Barn swallow
Black-winged stilt
Buff-spotted flufftail
Cape batis

Cattle egret
Collared pratincole
Common bulbul
Common cuckoo
Common waxbill
Corncrake
European bee-eater
European roller
European white stork
Great cormorant
Greater painted snipe
Green woodhoopoe
Hammerhead
Helmeted guineafowl
Hoopoe
House sparrow
Osprey
Peregrine falcon
Sacred ibis
Secretary bird
Small buttonquail
Southern ground-hornbill
Southern red bishop
Spotted flycatcher
Stonechat
Village weaver
White-helmet shrike
Zitting cisticola

SWEDEN

Barn swallow
Chaffinch
Common cuckoo
Common murre
Corncrake
Dunnock
Eurasian bittern
Eurasian dipper
European roller
European starling
Gray wagtail
Great auk
Great cormorant
Great crested grebe
Great tit
Gyrfalcon

Hoopoe
Horned lark
House sparrow
Mute swan
Northern fulmar
Northern gannet
Northern lapwing
Northern raven
Northern wryneck
Nuthatch
Osprey
Peregrine falcon
Puffin
Red crossbill
Red-throated loon
Rock pigeon
Ruddy turnstone
Snow bunting
Spotted flycatcher
Spotted nutcracker
Willow ptarmigan
Winter wren

SWITZERLAND

Barn swallow
Black tern
Chaffinch
Common cuckoo
Corncrake
Dunnock
Eurasian dipper
Eurasian golden oriole
European roller
European starling
European white stork
Gray wagtail
Great cormorant
Great crested grebe
Great tit
Hoopoe
House sparrow
Mallard
Mute swan
Northern lapwing
Northern raven
Northern wryneck

Nuthatch
Peregrine falcon
Red crossbill
Rock pigeon
Snow finch
Spotted flycatcher
Spotted nutcracker
Stonechat
Winter wren

SYRIA

Black-winged stilt
Cattle egret
Chaffinch
Collared pratincole
Common bulbul
Common cuckoo
Corncrake
Crag martin
Dunnock
Egyptian vulture
European bee-eater
European roller
European starling
Great bustard
Great cormorant
Greater flamingo
Hoopoe
House sparrow
Mallard
Northern gannet
Northern lapwing
Nuthatch
Peregrine falcon
Red crossbill
Rock pigeon
Spotted flycatcher
Stonechat
Winter wren

TAJIKISTAN

Barn swallow
Chaffinch
Common cuckoo
Crag martin
Egyptian vulture

Eurasian golden oriole
European roller
European starling
Great bustard
Great cormorant
Great crested grebe
Great tit
Hoopoe
House sparrow
Mallard
Northern raven
Peregrine falcon
Rock pigeon
Snow finch
Spotted flycatcher
Stonechat
Winter wren

TANZANIA

African broadbill
African jacana
African palm swift
African paradise-flycatcher
African pitta
African snipe
Bar-breasted mousebird
Barn swallow
Black-winged stilt
Buff-spotted flufftail
Cattle egret
Collared pratincole
Common bulbul
Common waxbill
Corncrake
Crab plovers
Eurasian golden oriole
European bee-eater
European roller
European white stork
Golden-winged sunbird
Gray go-away-bird
Gray wagtail
Gray woodpecker
Great cormorant
Great crested grebe
Greater flamingo

Greater painted snipe
Green woodhoopoe
Hammerhead
Helmeted guineafowl
Hoopoe
House sparrow
Leaf-love
Osprey
Ostrich
Peregrine falcon
Red-billed oxpecker
Rock pigeon
Rosy-breasted longclaw
Ruddy turnstone
Sacred ibis
Secretary bird
Shoebill
Small buttonquail
Southern ground-hornbill
Southern red bishop
Spotted flycatcher
Square-tailed drongo
Stonechat
Village weaver
White-helmet shrike
Wilson's storm-petrel
Yellow-fronted tinkerbird
Zitting cisticola

THAILAND

Arctic warbler
Asian fairy-bluebird
Australasian lark
Barn swallow
Barred eagle-owl
Baya weaver
Black bulbul
Black-and-red broadbill
Black-naped monarch
Black-winged stilt
Cattle egret
Common cuckoo
Common iora
Common myna
Coppersmith barbet
Crested tree swift

Dollarbird
Fiery minivet
Fire-breasted flowerpecker
Gray nightjar
Gray wagtail
Great cormorant
Greater painted snipe
Greater racket-tailed drongo
Green magpie
Helmeted hornbill
Hooded pitta
Hoopoe
Malaysian honeyguide
Northern lapwing
Northern wryneck
Orange-breasted trogon
Osprey
Peregrine falcon
Pheasant-tailed jacana
Purple sunbird
Rock pigeon
Ruby-cheeked sunbird
Ruddy turnstone
Rufous-collared kingfisher
Small buttonquail
Spotted munia
Stonechat
White-throated fantail
Zitting cisticola

TOGO

African jacana
African palm swift
African paradise-flycatcher
Barn swallow
Black tern
Black-winged stilt
Cattle egret
Collared pratincole
Common bulbul
Eurasian bittern
European bee-eater
European roller
Gray parrot
Gray woodpecker
Great blue turaco

Greater painted snipe
Green woodhoopoe
Hammerhead
Helmeted guineafowl
Hoopoe
Leaf-love
Northern wryneck
Osprey
Peregrine falcon
Rose-ringed parakeet
Ruddy turnstone
Sacred ibis
Secretary bird
Small buttonquail
Spotted flycatcher
Square-tailed drongo
Village weaver
White-helmet shrike
Wilson's storm-petrel
Yellow-fronted tinkerbird
Zitting cisticola

TRINIDAD AND TOBAGO

Blue-crowned motmot
Gray potoo
Hairy hermit
Oilbird
Rufous-tailed jacamar

TUNISIA

Barn swallow
Black-winged stilt
Collared pratincole
Common bulbul
Corncrake
Crag martin
Dunnock
Egyptian vulture
Eurasian bittern
European bee-eater
European roller
European starling
Gray wagtail
Great cormorant
Great crested grebe

Greater flamingo
Greater hoopoe-lark
Hoopoe
House sparrow
Northern gannet
Northern lapwing
Northern raven
Northern wryneck
Peregrine falcon
Rock pigeon
Ruddy turnstone
Small buttonquail
Spotted flycatcher
Stonechat
Winter wren
Zitting cisticola

TURKEY

Barn swallow
Black tern
Cattle egret
Chaffinch
Collared pratincole
Common bulbul
Common cuckoo
Corncrake
Crag martin
Dunnock
Egyptian vulture
Eurasian bittern
Eurasian dipper
Eurasian golden oriole
European bee-eater
European roller
European starling
Gray wagtail
Great bustard
Great cormorant
Great crested grebe
Great tit
Greater flamingo
Hoopoe
Horned lark
House sparrow
Mallard
Mute swan

Northern gannet
Northern lapwing
Northern raven
Northern wryneck
Nuthatch
Peregrine falcon
Red crossbill
Red-throated loon
Rock pigeon
Snow finch
Spotted flycatcher
Stonechat
Winter wren
Zitting cisticola

TURKMENISTAN
Barn swallow
Black-winged stilt
Cattle egret
Chaffinch
Collared pratincole
Common cuckoo
Common myna
Crag martin
Egyptian vulture
Eurasian bittern
Eurasian golden oriole
European bee-eater
European roller
European starling
Gray hypocolius
Great cormorant
Great crested grebe
Great tit
Hoopoe
Horned lark
House sparrow
Mallard
Northern lapwing
Northern raven
Nuthatch
Peregrine falcon
Red-throated loon
Rock pigeon
Spotted flycatcher

Winter wren

UGANDA
African broadbill
African jacana
African palm swift
African paradise-flycatcher
African pitta
African snipe
Bar-breasted mousebird
Barn swallow
Black-winged stilt
Buff-spotted flufftail
Cattle egret
Collared pratincole
Common bulbul
Common cuckoo
Common waxbill
Corncrake
Egyptian vulture
Eurasian golden oriole
European roller
European white stork
Golden-winged sunbird
Gray parrot
Gray woodpecker
Gray-crowned crane
Great blue turaco
Great cormorant
Great crested grebe
Greater painted snipe
Green woodhoopoe
Hammerhead
Helmeted guineafowl
Hoopoe
Leaf-love
Northern wryneck
Osprey
Ostrich
Peregrine falcon
Red-billed oxpecker
Rose-ringed parakeet
Sacred ibis
Secretary bird
Shoebill

Small buttonquail
Southern red bishop
Spotted flycatcher
Village weaver
White-helmet shrike
Yellow-fronted tinkerbird
Zitting cisticola

UKRAINE
Barn swallow
Black tern
Black-winged stilt
Chaffinch
Collared pratincole
Common cuckoo
Corncrake
Dunnock
Eurasian bittern
Eurasian golden oriole
European bee-eater
European roller
European starling
European white stork
Gray wagtail
Great bustard
Great cormorant
Great crested grebe
Great tit
Hoopoe
Horned lark
House sparrow
Mallard
Mute swan
Northern lapwing
Northern raven
Northern wryneck
Nuthatch
Osprey
Peregrine falcon
Red crossbill
Red-throated loon
Rock pigeon
Snow bunting
Spotted flycatcher
Spotted nutcracker

Stonechat
Winter wren

UNITED ARAB EMIRATES
Crab plovers
Egyptian vulture
European roller
Greater hoopoe-lark
Hoopoe
House sparrow
Northern lapwing
Osprey
Purple sunbird
Rock pigeon
Ruddy turnstone
Stonechat
Wilson's storm-petrel

UNITED KINGDOM
Barn owl
Barn swallow
Canada goose
Chaffinch
Common cuckoo
Common loon
Common murre
Corncrake
Dunnock
Eurasian bittern
Eurasian dipper
Eurasian golden oriole
European roller
European starling
Gray wagtail
Great auk
Great cormorant
Great crested grebe
Great tit
House sparrow
Mallard
Manx shearwater
Mute swan
Northern gannet
Northern lapwing

Northern raven
Northern wryneck
Nuthatch
Osprey
Peregrine falcon
Puffin
Red crossbill
Red-throated loon
Rock pigeon
Ruddy turnstone
Snow bunting
Spotted flycatcher
Stonechat
Willow ptarmigan
Winter wren

UNITED STATES
American anhinga
American avocet
American cliff swallow
American dipper
American goldfinch
American mourning dove
American robin
American white pelican
Anna's hummingbird
Apapane
Arctic skua
Arctic warbler
Baltimore oriole
Barn owl
Barn swallow
Belted kingfisher
Bishop's oo
Black rail
Black tern
Black-and-white warbler
Black-capped chickadee
Black-capped vireo
Black-winged stilt
Blue jay
Blue-gray gnatcatcher
Brown creeper
Brown pelican
Bushtit

Cactus wren
California condor
Canada goose
Cattle egret
Cedar waxwing
Chimney swift
Common loon
Common murre
Crested caracara
Eastern bluebird
Eastern phoebe
Eastern screech-owl
European starling
Gray catbird
Great auk
Great blue heron
Great cormorant
Great kiskadee
Greater roadrunner
Gyrfalcon
Harris's hawk
Hawaiian honeycreepers
Horned lark
House sparrow
House wren
Ivory-billed woodpecker
Killdeer
King eider
Kirtland's warbler
Laysan albatross
Laysan finch
Limpkin
Loggerhead shrike
Long-billed curlew
Magnificent frigatebird
Mallard
Manx shearwater
Mute swan
Northern bobwhite quail
Northern fulmar
Northern gannet
Northern raven
Osprey
Peregrine falcon
Plain chachalaca
Puffin

Red crossbill
Red-breasted nuthatch
Red-cockaded woodpecker
Red-throated loon
Red-winged blackbird
Rock pigeon
Roseate spoonbill
Rose-throated becard
Ruddy turnstone
Sandhill crane
Savanna sparrow
Snow bunting
Song sparrow
Sprague's pipit
Verdin
Western grebe
Western scrub-jay
Whip-poor-will
White-tailed tropicbird
Wild turkey
Willow ptarmigan
Wilson's storm-petrel
Winter wren
Wood duck
Wood stork
Wrentit
Yellow-bellied sapsucker
Yellow-breasted chat

URUGUAY
American anhinga
American cliff swallow
Barn owl
Baywing
Black-winged stilt
Cattle egret
Crested caracara
Gray potoo
Great kiskadee
Greater thornbird
Harris's hawk
House sparrow
King vulture
Limpkin
Magellanic penguin
Manx shearwater

Peregrine falcon
Red-legged seriema
Rock pigeon
Roseate spoonbill
Ruddy turnstone
Rufous hornero
Wilson's storm-petrel
Wood stork

UZBEKISTAN
Barn swallow
Black-winged stilt
Chaffinch
Collared pratincole
Common cuckoo
Common myna
Crag martin
Egyptian vulture
Eurasian bittern
Eurasian dipper
Eurasian golden oriole
European bee-eater
European roller
European starling
Great bustard
Great cormorant
Great crested grebe
Great tit
Hoopoe
Horned lark
House sparrow
Mallard
Northern raven
Pallas's sandgrouse
Peregrine falcon
Rock pigeon

VENEZUELA
Amazonian umbrellabird
American anhinga
Baltimore oriole
Barn owl
Barn swallow
Barred antshrike
Belted kingfisher
Black tern

Black-and-white warbler
Black-capped donacobius
Black-winged stilt
Blue-black grassquit
Blue-crowned motmot
Brown pelican
Cattle egret
Common trumpeter
Crested caracara
Gray antbird
Gray potoo
Great kiskadee
Greater flamingo
Guianan cock-of-the-rock
Hairy hermit
Harris's hawk
Highland tinamou
Hoatzin
Horned screamer
King vulture
Limpkin
Magnificent frigatebird
Oilbird
Osprey
Peregrine falcon
Red-billed scythebill
Roseate spoonbill
Ruddy turnstone
Rufous-browed peppershrike
Rufous-tailed jacamar
Scarlet macaw
Sharpbill
Spangled cotinga
Sparkling violet-ear
Sunbittern
Sungrebe
White-necked puffbird
Wilson's storm-petrel
Wire-tailed manakin
Wood stork

VIETNAM
Arctic warbler
Asian fairy-bluebird
Australasian lark
Barn swallow

Baya weaver
Black bulbul
Black-and-red broadbill
Black-crowned barwing
Black-naped monarch
Black-winged stilt
Cattle egret
Common cuckoo
Common iora
Common myna
Coppersmith barbet
Crag martin
Crested tree swift
Dollarbird
Eurasian bittern
Fire-breasted flowerpecker
Gray nightjar
Gray wagtail
Great cormorant
Great tit
Greater painted snipe
Greater racket-tailed drongo
Green magpie
Hoopoe
Northern wryneck
Orange-breasted trogon
Osprey
Peregrine falcon
Pheasant-tailed jacana
Purple sunbird
Rock pigeon
Ruby-cheeked sunbird
Ruddy turnstone
Saunder's gull
Small buttonquail
Spotted munia
Stonechat
White-throated fantail
Zitting cisticola

YEMEN
African palm swift
Cattle egret
Crab plovers
Crag martin
Egyptian vulture

European roller
Gray wagtail
Greater hoopoe-lark
Hammerhead
Hoopoe
House sparrow
Osprey
Peregrine falcon
Rock pigeon
Ruddy turnstone
Stonechat
Wilson's storm-petrel

YUGOSLAVIA
Common cuckoo
Corncrake
Crag martin
Egyptian vulture
Eurasian dipper
European bee-eater
European roller
European white stork
Gray wagtail
Great cormorant
Great crested grebe
Hoopoe
Horned lark
Mallard
Northern lapwing
Peregrine falcon
Rock pigeon
Snow bunting
Zitting cisticola

ZAMBIA
African broadbill
African jacana
African palm swift
African paradise-flycatcher
African pitta
African snipe
Bar-breasted mousebird
Barn swallow
Black-winged stilt
Buff-spotted flufftail

Cattle egret
Collared pratincole
Common bulbul
Common cuckoo
Common waxbill
Corncrake
Eurasian golden oriole
European bee-eater
European roller
European white stork
Gray go-away-bird
Gray-crowned crane
Great cormorant
Greater flamingo
Greater painted snipe
Green woodhoopoe
Hammerhead
Helmeted guineafowl
Hoopoe
House sparrow
Osprey
Ostrich
Peregrine falcon
Red-billed oxpecker
Rosy-breasted longclaw
Sacred ibis
Secretary bird
Shoebill
Small buttonquail
Southern ground-hornbill
Southern red bishop
Spotted flycatcher
Square-tailed drongo
Stonechat
Village weaver
White-helmet shrike
Yellow-fronted tinkerbird
Zitting cisticola

ZIMBABWE
African broadbill
African palm swift
African paradise-flycatcher
African pitta
African snipe
Bar-breasted mousebird

Barn swallow
Black-winged stilt
Buff-spotted flufftail
Cape batis
Cattle egret
Collared pratincole
Common bulbul
Common cuckoo
Common waxbill
Corncrake
Eurasian golden oriole
European bee-eater
European roller
European white stork

Gray go-away-bird
Gray-crowned crane
Great cormorant
Greater painted snipe
Green woodhoopoe
Hammerhead
Helmeted guineafowl
Hoopoe
House sparrow
Osprey
Ostrich
Peregrine falcon
Red-billed oxpecker
Rock pigeon

Rosy-breasted longclaw
Sacred ibis
Secretary bird
Shoebill
Small buttonquail
Southern ground-hornbill
Southern red bishop
Spotted flycatcher
Stonechat
Village weaver
White-helmet shrike
Yellow-fronted tinkerbird
Zitting cisticola

Index

Italic type indicates volume number; **boldface** type indicates entries and their pages; (ill.) indicates illustrations.

A

Abbott's boobies, *1:* 126

Abyssinian ground-hornbills, *3:* 653–54

Acanthisitta chloris. See Riflemen

Acanthisittidae. *See* New Zealand wrens

Acanthiza chrysorrhoa. See Yellow-rumped thornbills

Acanthizidae. *See* Australian warblers

Accentors. *See* Hedge sparrows

Accipitridae. *See* Eagles; Hawks

Aceros cassidix. See Sulawesi red-knobbed hornbills

Acridotheres tristis. See Common mynas

Actenoides concretus. See Rufous-collared kingfishers

Actinodura sodangorum. See Black-crowned barwings

Action Plan for Australian Birds, *4:* 1081

Actophilornis africanus. See African jacanas

Aechmophorus occidentalis. See Western grebes

Aegithalidae. *See* Long-tailed titmice

Aegithina tiphia. See Common ioras

Aegotheles insignis. See Feline owlet-nightjars

Aegothelidae. *See* Owlet-nightjars

Aepyronis maximus. See Elephant birds

Aethopyga species, *5:* 1209

Africa bay owls, *3:* 559

African black oystercatchers, *2:* 418, 419

African broadbills, *4:* 796–97, 796 (ill.), 797 (ill.)

African bulbuls. *See* Common bulbuls

African finfoot, *2:* 366–68

African flycatchers, *4:* 1060, 1061

African gray parrots. *See* Gray parrots

African jacanas, *2:* 404–5, 404 (ill.), 405 (ill.)

African palm swifts, *3:* 621–22, 621 (ill.), 622 (ill.)

African paradise-flycatchers, *5:* 1117–19, 1117 (ill.), 1118 (ill.)

African pittas, *4:* 812–13, 812 (ill.), 813 (ill.)

African snipes, *2:* 457–58, 457 (ill.), 458 (ill.)

Agelaioides badius. See Baywings

Agelaius phoeniceus. See Red-winged blackbirds

Agulhas long-billed larks, *4:* 905

Aitu swiftlets, *3:* 617

Aix sponsa. See Wood ducks

Ajaia ajaja. See Roseate spoonbills

Alaemon alaudipes. See Greater hoopoe-larks

Alagoas antwrens, *4:* 838

Alagoas tyrannulets, *4:* 853

Alaotra grebes, *1:* 92

Alaudidae. *See* Larks

Albatrosses, *1:* 41, 43, 44, **45–52**

Albert's lyrebirds, *4:* 888–89, 890, 891–93, 891 (ill.), 892 (ill.)

Alcedinidae. *See* Kingfishers

Alcidae. *See* Auks; Murres; Puffins

Alcids, *2:* 395, 396

Altricial chicks, *2:* 321

Amami woodcocks, *2:* 456

Amazonian umbrellabirds, *4:* 877–78, 877 (ill.), 878 (ill.)

American anhingas, *1:* 121–23, 121 (ill.), 122 (ill.)

American avocets, *2:* 424, 428–29, 428 (ill.), 429 (ill.)

American black rails, 2: 315

American cliff swallows, 4: 919–21, 919 (ill.), 920 (ill.)

American dippers, 4: 1005, 1007–9, 1007 (ill.), 1008 (ill.)

American goldfinches, 5: 1282–84, 1282 (ill.), 1283 (ill.)

American mourning doves, 3: 513–14, 513 (ill.), 514 (ill.)

American pearl kites, 1: 212

American redstarts, 4: 792

American robins, 4: 1014, 1015, 1022–23, 1022 (ill.), 1023 (ill.)

American white pelicans, 1: 139–41, 139 (ill.), 140 (ill.)

Amytornis striatus. See Striated grasswrens

Anas platyrhynchos. See Mallards

Anatidae. *See* Ducks; Geese; Swans

Andean condors, 1: 177

Andean flamingos, 1: 201, 202

Andean stilts, 2: 423

Andigena hypoglauca. See Gray-breasted mountain-toucans

Anhima cornuta. See Horned screamers

Anhimidae. *See* Screamers

Anhinga anhinga. See American anhingas

Anhingas, 1: 98, 99, **116–24**

Anis, 3: **545–51**

Anna's hummingbirds, 3: 636–38, 636 (ill.), 637 (ill.)

Anseriformes, 2: **241–45**

Ant thrushes, 4: **836–44**

Antbirds. *See* Ant thrushes

Antcatchers. *See* Ant thrushes

Anthreptes species, 5: 1209

Anthus spragueii. See Sprague's pipits

Anting behavior, 4: 1005

Antiphonal duets, 5: 1361

Antpittas. *See* Ant thrushes

Antshrikes. *See* Ant thrushes

Antwrens. *See* Ant thrushes

Apapanes, 5: 1289, 1291–92, 1291 (ill.), 1292 (ill.)

Aphelocoma californica. See Western scrub-jays

Apodidae. *See* Swifts

Apodiformes, 3: **610–14**

Apolinar's wrens, 4: 1039

Apostlebirds, 5: 1360

Aptenodytes forsteri. See Emperor penguins

Apterygidae. *See* Kiwis

Apteryx australis. See Brown kiwis

Ara macao. See Scarlet macaws

Arabian babblers, 4: 1026

Arabian ostriches, 1: 39

Arachnothera, 5: 1209

Aramidae. *See* Limpkins

Aramus guarauna. See Limpkins

Araripe manakins, 4: 866

Archer's larks, 4: 905

Arctic skuas, 2: 479–80, 479 (ill.), 480 (ill.)

Arctic terns, 2: 396

Arctic warblers, 4: 1058–59, 1058 (ill.), 1059 (ill.)

Ardea herodias. See Great blue herons

Ardeidae. *See* Bitterns; Herons

Arenaria interpres. See Ruddy turnstones

Artamidae. *See* Woodswallows

Artamus cyanopterus. See Dusky woodswallows

Ascension frigatebirds, 1: 110

Ash's larks, 4: 905

Asian dowitchers, 2: 454

Asian fairy bluebirds, 4: 960–61, 960 (ill.), 961 (ill.)

Asian frogmouths, 3: 586, 587

Asities, 4: **801–6;** 5: 1209

Astley's leiothrix, 4: 1027

Astrapia mayeri. See Ribbon-tailed astrapias

Astrapias, ribbon-tailed, 5: 1391–92, 1391 (ill.), 1392 (ill.)

Asynchronous hatching, 2: 476

Atoll fruit doves, 3: 505, 509

Atrichornis rufescens. See Rufous scrub-birds

Atrichornithidae. *See* Scrub-birds

Attagis gayi. See Rufous-bellied seedsnipes

Auckland Island teals, 2: 241

Audubon, John James, 4: 852, 933

Auklets, 2: 486

Auks, 2: 397, **486–95**

Auriparus flaviceps. See Verdins

Australasian figbirds, 5: 1340–41, 1340 (ill.), 1341 (ill.)

Australasian larks, 4: 906–7, 906 (ill.), 907 (ill.)

Australian brush-turkeys, 2: 270

Australian chats, 4: **1087–92**

Australian chestnut-backed buttonquails, 2: 328

Australian creepers, 5: **1145–50**

Australian diamond doves, 3: 504

Australian fairy-wrens, 4: **1070–78**

Australian frogmouths, 3: 585–86, 587

Australian greater painted snipes, 2: 408, 409, 410, 412

Australian honeyeaters, 4: 1087; 5: 1124, **1225–34**

Australian magpie-larks, 5: 1360, 1361, 1362–64, 1362 (ill.), 1363 (ill.)

Australian magpies, 5: 1372–74

Australian masked owls, 3: 557

Australian owlet-nightjars, 3: 592, 593

Buttonquails, 2: 316, 317, 326–32

C

Cacklers, red-breasted. *See* Gray-crowned babblers
Cactus wrens, 4: 1037, 1038, 1040–42, 1040 (ill.), 1041 (ill.)
Cage birds, 3: 523
   See also specific species
Calcium in eggshells, 1: 72
Calfbirds, 4: 874
California condors, 1: 147, 177, 181–82, 181 (ill.), 182 (ill.)
Callaeas cinerea. See Kokakos
Callaeidae. *See* New Zealand wattlebirds
Calypte anna. See Anna's hummingbirds
Calypturas kinglets, 4: 874
Campbell Island teals, 2: 241
Campephagidae. *See* Cuckooshrikes
Campephilus principalis. See Ivory-billed woodpeckers
Campylorhamphus trochilirostris. See Red-billed scythebills
Campylorhynchus brunneicapillus. See Cactus wrens
Canada geese, 2: 252–53, 252 (ill.), 253 (ill.)
Cape batises, 4: 1067–68, 1067 (ill.), 1068 (ill.)
Cape gannets, 1: 126
Cape puffbacks. *See* Cape batises
Cape sugarbirds, 5: 1231–32, 1231 (ill.), 1232 (ill.)
Capitonidae. *See* Barbets
Caprimulgidae. *See* Nightjars
Caprimulgiformes, 3: 555, 574–78
Caprimulgus indicus. See Gray nightjars

Caprimulgus vociferus. See Whip-poor-wills
Capuchinbirds, 4: 874
Caracaras, 1: 229–39
Cardueline finches, 5: 1289
Carduelis tristis. See American goldfinches
Cariama cristata. See Redlegged seriemas
Cariamidae. *See* Seriemas
Carolina parakeets, 3: 523
Carolina wrens, 4: 1037
Carrion, 1: 176
Cassowaries, 1: 1, 2, 3, **18–23**
Casuariidae. *See* Cassowaries
Casuarius bennetti. See Dwarf cassowaries
Casuarius casuarius. See Southern cassowaries
Catbirds
   black, 4: 998
   gray, 4: 998, 999–1000, 999 (ill.), 1000 (ill.)
Cathartidae. *See* New World vultures
Cattle egrets, 1: 145, 155–56, 155 (ill.), 156 (ill.)
Cave swiftlets, 3: 613, 616
Cavity nesters, 4: 831
   See also specific species
Cedar waxwings, 4: 979, 980, 981, 982–84, 982 (ill.), 983 (ill.)
Cephalopterus ornatus. See Amazonian umbrellabirds
Cercomacra cinerascens. See Gray antbirds
Certhia americana. See Brown creepers
Certhiidae. *See* Treecreepers
Chabert's vangas, 4: 972
Chachalacas, 2: 279–87
Chaetura pelagica. See Chimney swifts
Chaffinches, 5: 1280–81, 1280 (ill.), 1281 (ill.)
Chalcoparia singalensis. See

Ruby-cheeked sunbirds
Chamaea fasciata. See Wrentits
Chamaepetes unicolor. See Black guans
Channel-billed toucans, 3: 759
Chapman's antshrikes. *See* Barred antshrikes
Charadriidae. *See* Lapwings; Plovers
Charadriiformes, 2: **395–98**
Charadrius vociferus. See Killdeer
Charles mockingbirds, 4: 998
Chatham Island oystercatchers, 2: 419
Chatham mollymawks, 1: 48–49, 48 (ill.), 49 (ill.)
Chatham snipes, 2: 456
Chats, 4: **1013–24**
   Australian, 4: **1087–92**
   palmchats, 4: **988–90,** 989 (ill.), 990 (ill.)
   yellow-breasted, 5: 1261–62, 1261 (ill.), 1262 (ill.)
Chatterbox. *See* Gray-crowned babblers
Chestnut-backed mousebirds, 3: 639
Chestnut-backed sparrowlarks, 4: 904
Chestnut rails, 2: 357
Chickadees, 5: **1164–72**
Chicken-like birds, 2: **266–69**
Chickens, 2: 268–69
Chilean flamingos, 1: 202
Chilean tinamous, 1: 7
Chimney swifts, 3: 612, 618–20, 618 (ill.), 619 (ill.)
Chinese crested terns, 2: 478
Chionidae. *See* Sheathbills
Chionis minor. See Black-faced sheathbills
Chiroxiphia linearis. See Longtailed manakins
Chlamydera maculata. See Spotted bowerbirds

Chlidonias niger. See Black terns

Choco tinamous, 1: 7

Choughs, white-winged, 5: 1360

Chowchillas, 4: 1093–98

Christmas frigatebirds, 1: 110

Cicinnurus regius. See King birds of paradise

Ciconia ciconia. See European white storks

Ciconiidae. See Storks

Ciconiiformes, 1: 143–48

Cinclidae. See Dippers

Cinclosoma punctatum. See Spotted quail-thrushes

Cinclus cinclus. See Eurasian dippers

Cinclus mexicanus. See American dippers

Cinerous wattled birds. See Kokakos

Cinnamon-tailed fantails, 4: 1109

Cinnyris asiaticus. See Purple sunbirds

Cissa chinensis. See Green magpies

Cisticola juncidis. See Zitting cisticolas

Cisticolas, zitting, 4: 1053–54, 1053 (ill.), 1054 (ill.)

CITES (Convention on International Trade in Endangered Species)
    on eclectus parrots, 3: 528
    on helmeted hornbills, 3: 721

Clarion wrens, 4: 1039

Cliff swallows, 4: 913, 919–21, 919 (ill.), 920 (ill.)

Climacteridae. See Australian creepers

Climacteris rufa. See Rufous treecreepers

Cobb's wrens, 4: 1039

Cobeldick, William, 5: 1355

Cocks-of-the-rock, Guianan, 4: 879–80, 879 (ill.), 880 (ill.)

Cockerell's fantails, 4: 1109

Coleridge, Samuel Taylor, 1: 46

Colibri coruscans. See Sparkling violet-ears

Colies. See Mousebirds

Coliidae. See Mousebirds

Coliiformes. See Mousebirds

Colinus virginianus. See Northern bobwhite quails

Colius striatus. See Bar-breasted mousebirds

Collared pratincoles, 2: 437, 439–41, 439 (ill.), 440 (ill.)

Collared sunbirds, 5: 1209

Collocalia species, 3: 613

Colombian grebes, 1: 92

Colombian tinamous, 1: 7

Colonial nesters, 2: 396
    See also specific species

Columba livia. See Rock pigeons

Columbidae. See Doves; Pigeons

Columbiformes, 3: 504–7

Common barn owls, 3: 557, 560–62, 560 (ill.), 561 (ill.)

Common bulbuls, 4: 938 (ill.), 943, 944, 947–49, 947 (ill.)

Common buttonquails, 2: 328

Common cuckoos, 3: 545, 547–48, 547 (ill.), 548 (ill.); 4: 1061

Common diving-petrels, 1: 67, 68, 69–70, 69 (ill.), 70 (ill.)

Common ioras, 4: 956, 958–59, 958 (ill.), 959 (ill.)

Common loons, 1: 87–89, 87 (ill.), 88 (ill.)

Common murres, 2: 489–91, 489 (ill.), 490 (ill.)

Common mynas, 5: 1329–30, 1329 (ill.), 1330 (ill.)

Common potoos. See Gray potoos

Common redshanks, 2: 454

Common sunbird-asities, 4: 801, 802, 803, 804–5, 804 (ill.), 805 (ill.)

Common trumpeters, 2: 379–81, 379 (ill.), 380 (ill.)

Common waxbills, 5: 1299–1300, 1299 (ill.), 1300 (ill.)

Communal breeding, 5: 1140
    See also specific species

Condors, 1: 143, 146, 175, 176
    Andean, 1: 177
    California, 1: 147, 177, 181–82, 181 (ill.), 182 (ill.)

Congo bay owls, 3: 565

Congo swifts, 3: 617

Convention on International Trade in Endangered Species. See CITES

Cooling mechanisms, 1: 187

Coorong gerygones, 4: 1081

Coots, 2: 316, 356–65

Coppersmith barbets, 3: 750–51, 750 (ill.), 751 (ill.)

Coppery-chested jacamars, 3: 732, 735–36, 735 (ill.), 736 (ill.)

Coracias garrulus. See European rollers

Coraciidae. See Rollers

Coraciiformes, 3: 653–57

Coracina typica. See Mauritius cuckoo-shrikes

Cormorants, 1: 99, 100, 101, 116–24

Corncrakes, 2: 364–65, 364 (ill.), 365 (ill.)

Cortaplantas. See Plantcutters

Corvidae. See Crows; Jays

Corvus corax. See Northern ravens

Corvus species, 5: 1398

Corythaeola cristata. See Great blue turacos

Corythaixoides concolor. See Gray go-away-birds

Cotarramas. See Plantcutters

Cotinga cayana. See Spangled cotingas

European white storks, *1*: 171–73, 171 (ill.), 172 (ill.)

Eurylaimidae. *See* Broadbills

Eurypyga helias. *See* Sunbitterns

Eurypygidae. *See* Sunbitterns

Eurystomus orientalis. *See* Dollarbirds

Evaporation, *1*: 187

Exxon Valdez, *1*: 91

F

Fairy bluebirds, *4*: 955–61

Fairy-wrens, Australian, *4*: 1070–78

Falco peregrinus. *See* Peregrine falcons

Falco rusticolis. *See* Gyrfalcons

Falconets, *1*: 207, 229

Falconidae. *See* Caracaras; Falcons

Falconiformes. *See* Diurnal birds of prey

Falconry, *1*: 209, 230

Falcons, *1*: 207, 208–10, **229–39**; *2*: 318

False sunbirds, *4*: **801–6**

Families (Taxonomy), *4*: 861

See also specific family names

Fan-tailed berrypeckers, *5*: 1199–1201, 1199 (ill.), 1200 (ill.)

Fantailed cisticolas. *See* Zitting cisticolas

Fantailed warblers. *See* Zitting cisticolas

Fantails, *4*: **1105–14**; *5*: 1354

Feathers, grooming, *1*: 126

See also specific species

Feline owlet-nightjars, *3*: 594–95, 594 (ill.), 595 (ill.)

Ferruginous pygmy-owls, *3*: 555

Ficedula basilanica. *See* Little slaty flycatchers

Fieldfares, *4*: 1015

Fiery minivets, *4*: 936, 940–41, 940 (ill.), 941 (ill.)

Figbirds, *5*: **1337–44**

Finches, *4*: 789; *5*: **1278–87**, 1288

cardueline, *5*: 1289

cuckoo, *5*: 1308

Gouldian, *5*: 1298

grassfinches, *5*: **1296–1305**

Hawaiian, *5*: 1288

Laysan, *5*: 1293–94, 1293 (ill.), 1294 (ill.)

New World, *5*: **1244–57**

snow, *5*: 1323–24, 1323 (ill.), 1324 (ill.)

See also Weavers

Fire-breasted flowerpeckers, *5*: 1197–98, 1197 (ill.), 1198 (ill.)

Fire-eyes, fringe-backed, *4*: 838

Fish and Wildlife Service (U.S.), *2*: 243

on black-capped vireos, *5*: 1240

on cranes, *2*: 340

on Kirtland's warblers, *5*: 1266

on Laysan finches, *5*: 1294

on murrelets, *2*: 488

on New World warblers, *5*: 1260

Fish hawks. *See* Osprey

Fishing owls, *3*: 553, 565

Fishing with birds, *1*: 117

Flamingos, *1*: **200–206**

Flapped larks, *4*: 902, 903

Flightless birds, *2*: 318, 358; *3*: 518

Flood, Bob, *1*: 62

Flowerpeckers, *5*: **1194–1201**

Flufftails, *2*: 356, 360–61, 360 (ill.), 361 (ill.)

Flycatchers, *4*: 789

monarch, *5*: **1115–22**

Old World, *4*: **1060–69**

silky, *4*: 979–87

tyrant, *4*: 850–59, 861, 872, 882

See also Fantails; Gray hypocolius; Great kiskadees; Jacky winters

Flying jewels. *See* Hummingbirds

Fodies, *5*: 1306

Food and Drug Administration (FDA), on emu oil, *1*: 27

Forests, sclerophyll, *4*: 1095

Forktailed drongos, *5*: 1346

Formicariidae. *See* Ant thrushes

Forty-spotted pardalotes, *5*: 1204

Fowl, *2*: **294–302**

Fratercula arctica. *See* Puffins

Fregata magnificens. *See* Magnificent frigatebirds

Fregatidae. *See* Frigatebirds

Frigatebirds, *1*: 98, 99, 100, **109–15**

Fringe-backed fire-eyes, *4*: 838

Fringilla coelebs. *See* Chaffinches

Fringillidae. *See* Finches

Frogmouths, *3*: 575, 576, **585–90**, 591

Fruit doves, *3*: 505, 509

Fulmars, *1*: **53–60**

Fulmarus glacialis. *See* Northern fulmars

Furnariidae. *See* Ovenbirds

Furnarius rufus. *See* Rufous horneros

G

Galápagos cormorants, *1*: 116

Galápagos doves, *3*: 509

Galápagos penguins, *1*: 71, 73

Galbula pastazae. *See* Coppery-chested jacamars

Galbula ruficauda. *See* Rufous-tailed jacamars

Galbulidae. *See* Jacamars

Great kiskadees, *4:* 850, 856–57, 856 (ill.), 857 (ill.)

Great snipes, *2:* 455

Great spotted cuckoos, *3:* 545

Great spotted kiwis, *1:* 29, 30

Great-tailed grackles, *5:* 1268

Great tits, *5:* 1170–72, 1170 (ill.), 1171 (ill.)

Greater adjutant storks, *1:* 166

Greater anis, *3:* 545, 546

Greater flamingos, *1:* 203–5, 203 (ill.), 204 (ill.)

Greater hoopoe-larks, *4:* 908–9, 908 (ill.), 909 (ill.)

Greater melampittas, *4:* 1100

Greater painted snipes, *2:* 407, 408–9, 410–12, 410 (ill.), 411 (ill.)

Greater racket-tailed drongos, *5:* 1350–51, 1350 (ill.), 1351 (ill.)

Greater rhabdornis, *5:* 1188, 1190

Greater rheas, *1:* 13

Greater roadrunners, *3:* 545, 549–50, 549 (ill.), 550 (ill.)

Greater scythebills, *4:* 832

Greater thornbirds, *4:* 827–29, 827 (ill.), 828 (ill.)

Grebes, *1:* **90–97**

Green ioras, *4:* 957

Green magpies, *5:* 1398, 1405–6, 1405 (ill.), 1406 (ill.)

Green peafowl, *2:* 266

Green woodhoopoes, *3:* 710–12, 710 (ill.), 711 (ill.)

Greenbuls, *4:* 944, 945–46

Grenadier weavers. *See* Southern red bishops

Griffon vultures, *1:* 207

Grooming feathers, *1:* 126

Grosbeak weavers, *5:* 1306

Ground antbirds, *4:* 836

Ground cuckoo-shrikes, *4:* 935, 936

Ground-hornbills
Abyssinian, *3:* 653–54

southern, *3:* 717–19, 717 (ill.), 718 (ill.)

Ground jays, Hume's, *5:* 1398

Ground-rollers, *3:* 691, 692, 693

Grouse, *2:* 298

Gruidae. *See* Cranes

Gruiformes, *2:* **315–19**

Grus canadensis. See Sandhill cranes

Grus japonensis. See Red-crowned cranes

Guácharos. See Oilbirds

Guadalupe storm-petrels, *1:* 43

Guam boatbills. *See* Guam flycatchers

Guam flycatchers, *5:* 1116

Guam rails, *2:* 318, 359

Guam swiftlets, *3:* 617

Guans, *2:* **279–87**

Guianan cocks-of-the-rock, *4:* 879–80, 879 (ill.), 880 (ill.)

Guillemots, *2:* 486, 487

Guineafowl, *2:* **268–69, 288–93**

Gulls, *2:* **395–98, 475–85**

Gymnogyps californianus. See California condors

Gyrfalcons, *1:* 229, 234–35, 234 (ill.), 235 (ill.)

H

Haast brown kiwis. *See* Haast tokoeka kiwis

Haast tokoeka kiwis, *1:* 29, 32, 33

Haematopodidae. *See* Oystercatchers

Haematopus unicolor. See Variable oystercatchers

Hairy hermits, *3:* 632–33, 632 (ill.), 633 (ill.)

Hamerkops. *See* Hammerheads

Hammerheads, *1:* 143, 146, **160–65**, 162 (ill.), 163 (ill.)

Happy family. *See* Gray-crowned babblers

Harpactes oreskios. See Orange-breasted trogons

Harris's hawks, *1:* 213, 217–18, 217 (ill.), 218 (ill.)

Hatching, asynchronous, *2:* 476

See also specific species

Hawaiian creepers, *5:* 1288

Hawaiian crows, *5:* 1400

Hawaiian finches, *5:* 1288

Hawaiian honeycreepers, *5:* 1209, **1288–95**

Hawks, *1:* 207, 208, 209, **212–22**, 230

Hedge sparrows, *4:* **991–96**

Heliornis fulica. See Sungrebes

Heliornithidae. *See* Sungrebes

Helmet shrikes, *4:* 962, 964

Helmet vangas, *4:* 972, 973, 975

Helmeted guineafowl, *2:* 291–92, 291 (ill.), 292 (ill.)

Helmeted hornbills, *3:* 720–21, 720 (ill.), 721 (ill.)

Hemiprocne coronata. See Crested tree swifts

Hemiprocnidae. *See* Tree swifts

Hermits, hairy, *3:* 632–33, 632 (ill.), 633 (ill.)

Herons, *1:* 143, 144, 145, 146, **149–59**, 186

Highland tinamous, *1:* 8–10, 8 (ill.), 9 (ill.)

Himalayan accentors, *4:* 992

Himalayan vultures, *1:* 212

Himantopus himantopus. See Black-winged stilts

Himatione sanguinea. See Apapanes

Hirundinidae. *See* Swallows

Hirundo pyrrhonota. See American cliff swallows

Hirundo rustica. See Barn swallows

Hoatzins, *2:* **310–14**, 312 (ill.), 313 (ill.)

Hobbies, *1:* 229

Malaysian honeyguides, 3: 768, 769–70, 769 (ill.), 770 (ill.)

Malaysian plovers, 2: 446

Maleos, 2: 276–77, 276 (ill.), 277 (ill.)

Malimbes, 5: 1306

Mallards, 2: 247, 254–55, 254 (ill.), 255 (ill.)

Malleefowl, 2: 270, 273–75, 273 (ill.), 274 (ill.)

Maluridae. See Australian fairy-wrens

Malurus splendens. See Splendid fairy-wrens

Mamos, 5: 1288

Manakins, 4: 864–71

Mangrove fantails, 4: 1106

Manucodes, glossy-mantled, 5: 1389

Manus fantails, 4: 1109

Manx shearwaters, 1: 54, 56–57, 56 (ill.), 57 (ill.)

Marabou storks, 1: 166

Marbled murrelets, 2: 488

Marching eagles. See Secretary birds

Marsh tchagra, 4: 963

Marsh warblers, 4: 1052

Marshall's ioras, 4: 956

Martineta tinamous. See Crested tinamous

Martins
crag, 4: 922 (ill.), 923 (ill.), 2128–923
purple, 4: 914
white-eyed river, 4: 914–15

Masai ostriches, 1: 35

Masked bobwhites, 2: 308

Masked finfoot, 2: 366–68

Matthias fantails, 4: 1106, 1109

Mauritius cuckoo-shrikes, 4: 935, 937, 938–39, 938 (ill.), 939 (ill.)

Meadowlarks, 5: 1268

Meat, rotten, 1: 176

Megaceryle alcyon. See Belted kingfishers

Megalaima haemacephala. See Coppersmith barbets

Megapodes, 2: 267–68

Megapodiidae. See Moundbuilders

Megapodius layardi. See Vanuatu megapodes

Melampittas, 4: 1099, 1100

Melanocharis versteri. See Fan-tailed berrypeckers

Meleagris gallopavo. See Wild turkeys

Melichneutes robustus. See Lyre-tailed honeyguides

Meliphagidae. See Australian honeyeaters

Melodious larks, 4: 903, 905

Melospiza melodia. See Song sparrows

Menura alberti. See Albert's lyrebirds

Menuridae. See Lyrebirds

Merlins, 1: 229

Meropidae. See Bee-eaters

Meropogon forsteni. See Purple-bearded bee-eaters

Merops apiaster. See European bee-eaters

Mesites, 2: 316, 317, 320–25

Mesitornis variegata. See White-breasted mesites

Mesitornithidae. See Mesites; Roatelos

Mexican dippers. See American dippers

Microeca fascinans. See Jacky winters

Migrant shrikes. See Loggerhead shrikes

Migration, 1: 54, 145; 3: 613
See also specific species

Milk, crop, 3: 506, 509

Milky storks, 1: 166

Mimidae. See Mockingbirds; Thrashers

Minahass masked owls, 3: 559

Minas Gerais tyrannulets, 4: 853

Minivets, fiery, 4: 936, 940–41, 940 (ill.), 941 (ill.)

Mirafra javanica. See Australasian larks

Mississippi cranes, 2: 340

Mistletoebirds, 5: 1195

Mitchell's plovers, 2: 445, 446

Mniotilta varia. See Black-and-white warblers

Mockingbirds, 4: 997–1003

Moho bishopi. See Bishop's oos

Mohua ochrocephala. See Yellowheads

Moluccan woodcocks, 2: 456

Momotidae. See Motmots

Momotus momota. See Blue-crowned motmots

Monarch flycatchers, 5: 1115–22

Monarchidae. See Monarch flycatchers

Mongolian larks, 4: 903

Monkey-faced owls. See Common barn owls

Monogamy, 2: 327, 367
See also specific species

Montifringilla nivalis. See Snow finches

Moorhens, 2: 356–65

Morus bassanus. See Northern gannets

Motacilla cinerea. See Gray wagtails

Motacillidae. See Pipits; Wagtails

Motmots, 3: 653, 654, 655–56, 676–81

Moundbuilders, 2: 270–78

Mountain owlet-nightjars, 3: 592

Mountain plovers, 2: 446

Mountain-toucans, gray-breasted, 3: 759, 761–62, 761 (ill.), 762 (ill.)

Mourning doves, American, 3: 513–14, 513 (ill.), 514 (ill.)

Mousebirds, *3:* 639–43

Moustached tree swifts, *3:* 624

Moustached woodcreepers, *4:* 832

Mudnest builders, *5:* **1360–65**

Munias, spotted, *5:* 1303–4, 1303 (ill.), 1304 (ill.)

Murrelets, *2:* 397, 488

Murres, *2:* **486–95**

Muscicapa striata. See Spotted flycatchers

Muscicapidae. See Old World flycatchers

Musophagidae. See Plantain eaters; Turacos

Musophagiformes. See Plantain eaters; Turacos

Mute swans, *2:* 243, 249–51, 249 (ill.), 250 (ill.)

Mycteria americana. See Wood storks

Mynas, *5:* 1306, **1326–36**

N

Namaqua sandgrouse, *3:* 499–500, 499 (ill.), 500 (ill.)

Narrow-billed todies, *3:* 669, 672

Nectarinia, 5: 1208–9

Nectariniidae. See Sunbirds

Needle beaks. *See* Rufous-tailed jacamars

Neodrepanis coruscans. See Common sunbird-asities

Neophron percnopterus. See Egyptian vultures

Nesomimus macdonaldi. See Hood mockingbirds

Nests
    burrow, *2:* 414
    snakeskin, *5:* 1390
    See also specific species

New Caledonian crows, *5:* 1399

New Caledonian owlet-nightjars, *3:* 593

New Guinea forest rails, *2:* 356

New Guinea logrunners, *4:* 1093, 1094, 1095

New South Wales National Park, *4:* 1077

New World blackbirds, *5:* **1268–77**

New World finches, *5:* **1244–57**

New World quails, *2:* **303–9**

New World toucans, *3:* 654

New World vultures, *1:* 143–48, **175–85,** 187

New World warblers, *5:* **1258–67**

New Zealand dotterels, *2:* 446

New Zealand storm-petrels, *1:* 62

New Zealand wattlebirds, *5:* **1353–59**

New Zealand Wildlife Service, *5:* 1355

New Zealand wrens, *4:* **815–20**

Newtonias, red-tailed, *4:* 1062

Nicators, yellow-spotted, *4:* 945

Niceforo's wrens, *4:* 1039

Nighthawks, *3:* 602

Nightingale wrens, *4:* 1037

Nightingales, *4:* 789, 1014, 1016

Nightjars, *3:* 555, **574–78,** **602–9**

Nimba flycatchers, *4:* 1062

Nocturnal birds, *2:* 432
    See also specific species

Noisy scrub-birds, *4:* 895–97

Non-passerines, *4:* 791

Nonnula ruficapilla. See Rufous-capped nunlets

Nordmann's greenshanks, *2:* 456

Norfolk Island gerygones, *4:* 1081

North African ostriches, *1:* 35

North American Chimney Swift Nest Research Project, *3:* 620

North Island brown kiwis, *1:* 29

North Island kokakos, *5:* 1356–57, 1356–58

North Island saddlebacks, *5:* 1355

Northern bobwhite quails, *2:* 306–8, 306 (ill.), 307 (ill.)

Northern cassowaries, *1:* 20

Northern creepers, *5:* 1189

Northern fulmars, *1:* 58–60, 58 (ill.), 59 (ill.)

Northern gannets, *1:* 127–29, 127 (ill.), 128 (ill.)

Northern hawk owls, *3:* 565

Northern house wrens, *4:* 1038, 1039

Northern lapwings, *2:* 450–51, 450 (ill.), 451 (ill.)

Northern logrunners, *4:* 1094

Northern Pacific albatrosses, *1:* 45

Northern ravens, *5:* 1398, 1409–10, 1409 (ill.), 1410 (ill.)

Northern saw-whet owls, *3:* 565

Northern screamers, *2:* 262

Northern wrynecks, *3:* 777–78, 777 (ill.), 778 (ill.)

Notharchus macrorhynchos. See White-necked puffbirds

Nothocercus bonapartei. See Highland tinamous

Nucifraga caryocatactes. See Spotted nutcrackers

Nukupuus, *5:* 1288

Numida meleagris. See Helmeted guineafowl

Numididae. See Guineafowl

Nunlets, rufous-capped, *3:* 744–45, 744 (ill.), 745 (ill.)

Nutcrackers, spotted, *5:* 1407–8, 1407 (ill.), 1408 (ill.)

Nuthatches, *5:* **1173–81,** 1179 (ill.), 1180 (ill.)

Nyctea scandiaca. See Snowy owls

Podiceps cristatus. *See* Great crested grebes

Podicipedidae. *See* Grebes

Podicipediformes. *See* Grebes

Poecile atricapilla. *See* Black-capped chickadees

Pogoniulus chrysoconus. *See* Yellow-fronted tinkerbirds

Poisonous birds, 5: 1132

    See also specific species

Poisons, 1: 135

Polioptila caerulea. *See* Blue-gray gnatcatchers

Pollen's vangas, 4: 972, 973

Polyandry, sequential, 2: 327

Polyborus plancus. *See* Crested caracaras

Polygamy, 2: 327

    See also specific species

Polynesian swifts, 3: 617

Pomatostomidae. *See* Pseudo babblers

Pomatostomus temporalis. *See* Gray-crowned babblers

Ponapé fantails, 4: 1106

Poor-me-ones. *See* Gray potoos

Potoos, 3: 575, 576, **596–601**

Poughbills, 5: 1131

Powder downs, 1: 143, 149

Pratincoles, 2: **436–43**

Precocial chicks, 2: 321

Prince Albert's lyrebirds. *See* Albert's lyrebirds

Prionops plumatus. *See* White helmet-shrikes

ProAvesPeru, 4: 885–86

Procellaridae. *See* Fulmars; Petrels; Shearwaters

Procellariiformes. *See* Tubenosed seabirds

Promerops cafer. *See* Cape sugarbirds

Prunella modularis. *See* Dunnocks

Prunellidae. *See* Hedge sparrows

Psaltriparus minimus. *See* Bushtits

Pseudo babblers, 5: **1139–44**

Psittacidae. *See* Parrots

Psittaciformes. *See* Parrots

Psittacula krameri. *See* Rose-ringed parakeets

Psittacus erithacus. *See* Gray parrots

Psittirostra cantans. *See* Laysan finches

Psophia crepitans. *See* Common trumpeters

Psophiidae. *See* Trumpeters

Pterocles namaqua. *See* Namaqua sandgrouse

Pteroclididae. *See* Sandgrouse

Pterocliformes. *See* Sandgrouse

Pterocnemia pennata. *See* Lesser rheas

Ptilonorhynchidae. *See* Bowerbirds

Ptilonorhynchus violaceus. *See* Satin bowerbirds

Ptiloris victoriae. *See* Victoria's riflebirds

Ptyonoprogne rupestris. *See* Crag martins

Puerto Rican nightjars, 3: 577, 604

Puerto Rican todies, 3: 653, 669

Puffbacks, 4: 963

Puffbirds, 3: 725, 726, 727, **738–46**

Puffins, 2: **486–95**, 492 (ill.), 493 (ill.)

Puffinus puffinus. *See* Manx shearwaters

Puna rheas, 1: 13, 16

Purple-bearded bee-eaters, 3: 685–87, 685 (ill.), 686 (ill.)

Purple-crowned fairy-wrens, 4: 1071

Purple gallinules, 2: 401

Purple martins, 4: 914

Purple sunbirds, 5: 1213–14, 1213 (ill.), 1214 (ill.)

Purple swamphens, 2: 358

Purpletufts, buff-throated, 4: 874

Pycnonotidae. *See* Bulbuls

Pycnonotus barbatus. *See* Common bulbuls

Pygmy-geese, 2: 241

Pygmy-owls, 3: 555, 565

Pygmy tits, 5: 1151, 1152, 1153

Q

Quail thrushes, 4: **1099–1104**

Quails, 2: 266

    See also New World quails

Queleas, 5: 1306, 1309

Quetzals, resplendent, 3: 649–51, 649 (ill.), 650 (ill.)

R

Radiation, Great Australasian, 5: 1146

Rail-babblers, 4: 1099, 1100, 1101

Rails, 2: 315–19, 345, **356–65**

Rainbow lorikeets, 3: 535–36, 535 (ill.), 536 (ill.)

Rainforests, 2: 280

    See also specific species

Rallidae. *See* Coots; Moorhens; Rails

Ramphastidae. *See* Toucans

Ramphastos toco. *See* Toco toucans

Raphidae. *See* Dodos; Solitaires

Raphus cucullatus. *See* Dodos

Raptors. *See* Birds of prey

Raras. *See* Plantcutters

Raso larks, 4: 905

Ratites, 1: **1–4**, 7, 12, 18, 24, 29

Ravens, 5: 1398, 1400, 1409–10, 1409 (ill.), 1410 (ill.)

Razorbills, 2: 487

Recurvirostra americana. *See* American avocets

Recurvirostridae. *See* Avocets; Stilts

Ruffs, 2: 455
Rufous babblers, 5: 1139, 1140
Rufous-bellied seedsnipes, 2: 466–67, 466 (ill.), 467 (ill.)
Rufous-breasted hermits. *See* Hairy hermits
Rufous-browed peppershrikes, 5: 1241–43, 1241 (ill.), 1242 (ill.)
Rufous-capped nunlets, 3: 744–45, 744 (ill.), 745 (ill.)
Rufous-collared kingfishers, 3: 664–65, 664 (ill.), 665 (ill.)
Rufous fantails, 4: 1106, 1107, 1108
Rufous horneros, 4: 822, 823, 824–26, 824 (ill.), 825 (ill.)
Rufous-necked wood-rails, 2: 357
Rufous potoos, 3: 596
Rufous scrub-birds, 4: 895–900, 898 (ill.), 899 (ill.)
Rufous-tailed jacamars, 3: 732, 733–34, 733 (ill.), 734 (ill.)
Rufous-tailed plantcutters, 4: 881–82, 883
Rufous treecreepers, 5: 1146, 1147, 1148–50, 1148 (ill.), 1149 (ill.)
Rufous vangas, 4: 976–77, 976 (ill.), 977 (ill.)
Rupicola rupicola. See Guianan cocks-of-the-rock
Rusty-belted tapaculos, 4: 848–49, 848 (ill.), 849 (ill.)

S

Sacred ibises, 1: 193, 194–95, 194 (ill.), 195 (ill.)
Saddlebacks, 5: 1353, 1354, 1355
Saffron toucanets, 3: 759
Sagittariidae. See Secretary birds
Sagittarius serpentarius. See Secretary birds
St. Helena plovers, 2: 446
San Clemente loggerhead

shrikes, 4: 970
Sandgrouse, 3: 497–503
Sandhill cranes, 2: 334, 339–40, 339 (ill.), 340 (ill.)
Sandpipers, 2: 397, 453–63
Sandstone shrike-thrushes, 5: 1132
Sangihe shrike-thrushes, 5: 1132
São Tomé sunbirds, 5: 1208
Sarcoramphus papa. See King vultures
Sarothrura elegans. See Buff-spotted flufftails
Sarus cranes, 2: 315
Satanic-eared nightjars, 3: 577, 604
Satin bowerbirds, 5: 1383–85, 1383 (ill.), 1384 (ill.)
Satyr tragopans, 2: 300–301, 300 (ill.), 301 (ill.)
Saunder's gulls, 2: 481–82, 481 (ill.), 482 (ill.)
Savanna sparrows, 5: 1255–57, 1255 (ill.), 1256 (ill.)
Saw-whet owls, northern, 3: 565
Saxicola torquata. See Stonechats
Sayornis phoebe. See Eastern phoebes
Scarlet-collared berrypeckers, 5: 1196
Scarlet macaws, 3: 532 (ill.), 533–34, 533 (ill.)
Schetba rufa. See Rufous vangas
Schlegel's asities, 4: 801, 802, 803
Scimitar babblers, 4: 1025
Scissor-tailed flycatchers, 4: 850
Sclater's larks, 4: 905
Sclerophyll forests, 4: 1095
Scolopacidae. *See* Sandpipers
Scopidae. *See* Hammerheads
Scopus umbretta. See Hammerheads

Screamers, 2: 241–45, 261–65
Screaming cowbirds, 5: 1276
Screaming pihas, 4: 872
Screech-owls, 3: 553, 567–69, 567 (ill.), 568 (ill.)
Scrub-birds, 4: 895–900; 5: 1146
Scrub-jays, western, 5: 1403–4, 1403 (ill.), 1404 (ill.)
Scrub robins, 5: 1123, 1127–28 (ill.), 1127 (ill.), 1128 (ill.)
Scythebills
   greater, 4: 832
   red-billed, 4: 833–35, 833 (ill.), 834 (ill.)
Sea eagles, 1: 212
Seabirds, 1: 101
Secretary birds, 1: 207, 223–28, 225 (ill.), 226 (ill.)
Seed-eaters, 5: 1288
   See also specific species
Seedsnipes, 2: 396, 464–68
Semnornis ramphastinus. See Toucan barbets
Semper's warblers, 5: 1260
Senegal thick-knees, 2: 431
Sequential polyandry, 2: 327
Seriemas, 2: 316, 317, 318, 382–86
Seychelles sunbirds, 5: 1208
Seychelles swiftlets, 3: 617
Shakespeare, William, 3: 555; 5: 1327
Shanks, 2: 454
Sharp-tailed sandpipers, 2: 455
Sharpbills, 4: 860–63, 862 (ill.), 863 (ill.)
Shearwaters, 1: 43, 53–60
Sheathbills, 2: 396, 469–74
Shoebills, 1: 143, 145, 186–91, 188 (ill.), 189 (ill.)
Shore plovers, 2: 445, 446
Shorebirds. *See* Charadriiformes
Short-eared owls, 3: 554
Shovel-billed kingfishers, 3: 655